Samuel W. Mitcham, a gradua
General Staff College, is an a
Henderson State University ir

By the same author

Triumphant Fox: Erwin Rommel and the Rise of the Afrika Corps
Rommel's Desert War: The Life and Death of the Afrika Corps
Rommel's Last Battle: The Desert Fox and the Normandy Campaign
Hitler's Legions: The German Army Order of Battle, World War II

SAMUEL W. MITCHAM JR

Hitler's Field Marshals and Their Battles

GRAFTON BOOKS

A Division of the Collins Publishing Group

LONDON GLASGOW
TORONTO SYDNEY AUCKLAND

Grafton Books
A Division of the Collins Publishing Group
8 Grafton Street, London W1X 3LA

Published by Grafton Books 1989

First published in Great Britain by
Leo Cooper Ltd 1988

A CIP catalogue record for this book is available
from the British Library

ISBN 0-586-20553-5

Printed and bound in Great Britain by
Collins, Glasgow

Set in Baskerville

Contents

LIST OF TABLES

Illustrations

1. Werner von Blomberg
2. Walter von Brauchitsch
3. Ewald von Kleist
4. Walter von Reichenau
5. Ritter Wilhelm von Leeb
6. Fedor von Bock
7. Wilhelm Keitel
8. Erwin Rommel
9. Siegmund Wilhelm List
10. Baron Maximilian von Weichs
11. Friedrich Paulus
12. Erich von Manstein
13. Georg von Kuechler
14. Ernst Busch
15. Gerd von Rundstedt
16. Guenther von Kluge
17. Walter Model
18. Erwin von Witzleben
19. Ferdinand Schoerner
20. Hermann Goering
21. Erhard Milch

Acknowledgements

The author and publishers are grateful to the Robert Hunt Library for permission to reproduce illustrations Nos. 1–14, 16, 17, 20–23, 26, 28–31, 33, 35–38 and 42. Nos. 25 and 27 are reproduced by kind permission of the Imperial War Museum and Nos. 15 and 24 by kind permission of the US National Archives.

List of Maps

Map 1

Map 2

Map 3

WESTERN EUROPE

Acknowledgments

I would like to thank my academic mentor, Dr. Charles S. Aiken of the University of Tennessee, for his help in developing my career. I would also like to express my thanks to the staffs of the National Archives of Washington, D.C., and of the Historical Staff of the Air University, Maxwell Air Force Base, Alabama, for their assistance in the preparation of this book. My friends Friedrich von Stauffenberg and Dr. Roz McKeown-Ice also deserve special mention for their kind assistance.

Sincere gratitude is also expressed to Paula Leming, Professor of Foreign Languages at Henderson State University, Arkadelphia, Arkansas, for her valuable assistance in the preparation of this manuscript. I would also like to thank Dr. Sidney R. Jumper of the University of Tennessee for his advice and aid along the way.

I would be ungrateful indeed if I did not thank my parents, Mr. and Mrs. Wayne Mitcham, and my brothers, Steve and Mark, for everything they have done for me over the years.

Thanks go to Miss Donna Pounds – proof reader extraordinaire – and to Doctors Charles D. Dunne and Joe T. Clark of Henderson State University for all their assistance. Finally I would like to thank all those members of the staff of the Huie Library who assisted in the completion of this project, especially the long-suffering Barbara Roberts who very kindly put up with my insatiable requests for inter-library loans.

15

1

Werner von Blomberg

IT WAS SUNDAY, January 29, 1933, and an atmosphere of tension hung over Germany like a cloud of poisonous gas. The paraphernalia of the last election campaign still littered the cities, and the sound of Nazi jackboots seemed to haunt the streets, which resembled urban battlefields in many parts of the country. In a very real sense they had been: more than one hundred and fifty people had died in electioneering violence and rioting in the province of East Prussia alone, and still the issue had not been settled. Nevertheless, the tide seemed to many to have turned against Adolf Hitler and his struggling Nazi Party. The results of the balloting were not conclusive, but it was obvious to even the most disinterested observer that the former Austrian house painter with the Charlie Chaplin moustache had suffered a major setback.

Although still the largest party in the all-important Reichstag, the Nazis had lost 34 seats, and two million of their former voters had deserted them. Their arch-enemies, the Communists, had gained another 11 seats, and the National Party, which supported the government, had gained nearly one million votes. The Nazis still controlled 196 seats, but their opponents held 349, and the Nazi position was weaker now than it had been in months. To make matters worse, the party was on the verge of financial bankruptcy. Hitler paced up and down in his Berlin hotel room for hours, stopping only long enough to threaten to commit suicide if the party collapsed.[1]

The Nazi Party was not the only political force in Germany facing collapse that fatal day: in Berlin, the Weimar Republic was dying. Chancellor Kurt von Schleicher, the skilful manipulator, was desperately struggling to keep it alive, despite the fact that he had virtually no national popular following and was opposed by 90 percent of the deputies in the Reichstag. He had attained his high office through intrigue; now the aging President of the Republic, Field Marshal Paul von Hindenburg, had abandoned him. The hero of the First World War was even now considering who to name in his stead. Schleicher had one chance of retaining power and one only – the Army.

At the end of January 1933, a military *putsch* seemed a very real possibility. Count Wolf von Helldorf, the police president of Berlin and a high-ranking Nazi, certainly thought so. He had placed six battalions of police on alert and was ready to seize the Defense Ministry if necessary. The cast of characters also seemed right for such drastic action. Schleicher himself was a General Staff officer, a major general, former head of the Armed Forces Office and an ex-Minister of Defense. The Commander-in-Chief of the Army, General of Infantry Baron Kurt von Hammerstein-Equord, was a loyal supporter of his friend Schleicher and owed his position to the Chancellor's intrigues. He was perfectly willing to remove Hitler from the political scene by force, even by assassination if necessary.[2] The Chief of the *Truppenamt* – the Chief of the General Staff in everything but name and the second most important man in the German armed forces – was Lieutenant General Wilhelm Adam, who also owed his high position to his colleague, the Chancellor. However, if Schleicher had his friends installed in high places, he had also made enemies in his devious and ruthless climb to the top. One of these was a wealthy, reactionary politician named Franz von Papen.

In those days of economic depression and unstable party politics, governments in Germany rose and fell with amazing rapidity. With Schleicher's help, Papen had replaced Heinrich Bruening of the Catholic Center Party as Chancellor in June 1932, but his own government lasted less than six months. As part of their arrangement, Papen had appointed Schleicher Minister of Defense. Schleicher then double-crossed Papen, ousted him, and took the Chancellorship for himself. Papen had never forgiven Schleicher for betraying him. Now he got even. He persuaded President von Hindenburg to name former Chief of the General Staff General Werner von Blomberg as the new Minister of Defense. If allowed to stand, this appointment would rob Schleicher of his last trump card and signal the end of his régime. Blomberg was even now on his way from Switzerland to see Hindenburg, who would no doubt promulgate the appointment as soon as he arrived. Chancellor Schleicher now played his last card: conspiring with General Hammerstein, he decided to have Blomberg intercepted.[3]

Was Hammerstein planning to launch a military coup in favor of Schleicher that fateful day? We do not know for sure, but it seemed almost certain that he was. Hammerstein was fanatically anti-Nazi and blindly obedient to Schleicher. (Later he actively plotted to murder Adolf Hitler at the height of the Fuehrer's popularity, long before the Second World War broke out.) He suggested to Schleicher that they arrest President Hindenburg and dispatched his adjutant, Major von Kuntzen, to meet Blomberg at the railroad station and bring him to the Bendlerstrasse, where Hammerstein had his headquarters. Blomberg was also met on the platform by Colonel Oskar von Hindenburg, the son of the aging field marshal, who told him to report to the president immediately.

At the Anhalter Bahnhof, the railroad station in Berlin, at 8:30 A.M. on January 30, 1933, Werner von Blomberg made a momentous decision – the first of many. He ignored Hammerstein's orders and went directly to Paul von Hindenburg, who quickly swore him in as Minister of Defense.[4] He promoted him to general of infantry at the same time. Blomberg swore that the military would support a new government, which Hindenburg planned to announce that very day. The anti-Nazis had now lost control of the armed forces. Schleicher was finished. Within a few hours he was replaced as Chancellor of the Republic by Adolf Hitler. His rule had lasted only fifty-seven days. Franz von Papen was named Vice Chancellor in the new administration.

Hitler never forgot that Blomberg and the Army had rallied behind him that decisive day. Later, addressing the Nazi Party rally at Nuremberg on September 23, 1933, he told his followers: "If in the days of our revolution the Army had not stood on our side, then we would not be standing here today."[5] It was a decision both Blomberg and the Army would have ample cause to regret.

WERNER EDUARD FRITZ von Blomberg was born in Stargard, Pomerania, on September 2, 1878, the oldest child of Lt. Col. Emil and Emma von Blomberg. He had two brothers, both of whom became officers and were killed in action in World War I.[6] Tall, broad-shouldered, handsome, and physically impressive, Werner von Blomberg seemed destined for a military career from his boyhood. In 1894 he enrolled as a cadet in the Hauptkadettenanstalt at Gross-Lichterfelde and three years later, on March 13, 1897, was commissioned as a *Leutnant* (second lieutenant) in the 73rd Fusilier Regiment.* He was nineteen years old. Young Blomberg's next seven years were spent in the infantry, a branch he would be associated with throughout his career. On April 4, 1904, he married Charlotte Hellmich, who was to give him two sons and three daughters in the next two decades. Apparently they were quite happy together. Blomberg would be very lonely following her death in 1932, but this is getting ahead of our story.[7]

Those were days of slow promotions in the peacetime Imperial Army, and Blomberg was not promoted to *Oberleutnant* (first lieutenant) until May 18, 1907, just before his thirtieth birthday. Promotions came more rapidly after that, for Blomberg had learned his profession well. He had attended the War Academy (1904–07), graduated, and became a member of the prestigious General Staff in 1908. He served on the Greater General Staff in Berlin for the next three years (mainly in the Topographical Section), was promoted to captain in early 1911, and spent the next year on the General Staff of the Army. During this period he visited Paris, a city he came to admire greatly. In 1912 he was transferred to the garrison at Metz, on the French border, and in January 1914 was given command of a company in the 103rd Infantry Regiment, which formed part of the garrison of Metz.[8] When World War I broke out, he was named General Staff Oficer with the 19th

---

*See Appendix I for a table of equivalent ranks between the German and US Armies.

Reserve Division. Serving on the Western Front, Blomberg distinguished himself as a planner and organizer, for which he was
decorated with the *Pour le Mérite* (the "Blue Max"), Imperial
Germany's most coveted decoration. He had a brilliant war record
as a staff officer. Captain von Blomberg subsequently served as
General Staff Officer with XVIII Reserve Corps (1916–17) and the
7th Army (1917–19),[9] and got too close to the front at least once,
for he was wounded by French artillery fire when he left a
protective bunker too early.[10] Promoted to major in 1916, his career
seemed secure, despite Germany's collapse in November 1918.[11]

The Treaty of Versailles, which was signed in June 1919,
restricted the German Army to 100,000 men, only 4,000 of whom
could be officers. Blomberg was, of course, one of those selected for
retention in the new *Reichsheer*, as the German Army under the
Weimar Republic was called. He was Chief of Staff of the Doeberitz
Brigade in 1920, the year he was promoted to lieutenant colonel.
From May 1, 1921, he was Chief of Staff of Wehrkreis V (Military
District V), headquartered at Stuttgart. In 1924 General Hans von
Seeckt, Commander-in-Chief of the Army, brought him to the
Reichswehr Ministry as chief of army training. He became a full
colonel in 1925.[12]

General von Seeckt fell from power in October 1926, and was
replaced by Colonel General Wilhelm Heye. Heye found Blomberg
both likeable and intelligent and, in 1927, promoted him to acting
major general and appointed him chief of the Troop Office
(Truppenamt), which meant Blomberg was actually Chief of the
General Staff, although that title was denied to him under the terms
of the Treaty of Versailles, which officially outlawed the General
Staff. Heye soon openly viewed the Pomeranian as his heir-
apparent. Werner von Blomberg was only forty-eight years old.[13]

Like his predecessors, General Heye sought to circumvent the
Treaty of Versailles, which hamstrung the German Army in the
1920s and early 1930s. Of the four major innovations of World War
I – tanks, airplanes, submarines, and poisonous gas – Germany
was denied all four. The Reichsheer evaded some of these restrictions by setting up training bases in Russia, via secret arrangements with the Communists. Blomberg soon became deeply
involved in this secret military development, and visited the Soviet
Union in the late 1920s. He was impressed with the Soviet Army

and the totalitarian government. Here the military seemed to enjoy both power and respect, unlike in democratic Germany. "I was not far short of becoming a complete Bolshevik myself," Blomberg confessed later.[14]

In this statement, Blomberg exhibited one of his basic character flaws: he had a bit of Pollyanna in him. He was given to flights of romantic fantasy. He saw the possible positive benefits that a totalitarian form of government could have for the German Army and nation, but was blind to its hidden pitfalls and negative consequences. This naive shortsightedness did not, of course, hinder Blomberg's military advancement under Heye. He was promoted to major general with permanent rank in 1928, and to lieutenant general in 1929.[15]

Blomberg's success and favor with his chief led to his first clash with Kurt von Schleicher, who was then chief of the Ministry Office *(Ministeramt)* of the Defense Ministry. This ambitious and unscrupulous major general was jealous of Blomberg, because he coveted the post of Commander-in-Chief of the Army himself. Schleicher's mental process at this time is easy to follow: Blomberg was in the way of his advancement; therefore, Blomberg must be removed. The idealistic Chief of the General Staff was not mentally equipped to match Schleicher in a battle of intrigue. Schleicher went to his close personal friend, Defense Minister Wilhelm Groener, who owed his own appointment to a previous Schleicher intrigue, and saddled Blomberg with responsibility for some illegal border security measures. Blomberg was forced to step down as Chief of the General Staff.[16]

General Heye had to intervene personally to save Blomberg's career at all. He sent the unfortunate officer on a temporary duty trip to the United States, to allow the affair to cool down, and then transferred him to the command of Wehrkreis I, the isolated military district of East Prussia, in late 1929. It seemed to be a dead-end job, but at least Blomberg remained on active duty. He was replaced as Chief of the General Staff by Schleicher's nominee, Lieutenant General Kurt von Hammerstein, who eventually succeeded Heye as Commander-in-Chief of the Army on October 18, 1930.[17]

At his new headquarters in Koenigsberg, Blomberg took up his first command since he'd been a lieutenant. Like the other

Wehrkreise at this time, Wehrkreis I was a corps-level headquarters with a specific territorial responsibility. It had a few General Headquarters and border troops under its control, but only one division: the 1st Infantry. Unlike the other military districts, however, it was separated from the rest of Germany by the Polish Corridor. Surrounded by a hostile and numerically superior enemy, and without aircraft, tanks, or heavy artillery, it was not in an enviable position. From the day he assumed command, General von Blomberg was gravely concerned about a Polish invasion.

In East Prussia, Blomberg clearly demonstrated a second character flaw: he was too susceptible to outside influences and powerful personalities. The most powerful character Blomberg dealt with in Koenigsberg was Colonel Walter von Reichenau, his energetic and intelligent Chief of Staff. Reichenau was one of the earliest and most capable pro-Nazi officers in the German Army. Reichenau saw no reason why the paramilitary Nazi storm trooper (*Sturmabteilung*, or SA) units should not be used as military auxiliaries under the Wehrkreis control in case of war with Poland, and Blomberg agreed with him.[18] It was thus definitely in Blomberg's interests to maintain friendly contacts with the Nazis. Blomberg wrote later: "National Socialism, insofar as its main emphasis was on nationalism, was very close to me in the threatened, separated province of East Prussia."[19]

Blomberg first met Hitler in August 1930, when the Nazi leader visited Koenigsberg during an election campaign. The two agreed on Hitler's Eastern policies in general and on the issue of using Brownshirts as auxiliaries in particular. The general was impressed by the former corporal. He concluded that Hitler would eventually do for the German Army what the Communists had done for the Soviet military: turn it into a truly national force, with the support and good will of the people. Blomberg's support of the Nazis can be dated from this meeting. Unlike Reichenau, however, Blomberg was more attracted to Hitler personally than to the Nazi Party's philosophy.

In 1931, Blomberg had a riding accident and suffered a serious brain concussion. This, perhaps coupled with the death of his wife, led to an increase in Blomberg's nervousness and instability. As a result, Chancellor Heinrich Bruening asked Groener to remove Blomberg from his command in early 1932. This request was promptly complied with, and Blomberg was named Chief of the German Military Delegation to the International Disarmament Conference at Geneva the same year. This new post gave Blomberg direct access to President Paul von Hindenburg, which was very rare in those days. The impressive-looking Pomeranian was now in a position to influence the aging field marshal during a period of German history in which influence was everything. Blomberg's negative reports to Hindenburg on Bruening's disarmament policy contributed to the fall of the government in June. Bruening was succeeded by Franz von Papen and then, six months later, by Schleicher.

When Hindenburg decided to depose Chancellor von Schleicher in early 1933, Goering testified later, Blomberg's selection as Defense Minister was all Hindenburg's idea; the Nazis had nothing to do with it, although Hitler was certainly not displeased. Hindenburg's son Oskar and Franz von Papen also influenced the decision, and were probably the leading motivators behind it.[20] Shortly afterward, no doubt at Blomberg's instigation, his friend, Colonel Oskar von Hindenburg, was promoted to major general.[21]

AS SOON AS he took office, Blomberg began to dismiss Schleicher's men and bring in his own. Major General Kurt von Bredow was retired and replaced in the Ministry Office by von Reichenau; General Wilhelm Adam, who had succeeded Hammerstein, was ousted as the Chief of the General Staff in favor of General Ludwig Beck; and Lieutenant Colonel Eugen Ott was sent to Japan to make room for Colonel Fritz Fromm as Chief of the Armed Forces Branch of the Defense Ministry. Since he could not overtly sack Hammerstein for political reasons, Blomberg isolated him completely and froze him out of the decision-making process, which was a major factor in Hammerstein's decision to retire in January, 1934.[22]

In the beginning, Hitler got along well with Blomberg. At the first cabinet meeting, held in the afternoon of January 30, 1933, Blomberg declared his unquestioning loyalty to the Fuehrer. Four days later, Hitler met with his top generals in Hammerstein's Bendlerstrasse apartment (Blomberg did not yet have quarters in Berlin). He was nervous in front of the generals, but spoke for two and a half hours on his intention to reintroduce conscription, on the task of rearming the military, and on Germany's need for

Lebensraum ("living space") in the East. After the meeting broke up, Blomberg was especially enthusiastic about the Nazi program. He immediately began to establish his basic policy, which was one of collaboration between the régime and the armed forces. He started by ordering the Army to set up short, weekend training courses for the SA.[23]

The Jewish writer Bella Fromm described Blomberg in 1933 as "A reasonable man, except for his blind adoration of Hitler. . . . A Prussian soldier all his life, he is nevertheless amazingly well-bred. He has a good critical sense, and mental agility. Yet now he started to praise Hitler. His eyes shone with genuine rapture." He called Hitler "one of the greatest men of all time."[24]

The Nazification of the Army was a gradual process, made possible because it was largely done internally, thanks to von Blomberg. On May 15, 1933, he ordered all *Wehrmacht* (Armed Forces) members to salute all uniformed members of the National Verbaende and their colors at rallies and parades. (The National Verbaende referred to all armed formations of the Nazi Party, including the SA, SS, National Socialist Motor Corps (NSKK) and the Hitler Youth, as well as to the non-Nazi Stahlhelm and other veterans' organizations.) Soldiers and sailors were also instructed to avoid even the appearance of indifference to the "National Movement." Blomberg ordered them to give the Nazi (Hitler) salute when others were doing so. They were to join in nationalistic singings as well.[25]

In early July, following negotiations with the SA, Blomberg agreed to increased Army-Party contact which, in practical terms, meant increased distribution of Nazi propaganda in the lower, less sophisticated ranks of the armed forces. He also conceded to the disbandment of the Kuratorium, a national youth organization. It was to be replaced by the *Ausbildungswesen* (AW), under SA *Obergruppenfuehrer* (Lieutenant General) Krueger. Blomberg had wanted these young people – a major source of future recruits – placed under the non-Nazi Stahlhelm veterans' organization as a balance against SA Chief Ernst Roehm, so this agreement represented a major concession by the armed forces and a major opportunity for the Nazis to subvert the impressionable youth. In exchange for the AW, the SA agreed to supply 250,000 reservists to the Army in case of an emergency.[26] Since Hitler would probably have ordered their mobilization under military command in case of crisis in any event, the SA's agreement to these terms constituted hardly any concession at all.

On September 19, 1933, Blomberg directed servicemen to salute uniformed members of the Nazi Party. If the serviceman was in plainclothes, he was to use the Nazi salute. This order was so unpopular that Blomberg issued a second directive on October 4, restating it with emphasis. Less than two weeks later a lieutenant in the 15th Infantry Regiment was hit in the face by Brownshirts because he failed to salute their flag. Blomberg immediately summoned the young man to his office and sentenced him to three days' house arrest: a most unusual measure for a Defense Minister to take against a junior officer who, after all, was the one who had been struck.[27]

Blomberg went one step further on February 25, 1934, when he ordered all servicemen to wear the *Wehrmachtsadler* (Armed Forces' Eagle) on their tunics. In its claws, the eagle clutched a swastika.[28] The symbol of the Party now became a part of the everyday uniform of every soldier and sailor, but more drastic steps were yet to come.

On December 8, 1933, Blomberg issued his first anti-Semitic order: he instructed local commanders to honor any storm-trooper ban against Jewish shops. Three days after the Wehrmachtsadler directive, he imposed racial restrictions on the Armed Forces. Jews were to be retired from the military, and no more "non-Aryans" were to be allowed into the service. The order was softened by paragraphs excluding Jewish war veterans from the discriminatory clauses, and the Army was to determine who was non-Aryan, so the order affected fewer than fifty people, but it was distinctly anti-Semitic nonetheless. A further order, dated July 15, 1935, forbade servicemen from patronizing Jewish-owned shops.[29]

On April 4, 1934, Blomberg dictated that the Armed Forces hold National Socialist political doctrine classes for its soldiers and sailors twice a week. This indoctrination was carried one step further on January 30, 1936, when Blomberg ordered a special course of Nazi political instruction and training be instituted in all officer training schools, staff colleges, and in the War Academy. The following year this course of instruction was extended down to the Wehrkreis level.[30]

In July 1935, Blomberg issued a secret order commanding officers to accept the Nazi world view. Henceforth, by order of the Minister of War, the military officers were supposed to accept the Hitlerian philosophy, as well as the political views of the Nazi Party. Only men who publicly endorsed National Socialism were to be commissioned in the future. On April 1 of the following year, he prohibited servicemen from marrying non-Aryans. Even if only one of the bride-elect's grandparents was Jewish, the marriage was to be forbidden. Within two months he ordered that politically unreliable officers be reported to the Gestapo. Other Blomberg orders restricted the prerogatives of chaplains, decreed that attendance at the Barracks Evening Hour religious services and church parades was no longer mandatory, and that members of the armed forces were to treat members of the SS as comrades.[31]

As the Army collaboration with the Nazis grew closer, Blomberg's personal popularity with the Officers' Corps declined accordingly. Where before he had been referred to as "Siegfried with a monacle," his new nicknames were heard more and more frequently. He became known as the Rubber Lion (*"Gummi-Loewe"*) and Hitler's Boy Quex (*"Hitler-Junge Quex"*), after an idealized and adventurous boy in the Hitler Youth, seen frequently on German cinema screens at the time. None of this, however, affected Blomberg's personal advancement. On August 30, 1933, only seven months after Hitler's rise to power, the Fuehrer promoted Blomberg to colonel general. On May 31, 1935, Hitler appointed Blomberg Commander-in-Chief over all three services (including Goering's Luftwaffe), making him the most powerful peacetime general in German history: quite a rise for a man who spent over ten years as a second lieutenant! Finally, on April 20, 1936, he reached the pinnacle of his military career: Hitler used the occasion of his own forty-seventh birthday to promote the Rubber Lion to field marshal.[32]

In most things Blomberg got along very well with Hitler, especially in the mid-1934 to early 1937 period. There were three fundamental reasons for this successful relationship: 1) Blomberg was doing what Hitler wanted him to do; 2) Hitler was not yet completely secure politically (he was not yet the all-powerful dictator he later became); and 3) Hitler still respected his generals' opinions, and did not yet consider himself the greatest warlord of all history. In any event, Blomberg experienced little of the amateurish interference that future field marshals would have to endure. When Hitler suggested changes in the armed forces during this period, they were usually just that: suggestions. Hitler, for example, wanted the SA trained by the Reichsheer as a reserve military formation under party control, but Blomberg objected and the matter was dropped. When Himmler was agitating for an expansion of the *Waffen-SS* (Armed SS) beyond its original three regiments, Blomberg objected again, and the expansion was killed. However, the Rubber Lion roared the loudest when Ernst Roehm tried to usurp the Army's traditional role as defender of the nation and to make the storm troopers, in effect, the new armed forces of Germany.

Friction between Roehm and Blomberg began almost from the beginning of the Nazi régime. However, after December 1, 1933, when Hitler made the SA an official branch of the government, elevated Roehm to the cabinet as Minister Without Portfolio, and gave him a seat on the Reich Defense Council, the Roehm-Blomberg arguments became heated and then furious. At one point Roehm stated with great harshness that Blomberg did not understand the role of the SA in the new state any more than the deposed Schleicher had. The implications of this remark were not lost on Blomberg.[33]

Finally, on April 11, 1934, Blomberg brought the issue to a head. He joined Hitler on the cruiser *Deutschland* from Kiel to Koenigsberg, where they were to attend the spring maneuvers in East Prussia. Blomberg was accompanied by Admiral Erich Raeder, the Commander-in-Chief of the Navy, and the straitlaced General of Artillery Baron Werner von Fritsch, who had replaced Hammerstein as Commander-in-Chief of the Army less than three months before. The politician and his commanders-in-chief quietly came to an arrangement. The eighty-six-year-old President von Hindenburg was dying of old age, and Hitler wanted to combine the offices of Chancellor and President himself, in order to consolidate his power. In return for their support in this venture, Hitler agreed to suppress the SA. Blomberg and Raeder agreed immediately, but Fritsch said he wanted to consult his generals first. The meeting of the generals took place at Bad Nauheim on May 16, 1934, under Fritsch's chairmanship. Blomberg arrived late and found three men had been nominated to succeed Hindenburg: Hitler; Crown Prince Wilhelm, who favored a restoration of the monarchy; and General Ritter Franz von Epp, a champion of rearmament. Hitler was well behind the other two contenders in popularity until Blomberg arrived and told them of the "Pact of the *Deutschland.*" The generals then unanimously voted to accept Hitler under those conditions.[34] Hitler, however, hesitated to suppress his SA followers, so the anti-Nazi right wing acted, almost for the last time.

Franz von Papen, the former General Staff officer, started the process by giving a tough and courageous anti-Nazi speech at the University of Marburg on June 17. Propaganda Minister Dr. Joseph Goebbels was singled out for scorn. Goebbels suppressed the speech and let loose a storm of anti-right-wing propaganda. Three days later, on June 20, Vice Chancellor Franz von Papen, Foreign Minister Baron Constantin von Neurath, and Finance Minister Count Lutz Schwerin von Krosigk submitted their resignations. Hitler refused to accept them, but he was clearly shaken. Rumors of a counter-revolution were circulating freely in Berlin. President Hindenburg was said to be considering declaring martial law and turning power over to the Army. The Chancellor decided to visit Hindenburg at his Neudeck estate to discuss the situation.

Hitler was met on the steps of Neudeck by General von Blomberg. No Rubber Lion now, the tall, monocled Minister looked and sounded like a cold, pure-bred Prussian. He informed Hitler in no uncertain terms that, unless the present state of tension and crisis were dispelled, the President would declare martial law and the Army would take over the government. Ushered into Hindenburg's presence a few minutes later, he received the same message from the old field marshal's own lips. Blomberg stood right beside Hitler throughout the entire interview; he would not allow Hitler a private conference with the head of state. Less than half an hour after he arrived. Hitler was on his way back to Berlin, but he had got the message: Roehm must go and the storm troopers must be suppressed, or Hitler himself would be deposed by the Minister of Defense.

Nine days later, on June 30, Hitler acted. He personally arrested Roehm and had him shot, along with at least 116 others.[35] The number of dead probably exceeded 400. Among those killed were two generals: Kurt von Schleicher and his former lieutenant, Kurt von Bredow. By no means all of the dead were SA men: former politicians, old enemies, and an indiscreet religious minister (who knew too much about one of Hitler's love affairs) were all murdered. One respected music critic named Willi Schmid was taken out and killed by accident – the SS men were supposed to kill a man named Willi Schmidt. These excesses resulted in a storm of protest from the senior officers, but Blomberg stood by the "Pact of the *Deutschland*." He made sure that Hindenburg sent a message publicly congratulating Hitler for his actions. At a Cabinet meeting the next day, July 3, Blomberg expressed the armed forces' approval for the promulgation of a decree declaring the Blood Purge legal, since it was in the defense of the state.[36]

Hindenburg died on August 2, 1934. Hitler assumed office of President and promised that Blomberg would be his deputy for military affairs, just as Nazi Party Chief Rudolf Hess was his deputy for party affairs. The implication was clear: the Army would have a free hand in its own field, as long as it remained clear of politics. And that is exactly what happened – for over two years. During that period, Blomberg began Germany's military expansion.

SINCE 1921, THE Reichsheer had consisted of seven Wehrkreise: I at Koenigsburg, II at Stettin, III at Berlin, IV at Dresden, V at Stuttgart, VI at Muenster, and VII at Munich. Each had a territorial responsibility, and each had one infantry division, which bore the same number as its Wehrkreis. The Wehrkreise were subordinate to one of two "army groups" (*Gruppenkommandos*), which were army-level headquarters. Army Group 1, headquartered in Berlin, was responsible for northern and eastern Germany and included Wehrkreise I, II, III, and IV, while Wehrkreise V, VI, and VII in southern and western Germany were subordinate to Army Group 2 at Kassel. In addition, the Reichsheer had three cavalry divisions: the 1st at Frankfurt-an-der-Oder, the 2nd at Breslau, and the 3rd at Weimar. They had no territorial responsibilities, but were directly subordinate to the army groups. The 1st and 2nd Cavalry divisions were under Army Group 1, and the 3rd Cavalry was commanded by Army Group 2. Both army groups were directly subordinate to the Commander-in-Chief of the Reichsheer in Berlin. Each infantry division had about 12,000 men, while each cavalry division mustered about 5,300 men.[37] This organization provided Blomberg (and later Brauchitsch) with an excellent structure with which to carry out Germany's military expansion.

As early as October 1934, Hitler ordered Blomberg to increase the size of the Army from 100,000 to 300,000 men. Blomberg and Fritsch planned to expand it from ten to twenty-one divisions under the existing Wehrkreis structure. Each Wehrkreis would become a true corps headquarters, controlling three divisions each. However, by the time Hitler reintroduced conscription and publicly announced German rearmament on Saturday, March 16, 1935, the plans had been changed. Now Germany was to have 36 divisions. To meet these requirements. Blomberg created three new Wehrkreise. The 2nd and 3rd Cavalry divisions were disbanded and their headquarters were used to form Wehrkreis VIII at Breslau and Wehrkreis IX at Kassel, respectively. Later that year a new Wehrkreis headquarters (X) was formed at Hamburg. Near the end of the year a third army group was set up at Dresden under Fedor von Bock. He joined Gerd von Rundstedt at Berlin and Ritter Wilhelm von Leeb at Kassel as Germany's army group commanders. All later became field marshals, as did several 1936 Wehrkreise commanders: Walter von Brauchitsch (I), Erwin von Witzleben (III), Sigmund von List (IV), Guenther von Kluge (VI), Reichenau (VII), and Ewald von Kleist (VIII). Hitler's Council of Marshals was already taking shape.[38]

The new Wehrmacht Defense Law, which was published on May 21, 1935, led to the creation of a new command structure. At the top, of course, was Hitler, who assumed the title of Supreme Commander of the Armed Forces (*Der Oberste Befehlshaber der Wehrmacht*). Blomberg, his deputy in military affairs, changed his title from Minister of Defense to Minister of War and Commander-in-Chief of the Armed Forces (*Oberbefehlshaber der Wehrmacht*). The Reichswehr was renamed the Armed Forces (*Wehrmacht*); the Reichsheer became the Army (*Heer*), while the Reichsmarine became the Navy (*Kriegsmarine*). At the same time the Air Force (*Luftwaffe*) was created as a separate branch under Hermann Goering. All three branches came under the Wehrmacht (Blomberg), much to Goering's disgust. The Truppenamt was also renamed. It became the General Staff of the Army as, in fact, it had been all along.[39]

Shortly after compulsory military service was reintroduced, the revitalization of the Army took a major symbolic step forward when the War Academy in Berlin was reopened. The historic training ground of General Staff officers, it had been established by Scharnhorst in 1810 but had been closed by the victorious Allies in 1920. Now, on October 18, 1935, it was reopened on the 125th anniversary of its birth. Blomberg joined Hitler at the ceremonies, as did a host of dignitaries, past and present. Field Marshal August von Mackensen, who had won the great victory over the Russians at Gorlice in 1915, was there, as was Colonel General Hans von Seeckt, Goering, Fritsch, Beck, Rundstedt, Witzleben, and others – a sure mark of the Officer Corps' approval of Hitler's plans for arming his Reich. General of Infantry Kurt Liebmann was named the first Commandant of the Academy. His corps-level rank was an indication of the importance attached to his post.

Another high-level training facility was created in October 1935, when the Armed Forces Academy was opened in Berlin. It was headed by General Wilhelm Adam, the Wehrkreis VII commander whom Blomberg had removed from his post as Chief of the General Staff in 1933. Adam was succeeded in his Wehrkreis command by Reichenau, who felt he needed field command experience.[40] Blomberg would have cause to regret the absence of Reichenau's strong personality and firm hand in the days ahead.

AUTHOR DAVID IRVING called Blomberg "an officer of considerable vision" for the role he played in creating the Luftwaffe,[41] and he was absolutely correct. Despite his subservience to Hitler and his political ineptitude, no one can doubt that Blomberg was technically proficient. In the summer of 1933, he informed his commanders that the Geneva Disarmament Conference would come to nothing and that Germany must secretly rearm. He listed three specific elements that must go into this effort: 1) an air force; 2) a panzer arm; 3) an élite officer corps, especially in the panzer arm.

In 1933, as soon as the Air Ministry was formally established, Blomberg transferred his Air Operations Staff to it. Even though an infantry officer by training, he recognized the need for a strong air force and gave up some of his best and most promising Army officers to the new branch. In 1933 alone, he transferred 550 officers with aviation experience to the clandestine Luftwaffe. These were followed later by about 4,000 additional junior officers and NCO volunteers. Later, at the funeral oration for Walter Wever, the first

Chief of the General Staff of the Luftwaffe, who was killed in an air accident on June 3, 1936, Goering paid indirect tribute to Blomberg's magnanimity: "I acquired him through the generosity of the Army. He was one of many other outstanding officers. In Wever, the Army gave me its best. From day to day, as our work brought us together, I realized that I had been given the best of them all."[42]

Blomberg also played a role in the development of the panzer arm. Ludwig Beck and others would have killed the blitzkreig in its infancy by reducing the armored formations to nothing but infantry support units, and Fritsch was no great panzer advocate, either. Blomberg overrode them all by ordering the creation of three panzer divisions. They were activated on October 15, 1935. The 1st Panzer was formed at Weimar under Lieutenant General Baron Maximilian von Weichs. The 2nd Panzer was created at Wuerzburg under Colonel Heinz Guderian, while the 3rd Panzer was formed in Berlin, under Lieutenant General Ernst Fessmann.[43]

The expansion of the armed forces further enhanced Blomberg's policy of Army-Nazi collaboration by converting some of the older officers to his ideas, by bringing pro-Nazi officers into or back into the service, and by creating new command slots, which Blomberg often filled with pro-Hitler officers. Younger officers during this era tended to have a much stronger National Socialist orientation than older ones, and the ages of the average officer dropped markedly. The average colonel in 1930, for example, was more than fifty-two years old. Six years later the average colonel was only forty-three. The typical lieutenant colonel in 1930 was forty-seven and a half years old; by 1936, the average "light" colonel was less than forty. The age of the average major declined from forty-one to thirty-five and a half over the same period. The total number of general officers increased 400 percent in just four years, from 42 in 1932 to more than 150 in 1936, and was still growing as more divisions and Wehrkreise were created. The number of full colonels grew from 105 to 325 during the same period.[34] Propaganda, Blomberg's policies, and the prospect for rapid promotion caused many officers who had initially been suspect of Hitler to now enthusiastically endorse the new régime. Overt opposition to Nazism became rare after 1935, although it still existed beneath the surface.

BLOMBERG'S STANDING WITH the Fuehrer began to decline in 1936, during the Rhineland crisis. The field marshal had no doubt annoyed Hitler earlier by pleading for better treatment for the Jews, but Hitler ignored these unofficial requests. To Hitler, however, Blomberg's conduct during the remilitarization of the Rhineland showed a distinct lack of nerve.

German military forces had not been permitted in the Rhineland since the Treaty of Versailles. Hitler ordered the region reoccupied on March 1, 1936, and, although Blomberg favored a negotiated settlement, he dutifully issued the preliminary directive to subordinate commanders the next day; after all, contingency plans for this action had existed since May 1935. Three days later he set March 7 as the date for the operation to begin. That morning three battalions crossed the Rhine. One headed for Aachen, another for Trier, and the third for Saarbruecken. Blomberg was nervous from the first, but his mental agitation grew worse when the French responded by concentrating thirteen divisions near the German frontier. On March 9 Blomberg lost his nerve completely and begged Hitler to let him withdraw the troops. The Fuehrer tersely told the War Minister that he had weak nerves. Allied diplomats tried to pressure him into withdrawing. Hitler then threatened to send six more divisions into the Rhineland, even though he had only about four brigades available. The Allies backed down and Hitler had his way – a pattern that would repeat itself several times in the next three and a half years.[45] Hitler later commented that Blomberg behaved like a "hysterical maiden" during this crisis.[46] He told von Rundstedt that Blomberg's proposal to withdraw was nothing less than an act of cowardice.[47]

Hitler chalked up another black mark against Blomberg that summer when the field marshal opposed German involvement in the Spanish Civil War. The Prussian's opinion was that Germany had too much to lose and too little to gain by dabbling in the tricky politics of the Mediterranean. Blomberg's opposition was frank and open: he was against the adventure and he did not care who knew it. He may have been right, too, from a strategic point of view, but Hitler took the chance – and won again.

From 1936, Blomberg's strategic planning became more and more defensively oriented in nature. At the heart of his cautiousness was his belief that the German Army had expanded too rapidly and that its recruits were not yet ready for war. The expansion continued, nevertheless, and well beyond the initial thirty-six-division Army. In 1936, two more Wehrkreise were created: XI at Hanover and XII at Wiesbaden in the remilitarized Rhineland. This was followed in 1937 by the establishment of Wehrkreis XIII at Nuremberg, under Baron von Weichs. Further, there were three new corps without territorial responsibilities, to control the new mobile divisions: XIV Corps under General Gustav von Wietersheim controlled the new motorized divisions (the 2nd, 13th, 20th, and 29th); XV Corps under General Hermann Hoth directed the 1st, 2nd, and 3rd Light divisions (and later a fourth); and XVI Corps under Guderian was responsible for the three panzer divisions. Headquarters, Army Group 4, was activated at Leipzig in late 1937 to control the XIV, XV, and XVI Corps. Also nonterritorial, it was commanded by von Brauchitsch, who was succeeded at Wehrkreis I by General Georg von Kuechler.[48]

Despite the growing strength of the Army, Blomberg's deteriorating position was further damaged in the Hossbach Conference of November 5, 1938. Besides the Minister of War, Goering, Fritsch, Admiral Raeder, and Foreign Minister von Neurath participated. (The discussion was recorded for posterity by Colonel Fritz Hossbach, Hitler's Wehrmacht adjutant, which is why historians have given the conference that name.)

Hitler revealed that he planned to implement the first step in his Lebensraum agenda by launching a blitzkreig attack on Czechoslovakia in 1938, instead of the 1943-45 period, as originally planned. He also planned to incorporate Austria into the Reich in 1938. He did not believe the Western Allies would honor their treaty obligations in central Europe. He assured his shocked audience that Great Britain had already written off Czechoslovakia, and France would follow suit. If he proved wrong, however, the Army must be prepared to act with lightning speed.

Blomberg and Fritsch made it clear that the Army was not yet ready to fight a major European war. They warned Hitler against underestimating the strength of the French Army, or of the Czechoslovakian fortifications. They were also quite worried about the prospect of a war on two fronts. Blomberg was especially outspoken in opposing the invasion of Czechoslovakia, and Neurath also spoke out against war. Raeder said very little during the four-hour discussion.

Hitler was disturbed and unhappy over his generals' attitudes. He had expected them to want war as much as he did and was disappointed over their obvious lack of enthusiasm.[49]

Blomberg became nervous and upset after the Hossbach Conference. Apparently frightened by his own courage, the Rubber Lion now retreated from his opposition to the Fuehrer. In mid-December, he approved a draft for Operation Green, the invasion of Czechoslovakia, which stated that Prague could be successfully attacked even before the Wehrmacht was completely prepared for war providing she was deprived of all of their allies except Russia. Blomberg's vacillation led to animosity with Fritsch, whose attitude remained unbending, even in the face of Hitler's hostility.

To complicate matters further, the Nazi Party was attempting to harass the divisional chaplains again. Fritsch and Beck appealed to Blomberg, but it took a great deal of effort on their part to induce the field marshal to go to Hitler and protest against the Party's meddling in the internal affairs of the military again.[50]

ON DECEMBER 15, 1937, Colonel Alfred Jodl of the OKW staff noted in his diary that Blomberg was "highly excited" for some unknown reason. The War Minister then departed for a week "to some unknown place."[51] Actually he was off to Oberhof, where he spent a week with his girlfriend. Author Telford Taylor called him "moonstruck."[52]

The object of his affections was twenty-four-year-old Eva Gruhn, a stenographer with the Reich Egg Marketing Board. She was described as pretty, petite, and fair-haired, with gray-blue eyes and "a generous mouth."[53] Matthew Cooper believes that Blomberg met her during one of his jaunts to the Berlin nightclub district. He was aware that she had a past but did not know it included prostitution and posing for pornography.[54]

Werner von Blomberg was a lonely man. A widower since 1932, his five children were now grown; in fact early that year his youngest daughter had become engaged to Lieutenant Karl-Heinz Keitel, the eldest son of General of Artillery Wilhelm Keitel, who had replaced Reichenau in the Ministry Office. After his week at Oberhof, Blomberg headed for Munich, where he delivered the funeral oration for General Erich Ludendorff at the Feldherrnhalle on December 22. Here he sought out Hermann Goering for advice.

Goering had married a divorced actress after the death of his first wife, and Blomberg was concerned about the objections the strait-laced Prussian Officers' Corps might have to his marrying a commoner, and one younger than most of his children at that.

Much to Blomberg's relief, Goering heartily approved of the match. That was what National Socialism was all about, he said. There was no reason the field marshal should not marry a girl from the working class. Goering even offered to intercede with Hitler on the minister's behalf.

There was another problem, Blomberg said hesitantly. There was a rival. . . . No problem, the happy Goering announced. A few days later the rival was on a boat heading for South America. Whatever else one can say about Hermann Goering, he knew how to get things done.

Later that day Blomberg met with Hitler at his private, unpretentious Munich apartment on Prinzregenten Platz. Blomberg asked Hitler's permission to marry a government typist of modest background. (It was common practice for German officers to request their superiors' permission to marry in those days, and their applications were not always approved.) Hitler, however, consented immediately.[55] He and Goering would be the principal witnesses.

The ceremony took place at the War Ministry on January 12, 1938. There was reason for haste: Fraulein Gruhn was pregnant. The ceremony was extremely private; not one member of the Blomberg family was present. His only personal friend at the wedding was Captain Hans von Friedelburg, his former naval adjutant. Not even Reichenau knew about the wedding until later. The press hardly noticed the event.[56]

The newlyweds went first to Leipzig and then headed for Italy. Their honeymoon was spoiled, however, by the death of Blomberg's mother, who lived with her daughter at Eberswalde, not far from Berlin. Blomberg attended the funeral but gave the mourners no opportunity to express their condolences or to meet his new bride. The field marshal and his wife were the first to leave the cemetery.[57]

Meanwhile, in an obscure corner of the Berlin Police Department, a minor official named Curt Hellmuth Muller of the criminal police came across a photograph of Blomberg's wife – in the nude.

A further search uncovered the following facts: Eva Gruhn's father had died when she was five. Her mother had run a massage parlor, a designation that was used as cover for a brothel. Eva was a problem child and, at age eighteen, left home and moved into an apartment with her lover, a 41-year-old Czech Jew. It was he who arranged for a Polish photographer to take the pornographic pictures, for which she was arrested. She also had a record as a prostitute.[58]

Count Wolf-Heinrich von Helldorf, the Police President of Berlin, was horrified when the dossier reached his desk. Helldorf's loyalties were mixed. Although a staunch Nazi at the time, he was also an aristocrat and a member of the Officer Corps. He had served in the First World War as an officer of Hussars, and later had fought with the Rossbach Freikorps against the Poles. His official duty was clear: by regulations, he should take the file to Heinrich Himmler, the SS leader and head of the German police. Helldorf went to the War Ministry instead.[59]

Helldorf apparently attempted to see Blomberg, but he was out, so he took the dossier to Keitel. After some discussion, Helldorf suggested that they burn the file. Wilhelm Keitel had personal and family ties with Blomberg, but he lacked moral courage. He suggested, instead, that the file be turned over to Hermann Goering.[60]

The next day, Saturday, January 22, 1938, Helldorf gave the dossier to the Commander-in-Chief of the Luftwaffe. Goering immediately saw an opportunity here. He wanted to be Minister of War himself, and he was jealous of Blomberg for representing Germany at the coronation of King George VI in England the year before. General von Fritsch would have to be eliminated also, but Hermann Goering was up to that task as well, as we shall see.

"Blomberg has married a whore!" the Chief of the Luftwaffe announced to Adolf Hitler at Berchtesgaden on Monday, January 24, as he handed the explosive dossier over to the Fuehrer. Unlike his deputy, Hitler was not pleased at all. He mumbled something to the effect that if a German field marshal could do this, then anything in the world was possible.[61] Goering lamented his role as the bearer of bad news, but Blomberg would have to be dismissed. Hitler was not sure at first that this step was necessary, but Goering assured him that it was. The Prussian Officer Corps would not stand for this outrage, he said.

Goering was certainly right on that point. The Corps was already considerably upset over the marriage, as well as some strange telephone calls – from prostitutes – congratulating stiff-necked and proper generals on having one of their number as the First Lady of the Armed Forces. Blomberg was already unpopular with many of the generals because of his pro-Nazi policies. Generals Beck and von Fritsch were already demanding his resignation.[62]

Goering personally confronted Blomberg with the news about his wife that very day. Blomberg was shocked, as one might well imagine. His world was suddenly collapsing around him. He offered to divorce his wife at once. That was not enough, Goering said, politely but firmly. The Army High Command was already demanding his resignation, he said, as indeed it was. He told Blomberg that he would have no choice but to comply.

The following day Hitler summoned Blomberg into his presence and dismissed him. Jodl recorded that the Fuehrer treated the ruined man with "superhuman kindness," and this indeed seems to have been the case. He told Blomberg to go into exile for a year and gave him 50,000 Reichsmarks to take a trip around the world. There would be no special court of honor to consider the case, as some officers demanded – Hitler would see to that, he said. He even consulted the field marshal on who should be his successor as Minister of War. Ironically, Blomberg recommended Goering, but Hitler rejected this notion out of hand. Goering was too lazy, he said. Blomberg, deeply wounded over how quickly and unanimously the Officer Corps had turned against him, then suggested that Hitler assume the title of Minister of War himself.

It is possible that Hitler had not considered this solution until that moment, but it certainly appealed to him, and he assumed Blomberg's post one week later. Hitler's first field marshal had performed his last great disservice to the Officer Corps. In their next-to-last meeting, Adolf Hitler said to Blomberg: "As soon as Germany's hour comes, you will again be by my side, and everything that has happened in the past will be forgotten."[63]

Blomberg left Berlin on January 27, 1938, after one last visit with Hitler, who wished him *bon voyage*. He went to Italy, to resume his honeymoon and begin his exile. A few days later Blomberg was visited by Admiral Raeder's OKW adjutant, Lieutenant Baron Hubertus von Wangenheim, who found the couple on the beautiful island of Capri. Wangenheim was supposed to ask Blomberg to divorce his wife for the sake of the Officer Corps. The overly enthusiastic young naval officer, however, grossly exceeded his instructions. He invited Blomberg to commit suicide and even tried to thrust a revolver into the disgraced field marshal's hands! Blomberg declined the weapon, commenting that von Wangenheim apparently had quite a different view of life than he did. Wangenheim then indignantly informed the bridegroom that he had nothing but contempt for him, and stalked out.[64]

The sequel to this incident proves that Blomberg still had a few friends left in Berlin. Keitel, now Commander-in-Chief of OKW, the High Command of the Armed Forces, sacked Wangenheim, and Goering, perhaps with a guilty conscience, demanded that Wangenheim be dismissed from the service and even threatened to have him shot. Raeder, however, protected the lieutenant and allowed him to remain in the Navy.[65]

Frau von Blomberg miscarried while the couple were in Italy.[66] After her recovery they took a trip to Cairo, Ceylon, India, the East Indies, and Singapore before returning to Germany in late January 1939, at the end of Blomberg's period of exile. They settled in the town of Bad Wiessee, Bavaria, and lived there, in obscurity and total retirement, until the end of the war.[67]

After the initial shock of the scandal and disgrace wore off, Blomberg, who was always romantically inclined, apparently forgave Eva completely, and lived quite happily with his wife until his arrest by the Allies after the collapse of the Third Reich. As early as January 27, 1938, when Keitel urged him to get a divorce, Blomberg indignantly responded that he loved her. He was now aware of her past, he said, but she had been earning a honest living for some time, and he would rather shoot himself than leave her.[68] He had changed his tune completely since he spoke to Goering three days before, but he did not change it again.

When the war broke out in September 1939, Blomerg wrote to Hitler and asked to be re-employed, hinting he would even accept command of a corps – a position well beneath his rank (see Appendix II for the hierarchy of the German units along with their strengths and the normal ranks of their commanders). Hitler, however, now knew the depth of bitterness the senior generals held for Blomberg. He sent the retired marshal word – indirectly – that he could not use Blomberg as long as he remained with his wife.[69]

This ended the matter: Blomberg preferred Eva to the Army and was not employed again.

Blomberg was now completely isolated and friendless, as far as the Officer Corps was concerned. Even Reichenau deserted him. On one occasion during the war, the two men and their wives happened to be in the same restaurant. Neither gave any sign of recognition.[70] In his rambling, unpublished *Memoirs*, which are historically useless,[71] Blomberg pathetically commented that he expected better treatment from Reichenau.

Strangely enough, it was Adolf Hitler who remembered him with gratitude. On May 20, 1940, the day the panzers reached the English Channel and sealed the doom of France, Hitler was understandably overjoyed. In the middle of his victory celebration he paused for a minute and said: "I must not forget how much I owe to Field Marshal von Blomberg at this moment. Without his help, the Wehrmacht would never have become the magnificent instrument that has reaped us this magnificent victory."[72]

For his former services, Hitler saw to it that Blomberg continued to draw his full marshal's salary until the end of the war. Both of Blomberg's sons – Alex and Henning – were killed in action during the conflict. Despite these tragedies and a growing sense of isolation and frustration, Blomberg continued to believe in final victory until the end.[73] Arrested by the Americans at the end of the war, he testified at Nuremberg. Among other things, he said: "Before 1938–39 the German generals were not opposed to Hitler. There was no reason to oppose him since he produced the results which they desired."[74]

Even in prison at Nuremberg, many of Blomberg's former colleagues and subordinates continued to cut and shun him. Brauchitsch, for example, refused even to visit Blomberg on his deathbed. To those who would associate with him, however, Blomberg sooner or later remarked that his second marriage was a happy one.[75]

Field Marshal Werner von Blomberg had done a great deal toward the Nazification of the Armed Forces and had helped to furnish Hitler with the weapon he needed to wage World War II. Suffering from cancer, he died "a pathetic, bedridden old man," on March 14, 1946, while in American detention at Nuremberg.[76] He was buried without ceremony in an unmarked grave.[77]

2

Walter von Brauchitsch

THE LAST PROFESSIONAL soldier to be Commander-in-Chief of the German Army in the Second World War was Walter von Brauchitsch. He was a compromise candidate; indeed, the word "compromise" seems to be synonymous with his entire career in high command. History has dealt harshly with him, as well it should: he surrendered much to the Nazis in order to realize his personal ambitions. He sacrificed the remnants of the Army's independence out of subservience to Hitler; the General Staff's hegemony in military affairs to Hitler's creature, the OKW; and the careers of many of his colleagues and friends in order to make room at the top for generals more favorable to the Fuehrer. In the end his reward for his compromises turned to ashes in his mouth. His health broke, he retired in obscurity and disgrace, and died, nearly blind, in an enemy prison. It is not an attractive story.

WALTER VON BRAUCHITSCH was born in Berlin on October 4, 1881, the son of a Prussian general of cavalry. Destined for a career in the Army, he was raised in and around the Imperial Court and as a youth was a member of the Corps of Pages. Martially handsome, he served for a time as personal page of Empress Augusta Victoria. On March 22, 1990, at age eighteen, he was commissioned *Leutnant* (second lieutenant) in the élite 3rd Foot Guards Regiment, but transferred to the 3rd Guards Field Artillery Regiment the following year. He was associated with the artillery for the rest of his career; in fact, his positive innovations in that branch have been largely overlooked. It was Brauchitsch, however, who played a major role in developing the 88mm gun as both an anti-tank and anti-aircraft weapon. This "88" was later mounted on the PzKw V "Tiger" and PzKw VI "Panther" tanks and was both feared and respected by a generation of American soldiers, who generally considered it to be the finest tank gun used in the Second World War.[1]

Lieutenant von Brauchitsch's career developed normally enough for a Prussian general-elect. He did his artillery training and troop duty, became the adjutant of an artillery battalion in 1906, and adjutant of the 3rd Guards Field Artillery in April 1909. Six months later he was promoted to first lieutenant and, on December 29, 1910, married the noble-born but reportedly unattractive and emotionally cool Elizabeth von Karstedt, while he was a student at the War Academy. Duly graduated in 1912, he received the distinctive red leg stripes of a General Staff officer. He was assigned to the Greater General Staff in Berlin in 1912, was promoted to captain in 1913, and was on the General Staff of the Army in 1914, when World War I broke out.[2]

Brauchitsch spent the entire war on the Western Front as a General Staff officer, first with XVI Corps (1914–15), then with the 34th Infantry Division (1915–18), the 1st Guards Reserve Division (1918), and the Guards Reserve Corps (1918). He emerged from the conflict with the rank of major and the Hohenzollern House Order, a high decoration in the Imperial Army.[3] He was accepted into the 100,000-man Reichsheer as a matter of course.

During the days of the Weimar Republic, Brauchitsch continued his steady but unspectacular climb. He was on the staff of Wehrkreis II, then was attached to Artillery Command II, before serving a year's troop duty as commander, 2nd Battery, 2nd Field Artillery Regiment (1921–22). He was transferred to a staff job on the Truppenamt for three years, before serving two more years' troop duty as Commander, II Battalion, 6th Artillery Regiment (1925–27). Next he became Chief of Staff of Wehrkreis VI at Muenster (1927–30), before returning to the General Staff at

Berlin, where he became Director of Army Training in the Truppenamt (1930–32) and Inspector of Artillery (1932–33). He was preparing to take up his new post as Commander of Wehrkreis I at Koenigsberg when Hitler became Chancellor. Brauchitsch's promotions had also come regularly: lieutenant colonel (1925), colonel (1928), major general (1930), and lieutenant general (1933).[4]

Brauchitsch's attitude toward the Nazis varied from cool aloofness to outright hostility. He dealt firmly with Erich Koch, the rabid Nazi Gauleiter of East Prussia, and even ejected SS units from Wehrkreis maneuvers when they displeased him. Watching the Nazi Party Rally in Nuremberg, he told General Wilhelm Adam that he wished it were possible for him to live abroad. Later, when Goebbels spread an unflattering rumor about his private life, Brauchitsch challenged him to a duel. He professed to be a deeply religious man and was known to keep a Bible on his bedside table, which he turned to for comfort and solace.[5] Certainly he was not considered a Nazi appeaser by his fellow generals at this point in his career. In fact, he was highly thought of as a "distinguished representative of the Prussian aristocratic tradition," to quote author Harold C. Deutsch.[6] Army Commander-in-Chief General Werner von Fritsch called him his "best horse,"[7] and gave him command of Army Group 4 at Leipzig in 1937. Now a general of artillery, Brauchitsch controlled XIV, XV, and XVI Corps: all of the German panzer, mechanized, and motorized divisions – the Reich's entire mobile strike force. It was an assignment of great responsibility and an indication of even greater things in the future. Far from seeing himself on the threshold of a great career, however, Brauchitsch considered his career near its end. He faced the prospect of retiring in disgrace and of living in retirement, ostracized by his friends and fellow officers, eking out an existence with inadequate financial means. The reason for this bleak attitude was a woman or, more precisely, two women.

Brauchitsch's wife, according to General Curt Siewert, was an unattractive "governess type," lacking in warmth and femininity.[8] They had been living apart for about five years, although Brauchitsch had engaged in at least one extramarital affair while they were together. The other woman was a divorcée named Charlotte Rueffer, a beautiful and sexy daughter of a Silesian judge, whom Brauchitsch had met in Breslau in 1925 or 1926. He had asked his wife for a divorce then, but she refused. The illicit relationship ended for at time, and Charlotte married a bank director named Schmidt, but he drowned in a bathtub during a visit to Berlin, so Charlotte was free to resume their liaison when Brauchitsch returned from East Prussia in 1937.

By early 1938, Brauchitsch was determined to marry Frau Rueffer, but his wife was unwilling to grant him a divorce without a large lump-sum cash settlement. The general was preparing to pay much of his salary in alimony, but this did not satisfy Frau Brauchitsch: she wanted a lump sum or she would contest the divorce, which would result in a scandal that would end Brauchitsch's career. A divorce was bad enough in the 1930s, but the straitlaced Prussian Officer Corps would never tolerate a scandal. Brauchitsch decided to push ahead nevertheless, even if it ended the only career he had ever known. He considered his present situation intolerable.[9] Then, suddenly, he found himself not only happily divorced but his ex-wife satisfied and financially secure – the scandal suppressed by no less a personage than the Head of State – and himself promoted to colonel general and named Commander-in-Chief of the German Army! Here is how it happened.

AS WE HAVE seen in chapter 1, Field Marshal Werner von Blomberg was relieved of his position as Minister of War on January 26, 1938, when it was discovered that he had married a former prostitute. The next in line for this post was Colonel General Baron Werner Thomas Ludwig von Fritsch, the C-in-C of the Army. The idea of appointing this tough, independent-minded Prussian, however, was intolerable to Hitler, who despised him. Fritsch was openly anti-Nazi, hated the SS, and had made it quite clear in the Hossbach Conference of November 5, 1937, that he opposed Hitler's aggressive plans. Hermann Goering – who coveted the Defense Minister's job himself – knew that he would have to get rid of Fritsch before he could assume Blomberg's mantle, so he teamed up with Himmler and Reinhard Heydrich, the chief of the SD (*Sicherheitsdienst*, or Security Service) to frame Fritsch. On January 25, at the same time he presented Hitler the police dossier on Frau Blomberg, Goering handed Hitler another document – prepared by Himmler and Heydrich – charging Fritsch with homosexual offenses. It also charged Fritsch with having paid blackmail to an ex-convict named Hans Schmidt since 1935, to keep Fritsch's activities secret. All these charges were purely fictitious, of course, but Hitler took them seriously. That same day, despite orders to the contrary, Colonel Hossbach warned Fritsch what was afoot. Fritsch was furious. The next day, Hossbach ignored the damage it could do to his own career and informed Hitler of his insubordination. He urged the Fuehrer to give Fritsch a hearing so he could deny the charges. To his surprise, Hitler readily agreed.

The fateful meeting took place in the library of the Chancellery that same evening. Fritsch gave his word of honor that the charges were completely false. To his horror, Himmler then produced Schmidt, who identified von Fritsch as the man he had caught in a homosexual act with an underworld character named "Bavarian Joe" in a dark alley near the Potsdam railroad station. The creature swore to Hitler that Fritsch had been paying him blackmail money for years.

Fritsch was literally too outraged to speak. Nothing in his background, after all, had prepared him for this! Hitler, however, took Fritsch's silence as an indication of guilt and asked for his resignation. The Baron refused, demanding a trial by a military Court of Honor instead. Unfortunately for him, Hitler saw his chance to rid himself of a troublesome obstacle and was not about to turn the case over to a more objective body. He sent Fritsch on indefinite leave, in effect relieving him of his command. The next day, Hitler was discussing possible successors to Fritsch, as well as von Blomberg.[10]

By January 28, Hitler had decided to take over Blomberg's duties himself. General Wilhelm Keitel would be his principal military deputy as Commander-in-Chief of the Armed Forces High Command (OKW), to which the High Command of the Army (OKH) would be subordinate under the new organizational structure. Reichenau, who had been recommended by Blomberg, was the leading candidate to succeed Fritsch. Keitel, however, opposed Reichenau because too many senior generals would refuse to serve under him. The Army could not stand another shock after the Fritsch and Blomberg scandals, he said. Other possible nominees were suggested. Rundstedt was turned down as too old, Joachim von Stuelpnagel was "disloyal" (i.e., anti-Nazi), and the deeply religious Ritter Wilhelm von Leeb was rejected out of hand. Finally, Keitel mentioned Brauchitsch. The Chief of OKW praised him as a nonpolitical soldier, an authority on organizational and training matters, and a proven commander. Hitler remembered that Blomberg had recommended Brauchitsch after Reichenau, but was unenthusiastic, possibly recalling reports of Brauchitsch's anti-Nazi behavior in East Prussia. Finally he agreed to meet with the Army Group 4 commander to form his own opinion. Keitel quickly summoned Brauchitsch to Berlin.[11]

General Brauchitsch met with Hitler the next day, January 29. He had found out from Keitel that there were strings attached to the new post, but he was prepared to compromise. He was "ready to agree to everything," Jodl recorded in his diary.[12]

Hitler, however, still preferred Reichenau, possibly because he knew of von Brauchitsch's domestic situation. One thing he did not need at this juncture was another scandal. Besides, Reichenau was genuinely pro-Nazi, whereas Brauchitsch was not.

On January 31, Hitler met with Gerd von Rundstedt, now the senior general on active duty. Rundstedt, to Hitler's displeasure, warmly recommended General Ludwig Beck, the strongly anti-Nazi Chief of the General Staff. When Hitler brought up Reichenau's name, Rundstedt flatly rejected the idea. With the Fritsch matter still unresolved, Hitler was in no position to buck the senior and most influential Army general, so he brought up the possibility of appointing von Brauchitsch. Rundstedt praised Brauchitsch warmly and said that he was entirely acceptable to the Army.[13]

Reichenau was effectively eliminated as a candidate after this meeting, although Hitler continued to bring up his name, probably to squeeze more concessions out of General Brauchitsch.

Meanwhile, Keitel summoned one of Brauchitsch's sons (probably future Luftwaffe Colonel Bernd von Brauchitsch) and sent him to his mother, to appeal to her to grant Brauchitsch a divorce. She agreed to do so in writing, providing her financial demands were met.

Goering, who opposed the hardheaded Reichenau, also got into the act. On February 1 he was examining Brauchitsch's appointment. Georing no doubt discovered that Charlotte Rueffer, the object of Brauchitsch's affections, was a fanatical Nazi and obviously had a great deal of influence over the general. He recommended that Hitler pay off Frau von Brauchitsch and promulgate the appointment.

From the moment he involved the Nazis in his private life, Brauchitsch ceased to be a free agent. His choices, however, were clear: come to an arrangement with Hitler, in which case all of his problems would be solved; he would be able to marry the beautiful woman he loved, and simultaneously he would reach the peak of his profession as well. The other option was to retire in semi-disgrace, with financial difficulties, married to a woman whom he did not love but would nevertheless have to support for the rest of his life. His choices remind one of a scene from *The Devil and Daniel Webster*, except in this case Lucifer wore a Charlie Chaplin moustache.

Brauchitsch met with Hitler again on February 2 and agreed to almost all of his demands. Almost was not good enough for the Fuehrer, however. The next morning Jodl found Keitel very depressed. Hitler and Goering, he said, were now leaning toward Reichenau after all. Keitel was afraid that the Army would not stand for Reichenau's appointment. Beck would certainly not serve under him; neither would Franz Halder, the Deputy Chief of the General Staff. He feared mass resignations. Near despair, Keitel asked for an appointment with Hitler.[14]

We do not know all of the details of the negotiations of January 31–February 3, 1938, but their results are known only too well. Brauchitsch was promoted to colonel general and appointed Commander-in-Chief of the Army on February 4. He accepted without protest the new command structure, with Keitel as Chief of the High Command of the Armed Forces. The Army thus lost its previously undisputed hegemony in German military affairs. He also accepted Hitler's assumption of the War Minister's portfolio without demur and promised to bring the Army even closer to the National Socialist philosophy. Frau Brauchitsch received a cash payment, variously reported as between 80,000 and a quarter of a million Reichsmarks from Nazi Party coffers. And heads rolled.

Brauchitsch had agreed to numerous personnel changes in the highest levels of the Army. A great many careers were sacrificed as stepping stones for Brauchitsch's advancement. The first to go was Lieutenant General Viktor von Schwedler, the Director of the Army Personnel Office, and his two principal deputies, Colonels Adolf

Kuntzen and Hans Behlendorff, who had constantly resisted Nazi attempts to obtain favorable appointments for their sympathizers within the Army.[15] Schwelder was succeeded by Colonel Bodewin Keitel, the brother of the new OKW chief, whom the Nazis considered reliable.

The most important officer to depart was General Wilhelm von Leeb, the Commander of Army Group 2, who was second only to Rundstedt in seniority. Too strong a Catholic for Hitler, he was retired with the honorary (*"charakterisierte"*) rank of colonel general. The pro-monarchist Ewald von Kleist and the Bavarian aristocrat Franz Kress von Kressenstein, the commanders of Wehrkreise VIII and XII, repectively, were also forced into retirement. Other retirees included Oswald Lutz, the first General of Panzer Troops; General Guenther von Pogrell, the Inspector of Cavalry; General Kurt Liese, the Chief of Ordnance; and Lieutenant General Guenther von Niebelschuetz, the Inspector of Army Schools. Franz Halder, Deputy Chief of the General Staff for Training, was also on Hitler's list, but he was saved by the personal intervention of Keitel. Future Field Marshals Georg von Kluecher, Baron Maximilian von Weichs, Guenther von Kluge, and Erwin von Witzleben were also retired. Rundstedt escaped the initial purge, but was retired in November, along with Curt Liebmann and Wilhelm Adam. During the same period, Generals Hermann Geyer, Wilhelm Knochenhauer, and Wilhelm Ulex, Commanders of Wehrkreise V, X, and XI, respectively, were sacked. Colonel Friedrich Hossbach, Hitler's "disloyal" adjutant, also lost his job for informing Fritsch of the conspiracy against him. In all, sixteen senior Army generals were retired and forty-four others were transferred to other duties.[16] They were replaced by men who were regarded as pro-Nazi at the time.

Telford Taylor summarized the situation well when he wrote: "To achieve his new position, Brauchitsch stooped to the meanest concessions and put himself under permanent obligation to Goering and Keitel as well as to Hitler. For this dismal surrender of principle for position, the officers' corps paid soon and dear."[17] He was right about that.

A sequel to the events of February 1938 occurred a year later. It demonstrates the depths of Brauchitsch's hypocrisy and reflects rare credit on Hitler. A young lieutenant impregnated a girl from a good family. He immediately offered to do the honorable thing and marry her, but this did not satisfy Brauchitsch, who petitioned to dismiss the young man from the service. When the case came before Hitler, he became very angry. This was typical of aristocratic generals like Brauchitsch, he snapped: he carried on an adulterous affair with his second wife while still married to his first, and yet he wanted to ruin the career of a young man who was behaving more honorably than Brauchitsch himself had done. Hitler set the dismissal aside, instructing Brauchitsch to apply the same moral standards to his subordinates that he applied to himself.[18]

WITHIN FIVE WEEKS of taking office, Brauchitsch tried to renege on his acceptance of the OKW-dominated command structure. He supported the efforts of Ludwig Beck who, along with Deputy Chief of the General Staff for Operations Erich von Manstein, submitted a memorandum proposing that the Army have predominance in any Wehrmacht command. Keitel, strongly supported by Goering, successfully resisted the proposal, and Walter von Brauchitsch's standing suffered its first decline in Adolf Hitler's eyes. Very soon thereafter, Manstein was transferred from the General Staff to command of the 18th Infantry Division. He was replaced by Halder.[19]

Within six weeks of Brauchitsch's assumption of command, Hitler's *Blumenkriege* – flower wars – began. This series of bloodless, diplomatic conquests began with a sudden diplomatic *coup* over Austria, which was incorporated into the Third Reich on March 12, 1938. "It came as a complete surprise to me!" Brauchitsch later testified at Nuremberg, and indeed he played no part in it. He does not even seem to have been in Berlin at the time.[20]

Hitler's next target was Czechoslovakia, where more than three million Germans had been marooned on the wrong side of the border imposed on Germany by the Treaty of Versailles. The Prague government had discriminated against them for years, especially in the courts, where they were dealt with more harshly than Czechs and were much less likely to receive justice than others. Czechs also received preferential treatment in other areas, such as civil service employment and government appropriations. No effort was made to assimilate them, and as a result they were a fertile breeding ground for Nazi agitation in 1938.

The Sudetenland crisis began on April 24 when Konrad Henlein, Chief of the Nazi Party in Czechoslovakia, set forth a program calling for autonomy for the Sudetenland. It was worded to sound reasonable enough to the international community, but Henlein (and Hitler) knew Czech President Eduard Benes would reject it.[21]

Brauchitsch was on the horns of a dilemma during the Sudetenland crisis. He believed, as did the vast majority of the German people, that the lands in question should be returned to Germany, but he seriously doubted that they could be taken, because France and Great Britain were allied with Czechoslovakia. He was also caught between two influences: his Nazi wife, and Generals Beck and Halder, who condemned Hitler's plans because they would, the generals thought, make a general European war inevitable. The specter of a two-front war of the type that killed the Second Reich in 1918 began to haunt the weak-willed Commander-in-Chief of the Army.

The crisis deepened on May 21 when Czech police shot and killed two Sudeten farmers and Prague mobilized some 200,000 soldiers on the pretext that Germany had concentrated troops in Silesia and Saxony, on the Czechoslovakian border. Britain, France, and the Soviet Union all backed the Czech action. Hitler was outraged, for he had done nothing of the kind. He intended to, it is true, but the Allies did not know that, and he was furious at being accused of a crime he had not yet committed. He decided to resolve the Sudetenland question by the end of 1938, even if it meant a general European war.[22] On May 28 he called Goering, Brauchitsch, Keitel, Beck, Raeder, Ribbentrop, and Neurath to the Reich Chancellery in Berlin, where he expressed his "unshakable will that Czechoslovakia shall be wiped off the map."[23]

Apparently the real Czech motive behind their partial mobilization was to have troops on hand in the Sudetenland for the municipal elections, held the next day. Henlein's followers provoked general disorder. There were riots in the Sudetenland, reports of Czech outrages against people of German ancestry, and a general deepening of the crisis. Two days later, on May 30, Hitler signed the directive for Operation Green, the military invasion of Czechoslovakia. It set the attack day for October 1 at the latest.

Ludwig Beck also disliked Czechoslovakia and wanted the

Sudetenland returned to Germany, but not at the price of a general war, which he was convinced Germany could not win. He therefore began to conspire against Hitler. Beck, however, was not a man of action; furthermore, the Chief of the General Staff had no troops directly under his command. Any successful military *coup d'etat* against the Nazi régime would have to have the support of the Commander-in-Chief of the Army. With this in mind, Beck asked for an appointment with Brauchitsch on May 30, just two days after Hitler had revealed his intentions toward Prague. Brauchitsch, however, guessed the purpose of Beck's visit. He sent word back that he was going on a short but immediate leave and would see Beck when he returned.[24] Actually, Brauchitsch was hedging. He did not want a war for which he knew Germany was not prepared, but he shrank from personally doing anything to prevent it. Later he said: "Why, in heaven's name, should I, of all men in the world, have taken action against Hitler? The German people had elected him, and the workers, like all other Germans, were perfectly satisfied with his successful policy."[25]

Beck continued his anti-war campaign via a series of memoranda throughout June and July, in which he clearly pointed out the ultimate hopelessness of Germany's isolated military position. The memorandum of July 16 was perhaps the most important. It enumerated the dangers of a two-front war, forcefully objected to Hitler's policy-by-intuition, and spelled out Germany's lack of readiness for a general conflict. One must keep in mind that the German rearmament program had only started in earnest less than four years before and armies can expand only so fast, especially since there were only 100,000 men in service in 1935 to begin the process. Despite its enthusiasm for Hitler's policies, Nazi Germany still had a serious shortage of trained soldiers in 1938.[26]

Beck finally met with Brauchitsch on July 29. Backed by several important generals, including Wilhelm Adam, the Commander-in-Chief-designate of the Western Front, he finally pressured Brauchitsch into calling a secret meeting of the top commanders to discuss the deteriorating international situation and the military threat it posed to Germany.

The fateful meeting took place on August 4. Not trusting Brauchitsch to show moral courage, Beck wrote a speech for him, in which he described Germany's isolated position. It stated that Germany would not be ready for war before 1941 and that Hitler must act in accordance with these views.

Brauchitsch did not read the speech Beck had prepared, but he did let the Chief of the General Staff read his memo of July 16 to the generals, who were deeply impressed. General Adam then stood up and spoke in support of Beck. Operation Green, he said, left him with only five active-duty divisions in the west, along with four reserve divisions and the over-age troops of the Landwehr (thirty-five to forty-five years of age). He predicted that these would be quickly overrun by the French, who had about one hundred divisions. Thus encouraged, Brauchitsch admitted that he shared the concerns of Beck and Adam and even commented that a European war would mean the end of German culture. Beck asked if any of the generals disagreed that a war with Czechoslovakia and her allies would be militarily foolish. None did, but there the unanimity ended.

Beck wanted the Commander-in-Chief to lead the generals *en masse* to Hitler and demand that he change his policy. General Kluge even called for mass resignations, which he felt would force Hitler to reconsider. Brauchitsch, however, did not want to lead such a military revolt – albeit peaceful – and von Rundstedt also advised him to tread carefully, perhaps fearing that he would be sacked and replaced by the hated Reichenau. Reichenau, although he opposed the war, said the decision was one for Hitler alone to make. General Ernst Busch echoed von Reichenau's sentiments and spoke of obedience and the oath of loyalty. Most of the commanders said very little or nothing at all. The meeting ended without any overall agreement but with some results, even though they were indirect.[27]

Brauchitsch knew that Hitler would now hear of Beck's memorandum of July 16, so he showed it to him. Hitler found his distrust of Beck confirmed. He encouraged Brauchitsch to avoid Beck and deal directly with General Halder, the Deputy Chief of the General Staff. Brauchitsch did as the Fuehrer suggested. He also half-heartedly conveyed the generals' misgivings about Operation Green, but when Hitler stood firmly for the plan, Brauchitsch quickly gave in. Hitler privately remarked that he would take

Czechoslovakia with one set of generals, and then would face France with a new set.[28] Perhaps with this idea in mind, he held a luncheon for junior officers at the Berghof on August 10. Present were all of the chiefs of staff-designees for the Army and Luftwaffe commands earmarked for the campaign. Brauchitsch and Beck were excluded from the guest list. Fritsch would never have tolerated such a flagrant breach of protocol. Brauchitsch never uttered a word of protest.[29]

After lunch, Hitler made a three-hour speech to the officers. If Hitler's purpose was to convince the junior generals of the feasibility of Green, he failed miserably. When the Fuehrer told them that the French would not penetrate the western fortifications, General of Infantry Gustav von Wietersheim, the senior officer present, challenged him. He repeated Adam's assessment that the Western Front could not be held for three weeks. Upon hearing this, Hitler flew into a rage. He called the generals defeatists and scoundrels. Finally, he assured Wietersheim that the fortifications could be held for three years. The officers were overwhelmed by this display of temper by the Head of State. No one else dared protest against Hitler's invasion plans.[30]

If Hitler's purpose in holding the Berghof luncheon was to send a message to his senior generals that he would tolerate no opposition to his plans and could do without them, he succeeded admirably. Five days later, on August 15, Hitler attended a field exercise at the Jueterbog Maneuver Area and again spoke to his senior generals of his unshakable determination to smash Czechoslovakia. This time there were no protests.

After the meeting, Beck asked to speak privately to von Brauchitsch. The Commander-in-Chief, however, refused, stating that he was going on another leave! Beck was furious. When he finally did manage to secure an interview with Brauchitsch on August 18, the C-in-C told Beck that Hitler had issued an order demanding unconditional obedience from all commanding generals *and* from the Chief of the General Staff. Brauchitsch was now all too willing to comply, but Beck refused to. The two generals exchanged harsh words. Brauchitsch was obviously tired of the pressure the Chief of Staff was putting on him to act against Hitler. Finally Beck submitted his resignation and called upon Brauchitsch to do the same. He refused, saying: "I am a soldier. It is my duty to obey."

With the departure of Beck, the weak-willed Brauchitsch lost a troublesome subordinate who tried to motivate him into doing what he knew was right, even if it meant opposing Hitler. Brauchitsch was glad to see Beck go. He was replaced by General Halder.

WE WILL NOT go into the tactical details of the Czech campaign here, because it was never launched. One aspect of it, however, is significant: Hitler interfered with it.

Brauchitsch and Halder planned a giant pincer movement in Moravia to achieve a quick, decisive victory; however, Hitler objected. He wanted more emphasis placed on a frontal assault.

The decisive conference took place at Nuremberg, beginning at 10 P.M on the night of September 9, with Halder presenting a lengthy defense of the Army's plan. He echoed von Brauchitsch's sentiments and stated that Germany needed a speedy victory. Hitler's plan would allow the Czech Army to escape into Slovakia, giving the Allies time to intervene in the West, while the bulk of Germany's ground forces were tied up in the East.

Hitler argued that too much depended on the success of the pincer movement in the Brauchitsch/Halder plan. He decided that it should be attempted but not relied upon. At last he suggested a compromise that, in effect, called for the adoption of both plans, because it divided the mobile forces between the armies of Rundstedt, Reichenau, and List.[31]

The soldiers would not agree to the compromise because it was a division of forces and reduced the chances for a quick, decisive victory by weakening the pincers. Brauchitsch left most of the technical aspects of the discussion to Halder but once again urged Hitler to postpone the invasion until the danger of war on two fronts could be avoided. Hitler viciously accused him of lacking nerve. Keitel also turned on him, stating that he would not tolerate "criticism" and "defeatism" from OKH. He accused the Army generals of being jealous of the Fuehrer and of seeing him as a World War I corporal and not as the greatest statesman since Bismarck.[32] Halder, whose schoolmaster appearance belied his toughness, still would not give in. Finally, about 4 A.M., Hitler grew tired, lost his patience, and gave up his attempts at persuasion. He ordered his compromise plan be adopted.[33] Brauchitsch then surprised everybody by declaring his unquestioning loyalty to the

Fuehrer. After the OKH generals had gone, Hitler turned to Keitel and bemoaned the fact that the Nazi Gauleiters could not command his armies, because they had "guts" as well as faith in the Fuehrer.[34]

Since the Czechoslovakian invasion was cancelled after the Munich accords, it is impossible to state definitely who was right or how well Hitler's plan would have worked. Its adoption, however, amounted to a major defeat for the Army, for it represented Hitler's first intervention in detailed military planning. It also proves that Hitler was meddling in Army operational planning as early as 1938, not 1940 – the year commonly cited by historians.

MEANWHILE, GENERAL HALDER joined the anti-Hitler conspiracy, which was preparing to launch a revolt against the Nazis, arrest Hitler, and establish a military government (see chapter 19). On September 28 the crisis reached its peak. The Czechs had assembled an 800,000-man field Army behind strong frontier fortifications; the French had partially mobilized and could send 65 divisions against Adam's weak armies; and the British fleet was ready to put to sea in support of the Czechs. Meanwhile, German armor rumbled down the Wilhelmstrasse in what was supposed to be a parade, but the few Berliners who watched it did so stone-faced. They did not want war. German citizens, fearing air raids, fled the cities in the western areas in droves. On September 28, Halder stood ready to issue the orders initiating the military revolt the next day, providing Brauchitsch would approve. Brauchitsch vacillated, however: he simply could not decide what to do.[35]

In the middle of all this, Brauchitsch's divorce became final on August 4. On September 23 he finally got his heart's desire and married Charlotte Rueffer. After that, anti-Hitler conspirator Ulrich von Hassell wrote in his diary, Brauchitsch "became heavily involved with the Nazis, largely through the influence of his 200 percent rabid Nazi wife."[36] The new Frau von Brauchitsch had been a devoted Nazi long before 1933. Her influence with the colonel general was obviously very strong, and she had the habit of reminding him "how much we owe the Fuehrer" every time Halder and the others had convinced him to stand up to Hitler. They attributed Brauchitsch's habit of changing his position overnight to her pro-Nazi influence.[37]

Brauchitsch could never bring himself to act against Hitler. Fate intervened on his behalf this time, however. In the early morning of September 30, France, Britain, Italy, and Germany signed the Munich Agreement, awarding the Sudetenland to Germany. The Prague government, which had not even been invited to the conference, was left without allies and had not choice but to yield. The occupation of the Sudetenland took place October 1–10, 1938. With the loss of these territories, Czechoslovakia also lost her strong frontier fortifications and, in effect, became a defenseless state.

The Munich accords were supposed to protect the remainder of Czechoslovakia, but they did just the opposite. Poland now stepped forward and demanded and received the Teschen region. Hungary submitted its territorial claims to the "arbitration" of German Foreign Minister Joachim von Ribbentrop and Italian Foreign Minister Count Galeazzo Ciano, and was awarded a sizable part of southern Slovakia. Encouraged by German Foreign Minister Joachim von Ribbentrop and his state secretary, Ernst Weizsaecker, the Slovakian Diet in Bratislava declared its independence on March 14, 1939, while Hungarian troops occupied Ruthenia, the eastern tip of Czechoslovakia. Finally, two days later, aging Czechoslovakian President Dr. Emil Hacha capitulated completely. He signed a document surrendering what was left of Bohemia and Moravia to the Third Reich as a "Protectorate." These areas were occupied by the Wehrmacht the same day. Czechoslovakia had ceased to exist.

POLAND WAS WALTER von Brauchitsch's campaign. Like most Germans at the time, he believed that the Polish Corridor and the Free City of Danzig, which had been awarded to Warsaw by the Treaty of Versailles, rightfully belonged to Germany and should be returned to her. As the date of the attack grew near, Dr. Hjalmar Schacht, the President of the Reichsbank and former Minister of Economics, said that he intended to go to Zossen (the new headquarters of OKH) to remind Brauchitsch that his oath to the Constitution did not permit a declaration of war without the consent of the Reichstag. Brauchitsch sent word back that if Schacht set one foot in OKH without his permission, he would have him arrested. Beck also sent Bauchitsch a letter, appealing to him to stop the invasion before it was too late. Brauchitsch did not even bother to reply.[38]

Although vastly overrated by both the foreign and domestic news media, the strength of the Wehrmacht was much greater in 1939 than at the time of the Sudetenland crisis. The Army was training about 250,000 conscripts a year and trained reservists were now available. The old Mark I and Mark II panzers (PzKw I and PzKw II, respectively) were gradually being phased out for the vastly superior Mark IIIs and Mark IVs (PzKw III and IV) models.* The deficiencies in the mobilization plans had been made clear under actual conditions in September 1938, and Brauchitsch had corrected them. The West Wall, a poor joke in 1938, was much stronger in 1939, and more divisions were available in 1939 than at the time of the Czech crisis. Finally, the strong and hostile Czech Army no longer existed. The twenty-five or so divisions required to guard this flank were now free for employment elsewhere.

Unlike the year before, Hitler did not interfere in either the planning or execution of military operations against Poland. Brauchitsch's scheme of maneuver was based on the assumption that the Poles would defend western Poland, where the country's major industries were located. For the attack, the German forces in the East would be divided into two Army groups. Army Group North (under General von Bock) would consist of 3rd Army in East Prussia and 4th Army in Pomerania. They were to cut off and destroy the Polish forces in the Corridor and establish contact between East Prussia and the rest of the Reich. Meanwhile, other elements of the 3rd Army were to advance on Warsaw from the north.

Rundstedt's Army Group South consisted of the 8th, 10th, and 14th Armies. The 10th Army (Reichenau) was by far the strongest. Its mission was to break through the southern Polish frontier and head directly for Warsaw, with the 8th and 14th Armies advancing on its left and right, respectively. Army Group C (under Ritter Wilhelm von Leeb) would guard the Western Front with the weak 1st, 5th, and 7th Armies. Table 1 shows the strengths of the German armies in the East.

---

*See Appendix IV for German tank characteristics.

Table 1

STRENGTHS OF THE GERMAN ARMIES vs. POLAND, 1939

3rd Army (Kuechler)	320,000*
4th Army (Kluge)	230,000
Army Group North Reserves	80,000
Total, Army Group North (Bock)	630,000
8th Army (Blaskowitz)	180,000
10th Army (Reichenau)	300,000
14th Army (List)	210,000
Army Group South Reserves	196,000
Total, Army Group South (Rundstedt)	886,000
Grand Total (Brauchitsch)	1,516,000

*Includes SA, frontier, and miscellaneous units.

SOURCES: Taylor, p. 313; Kennedy, p. 77.

The Polish Army in 1939 exceeded the strength of Brauchitsch's forces in raw numbers, but its equipment was hopelessly outdated and it had only a few obsolete tanks and a poor Air Force. Poland had only 280,000 men in the peacetime Army, but it depended on mobilizing 1,500,000 first-line reservists and 560,000 second-line reservists (ages forty-three to fifty-two). If they had been allowed to complete their mobilization, the Poles would have fielded twenty-eight regular infantry divisions, fifteen reserve divisions, two mountain divisions, eleven regular cavalry brigades, and a mechanized infantry brigade, as well as several anti-aircraft regiments and tank battalions and two air divisions (Poland had no separate air force).[39] Map 4 shows the German dispositions on August 31 during the Polish campaign.

Map 4

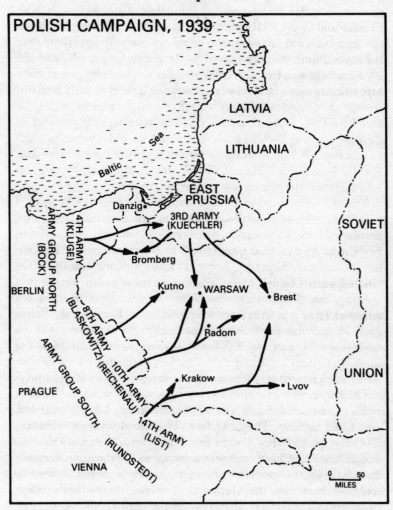

POLISH CAMPAIGN, 1939

LATVIA

LITHUANIA

Baltic   Sea

EAST PRUSSIA

Danzig

3RD ARMY (KUECHLER)

SOVIET

4TH ARMY (KLUGE)

ARMY GROUP NORTH (BOCK)

Bromberg

BERLIN

Kutno

WARSAW

Brest

8TH ARMY (BLASKOWITZ)

10TH ARMY (REICHENAU)

Radom

ARMY GROUP SOUTH

PRAGUE

Krakow

UNION

Lvov

14TH ARMY (LIST)

(RUNDSTEDT)

VIENNA

0   50
MILES

THE POLISH CAMPAIGN, 1939. Directed by Field Marshal Walter von Brauchitsch, the German Army conquered Poland in thirty-six days in the first blitzkrieg campaign, with no interference from Hitler. Both Army group commanders and four of the five Army commanders in this operation were eventually promoted to the rank of field marshal.

Brauchitsch did not give the Poles time to complete their mobilization. He had scheduled a number of maneuvers in East Prussia and eastern Germany in August 1939, so that the initial concentration did not appear to be a hostile act. When Hitler gave the signal, units rapidly moved to their assembly areas, and the invasion began at 4:45 A.M. on September 1. The Poles played right into Brauchitsch's hands by concentrating a third of their forces in or near the Corridor, and most of the rest on the frontier, just as he had hoped. As a result, as early as the morning of September 5, Brauchitsch and Bock had concluded that the Poles were "practically beaten."[40] The Polish government fled Warsaw the next day, and by September 7 Halder was already engaged in working out schedules for the transfer of troops to the west.

Brauchitsch wanted to avoid a battle for the center of Warsaw if he could, but the capital's garrison put up a spirited resistance despite its hopeless situation, so he ordered 3rd and 10th armies to begin a heavy and continuous artillery bombardment on September 20. Six days later, 8th Army launched a major assault on the city, supported by 3rd Army. The Poles tried to obtain a truce that evening, but Brauchitsch refused to allow it. He instructed 8th Army to agree to a truce only if General Julius Rommel, the Polish garrison commander, wanted to surrender. He did so at 2 P.M. on September 27, and 140,000 Polish soldiers (more than 16,000 of them wounded) capitulated.[41] The last remnants of the Polish Army surrendered on October 6. The campaign had lasted thirty-six days.

The Germans suffered a total of 8,082 killed, 27,278 wounded, and 5,029 missing. They had lost 217 tanks destroyed, including 89 PzKw Is, 83 PzKw IIs, 26 PzKw IIIs, and 19 PzKw IVs. The Polish Army had been completely destroyed. Of the approximately 800,000 men the government had managed to mobilize, 694,000 were captured by the Germans. The rest were either killed, captured by the Russians (who invaded eastern Poland on September 17), managed to hide inside Poland, or fled to Rumania or Hungary.[42]

Poland was the only operation Brauchitsch was allowed to direct without considerable interference from Hitler. He demonstrated solid generalship during this campaign, although he did use his panzer forces piecemeal and was subject to being overcautious.

These failures, however, must be regarded as minor. It is undeniable that the German Army under Brauchitsch won a major victory in the Polish campaign.

DURING THE OCCUPATION, Brauchitsch was careful not to incur Hitler's displeasure over the question of the Polish Jews. At this time Hitler was speaking in terms of deportation, rather than extermination, although some murders were already taking place. Brauchitsch ordered the Army not to interfere with the SS operations or "police" task forces.

BRAUCHITSCH OPPOSED GOING to war against the Western Allies. He (and Halder) hoped that the Allies would come to terms with Germany or try to take the offensive themselves. When Hitler made a long speech to his commanders on September 17, he permitted no discussion but instead ordered Brauchitsch to concentrate his forces in the West as soon as possible and to inform him of the earliest possible date at which the buildup could be completed.[43]

The OKH commander presented his plan for the invasion of the West to Hitler on October 7. Plan Yellow, as it was called, was an unimaginative rehash of the Schlieffen Plan of the 1900s. It called for a massive attack by Bock's Army Group B on Belgium and northern France with seventy-five divisions, with the main effort in the Liege-Namur sector. Rundstedt's Army Group A would launch a secondary attack in the center, while Leeb's Army Group C would remain on the defensive to the south. Under it, the panzer and motorized forces would advance through the marshy Low Countries, pivot southwest, and enter France from the north, thus outflanking the Maginot Line fortifications on the left. Brauchitsch said he opposed the immediate execution of the plan due to the need to stockpile ammunition, because of equipment and supply problems, and because the shorter days and foggy winter weather would minimize Luftwaffe support.[44]

Hitler did not like Brauchitsch's plan or comments at all. In mid-October he rejected Brauchitsch's objections and set the date for the execution of Yellow for the third week in November. Cancellation would depend on the weather, not the objections or difficulties of the Army.

The first detailed draft of Plan Yellow was issued on October 19. It was presented to Hitler by Keitel. Six days later the Fuehrer called Brauchitsch and Halder to the Reich Chancellery to discuss Yellow. Rather than use the modified Schlieffen Plan, which had been tried in World War I and failed then, Hitler brought up the possibility of a main attack south of the Meuse, coupled with a secondary offensive in the Low Countries, to draw the main British and French Armies into Belgium, where they could be cut off and destroyed. This suggestion took Brauchitsch and Halder by surprise. Debate on the relative merits of the two plans raged for some time, but no decision was reached.

Hitler set the date for the invasion of France as November 12, 1939. At noon on November 5, Brauchitsch met with Hitler and fatally wounded his own military career. Besides advancing the very valid points that the Army was unready and that the wet winter weather would enhance the advantages of the defense by impeding the advance of the panzers and limiting the hours of daylight during which the Luftwaffe could operate, he made the rather stupid comment that the German infantry in Poland had shown little spirit in the attack. He even spoke of "mutinies" in some units, of indiscipline at the front, and even invited comparisons of the state of the Army in 1939 to that of 1918, when the Second Reich collapsed.

These last arguments were simply not true. Hitler, realizing that Brauchitsch was lying, lost his temper and was soon in a white rage. He demanded to know the identities of the units involved. He would fly to them that very day and investigate, he screamed. He seized the general's notes and threw them into his safe. He yelled that it was incomprehensible to him how a commander-in-chief could blacken the reputation of the entire Army in this manner. "Not one frontline commander mentioned any lack of attacking spirit to me!" he roared.[45] He demanded that Brauchitsch furnish him with the detailed reports of the incidents in question, along with copies of the death sentences handed down as a result of them. Finally, he stormed out of the door and slammed it behind him, leaving von Brauchitsch pale and trembling. Even after he got back to Zossen later that day, von Brauchitsch was unable to speak coherently for some time. Hitler later dismissed the entire report as a pack of lies.

The conference of November 5 totally routed Brauchitsch.

Whereas before this date he vacillated on the subject of an anti-Hitler putsch, he never again showed the slightest indication of supporting a coup.

Hitler would not speak to Brauchitsch for weeks after this conference. On January 18, 1940, for example, Colonel Adolf Heusinger, the deputy chief of the operations branch at OKH, told General Manstein that Hitler had not seen Brauchitsch since November 5.[46] On November 23, in fact, Hitler expressed strong disapproval of Brauchitsch and added that it was unfortunate that there was no suitable replacement for him.[47]

Brauchitsch's stock sank even lower with Hitler at the end of January 1940, when Hitler's chief military adjutant, Colonel Rudolf Schmundt, returned from a visit to the Western Front in a state of great excitement. With him he carried an alternate plan for the

Map 5

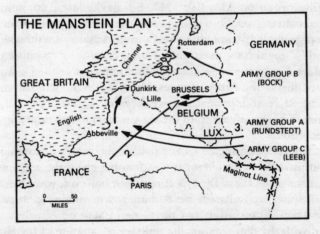

THE MANSTEIN PLAN was the brainchild of Lieutenant General (later Field Marshal) Erich von Manstein, Chief of Staff of Army Group B. It consisted of three stages: Army Group B invades the Low Countries (1), inducing the Allies to commit their mobile reserves to that sector (2). Then the main German forces attack through the Ardennes and drive to the Channel (3), cutting off the main Allied forces. The plan worked exactly as Manstein envisioned it.

western campaign. It was the brainchild of Lieutenant General Erich von Manstein, Rundstedt's brilliant Chief of Staff. The Manstein Plan called for an attack in the Low Countries to draw the Allied reserves north. Then the main attack would be launched to the south, through the Ardennes to the English Channel, cutting off the main enemy armies in Belgium (Map 5). Hitler was very happy about the plan, for it was essentially the same one that he had suggested in October! That it was proposed by Manstein, perhaps Germany's best young general, convinced Hitler both of his own genius and of the plan's feasibility. The fact that Brauchitsch had suppressed Manstein's ideas and refused to forward his memoranda to the Chancellery no doubt earned him more black marks in Hitler's book. The Fuehrer never seriously listened to Brauchitsch's advice again.

THE MANSTEIN PLAN worked exactly as its creator said it would. The invasion began on May 10, 1940. Six weeks later, on June 21, France surrendered. Overjoyed in victory, Hitler decided to reward his top generals by promoting them to field marshal. Although he probably would have preferred to have replaced Brauchitsch, he could hardly promote the others without promoting the Commander-in-Chief of the Army. Besides, Hitler's attitude had mellowed; now he at least tolerated the weak-willed C-in-C. On July 19 Brauchitsch was advanced to the rank of field marshal, along with eleven others.

Brauchitsch had mixed feelings about the proposed invasion of Britain in 1940 but thought it was feasible given the right set of circumstances. One of these prerequisites, however, was air superiority, which the Luftwaffe never managed to obtain, so there was no invasion. Brauchitsch and the General Staff nevertheless went ahead with the planning for the military occupation of the British Isles. On September 9, 1940, he signed a directive that after the occupation all males from seventeen to forty-five years of age would be transported to the Continent; in other words, most of the adult male population of the United Kingdom would become slave laborers in Nazi Europe.[48] This order, perhaps more than any other, demonstrates how far Brauchitsch was willing to go to please his master and keep his job.

AS EARLY AS July 2, 1940, Brauchitsch had instructed Halder to examine the possibility of invading Russia, so he was not surprised on July 21, when Hitler summoned him to Obersalzburg and announced his intention of conquering the Soviet Union. The next day he told Halder to begin the detailed planning. Halder asked Colonel Hans von Greiffenberg, the chief of OKH's operations branch, to pick a special assistant to prepare a working plan. Two days later Major General Erich Marcks, Chief of Staff of the 18th Army, was given the task.[49]

The Marcks Plan was submitted to Hitler on August 5. The objective of the campaign was to defeat the Soviet Army so thoroughly that Russia could never again threaten Germany. The Army was to seize all of the territory west of the Rostov-Gorki-Archangel line. The main objective of the campaign was Moscow.

The plan called for the attack forces to be divided into Army Groups North and South. Army Group North was to have 68 of the 147 available divisons and was assigned the task of taking Moscow. Its secondary objective was Leningrad. Army Group South (35 divisons) was to take Kiev and then Rostov. Forty-four divisions were to be initially held in OKH reserve.

Surprise and speed were to be the keys to victory in Russia, according to General Marcks. Panzer and motorized forces, closely supported by the Luftwaffe, were to break through Soviet lines and push rapidly toward the objectives, while infantry divisions were to follow as quickly as they could, encircling and destroying bypassed Russian formations on the way. Marcks estimated that it would take nine to seventeen weeks to carry out the operation.[50]

Although the number of army groups used was later expanded to three, the Marcks Plan remained the basis of the German strategy until the invasion began. Hitler disagreed with only one part of it, but it was major: he did not consider the capture of Moscow particularly important and would therefore not commit himself on what was to be done after the main Soviet armies were destroyed in western Russia (formerly eastern Poland), Belorussia, the Baltic States, and the Ukraine.

Brauchitsch never once questioned Hitler or OKW about the necessity or advisability of invading the Soviet Union, despite the fact that it would result in the dreaded two-front war. When the three army group commanders were informed of the planned invasion, all three protested to Brauchitsch, but the C-in-C replied only that he shared their fears but could do nothing. He did not say a word when Hitler commanded that the Army launch a "race war without pity."[51] He did not even oppose the Commissar Order of May 1941, in which Hitler decreed that the political officers attached to the Red Army were to be shot out of hand, even after they had surrendered. Several officers demanded that he protest against it, but Brauchitsch refused to risk the wrath of the Fuehrer. He had given up. Manstein wrote: "I am convinced that he wore himself out mentally in his struggle with a man of such ruthless will. . . . Brauchitsch choked down his vexation and anger, particularly as he was no match for Hitler dialectically."[52]

Table 2

GERMAN ORDER OF BATTLE, EASTERN FRONT, June 22, 1941

High Command of the Army (OKH): Brauchitsch

Army Group North (Leeb)
    18th Army (Kuechler)
    4th Panzer Group (Hoepner)
    6th Army (Busch)
    1st Air Fleet (Keller)

Army Group Center (Bock)
    3rd Panzer Group (Hoth)
    9th Army (Strauss)
    4th Army (Kluge)
    2nd Panzer Group (Guderian)
    2nd Air Fleet (Kesselring)

Army Group South (Rundstedt)
    1st Panzer Group (Kleist)
    6th Army (Reichenau)
    17th Army (Heinrich von Stuelpnagel)
    11th Army (Schobert)
    4th Air Fleet (Loehr)

The invasion of the Soviet Union began on June 22, 1941. Table 2 shows the initial order of battle of the German Army on the Eastern Front, and Map 6 shows the first phase of the campaign.

Map 6

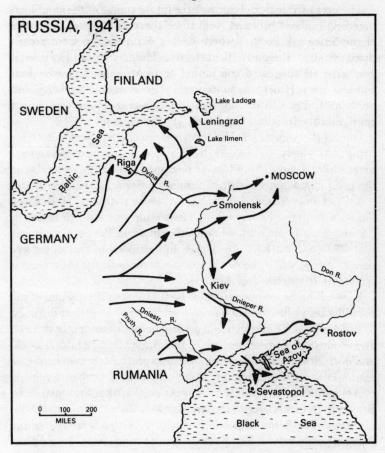

RUSSIA, 1941. Germany invaded Russia with three army groups on June 22, 1942. The operations were nominally directed by Field Marshal Walter von Brauchitsch, Commander-in-Chief of the Army, but he suffered from considerable interference from Hitler and was unable to take Moscow. During the subsequent Soviet counteroffensive, Brauchitsch was made a scapegoat for this failure and was retired in disgrace on December 19, 1941.

The Wehrmacht quickly overcame the Soviet frontier defenses and achieved complete tactical surprise. Some units drove more than two hundred miles inside Russia within five days. On the other hand, Hitler was bypassing Brauchitsch and giving orders directly to the army group commanders by June 25.

The great strategic debate over the future course of the campaign raged throughout July and August 1941, especially after the Battle of the Smolensk Pocket, where Bock's Army Group Center captured 300,000 Russians. Brauchitsch, Halder, Bock, Hoth, and Guderian all advocated continuing on to Moscow, and even Jodl was won over. Hitler was supported in his views only by Keitel and Schmundt, his OKW advisers – yes-men without any direct responsibility for the conduct of operations.

During the arguments, Hitler severely castigated Brauchitsch for being too easily influenced by his army group commanders; meanwhile, Army Group Center remained idle for three weeks, as the good campaign weather of summer passed. In the end, Hitler could not be persuaded. On August 24 he detached Hoth's 3rd Panzer Group from Army Group Center and sent it north to join in the attack on Leningrad, while Guderian's 2nd Panzer Group was sent south against Kiev. Bock was thus stripped of four of his five panzer corps, while the Soviets desperately built up their central sector for the defense of Moscow.

Kiev fell on September 16, and the subsequent liquidation of the Kiev Pocket yielded 667,000 prisoners. Hitler now seemed disposed to end the initial campaign and go into winter quarters. Both Leeb and Rundstedt favored this plan, but Brauchitsch, Halder, Bock, and Kesselring all felt an attempt to capture Moscow should be made. Hitler allowed himself to be convinced – probably not too much against his will.[53] He then went even further and instructed Brauchitsch to advance to the Archangel-middle Volga-Astrakhan-Caucasus line before the onset of winter. These were incredibly unrealistic objectives. The German armies would have done well to capture Moscow, Leningrad, and Rostov.

By sending them racing all over Russia, Hitler had contributed greatly to the wear on his panzers. Tank units had less than 50 percent of their authorized strength when Operation Typhoon, the final drive on Moscow, began on September 26. Due to the already excessive wear on the tanks, it was not considered advisable to bring Guderian's 2nd Panzer Group back to Smolensk. He was to attack from where he was toward Tula, south of the city. Hoth, strangely, was ordered to drive his 3rd Panzer Group toward the upper Volga, north of Stalin's capital. Moscow was to be taken by Kluge's 4th Army and Hoepner's 4th Panzer Group, which had been transferred to Bock from Army Group North in mid-September (see chapter 5). The panzer groups were redesignated panzer armies on October 6, but received no additional units.

Brauchitsch had now been contending with Hitler's rudeness and ruthlessness for four years. He had lived on a steady diet of humiliation, anger, hatred, frustration, and fear, day-in and day-out. As early as July 28, 1941, Halder had noted in his diary that Brauchitsch was at the end of his tether, "and hides behind an iron mask of manliness so as not to betray his complete helplessness."[54] On November 10 Brauchitsch had his first heart attack. In the hospital he was told that he had a malignant cardiac disease that was probably incurable.[55] He nevertheless returned to duty in mid-November, more determined than ever to capture Moscow.

It simply could not be done. The German Army had expected the Russian campaign to be another *blitzkrieg* victory and had not provided either the equipment or clothing for a winter campaign. After a promising start, Typhoon bogged down in the Russian mud by mid-October. Army Group Center was at the end of a thousand-mile supply line, and only 30 percent of the German transport vehicles were still operating. Infantry divisions were down to two to three thousand men and low on ammunition; still they pushed forward again on November 16, only to be hit by the full impact of the Russian winter. The German units lacked cold-weather lubricants and soon the moving parts of machine guns and artillery pieces were frozen. Wounded men often froze to death where they fell. Meanwhile, Walter von Brauchitsch had had enough. Sick in body and spirit, and probably realizing that he would be made the scapegoat for the Wehrmacht's first major defeat, he submitted his resignation on December 6. Hitler paced up and down the room for ten minutes before replying that he could not allow a change in command at that moment. Brauchitsch got up and left the room without saying a word.[56]

Meanwhile, that same day, Stalin threw all his reserves into a massive winter offensive from the Baltic to the Black Sea, aimed at nothing less than decisively defeating the Wehrmacht all along the Eastern Front, as well as totally destroying Army Group Center. Hitler responded by issuing his first hold-at-all-costs order. Every soldier was to stand and, if necessary, die where he stood. Flanks were to be ignored; not one step back was to be permitted, even if the units in question were encircled.

On December 16, Colonel Schmundt informed Hitler that von Brauchitsch had secretly discussed limited withdrawals with von Bock, von Kluge, and Guderian. Arrangements for setting up a winter line had also been discussed. Hitler immediately cancelled these plans and demanded that the troops hold where they were, regardless of the situation on their flanks or in their rear. Three days later Hitler dismissed von Brauchitsch. Their final meeting, which lasted two hours, was acrimonious. In the end Hitler shouted that he was assuming command of the Army himself because he knew of no general who was capable of instilling the National Socialist spirit into the Army. But, he added in a soft voice, "We will remain friends."[57]

News of Brauchitsch's retirement was announced without preface to the entire world. Hitler named himself C-in-C of the Army. The next day the disgraced field marshal left Zossen for the last time. He never saw Hitler again.[58]

Like Blomberg before him and many after, Brauchitsch retired into obscurity. He was kept under quiet surveillance by the Gestapo for a time as a possible dissident, but this watch was soon dropped. The former Commander-in-Chief of the Army was now just a tired, sick, and broken old man.

Predictably, Hitler blamed Brauchitsch for the defeat in Russia in the winter of 1941/42. On March 15, 1942, Hitler described him to Goebbels as "a vain, cowardly wretch."[59]

On August 3, 1944, two weeks after the nearly successful attempt on Hitler's life, Brauchitsch wrote a letter to the Fuehrer, dissociating himself from the conspiracy of July 20 and offering his services once more. On August 19 he issued a public proclamation, condemning the conspirators in strong terms and welcoming Himmler's appointment as Commander-in-Chief of the Replacement Army. By now Hitler's opinion of Brauchitsch had improved considerably because of his previous support of the V-2 rocket project. Brauchitsch's offer to return to active duty was not acted upon, however.[60]

Walter von Brauchitsch was arrested at his estate in Schleswig-Holstein by the British in early May 1945. Subsequently taken to England, he was returned to Germany with Manstein and Rundstedt and imprisoned in Muenster. By now he was practically blind. Despite his poor health, he was sent to "the bunker" at Nuremberg, and forced to share a two-man cell with five other men. Later he was transferred to Hamburg. He was scheduled to go on trial before a British Military Court as a war criminal in 1949, but he died of heart failure in the British Military Hospital at Hamburg-Barmbeck on October 18, 1948.

3

Ewald von Kleist

UNLIKE THE FIELD marshals described in the first two chapters, there is no hint of scandal in the career of Paul Ludwig Ewald von Kleist. He never compromised with the Nazis or anyone else. He was not involved in sexual scandals like Blomberg and Brauchitsch, nor was he a pro-Nazi like Blomberg, nor weak-willed like Brauchitsch, nor blindly obedient, like many generals. He was the prototype Prussian officer of the Old School who openly favored a restoration of the monarchy. And yet, he was not a conspirator. Hitler was the Head of State and Kleist accepted that fact. To the Prussian Officer Corps, an oath was a sacred, almost physical thing, and von Kleist swore an oath of allegiance to Hitler in 1934, along with the rest of the Army. He would never go back on it. In short, he was a Prussian soldier and nothing else. That is why Adolf Hitler detested him.

HE WAS BORN on August 8, 1881, in Braunfels an der Lahn, in the province of Hessen, from a long line of Prussian generals and aristocrats. Three field marshals came from his family, and one of his kinsmen, Field Marshal Count Friedrich von Kleist, won the Battle of Laon in France in 1814, against the great Napoleon himself.[1] Thirty-one members of his family held the *Pour le Mérite*.[2]

Kleist's own father was a professor of mathematics at a private secondary school.[3]

Ewald von Kleist joined the 3rd Royal Field Artillery Regiment as a *Fahnenjunker* (officer-cadet) in March 1900. He was commissioned second lieutenant on August 18, 1901, and became regimental adjutant in 1907. After attending the cavalry school at Hanover (1908–09), he was promoted to first lieutenant in 1910 and posted to the War Academy in Berlin, where he underwent General Staff training. Later that year he married Gisela Wachtel at Hanover and remained devoted to her for the rest of his life.[4]

Kleist graduated from the War Academy in 1912 and was assigned to the 14th Hussar Regiment at Kassel as a General Staff officer. Shortly before the outbreak of World War I, he was transferred to the staff of the 1st Prince's Own Hussar Regiment and was promoted to captain of cavalry (*Rittmeister*).

Captain von Kleist spent the next four years on the Eastern Front. In late 1914 he commanded a cavalry squadron in the Battle of Tannenberg,[5] where the Russian invasion of East Prussia was decisively defeated. He led his squadron for exactly one year, returning to General Staff duty on October 17, 1915, as a staff officer with the 85th Infantry Division, a *Landwehr* (reserve) division on the Eastern Front. On January 1, 1916, he was named adjutant of a brigade, and in June he became deputy divisional adjutant. At the end of the year he was named Ordnance Officer of XVII Corps. In 1917 he was named Chief of Staff of the Guards Cavalry Division. Following the Russian capitulation in early 1918, the Guards were transferred to the Western Front, and Kleist fought in the battles around Reims and in the Champagne and Maas River sectors. Toward the end of the war he was assigned to the staff of the 225th Infantry Division. After the armistice, Kleist served briefly with the Freikorps before joining the Reichsheer as a divisional chief of staff.[6]

From 1919 to 1931, Ewald von Kleist held various staff and training appointments. He was with the 13th Cavalry Regiment (1920–23), Instructor of Tactics at the Cavalry School at Hanover (1923–26), Chief of Staff of the 2nd Cavalry Division at Breslau (1927–28), and Chief of Staff of the 3rd Infantry Division and later Chief of Staff of Wehrkreis III, both in Berlin (1928–31). In 1931 he was named Commander of the élite 9th Infantry Regiment at

Potsdam. He was promoted successively to major (1922), lieutenant colonel (1926), colonel (1929), and major general (1932).[7] On February 1, 1932, he assumed command of the 2nd Cavalry Division at Breslau, replacing Gerd von Rundstedt, who moved up to the command of Wehrkreis III. Kleist was promoted to lieutenant general in 1935.[8]

Meanwhile, Gisela von Kleist gave him two children, both boys. Johannes Juergen Christoph Ewald von Kleist (called Ewald) was born in 1917 and later followed his father into the Army. During World War II he served as a captain of cavalry on the Eastern Front. Von Kleist's other son, Hugo Edmund Christoph Heinrich, who was born in 1921, also served in Russia, but as an agricultural specialist. His severe asthmatic condition made him medically unfit for combat duty.[9]

The 2nd Cavalry Division was dissolved in the expansion of 1936, but Kleist never moved. His HQ was converted into Headquarters, Wehrkreis VIII, and he was promoted to general of cavalry on August 1, 1936.[10] His new command included the 8th, 18th, and 28th Infantry divisions, as well as the 3rd and 4th Frontier Zone commands.[11] He supervised Hitler's military expansion in Silesia until February 1938, when he was forced into retirement by von Brauchitsch because of his pro-Royalist political views. As a departing honor, Kleist was authorized to wear yellow cavalry shoulder boards with the number "8" on them (for 8th Cavalry Regiment). Kleist wore these shoulder boards throughout World War II, instead of the traditional red shoulder boards of a general.[12]

Ewald von Kleist lived in comfortable retirement on his beautiful country estate at Weidebrueck, near Breslau, for a year and a half.[13] Despite his anti-Nazi views, however, his ability was never questioned by Hitler and his paladins. He was recalled to active duty in August 1939, at the age of 58, for the invasion of Poland. He commanded XXII Corps of General Siegmund Wilhelm List's 14th Army on the southern sector of the front. Initially in reserve, XXII was committed to action on September 4 with a panzer, a light, and a mountain division. Kleist distinguished himself by capturing the oil fields below Lvov and linking up with Guderian near the Bug River on September 17, thus cutting Poland in two.[14]

Kleist was given an extremely important assignment for the

French campaign. On February 29, 1940, Hitler approved his appointment as commander of the main panzer forces in the western campaign. These included General Georg-Hans Reinhardt's XLI Motorized Corps (6th and 8th Panzer divisions), Heinz Guderian's XIX Motorized Corps (1st, 2nd, and 10th Panzer divisions, plus the élite Grossdeutschland Motorized Infantry Regiment), and the three motorized infantry divisions of General Gustav von Wietersheim's XIV Motorized Corps. Five of the ten German panzer divisions were under Kleist's direct command, and two more were to support him to the north. Kleist was thus the first man to direct a panzer army, although the term would not be used officially for another year and a half. His XXII Corps Headquarters was temporarily renamed Panzer Group Kleist.[15]

Why was a cavalryman like Ewald von Kleist given such an important command? He was a conservative traditionalist who had not led tank forces until 1939 and, if he had performed well in Poland, his accomplishments were certainly not to be compared to Guderian's. In fact, Kleist had never been particulary well disposed toward the panzer arm, and always preferred the horse to the tank. The answer to the question was fundamental: the High Command of the German Army had not yet fully accepted the panzer branch or the concept of the blitzkrieg. They felt Kleist could keep a tight rein on the impetuous Guderian and prevent the tank advocates from endangering the success of the operation by their precipitate actions; in other words, Kleist's cautiousness was seen as a necessary counterbalance to Guderian's rashness.

PANZER GROUP KLEIST had the most critical mission of the entire French campaign: penetrate the Meuse River line and sweep to the English Channel as the all-important southern thrust of the Manstein Plan. If successful, he would cut off the main French and British armies north of Paris, which could easily win the entire war for Germany. Map 5 shows this offensive.

The Manstein Plan called for a quick advance through the difficult Belgian Ardennes and a rapid crossing of the Meuse, which was weakly defended, because the Allies considered a major armored advance by this route impossible. Kleist placed Reinhardt's corps on the northern flank of the group and Guderian on the south. Wietersheim, in group reserve, would follow behind Guderian with his motorized infantry, and the foot soldiers of List's 12th Army marched behind him. The 5th and 7th Panzer divisions of General Hermann Hoth's XV Panzer Corps, while not under Kleist's direct command, were assigned the task of crossing the Meuse and covering his northern flank.

Panzer Group Kleist moved out at 6 P.M. on May 9, 1940. It was a moonless night and progress was slow and difficult through the Eifel region, as the German Ardennes is called.[16] The storm broke across the Dutch, Belgian, Luxemburgian, and French borders at 4 A.M. on May 10. The Luftwaffe attacked Allied air bases and ground installations up to two hundred and fifty miles behind the front, while panzer grenadiers quickly overcame the Belgian frontier outposts. The French Cavalry Corps, which was supposed to cross into Belgium as soon as the Germans violated Belgian neutrality, did not move out until 10:30 A.M.: a slow start for the French. By the evening of the first day of the offensive, the spearheads of the 10th Panzer Division had made contact with the French 2nd Cavalry and 3rd Colonial Infantry divisions and were pushing them back toward the Meuse.[17]

Meanwhile, Hitler was overjoyed to learn that the British Expeditionary Force and the French 1st and 7th Armies, which included France's best units, were pouring into Belgium and Holland, believing the main German attack was coming through the Low Countries. "I could have wept for joy!" he exclaimed later. "They had fallen into the trap!"[18] Now, if the panzers could score their breakthrough and reach the English Channel, a decisive German victory was in sight.

The following day Kleist almost made a serious blunder. French cavalry forces tried to advance from Montmédy against his left flank. He ordered Guderian to halt his left-flank division, the 10th Panzer, and turn it south to meet the threat. Such a move would have diverted a third of XIX Motorized Corps from its objective and made the success of an attack across the Meuse at Sedan doubtful. Guderian emphatically objected to this move, and von Kleist yielded to his arguments. He ordered Wietersheim to safeguard the left flank against the French cavalry threat with elements of his XIV Motorized Corps.[19] The advance continued.

That day the German panzers defeated the French cavalry. The 2nd and 5th Light Cavalry divisions of the French 2nd Army fell back toward the main line of resistance behind the Meuse, or were forced to "take to the hills." This exposed the right flank of the French 9th Army's cavalry, which also began an immediate withdrawal.[20] By now General Gamelin, the French Commander-in-Chief, began to suspect that the Ardennes thrust might be the true focus of the German attack. His intelligence service had already identified four of Kleist's five panzer divisions, as well as Hoth's 5th and 7th Panzer divisions to the north. Gamelin ordered eleven French divisions to converge on the threatened sector with the highest railroad priority. The problem was that these divisions would arrive on the Meuse between May 14 and 21. This fact did not excessively worry Gamelin, however, because he did not expect Kleist to try to cross the Meuse until the infantry of List's 12th Army arrived, about May 19.[21]

On May 12 the last of the French cavalry fell back behind the Meuse, and all of the bridges in Kleist's sector were blown. The French cavalry, which was supposed to delay the Germans five to six days, had delayed them only three. General Huntziger, the Commander of the French 2nd Army, was alarmed, for it was his army that Guderian was barreling down upon. He demanded reinforcements, so the High Command assigned the French 3rd Armored and 3rd Motorized divisions to him, along with the 14th Infantry Division of the 9th Army, whose right wing faced Kleist's northern thrust (Reinhardt's XLI Motorized Corps). It would, however, take these units some time to reach their destinations.[22]

That day, May 12, Hitler sent Colonel Schmundt, his chief adjutant, to von Kleist's command post. The Fuehrer wanted to know if von Kleist planned to attempt a crossing of the Meuse the next day, or if he wanted to wait for List's infantry to arrive. Kleist replied that he intended to attack "at once, without wasting time." Hitler approved this decision and ordered the attacks be supported by the dive-bombers of General Baron Wolfram von Richthofen's VIII Air Corps.[23]

Kleist summoned General Guderian to his CP that evening and ordered him to attack across the Meuse in the vicinity of Sedan by 4 P.M. the next day, May 13. Guderian pointed out that he would only have two divisions for the assault, as the 2nd Panzer on his northern flank was still being held up by die-hard French resistance in the Semoy sector. He wanted to delay the crossing until his entire corps was up. Guderian's uncharacteristic cautiousness is no doubt attributable to a brush with death he had earlier that day during a rare French air attack. A French bomb had struck his headquarters at the Hotel Panorama in Bouillon and he had narrowly escaped. The window through which Guderian was watching had been shattered by a bomb fragment, and the general had been covered with glass splinters. Guderian was still shaken by the incident. Kleist overruled the panzer leader's objections and ordered him to attack with whatever forces were available. He issued similar orders to Reinhardt.[24]

Guderian's plan of attack was a concentrated thrust by his center division, the 1st Panzer, just west of Sedan. The division was reinforced with the Grossdeutschland Regiment. The corps artillery units were assigned to support the 1st Panzer, as were the bulk of the panzer artillery regiments of the neighboring divisions.

Sedan was defended by the French 55th and 71st Infantry divisions. Neither was of high quality. French General Grandsard, whose X Corps was responsible for the sector, described the soldiers of these divisions as "fat and flabby men in their thirties who had to be retrained."[25] Only 20 of the 450 officers of the 55th were regulars and the division had only about 25 percent of its authorized complement of 25mm anti-tank guns, even though the French had 520 such guns in storage – enough to equip ten divisions. The 71st Infantry was in even worse shape. It had less than half of its anti-tank and anti-aircraft guns, and 7,000 of its 17,000 men were either on leave or had reported sick. Morale was not high in either unit.[26]

The Grossdeutschland Regiment crossed the river in pneumatic and engineer boats. They landed at the western edge of Sedan and swung behind the city, taking the critical Marfee Heights about 7 P.M. They were followed across the river by the infantry of the 1st Motorized Brigade, 1st Panzer Division, which joined the others at the heights about 7:30 P.M Two infantry battalions of the 10th Panzer Division crossed the Meuse southeast of the city at nightfall and joined the others on the heights after dark. Meanwhile, German combat engineers assembled the first ferry in thirty-eight minutes and began transporting men and anti-tank guns across the Meuse. By midnight a sixteen-ton pontoon bridge had been built across the river at Glaire.[27]

The forward elements of Lieutenant General Rudolf Veiel's 2nd Panzer Division – the 5th Panzer Reconnaissance and 2nd Motorcycle battalions – finally came up on the right flank at 5 P.M. Guderian immediately ordered them across the river. They landed almost exactly at the junction of the French 55th Infantry and 102nd Fortress divisions, which was also the boundary between Huntziger's 2nd and Corap's 9th armies. At 5:10 P.M. the 55th Infantry Division reported that it had lost contact with the infantry on its left. A gap had been opened between the French 2nd and 9th armies – a gap that was never to be closed.[28]

Meanwhile, reports circulated through French artillery channels that German tanks were on Marfee Heights and had reached Bulson, a village about five miles south of Sedan. These reports were completely false, for not a single panzer had yet crossed the river, but the rumors soon reached the infantry as well. The colonels commanding the X Corps heavy artillery regiment and the artillery group supporting the 55th Infantry Division ordered their men to retreat, and then they disappeared. Most of the guns were abandoned as the 55th panicked. The roads were soon clogged with men who, in the words of General Goulard, were "terror-stricken and in the grip of mass hysteria."[29] The division disintegrated; some of the troops did not stop until they reached Reims, sixty miles away.[30] Soon Guderian held a bridgehead five miles wide and five miles deep. By dawn, he had an entire panzer brigade across the river.[31]

On the French side, everything was in confusion. Corap had ordered the 3rd Spahis Brigade and the 53rd Infantry Division to the Bar River (just west of Guderian's bridgehead), but only the 3rd arrived. Due to confused orders, the 53rd Infantry spent the night marching in circles and was not in position on May 14. It was a poorly trained unit in any event, as it had spent the winter constructing fortifications and then had been used for farming in the Seine-et-Oise.[32]

The French did launch a counterattack at 7 A.M., three hours later than planned, with the 213th Infantry Regiment and two battalions of infantry support tanks from X Corps reserve. Two panzers and two 88mm guns were knocked out, and the commander of the 1st Panzer Regiment was seriously wounded, but by 8:30 A.M. more than half of the French tanks were burning and the commander of the infantry regiment was dead. The left flank of the 71st Infantry Division was in full retreat (even though it had not yet engaged German ground forces) and under attack by Stuka dive-bombers. By nightfall the 71st had also ceased to exist. Huntziger nevertheless signaled Gamelin that the bridgehead was sealed off and that French units were still in possession of Marfee Heights.[33]

The French 3rd Armored Division, which had only been formed six weeks before, arrived in the area that morning but was immobilized until noon due to a lack of fuel. (French tanks were designed as infantry support vehicles and had only about one-third of the range of the German tanks.) It was preparing to counterattack south of Sedan at 3:30 P.M., along with the French 3rd Mechanized Division, but General Flavigny, the French XXI Corps commander, intervened. In accordance with French tactical doctrine of 1940 (which dated back to World War I), Flavigny viewed tanks and armored vehicles as infantry support weapons only. Accordingly, he cancelled the counterattack and dispersed the two divisions over a twelve-mile front. General Huntziger was in the process of moving his headquarters back to Verdun(!), so he was in no position to reverse Flavigny's decision.[34]

Kleist's decision to attack across the Meuse at once had been the correct one. On the afternoon of May 14, Guderian burst across the Bar River. The Chanoine Group of the French 2nd Army (the 5th Light Cavalry and 1st Cavalry brigades) put up stiff resistance but was unable to stop the panzer units. By nightfall the French cavalry was retreating to the south, while the remnants of the 53rd Infantry Division, which had been swamped piecemeal, were retreating in several directions. Guderian had captured more than forty guns and "thousands" of prisoners by nightfall.[35]

The French 9th Army began to disintegrate. "On the ground," Jacques Benost-Mechin wrote later, "Corap's ravished army scarcely even *looked* like a disciplined force."[36] The next day, May 15, French resistance in front of Guderian collapsed completely and the "dash to the Channel" began. Meanwhile, Gamelin called Huntziger and emphatically reminded him that he had been given the 3rd Armored Division to launch a counterattack. Huntziger delayed several hours before relaying the message to Flavigny, who also delayed several hours before passing it on to General Antoine Brocard, the divisional commander. Flavigny calculated that it would take twenty-four hours to reassemble the scattered division. Later that day, Huntziger relieved Brocard of his command for not assembling it quickly enough! Since a scapegoat had been found, all thought of a counterattack was forgotten.[37]

Meanwhile, to the north, Corap ordered the French 102nd Garrison Division to retreat. Up until now, this overaged, under-equipped static division had checked the entire XLI Motorized Corps – a magnificent feat of arms! As soon as it began to withdraw, however, Lieutenant General Franz Kempf's 6th Panzer Division threw an improvised bridge over the Meuse and roared across. Kempf fell upon the rear of the 102nd Garrison, which had had to abandon most of its heavy equipment and artillery on the Meuse due to a lack of transport. Soon the 102nd had also been overwhelmed and ceased to exist. The 8th Panzer Division followed Kempf across and by evening Reinhardt's spearheads had advanced forty miles.[38] Map 7 shows the advance of Panzer Group Kleist from May 15 to 20.

That night von Kleist ordered Guderian to halt until the bridgehead was consolidated. Guderian rushed back to see Colonel Kurt Zeitzler, the Panzer Group Chief of Staff, and then von Kleist himself. After a heated argument, Kleist agreed to allow another twenty-four-hours' advance, so sufficient space could be gained for an infantry corps to enter the bridgehead.[39]

On May 16, Guderian's advanced units moved ahead forty miles and were more than fifty-five miles west of Sedan. Reinhardt got the rest of his corps across the river and advanced several miles, destroying the entire French XLI Corps in the process.[40] He was only eleven miles from 9th Army Headquarters, where General Giraud had relieved Corap as commander. There was little Giraud could do, however. The gap in 9th Army's sector was now sixty-two miles wide. To make matters worse, XLI Motorized Corps mauled the French 2nd Armored Division that evening. The division's tanks were being shipped by rail to Signy-l'Abbaye, while its wheeled vehicles came up separately. The 6th Panzer just happened to drive right through the middle of this maneuver, separating the short-ranged tanks from the motorized column, which included their fuel trucks. The divisional artillery was caught on the road and destroyed before it could deploy, while most of the tanks were smashed at or near the railroad station at

Map 7

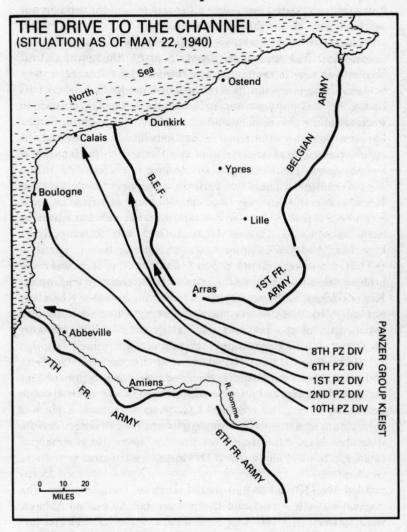

THE DRIVE TO THE CHANNEL
(SITUATION AS OF MAY 22, 1940)

THE DRIVE TO THE CHANNEL, MAY 1940. Panzer Group
Kleist broke through to the English Channel and isolated the British
Expeditionary Force, the Belgian Army, and the 1st French Army in
the Dunkirk Pocket in the Western Campaign of 1940. This victory
doomed France, which surrendered to Hitler the following month.

Singy. Some of them had not even been taken off the flatcars. The 2nd Armored's signal units were also overrun, and the division was scattered and thoroughly disorganized.[41]

France only had four armored divisions when the campaign began. Hoth had already destroyed the first to the north, and the second was now in remnants. The third was the Huntziger, who was retreating to the southwest. The fourth, under Colonel Charles de Gaulle, was not yet completely organized. There was panic in Paris when the government learned that not a single division stood between them and the panzers, as Gamelin had committed the entire strategic reserve to Belgium and Holland on the first day of the campaign. The French officials decided to evacuate the seat of the government to Tours that very afternoon, never suspecting that Kleist's objective was the Channel coast and not Paris.

There was fear on the German side, also, but with less cause. As early as May 15, Colonel General Gerd von Rundstedt, the Commander of Army Group A, was considering halting Kleist on the Oise, some seventy miles from Sedan. On May 16 he did order a twenty-four-hour halt, so the infantry could come up and protect Kleist's flanks, and Brauchitsch endorsed the decision. Kleist was not upset by these orders, for they corresponded with his own instructions of the previous day. Then came a dispatch from Guderian reporting on the day's progress and informing Kleist that he planned to continue the advance on the morrow. Guderian commented later that he never dreamed, after the successes of May 16, that the orders to halt were still in effect. Kleist never thought otherwise; in fact, he considered Guderian's dispatch a piece of rank insubordination. He immediately sent further orders demanding that XIX Motorized Corps halt at once. He commanded Guderian to meet him at the XIX Corps forward airstrip at 7 A.M. the next day.[42]

Ewald von Kleist had had about enough of Heinz Guderian. The panzer leader was undoubtedly brilliant, but he was not an easy man to work with. He was considered a maverick and had had difficulties with Kluge and Bock in Poland. It was also generally known that he was less than thrilled about Kleist's appointment to Panzer Group Command, and the two had already clashed, as we have seen. As soon as he landed at the airstrip, Kleist began to upbraid Guderian violently for disobeying orders. Guderian was not the type of man to take a reprimand quietly, and a vehement argument began. It ended with Guderian demanding to be relieved of his command. Kleist was "momentarily taken aback,"[43] but backing down was not his nature, either. He sacked Guderian on the spot.

Historians have looked down on Kleist for relieving Guderian, but this author does not. I consider it highly unlikely that Kleist would have relieved Guderian had he not literally asked for it. Guderian did have a fractious nature, but he was a tank genius; Kleist, who respected his talent if not his nature, would not have sacked him out of hand. Later, in Russia, Kleist showed a reluctance to relieve senior commanders. He just wanted to have his orders obeyed – insisted upon it, in fact, as any officer must. If Guderian did not want to be relieved, he should not have demanded it.

Later that day, May 16, Colonel General List, the commander of the 12th Army, straightened out the matter. He told Guderian that the order to halt had come from Hitler, not Kleist, and that Guderian would not be allowed to resign his command. Army Group A expected the halt order to be obeyed, he said, although a "reconnaissance in force" would be permitted. Corps Headquarters was to stay where it was. Then he went to Panzer Group Headquarters to smooth Kleist's ruffled feathers.

Guderian interpreted List's order as a green light to continue his advance. He went forward with his panzers as part of an "advanced" corps headquarters. He was more careful this time, however, and set up his communications in such a manner that higher headquarters could not intercept his messages.[44]

May 17 saw the counterattack of Charles de Gaulle's French 4th Armored Division. Much was made of it later for political reasons, but it did not jeopardize the advance at all and was, in fact, easily beaten off. The 4th Armored was not in particularly good condition from the beginning. It was still in the organizational phase when the invasion began and had never been on a tactical maneuver as a unit, and it had little or no infantry support. Many of its tank crews were trained to fight in light tanks, but then had been given heavy "B" tanks. Due to a shortage of ammunition, they had been allowed to fire only one practice round from their 75mm main battle guns before being sent into battle against Germany's élite

Panzer Corps. Soon the 4th Armored was under Stuka attack and in retreat.[45] Unlike the other French divisions Panzer Group Kleist had faced, however, it did not fall apart completely, which says something for de Gaulle's leadership.

The German High Command regained its nerve, and the halt order was revoked on May 18. Guderian and Reinhardt were directed to break the Canal du Nord line, behind which the Allies were desperately trying to establish a solid front forward of the English Channel. The infantrymen of the British 23rd and 12th Infantry divisions occupied their sectors as ordered, but the French units assigned to defend the fourteen miles south of the canal failed to arrive. Also, two British territorial divisions had no artillery in support when they were attacked by the 1st, 2nd, 6th, 7th and 8th Panzer divisions, with the 5th and 10th Panzers close at hand. The line did not hold for long.[46]

General Giraud tried to organize a counterattack with the French 1st Mechanized Division but got nowhere. The division had been so thoroughly dispersed over the 1st North African Infantry Division's front that it was not reassembled by 10:30 P.M., when Reinhardt's tanks slashed through to Le Catelet, where Giraud was setting up a new command post. The headquarters of the French 9th Army was quickly overrun. Giraud escaped alone across the open countryside.[47] He was picked up the next day. French sources say he was captured by a panzer detachment; German sources say it was a field kitchen unit. The reader may take his pick. In any event, the French 9th Army had ceased to exist.

Meanwhile, there was near hysteria in the high commands on both sides of the line. Hitler loudly accused Brauchitsch and Halder of advancing too rapidly and jeopardizing the entire campaign. French Prime Minister Paul Reynaud, who had more cause to worry, sacked sixty-eight-year-old Marshal Gamelin and replaced him with seventy-three-year-old Marshal Maxime Weygand. He also brought eighty-four-year-old Marshal Henri Pétain into the government as vice premier. So much for new blood. Both were poor choices. Pétain was a defeatist, and Weygand hated the British in particular and all politicians in general. His first act as Command-in-Chief was to go to bed. He did not issue a single order until May 21.[48]

The panzer advance continued on May 19, depsite the Fuehrer's nervousness. Lord Gort, Commander of the British Expeditionary Force (BEF), was already suggesting to the War Office that an evacuation might be necessary. He ordered the air component of the BEF to return to the United Kingdom. Meanwhile, the 8th Panzer Division overtook and smashed the 70th Infantry Brigade (of the British 23rd Infantry Division). By nightfall the 70th had fewer than two hundred and fifty men left. Further west, the 1st Panzer Division established a bridgehead across the Somme near Peronne and captured several French staff officers.[49]

The next day, May 20, elements of the 2nd Panzer Division took Abbeville against weak resistance. About 7 P.M. that night, a panzer battalion reached the English Channel at Noyelles. More than 400,000 French and British troops now were isolated in what became known as the Dunkirk Pocket.[50]

The Allies threw a scare into the entire German High Command on May 21 when they launched an armored counterattack at Arras. Although it was repulsed by Major General Erwin Rommel's 7th Panzer Division and SS Lieutenant General Theodor Eicke's 3rd SS Motorized Division of Hoth's XV Motorized Corps, it reminded Hitler, Rundstedt, and Kleist that the "Panzer Corridor" was still 156 miles long and only 25 miles wide at the narrowest point. Rundstedt held back XV Motorized Corps as an army group reserve, while Reinhardt felt compelled to keep the 8th Panzer Division to the east, to guard against another Allied counterattack. Kleist also made a serious mistake: he took the 10th Panzer Division away from XIX Corps and placed it in panzer group reserve on May 22. Guderian had planned to use it to take Dunkirk.[51]

Guderian pushed on toward the Channel ports of Calais and Boulogne on May 22 with his two remaining divisions, but now Rundstedt intervened and ordered Kleist not to attack these ports until the situation at Arras had been settled. As a result, five more hours were lost. Finally, early in the afternoon, Guderian was allowed to advance again, and Kleist decided to return the 10th Panzer Division to him. Guderian quickly rushed it to Calais, to relieve the better-equipped 1st Panzer for an attack on Dunkirk. With Calais and Boulogne sealed off, this was the only port left through which the Allies in the northern pocket could escape.

So far the nervousness, hesitation, and delays by the headquarters above the corps level had not really caused serious consequences.

On May 23, however, Adolf Hitler issued his famous "halt order," which allowed 224,585 British and 112,546 French troops to escape from Dunkirk via naval evacuation to England.[52] Without these 337,000 men, London might well have accepted Hitler's offer for an armistice. Rundstedt favored a halt, but Guderian, Halder, and Brauchitsch did not (although Brauchitsch's objections to Hitler's interference in tactical operations were halfhearted, as usual).

Kleist's attitude appears to have been mixed. He did report that his tank losses exceeded 50 percent (in casualties and breakdowns) – a figure that was probably inflated by about 20 percent;[53] however, when the initial order to halt came from Army Group A Headquarters on May 22, Kleist kept right on advancing. "I decided to ignore it," he said after the war. He pushed on with XLI Motorized Corps across the Aire-St. Omer Canal to Hazebrouck, cut the British main line of retreat, and narrowly missed capturing Lord Gort.[54] Upon receipt of the second order (on May 23, and from Fuehrer Headquarters), which repeated the instructions more strongly, he withdrew to the Aire-St. Omer Canal as ordered and remained there for three days. The real culprits at Dunkirk were Hitler and Goering. Goering assured the Fuehrer that the Luftwaffe alone could destroy the enemy – which it could not do. Hitler, of course, bears the final responsibility, since he accepted Goering's word and, incredibly enough, seemed to think his purposes might be better served if the BEF escaped. He seems to have thought that the British would be more likely to negotiate an armistice if they were not totally humiliated. It is difficult to follow his logic, however.

FOLLOWING THE HALT order, the German panzer troops performed much-needed maintenance on their vehicles, rested, and moved south for the final offensive against France. Guderian got his heart's desire: XIX Corps was temporarily redesignated Panzer Group Guderian and took control over General Rudolf Schmidt's XXXIX Motorized Corps and Reinhardt's XLI. Kleist retained XIV Motorized Corps and assumed control over General Erich Hoepner's XVI Motorized Corps. Kleist now directed four panzer, two infantry, and two SS motorized divisions, plus an army motorized division and the Grossdeutschland Regiment.[55]

The second phase of the campaign amounted to little more than a gigantic mopping-up operation, for France's best divisions had already been destroyed. The final drive began on June 5. Hoepner struck along a six-kilometer front with a density of more than one hundred tanks per kilometer, against the weak French 6th Army, which was soon in full retreat. When France surrendered on June 21, XVI Motorized was in Lyons and XIV Motorized Corps was in the Bordeaux area, near the Spanish frontier.[56]

For his services in France and Belgium, Ewald von Kleist was promoted to colonel general on July 19, 1940.[57] After a brief period of occupation duty he was sent east, where Hitler had new enemies to face. Except for a few brief periods of leave, Kleist would remain on the Eastern Front for the rest of his career.

KLEIST'S XXII CORPS was redesignated Headquarters, First Panzer Group in early 1941 and was earmarked to spearhead the German invasion of Greece. In March 1941 it was assembled in the vicinity of Sofia, Bulgaria. On the night of March 26/27, however, the pro-Axis government of Premier Dragisha Cvetkovic in Yugoslavia was overthrown and replaced by a *junta* under General Richard D. Simovic, the former commander of the Yugoslav Air Force.[58] Hitler quickly decided to invade Yugoslavia as well as Greece, and 1st Panzer Group was assigned the task of launching a surprise attack on April 8, advancing along the Nis-Kragujevac-Belgrade line and capturing the Yugolav capital as rapidly as possible. Because the terrain in south-eastern Yugoslavia is mountainous, the roads few and primitive, and the best enemy troops could be expected to defend the capital, Kleist's task was by no means considered easy.[59]

Under his command on April 8, Kleist had Wietersheim's XIV Motorized Corps (5th Panzer, 11th Panzer, 294th Infantry, and 4th Mountain divisions) and General Joachim von Kortzfleisch's XI Corps (60th Motorized Infantry Division plus some minor units).[60]

Kleist's attack initially met stiff but short-lived resistance from the Yugoslav 5th Army, which was crumbling by evening. Kleist took Nis on April 9 and ordered his spearhead, the 11th Panzer, to continue the advance to the northeast against Belgrade, while the 5th Panzer Division turned south to cut off the Yugoslav forces in the Leskovac area. Advancing rapidly up the Morava Valley, Kleist smashed the right wing of the Yugoslav 6th Army on April 11 and 12. By the evening of April 12 he had advanced about one hundred and twenty-five miles and was less than forty miles from Belgrade.[61] He entered the city at the head of the 11th Panzer Division at 6:30 A.M. on April 13 and is sometimes given credit for capturing the Yugoslav capital.[62] However, elements of the 2nd SS Motorized Infantry Division "Das Reich," under SS First Lieutenant (*Obersturmfuehrer*) Klingenberg, had entered the city from the north at 5 P.M. the previous day, freed the members of the German Foreign Ministry (who had been interned), and accepted the surrender of the city from the mayor at 7 P.M. on April 12.[63] Map 8 shows the German campaign in Yugoslavia up to the capture of Belgrade.

IMMEDIATELY AFTER THE Yugoslav capitulation, First Panzer Group redeployed to southern Poland for the invasion of the Soviet Union. Here, Kleist was assigned five panzer, two motorized, and two SS motorized divisions under XLVIII Panzer, III Panzer, and XIV Motorized corps.[64] His forces deployed on the left wing of Field Marshal von Rundstedt's Army Group South, between Reichenau's 6th and General Karl-Heinrich von Stuelpnagel's 17th armies. His initial objective was to advance to the Dnieper in the vicinity of Kiev. Then he was to pivot southeast and drive toward the Black Sea to secure the Dnieper crossings and to prevent the eastward escape of the two Russian fronts (i.e., army groups) of Soviet Marshal Semën Mikhailovich Budenny. His long-range objective was the city of Rostov on the Sea of Azov.[65]

Stalin had deployed his best formations under his most able generals on the southern sector, probably with an eye to a future invasion of Rumania. Such a move would deprive Hitler of the Ploesti oil fields, which were considered vital to his war effort. Indeed, while Hitler was busy in the West, Stalin had forced Rumania to cede the provinces of Bessarabia and North Bukovina to him. He had also gobbled up the Baltic states of Latvia, Estonia, and Lithuania, invaded Finland, and made territorial demands on Turkey. He had incorporated some 175,000 square miles of territory and 20,000,000 people into his empire, and was talking about more. He was not at all pleased when Hitler crushed France in six weeks.

First Panzer Group crossed the frontier into Russia on June 22,

Map 8

THE YUGOSLAVIAN CAMPAIGN, APRIL 1941. Yugoslavia was conquered in less than two weeks by Colonel General Baron von Weichs' 2nd Army and Kleist's 1st Panzer Group. Following this victory, both Kleist and Weichs were sent to the east for the invasion of the Soviet Union. Weichs later returned to the Balkans as Commander-in-Chief, OB Southeast, in mid-1943.

1941. The terrain of the Galicia and western Ukraine regions through which it advanced was far from ideal for armored operations, since it was heavily forested with few roads. In places it was swampy, but the major difficulty Kleist faced was heavy resistance and the repeated counterattacks of the Russians. Within the first six days of the war, Kleist met counterattacks from the Soviet 9th, 19th and 23rd Mechanized corps. In all, Kleist's six hundred panzers faced 2,400 Soviet tanks,[66] many of which were technologically superior to his PzKw IIIs and IVs – the best tanks Germany had in 1941. His troops nevertheless reached Lvov on June 30 and broke the Stalin Line on July 6, despite several strong counterattacks. Zhitomir, about ninety miles from Kiev, fell on July 10, after 1st Panzer Group defeated heavy attacks from the 4th, 15th, and 16th Mechanized corps. That same day the Soviet 5th Army, reinforced with strong elements of the 9th, 19th, and 22nd Mechanized corps, emerged from the southern edge of the Pripyet Marshes and cut the panzer group's main supply route. Reichenau, following Kleist with his infantry, had to commit much of his army to clear the road.[67] And so it went through July and August. From June 22 to July 10 the panzer group advanced only 10 miles a day and even less after that – far from the rapid blitzkrieg Hitler had hoped for.[68]

Kleist turned south behind Tyulenev's South Front (of Budenny's Southwest Theater) in mid-July and, despite counterattacks against his left flank by the Soviet 26th Army, linked up with 17th Army at Pervomaysk, forming the first large encirclement on the southern sector of the Eastern Front. The pocket was cleared on August 8; 103,000 prisoners were taken, including two Soviet army commanders, along with 317 tanks and 1,100 guns captured or destroyed.[69]

Even before the Uman Pocket was cleared, the Russians counterattacked again, toward Boguslav, into the zone the 1st Panzer Group had vacated when it turned southward on Uman. Group von Schwelder (a few combat and miscellaneous rear-area troops were under the command of IV Corps Commander General Victor von Schwelder) delayed the Russians long enough for Kleist and Reichenau to restore the situation, but it was August 17 before Army Group South could resume the offensive.

First Panzer Group finally reached the east bank of the Dnieper on August 19, when the 9th Panzer Division attacked across the dam at Zaporozhye and established a bridgehead; the Russians, however, counterattacked violently and pushed them back to the west bank. It was another week before the 60th Motorized Division succeeded in seizing a Russian pontoon bridge at Dnepropetrovsk and establishing a bridgehead on the far shore. The Soviets counterattacked fiercely for three days, but Kleist reinforced the foothold with General Eberhard von Mackensen's III Panzer Corps. The bridgehead was also supported by around-the-clock aerial attacks by the Luftwaffe. By August 29 the 1st Panzer Group was steadily expanding the bridgehead eastward, and the entire Donetz Basin, one of the major industrial centers of the Soviet Union, was threatened. Two days later 17th Army also secured a foothold on the east bank at Kremenchug.[70]

On the evening of September 10, Kleist took over the Kremenchug bridgehead from 17th Army and began funneling Kempf's XLVIII Panzer Corps into it. At 9 A.M. the following morning, Lieutenant General Hans Hube's 16th Panzer Division broke out of the bridgehead through the defensive perimeter of the Soviet 38th Army and headed due north for Romny, followed by the 9th Panzer and 14th Panzer divisions. This sudden move took the Soviet High Command totally by surprise. Hube gained 43 miles in the first 12 hours. At 6:20 P.M. on September 14 he linked up with Lieutenant General Walter Model's 3rd Panzer Division of Guderian's 2nd Panzer Group near Romny, 130 miles east of Kiev. Kleist and Guderian had completed the largest encirclement of the entire war: five Soviet armies. By September 26 the battle was over. The final bag was 667,000 prisoners taken, and 3,718 guns and 884 armored vehicles captured or destroyed. Kempf's corps alone took 109,097 prisoners.[71] The entire Ukraine, the breadbasket of the Soviet Union, was now lost to Stalin.

AFTER KIEV, KLEIST'S group was upgraded and renamed 1st Panzer Army (on October 6), and headed south to begin his drive for Rostov, the final objective of the 1941 campaign. Even before the Battle of Kiev was over, the southernmost elements of 1st Panzer Army (III Panzer Corps) attacked southward from the Dnepropetrovsk bridgehead and destroyed three Soviet divisions at Novo-Moskovsk. After rolling up the Soviet Dnieper flank as far as Zaporozhye, 1st Panzer Army advanced east and then south, cutting behind the Soviet forces delaying Manstein's 11th Army at Melitopol. The 1st Panzer Division reached the Sea of Azov at Berdyansk (now Osipenko) on October 5, forming another Soviet pocket at Chernigovka. When the battle ended on October 10, the Soviet 18th Army had been destroyed, its commander killed, and more than 100,000 men, 212 tanks, and 672 guns captured. Kleist set out in immediate pursuit. Taganrog fell on October 12, and the Mius River, the last obstacle before Rostov, was reached on October 28. Then, however, the Russian rainy season arrived and "General Mud" took over. Kleist was not able to advance again until the ground froze on November 17.[72]

The spectacular victories of the previous three months, plus coping with the mud, had drained Kleist's fuel reserves; only about 30 percent of the trucks that had crossed into Russia were still running. Nevertheless the 4th Panzer Army advanced again on October 17, spearheaded by the 1st SS Motorized Division, which had been reinforced with the 1st Panzer Regiment of the 13th Panzer Division. The 60th Motorized and 14th Panzer divisions screened Rostov to the east while the SS and 4th Panzer took the city on the night of October 20. Counterattacks by ten Red Army divisions were beaten off.[73]

Rostov was not just a city of a half million people in 1941: it was seen as the gateway to the Caucasus, the Soviet oil regions, and to Iran. The Communists could not afford to leave it in German hands as a springboard for their 1942 summer offensive. Kleist warned Rundstedt on October 21 that Kleist's left flank was dangerously exposed, but there was little Rundstedt could do to help him.

The Russians began attacking the exposed flank that very day. Kleist was forced to shift his 13th and 14th Panzer divisions north and northwest to avert disaster. Then Soviet Marshal Semen Timoshenko launched his main attack against the 1st SS and 60th Motorized divisions on October 25. The Don River would have protected them in the summer, but now it was frozen solid. The line companies of the German division were down to one third of their authorized strength due to casualties and frostbite (they were still in their summer uniforms), but they held on for three days in temperatures of 14 degrees Fahrenheit.[74]

Rostov finally fell on November 28. Two days later Kleist was forced to withdraw his battered spearhead and requested permission to withdraw to the Mius. Hitler refused to allow any retreat whatsoever, but Rundstedt authorized it anyway. Hitler relieved him the same day. He was replaced by Field Marshal von Reichenau.

The gifted Reichenau could see no way out of the deteriorating situation either, except to allow Kleist to retreat. He obtained permission from Hitler within twenty-four hours of assuming command. Ewald von Kleist had gained the dubious distinction of suffering the first major defeat Germany experienced in the Second World War. It would not be its last – or his.

DURING THEIR WINTER offensive of 1941/42, the Soviets threw the Germans back on all fronts, but the Wehrmacht did not collapse despite temperatures that sometimes dipped as low as minus 50 degrees Fahrenheit. By the spring of 1942, the panzers were ready to attack again. Kleist commanded the 1st Panzer and 17th armies (as Army Detachment Kleist) in Operation Fridericus, which led to another battle of encirclement. When the fighting was over, 239,000 more Soviet troops had been captured, and 1,250 tanks and 2,026 guns had been captured or destroyed.[75]

Following Fridericus and the initial advance toward the Volga, Kleist's 1st Panzer Army was transferred south of Kharkov, where it joined Field Marshal List's newly formed Army Group A. First Panzer Army covered the left wing of the 17th Army when it recaptured Rostov on July 24. Weichs's Army Group B (formerly HQ, Army Group South) headed for the Volga and Stalingrad, while Army Group A thrust toward the Caucasus and the Baku oil region on the Caspian Sea. Meanwhile, Manstein's 11th Army was transferred to the north, to take Leningrad. By thus dividing his forces and sending them toward three separate objectives, Hitler had insufficient strength to take any of them. Army Group A bogged down in the Caucasus region in September.

Hitler's interference in the direction of military operations reached a new peak on September 9, when he relieved Field Marshal List and assumed command of Army Group A himself. He remained at his headquarters near Rastenburg, East Prussia, a thousand miles away. The day-to-day tasks were handled by List's former Chief of Staff, Lieutenant General Hans von Greiffenberg.

On November 21, 1942, Hitler finally gave up command of Army

Group A, which had not been able to advance for weeks. His successor was Colonel General Ewald von Kleist. Eberhart von Mackensen assumed command of the 1st Panzer Army. Kleist's only other army was the 17th, under Colonel General Richard Ruoff.

Kleist had warned Hitler against using the Hungarians, Italians, and Rumanians as flank protectors for the 6th Army during the drive on Stalingrad, but the Fuehrer would not listen.[76] The Soviets attacked the Rumanians north and south of Stalingrad on November 19 and 20, quickly broke through, and surrounded 6th Army on November 22. This disaster placed Kleist in a dangerously exposed position, for Stalin's victorious forces were closer to Rostov than Kleist's exhausted forces, and there was little to prevent the Red Army from seizing the city. Rostov was Army Group A's only land connection with the rest of the Russian Front. Nevertheless, Hitler would not give him permission to retreat until December 27.

When Colonel General Kurt Zeitzler, now Chief of the General Staff of the Army, finally convinced the Fuehrer to allow Army Group A to withdraw, the forward units of the 1st Panzer Army were on the Terek River, almost four hundred miles away. By January 20, 1943, the Soviets had pushed to within nineteen miles of Rostov, but were halted by the last reserves of the 4th Panzer Army (of Manstein's Army Group Don). The Soviets tried for three more weeks to cut off the retreat of the 1st Panzer Army, but were unsuccessful. Part of the Army, including XL Panzer Corps, had to retreat across the ice on the Sea of Azov. Finally, on February 6, the rearguard and last unit of the 1st Panzer Army, Major General Hermann Recknagel's 111th Infantry Division, blew up the Don River bridge south of Rostov in the very faces of the Soviet units trying to disarm the explosives.[77] First Panzer Army had escaped.

Kleist was now faced with the problem of holding the Kuban, across the Straits of Kerch from the Crimea. Army Group A lost command of 1st Panzer Army after it escaped, leaving Kleist with only the 17th Army (five German infantry and two mountain divisions, plus a Rumanian cavalry division, the Slovak Security Division, and some miscellaneous Eastern and Cossack cavalry units under the German V, XLIV, and XLIX Mountain corps), the Military Command Crimea (Headquarters, XLII Corps, with the 1st and 4th Rumanian Mountain divisions and the German

153rd Reserve Division), and the Rear Area Command A (454th and 444th Security divisions, each with two security regiments and no organic artillery). Only one unit was in army group reserve: the 381st Field Training Division, which was not fit for front-line duty. Starting on January 10, 17th Army had to abandon its footholds in the eastern Caucasus and swing north and east, to establish a defensive line covering the Kuban. They were under constant pressure from the 47th, 56th, 18th, 46th, 37th, 9th, 58th, and 44th Soviet armies but, using a series of improvised interception lines, managed to reach their assigned positions in only four weeks.

Stalin's forces tried desperately to break through the German rear-guards and overwhelm 17th Army before it could complete its maneuver and dig in. If successful, they would bag 400,000 German soldiers, complete with 110,000 horses, 26,500 motorized vehicles, and 2,085 guns: a haul larger than Stalingrad![78] If not, Hitler would maintain a foothold in Asia and might well be in a position to launch another offensive against the all-important oil fields in the summer of 1943. Stalin threw everything he could against Kleist, but was unable to disrupt the retreat or break the Kuban line. For this defensive success, Ewald von Kleist was promoted to field marshal on February 1, 1943.

Ironically, some of the successes for which Kleist owed his promotion were due to his ignoring Hitler's instructions concerning the persecution of the peoples who previously had lived under Communist domination. In September 1942, Kleist remarked: "These vast spaces depress me. And these vast hordes of people! We're lost if we don't win them over."[79] And win them over he did. With great foresight, he appointed two former military attachés to Moscow to his staff: Lieutenant General Ritter Oskar von Niedermayer and Major General Ernst Koestring, who had been born in Moscow. Niedermayer, who first retired from the Army in 1935, was a professor of geopolitics at the University of Berlin until he was recalled to active duty. He had organized and commanded the 162nd Infantry Division, which included men from Georgia, Armenia, Azerbaijan, Kazakstan, Turkestan, Iran, Afghanistan and other eastern territories who joined the German Army to fight Communism. Niedermayer was an outspoken critic of the Nazi policy treating the non-German peoples of the Soviet Union as subhumans (*Untermenschen*). He and Koestring provided Kleist with truly expert advice on the treatment of the occupied territories and their ethnic (non-Russian) peoples. As a result, 825,000 men were recruited in Russia to fight Communism, including Karachoevs, Kabardines, Ossets, Ingushts, Azerbaijans, Kalmucks, Uzbeks, and especially Cossacks. These men were largely recruited from Kleist's areas of operation. In September 1944, Hitler allowed these men to be incorporated into the Army of National Liberation under former Soviet General Vlassov, but by then Germany had lost almost all of its captured territory in the Soviet Union and the war was as good as lost. Kleist, however, was allowed to employ his foreign recruits as auxiliaries and in Cossack cavalry regiments.[80]

Gauleiter Erich Koch, the Reich Commissioner of the Ukraine, and Fritz Sauckel, Plenipotentiary for Labor Allocation (i.e., head of slave-labor importation for Nazi Germany), protested against Kleist's humane policies. Kleist had even gone so far as to order his subordinates to make sure that "voluntary" labor recruitment in occupied areas was really voluntary! Koch and Sauckel were furious. Their protests cut no ice with the Prussian cavalryman, however.[81] Kleist went so far as to summon SS and "police" officials to his headquarters and categorically informed them that he would tolerate no excesses in his area of command.[82]

Kleist's humane policy was quite successful and even elicited half-hearted praise from Joseph Goebbels, the Nazi Minister of Propaganda.[83] Had Kleist's ideas been implemented throughout the East, they conceivably could have changed the course of the war.

THE RUSSIANS MADE several attempts to break the Kuban Line, and even attempted an amphibious landing at Novorossiysk on the night of February 3/4, the only major Soviet amphibious landing attempted during the war. All of their efforts were checked with heavy casualties. All the while, Kleist was advocating the evacuation of the Kuban line with greater and greater urgency. Hitler stalled, however, fearing the repercussions such a move would have in Rumania and neutral Turkey. Finally, on September 3, he gave Kleist the order to go ahead with the evacuation. The word came none too soon, for the Soviets were nearing the Perekop Isthmus at the northern edge of the Crimea. If they could seize this position before Army Group A could make good its escape, all of Kleist's forces would be trapped. Manstein, whose Army Group South was covering the retreat route, made it clear that he could not hold off the Red Army for long.

The Kuban foothold had served its purpose. For most of the summer it had attracted seven Russian armies with more than fifty divisions, which Stalin could have employed with devastating effect elsewhere. By September, however, it was clear that the Germans would never again launch a major offensive against the Caucasus, Stalin had sent many of his divisions elsewhere, and it was high time to get out of the Kuban. Over a period of 34 days, Kleist and his naval commander, Vice Admiral Scheurlen, ferried 227,484 German and Rumanian soldiers, 72,899 horses, 28,486 Russian auxiliaries, 21,230 motor vehicles, 27,471 horse-drawn vehicles, and 1,815 guns across the Straits of Kerch to the Crimea. The evacuation was completed on October 9. The Soviets launched a number of heavy attacks, supported by armor, but were repulsed with heavy losses. Seventeenth Army even succeeded in evacuating its supplies and damaged equipment. All it lost was the fodder for its horses.[84] Most of its units were hurried through the Crimea to Colonel General Karl Hollidt's reconstituted 6th Army, guarding the northern approaches to the Perekop Isthmus. Hitler assigned this army to Kleist after the Kuban evacuation.

Kleist's last campaign was characterized by increasing friction with Hitler over the Fuehrer's mishandling of the war. Kleist agitated for the abandonment of the Crimea from the time the Kuban evacuation was completed. He went so far as to issue the order to evacuate the peninsula on October 26, but Hitler countermanded it the same day. Even after the Soviets finally reached the Perekop Isthmus on November 1 and cut off 17th Army in the Crimea, Kleist continued to call for its evacuation by sea.

On several occasions, Kleist called for timely retreats that Hitler refused to authorize until they were absolutely forced on him, with much greater casualties as the result. Finally pushed behind the Bug, a line he could not hold with his depleted divisions, Kleist conspired with Hollidt and General Otto Woehler, the commander of the 8th Army on the southern wing of Army Group South, to ensure that the retreat to the Dnestr would be made in time. On March 26, 1944, he informed Zeitzler that he had taken over 8th

Army from Army Group South(!) and would issue the order to withdraw to the Dnestr that afternoon, with or without OKH's permission. Zeitzler asked him to see Hitler first. The field marshal replied that he would see the Fuehrer the next day, but only after he was sure that the withdrawal was ready to begin immediately. "Someone must lay his head on the block," Kleist told his chief of staff.[85] Ewald von Kleist had had enough.

Presented with a virtual *fait accompli*, Hitler authorized the withdrawal of the 6th and 8th armies on March 27, conditional only on Kleist's holding the bridgehead from Tiraspol to Odessa, the main supply port for the Crimea. The next day the two armies were in full retreat from the Bug, pursued by the Russian 8th Guards and 46th armies.[86]

Did this incident cost Ewald von Kleist his command and end his military career? It seems quite likely that this was the "straw that broke the camel's back" for both himself and Manstein. Hitler had wanted to relieve Manstein as early as the first part of 1943. Kleist had annoyed the Fuehrer by his constant calls for the evacuation of the Crimea; by his attitude toward "subhumans"; by advising him in November 1943 to appoint a First Quartermaster General of the Wehrmacht to direct operations on the Eastern Front; by his pro-monarchist views; and by his threat to take matters into his own hands if Hitler did not give him permission to retreat from the Bug. Hitler had said of the two field marshals as early as July 1943: "I can't trust Kleist or Manstain. They're intelligent, but they're not National Socialists."[87]

On March 30, the Fuehrer's personal Condor landed at Kleist's airstrip at Tiraspol to pick up the Commander-in-Chief of Army Group A. It then flew on to Lvov to collect Erich von Manstein. That evening on the Obersalzburg, Hitler presented them with the Knight's Cross with Oak Leaves and Swords – and relieved them of their commands. Hitler told both Manstain and Kleist that he approved of all that they had done, but the days of the master tacticians were over on the Eastern Front. What he needed now were commanders who could summon the last once of resistance from their troops.

Kleist took the opportunity of his last meeting with Hitler to recommend that he make peace with Stalin. Hitler assured him that there was no need to do so, as the Soviet Army was almost exhausted.[88]

Colonel General Zeitzler tendered his resignation when Hitler announced that he was sacking Kleist and Manstein. Hitler curtly rejected the resignation, but the attitude of the Chief of the General Staff (and former Chief of Staff of Panzer Group Kleist) probably explains why Hitler dealt with Kleist and Manstein in such a civilized manner.

Army Group A was redesignated Army Group South Ukraine and placed under the command of Colonel General Ferdinand Schoerner. Kleist went into retirement and was arrested by the Gestapo in 1944 in connection with the July 20 assassination attempt on Hitler, in which one of his cousins was deeply involved. Kleist himself knew of the resistance movement but had not reported it; therefore he was technically guilty of a crime, although not actively involved in the unsuccessful coup himself. The Nazis did not want to put such a respected field marshal on trial before the People's Court, especially after the execution of Field Marshal von Witzleben, so they released him.

Except for this brief interlude, Ewald von Kleist lived quietly in retirement at Weidebrueck from April 1944 until early 1945, when the Russians invaded Silesia. The field marshal emigrated to the tiny village of Mitterfels in lower Bavaria, while his oldest son, a captain on active duty, blew up the family home to prevent it from falling into the hands of the Russians.[89]

Von Kleist was variously reported as being captured by the British in Yugoslavia and as having surrendered to the Americans at the end of the war.[90] Author C. R. Davis, who interviewed members of the Kleist family, said that Kleist was taken into custody by a patrol from the US 26th Infantry Division on April 25, 1945. In any event he was held in a total of twenty-seven different prisons in the next nine years. He was turned over to the Yugoslavs in 1946, tried as a war criminal, and sentenced to fifteen years' imprisonment. Two years later he was extradicted to Russia, where he was charged with having "alienated through mildness and kindness" the population of the Soviet Union.[91] He remained in Russian captivity for the rest of his life.

In March 1954 the former Panzer Army commander was transferred to the Wladimir Prison Camp (a prison for German generals, located about one hundred and ten miles east of Moscow). Here the Russians allowed him to write and receive one postcard-size letter per month to his family – his first correspondence with them in eight and a half years.[92]

Field Marshal Ewald von Kleist died of "general arteriosclerosis and hypertension" at Wladimir on October 15, 1954 – the only one of Hitler's marshals to die in Soviet captivity. His eldest son, Ewald, was released from prison in 1956, after spending ten years in Siberia. He died in 1976. Frau Kleist died in West Germany in May 1958, and Kleist's youngest son succumbed in 1973. As of 1979, eight of the field marshal's grandchildren were alive in West Germany – although Ewald von Kleist never saw one of them.[93] He is buried in an unknown grave somewhere in the Soviet Union.

4

Walter von Reichenau

REICHENAU WAS ONE of the most exceptional of the field marshals. His appearance, except for his pale-blue eyes, was typically Prussian: stern features, monocled, cold, and forbidding. Yet he was innovative, liked automobile racing, swimming, tennis, boxing, and cross-country running. He was accessible and popular among the troops. He studied science and enjoyed meeting people from outside the military sphere – even foreigners. No automaton, he was very independent-minded and detested anything that smacked of traditionalism just for the sake of tradition. Above all he was ruthlessly ambitious.[1] Historian Walter Goerlitz called him "the most progressive thinker among the Army Commanders-in-Chief," but also "a man devoid of all sentiment, at times, indeed, a cold-blooded, brutal man."[2]

The son of a Prussian general, he was born in Karlsruhe on August 16, 1884. His mother was Silesian. Reichenau married Countess von Maltzan of Militsch, a noble Silesian family. She was related to the ancient Prussian house of Schwerin.

Reichenau joined the Army at age eighteen as a *Fahnenjunker* in the Prussian 1st Guards Field Artillery Regiment. He received his commission the following year (1904) and was promoted to first lieutenant in 1912. In May 1914 he was attending the War

Academy in Berlin, undergoing General Staff training, but returned to his regiment when the war broke out. He "served with valor" on the Western Front in World War I[3] as Adjutant of the 1st Guards Field Artillery and later as a General Staff officer with the 47th Reserve Division, VI Corps, and the 7th Cavalry Division. He worked for a time under Major General Max Hoffmann, the military genius who was closely associated with the Hindenburg-Ludendorff victory at Tannenburg. He emerged from the war as a captain with the Iron Cross, 1st Class, and the Hohenzollern House Order, among other decorations.[4]

Reichenau's rise in the Reichsheer was steady, but not spectacular. He was a General Staff officer with Wehrkreis VI at Muenster (1920–22) before serving a year's troop duty as commander of the 8th (Machine Gun) Company, 18th Infantry Regiment. Promoted to major in 1923, he served on the staff of Wehrkreis III in Berlin until the summer of 1926, when he took his first trip to England. Upon his return he received another Berlin staff appointment – this one with HQ, Army Group 1 – before being named Commander of the 5th Signal Battalion at Stuttgart on November 1, 1927. He was promoted to lieutenant colonel in April 1929.[5]

Following his promotion, Reichenau spent several months in England, where he engaged in language study and developed a great regard for the British, even to the point of speaking English and wearing English clothes at home. Upon his return to Berlin in the fall of 1929, he was named Chief of Staff to the Inspector of Signals at the Reichswehr Ministry, a position he held until February 1, 1931, when he was named Chief of Staff of Wehrkreis I in East Prussia. Exactly one year later he was promoted to full colonel.[6]

The two years Walter von Reichenau spent in East Prussia were pivotal, not only for himself but for the entire Officer Corps and, indeed, for the entire German nation. Until then, Reichenau's career had been fairly typical for a Prussian General Staff officer. In 1932, however, he met Adolf Hitler through his uncle, Friedrich von Reichenau, a retired diplomat and President of the German Overseas League. Friedrich von Reichenau was a Nazi and a great admirer of Hitler.[7] His nephew also decided to jump on the Nazi bandwagon, but admiration for the Fuehrer had little or nothing to do with this decision; rather, as Wistrich wrote, "he regarded the

National Socialists as an indispensable battering-ram against Marxism and planned to harness their revolutionary drive for his own career ends and the interests of the Army."[8]

Reichenau's commander, General Werner von Blomberg, was easily influenced by his more intelligent, pragmatic, and dynamic Chief of Staff, and soon Reichenau had almost complete sway over his superior. The colonel introduced the general to Hitler, who soon completely captivated Blomberg. Reichenau, the cool Machiavellian, had made his decision: he broke with the Prussian officer caste and, as Goerlitz wrote, was "the first military expert of real importance, who placed himself entirely without reservation at the dictatorship's disposal."[9]

Reichenau had calculated the odds and threw in his lot with the Nazis, not out of principle, but to further his own ruthless ambitions. He risked his career in doing so, but the gamble paid off on January 30, 1933, when Adolf Hitler became Chancellor of Germany and Werner von Blomberg was named Minister of War. Reichenau was immediately promoted to major general and became head of the Ministerial Office of the Reichswehr Ministry. Soon he was unofficially regarded as the chief liaison officer between the Army and the Nazi Party and was a favorite of Hitler, who greatly admired him. He was a frequent guest at Berchtesgaden in the early days of the régime.

In 1933, Reichenau's position and influence greatly exceeded his rank. He was one of the "Big Four" in the defense establishment, along with the War Minister, the Commander-in-Chief of the Army, and the Chief of the General Staff (Generals Blomberg, von Hammerstein, and Adam, respectively).[10] On Blomberg's behalf, he negotiated several agreements with the SA. These provided for Army control of 250,000 reserves from the Nazi paramilitary organizations in case of an emergency; for increased contact between the Army and the Party; and for more opportunities for the Nazis to distribute propaganda to the lower, less critical ranks of the military.[11]

Reichenau hoped that the SA and Army could peacefully coexist. He watched with increasing alarm as SA Chief Ernst Roehm gained more and more power. On November 6, 1933, the SA absorbed the Stahlhelm (Steel Helmet), Germany's principle veterans' organization, as well as the Kyffhaeuser Bund, another large veterans' group. Less than a month later the SA became an official branch of the government, and Roehm was given a seat on the National Defense Council. Roehm was demanding more and more say over military affairs. Reichenau tried to compromise with him, proposing that the military activities of the SA be expanded, but that the SA be put under Army control, as a sort of militia. Roehm rejected the idea.[12]

The Army and the Party now seemed to be on a collision course. Nazi Party Chief Rudolf Hess, no doubt at Hitler's suggestion, tried to defuse the situation in early 1934. He wrote an editorial in the Party's newspaper, the *Voelkischer Beobachter*, calling for more obedience from Party organizations (i.e., the Brownshirts). Four days later, on January 26, 1934, Hitler yielded to pressure from the Reichswehr and agreed to the formation of a Working Committee for the National Defense Council. The chairman of the new committee was Reichenau. The SA responded the same day by wrecking a social gathering of monarchist officers who were celebrating Wilhelm II's birthday at the Hotel Kaiser in Berlin. Naturally the Officer Corps was outraged by the incident.[13]

In this atmosphere of friction and tension, Blomberg finally forced anti-Nazi General Kurt von Hammerstein to retire from his position as Commander-in-Chief of the Army. Predictably, Blomberg nominated Reichenau for the post and Hitler heartily approved, but President von Hindenburg vetoed the selection. Blomberg's second choice (and the favourite of the Officer Corps), General Baron Werner von Fritsch, the commander of Wehrkreis III, received the appointment instead. He assumed his new office on February 1, 1934.

The next day, the Wehrkreise commanders and senior Army staff officers met in Berlin for a conference. Here General Beck, who had replaced Adam as Chief of the General Staff on October 1, 1933, rose and criticized Reichenau for making the Army too dependent on the SA for the frontier defenses against Poland. Fritsch agreed with Beck and claimed that the SA now had too much opportunity for ideological subversion. Under this pressure, Blomberg promised to end his policy of compromise with the SA.[14]

The next day Reichenau received a letter from Ernst Roehm. He asked Fritsch's permission to read it aloud to the commanders, and Fritsch consented. It said: "I regard the Reichswehr now only as a training school for the German people. The conduct of war, and therefore of mobilization as well, in the future is the task of the SA."[15]

The situation was now extremely volatile; an Army coup against Hitler and the Nazis was a distinct possibility. Reichenau had attached himself to the Nazis to such an extent that he could never go back. If the Nazis lost power, his career would be over. Therefore only one choice remained: the SA must be suppressed, and Ernst Roehm must die.

We do not know exactly what role Reichenau played in the elimination of the SA, but it was considerable. We do know that Reichenau conspired with Hermann Goering and SS Chief Heinrich Himmler against Roehm, and probably helped draw up the lists of men to be executed. On July 30, the "Blood Purge" of the storm troopers began. Before it ended, some one hundred and fifty Brownshirt leaders were taken out and shot by the SS.[16] Blomberg ordered the Army not to interfere in the executions, and Reichenau supplied arms to the SS just before the purge. Reichenau served as liaison officer between the killers and the Army, and Blomberg – undoubtedly guided by Reichenau – immediately and publicly endorsed Hitler's actions.

Hitler took advantage of the opportunity offered by the bloodletting to eliminate two of the more dangerous anti-Nazi Army officers – former Chancellor General Kurt von Schleicher and General Kurt von Brelow, Reichenau's predecessor in the Ministerial Office of the Reichswehr. Reichenau tried to whitewash the assassinations by issuing a communiqué stating that Schleicher had maintained "treasonable relationships with a foreign power," and had resisted when the police tried to arrest him. Schleicher's wife, according to Reichenau, had run into the line of fire and had also been killed.[17] Actually there had been no resistance; the Schleichers and von Brelow had been murdered by the Gestapo.

The death of Roehm and the decimation of the leadership of the SA eliminated the threat to Reichenau's career and moved him even further into the orbit of the Nazi Party. He was rewarded by an accelerated promotion to lieutenant general a year after the Blood Purge.[18] His next service for Hitler was less violent but equally far-reaching. At 9 A.M. on the morning of August 2, the eighty-seven-year-old President von Hindenburg finally died after a lengthy illness. Three hours later Hitler abolished the office of President, assumed the title of Fuehrer and Reich Chancellor, and realized his dream of becoming dictator of Germany. The same day, the soldiers of the Third Reich (as it now was) had to take an oath of loyalty – not to the Republic or the Constitution, but to the Fuehrer personally. The oath was written by Walter von Reichenau. It went: "I swear by God this sacred oath, that I will render unconditional obedience to Adolf Hitler, the Fuehrer of the German Reich and people, Supreme Commander of the Armed Forces, and that I am ready as a brave soldier to risk my life at any time for this oath."

This oath permanently diffused the possibility of a coup against Hitler by the vast majority of the Officer Corps, for it committed them to personal loyalty to Hitler himself. Many officers could not, in good conscience, break that oath without feeling that they would thereby dishonor themselves. Most of them would take no action to depose Hitler, even when the Army was in ruins and the enemy was at the very frontiers of the Reich. Reichenau's oath served him very well: there would be no officers' *putsch*; the party he had chosen would remain in power, and his personal career was assured.

In justice to Reichenau, it must be noted here that he could not have foreseen the events of 1941–45, or the long-range effects of his oath. Indeed, one might speculate that the unorthodox Reichenau, who was possibly the least tradition-bound of Hitler's field marshals, might well have personally led a coup against Hitler had he lived – that is, if he believed it might benefit his own career. Certainly one cannot imagine the pragmatic Reichenau taking something as abstract as an oath too seriously – if it ran counter to his own ambitions for Reichenau believed in Reichenau; everything else was secondary.

IN 1935 REICHENAU was, as always, considering another way to advance his career. He was constantly seeking new outlets for his abundant energy, and now it seemed that the road to the top of his profession no longer led through Berlin. One of the objections his opponents had raised to his appointment as Commander-in-Chief of the Army was that he had never commanded anything larger than a battalion. Very well: he would obtain a command. With his influence over Blomberg and his friendship with Hitler, he had no trouble obtaining one. Typically, he skipped the division level (which was more appropriate for his rank and seniority) and, on August 1, 1935, was promoted to lieutenant general, and on October 1 assumed command of Wehrkreis VII in Munich, replacing General Wilhelm Adam. He was succeeded in Berlin by Major General Wilhelm Keitel.[19]

Reichenau was promoted to general of artillery on October 1, 1936, shortly after returning from a trip to China, but his ambition was unsatisfied. In January 1938, when his old mentor Blomberg was in serious trouble for marrying a suspected prostitute, Reichenau refused to lift a finger to help him. "I had really expected different treatment from him [Reichenau]," Blomberg complained later.[20] Telford Taylor explained his attitude this way: "Reichenau, who, like Keitel, could hope for promotion as a result of Blomberg's misfortune, did nothing for his former superior."[21] Indeed, as far as we know, Reichenau never spoke to Blomberg again, despite the fact that Blomberg had once recommended Reichenau for the top post in the Army.

With Blomberg ousted and Fritsch on the way out due to trumped-up charges of homosexuality, Reichenau was looked upon by almost everyone as the leading candidate for the post of Commander-in-Chief of the Army. However, merely being a Nazi sympathizer was not yet sufficient qualification for this job in early 1938. Hitler, true enough, wanted to promote Reichenau, but General Gerd von Rundstedt, Commander of Army Group 1 and the most senior member of the Officer Corps, objected very strongly. Reichenau now paid the penalty for offending the ultra-conservative Prussian Officer Corps. Neither Beck nor his deputy, Franz Halder, would serve as Chief of the General Staff under Reichenau, and other senior officers also threatened to resign, forcing even Wilhelm Keitel, the newly appointed Commander-in-Chief of the High Command of the Armed Forces (OKW), to frankly inform Hitler that the Army would not stand for the shock of Reichenau's appointment. Keitel did not have much use for Reichenau either, as he makes clear in his memoirs.[22] Hitler vacillated for a few days, but February 4, 1938, named General

Walter von Brauchitsch C-in-C of the Army. As a consolation prize of sorts, Reichenau succeeded Brauchitsch as C-in-C of Army Corps 4, headquartered at Leipzig.

Unlike the other three army groups, Army Group 4 was non-territorial. Its new corps headquarters, numbered XIV, XV, and XVI, created only the year before, also had no territorial jurisdictions. Fourteen Corps controlled all four of Germany's motorized divisions (numbered 2nd, 13th, 20th, and 29th), while XV Corps directed the 1st, 2nd and 3rd Light divisions, which consisted of motorized infantry regiments, a reconnaissance regiment, and a tank battalion or regiment. Fourteen Corps directed all three panzer divisions (1st, 2nd, and 3rd). The corps were commanded, respectively, by Generals Gustav von Wietersheim, Hermann Hoth, and Heinz Guderian. Reichenau therefore had the tremendous responsibility of directing all of Germany's mobile divisions and creating new ones.

General von Reichenau tackled his new job with typical determination and saw to it that his units were properly trained and ready for war. His headquarters (which became HQ, 10th Army, upon mobilization) played a major role in the occupation of Austria. It was during this crisis that Hitler summoned Reichenau and Luftwaffe General Hugo Sperrle to Berchtesgaden. The Fuehrer wanted to bluff the Austrian Chancellor into submission, and he considered Reichenau and Sperrle to be his two most brutal-looking generals. The bluff worked. Later the same year (1938), Reichenau was slated to direct the main thrust of the invasion of Czechoslovakia, before the French and British signed the Munich Accords and surrendered the Sudetenland without a fight. The rest of Czechoslovakia was occupied the next year.

Reichenau was a good choice for the post of commander of Army Group 4. He was not a rigid disciplinarian, but treated his men "with a familiarity that did not breed contempt," to quote Matthew Cooper.[23] He even proved to have a sense of humor, and his men like him.

Reichenau's popularity extended only to the effective soldiers. He had no patience with the inefficient or lazy. His streak of ruthlessness still showed itself when he dealt with offenders. The punishment for being away from duty without leave (AWOL), for example, was not demotion, extra duty, or a short imprisonment: it was execution.

Almost alone of the senior generals, Reichenau supported the new tank technology. As early as the 1920s he was a panzer enthusiast. He translated several of the works of B. H. Liddell Hart, the British armor expert, into German and in 1933 ordered Krupp to begin a systematic program of panzer production under the cover of "agricultural tractors."[24] Reichenau's open mind, intelligence and innovative nature drove him to support the ideas of Heinz Guderian and made him, indirectly, a contributor to the development of the blitzkrieg; for he used his considerable power and influence to help build and later shield the panzer divisions from more conservative generals, such as Fritsch, Beck, and Otto von Stuelpnagel, who would have broken up the tank divisions and used the panzers only as infantry support weapons.

IN AUGUST 1939, Reichenau moved his headquarters (now designated 10th Army) to Oppeln and assembled his forces for the invasion of Poland. His Army was the largest of the five used in the invasion, and it was given the most difficult mission: penetrate the Polish frontier defenses, head directly for Warsaw, and take the Polish capital. Tenth Army also had the bulk of Germany's mobile forces: two panzer, three light, and two motorized divisions, as well as six infantry divisions, under XI, XVI, IV, XV, and XIV corps. His corps commanders were also an experienced group: General Emil Leeb (brother of the future field marshal), Erich Hoepner, Victor von Schwelder, Hermann Hoth, and Gustav von Wietersheim.[25]

Tenth Army penetrated fifteen miles on September 1, the first day of the invasion, and reached the Warta River the next day. The Poles tried to halt him on this river, but Reichenau established several bridgeheads in heavy fighting on September 3, while destroying the Polish 7th Infantry Division and scattered the Krakowska Cavalry Brigade. His advance continued toward the Pilica River and Warsaw.[26]

The Poles tried to concentrate against 10th Army on September 6, for Reichenau was now threatening the capital, as well as the lines of retreat of the Polish Lodz and Poznan armies. Reichenau, however, beat off heavy counterattacks against his northern flank with his panzer divisions, smashed the Polish 29th Infantry Division, and captured the commander of Poland's general reserve. By the end of the day he had bypassed the Lodz Army on his northern flank and all but enveloped the Krakow Army at Radom on his southern flank.[27]

Rundstedt, the commander of Army Group South, now directed Reichenau to destroy the Polish forces at Radom, an operation that would cause considerable delay in the advance on the Vistula, especially since he detached two of 10th Army's corps (XI and XVI) to 8th Army on Reichenau's left flank. In the Radom vicinity, the Poles had concentrated their 3rd, 7th, 12th, 19th, and 29th Infantry divisions, as well as what was left of the Krakowska Cavalry Brigade. Some of these units were in remnants, but they nevertheless constituted a considerable force, and it took most of Reichenau's strength to deal with them.[28]

Reichenau ordered IV Corps to attack the Radom Army from the west and southwest, while the mobile XIV Corps enveloped it from the north, and XV Corps enveloped it from the south. The fighting was heavy, but the advance panzer detachments reached the Vistula north and south of Radom by nightfall on September 8. Reichenau himself was the first German to cross the river: he swam it. Clearing the Radom Pocket delayed the exploitation phase of the operation, but by September 11 organized resistance had ended and 10th Army had taken 60,000 prisoners in the first major battle of encirclement fought by the German Army in World War II.[29]

The main Polish forces, some twelve infantry divisions and three cavalry brigades, were in the Kutno vicinity, about seventy miles due west of Warsaw, and were retreating toward the Polish capital, pursued by the 8th Army. Reichenau saw that he had a chance to cut off their retreat if he advanced rapidly enough. Using the 31st Infantry Division to screen Warsaw from the south, Reichenau hastily attacked toward the Warsaw-Kutno railroad with most of his army, spearheaded by the 1st Panzer and 4th Panzer divisions. By September 16 the bulk of the Polish Lodz and Poznan armies had been cut off and were in the process of being crushed by the 8th and 10th armies and the Luftwaffe. Reichenau had already taken 12,000 more prisoners.[30]

Except for the Siege of Warsaw, the rest of the Polish campaign was a mopping-up operation. Reichenau's artillery bombarded the city, but his initial infantry attacks were repulsed. On September 24 Blaskowitz's 8th Army assumed command of the forces besieging the Polish capital. The rest of 10th Army pushed on to the Bug River, which Stalin and Hitler had establshed as their Demarcation Line. On October 1 Reichenau was ordered to prepare to move his troops back to Germany.[31]

Although operational opportunities had diverted him from the mission of capturing Warsaw, Reichenau had performed well and perhaps brilliantly in the Polish campaign. He was decorated with the Knights' Cross and on October 1 was promoted to colonel general.[32]

In the initial plan for the invasion of France and the Low Countries, Reichenau's 10th Army (which was soon redesignated 6th Army) was placed under Bock's Army Group B and given the bulk of the panzer formations and the primary mission of destroying the main French and British armies in the field. Later, when the Manstein Plan was adopted, most of Reichenau's panzer units were transferred to Army Group A. He bitterly protested the loss of these formations. He was, after all, a leading tank advocate and had successfully led armored formations in Poland. A more rational move on the Germans' part would have been to place the tanks under Reichenau, instead of the conservative cavalryman, Ewald von Kleist, but this was apparently not considered. Reichenau's role was now secondary: overrun southern Holland and western Belgium and drive on to Brussels, forcing the Allies to commit their mobile forces against him. Army Group A would then attack to the south and drive on to the English Channel, cutting off the best Allied units in Belgium. For this operation, Reichenau was given IV, XI, and XXVII corps, plus Hoepner's XVI Motorized Corps. Reichenau controlled two panzer and fourteen infantry divisions, plus one motorized division.[33]

Reichenau clashed with Hitler over the Fuehrer's plan to launch the Western campaign in the fall of 1939, even if a delay meant conceding Belgium to the Allies. The winter weather would limit the value of Germany's two most important weapons: the panzer/ motorized forces and the Luftwaffe. He said so, loudly and in no uncertain terms.[34] Reichenau was never one to be overly diplomatic and was never too impressed by Hitler personally. Friction had developed between the two over Hitler's alliance with Italy (which Reichenau considered to be worse than useless) and his alliance with Japan (instead of China, as Reichenau advocated). Reichenau also no doubt resented being passed over for the post of Army C-in-C. Relations between the two continued to be strained until Reichenau's death.

On May 10, 1940, the Wehrmacht launched its western campaign. Reichenau faced part of the Dutch Army, the Belgian Army, and elements of the French 9th Army (under General Corap). The Belgians had twenty-four infantry divisions, fourteen of which were on the frontier. They planned to fight a delaying action on the Albert Canal from Antwerp to the Meuse, and then along the Meuse from Liège to Namur, until the Allies occupied the Dyle River line. Reichenau, however, quickly disrupted the Belgian forces and took the Albert Canal bridges at Briedgen, Veldwezelt, and Vroenhoven, while Hitler's paratroops neutralized the key fortress of Eben Emael. Reichenau's advance was so rapid that the Dutch Army could not make a stand on the Peel River, as it had planned. It fell back toward the center of Holland, exposing the Belgian left flank. Reichenau quickly poured troops into this area, widening the gap. As the Dutch and Belgians retreated in confusion the Allies rushed into Belgium from the south. They committed General Billotte's entire 1st Army Group, including the French 7th Army (Giraud), the British Expeditionary Force (Lord Gort), the French 1st Army (Blanchard), and the left wing of the French 9th Army. Hitler was overjoyed: the Manstein Plan was working to perfection.[35]

On the second day of the campaign, Reichenau wrecked the Anglo-French plan to hold at the Dyle. General Prioux's French Cavalry Corps had rushed forward from the river with two mechanized divisions, according to plan, to delay the German advance; but at 1 P.M. they ran into Reichenau's two panzer divisions, which were driving forward rapidly and with powerful Luftwaffe support. By 3 P.M. two of the best French divisions were in full retreat and General Prioux was conceding defeat, signalling General Billotte that he had not been able to hold off the Germans long enough for the infantry divisions of the French 1st Army to reach the Dyle.[36]

Meanwhile, elements of the French 7th Army crossed Belgium

and entered southern Holland. Here, on May 12, they clashed with Reichenau's fast-moving forces in the vicinity of Breda. They were unable to make contact with the Dutch Army. Later that evening Billotte ordered them back to the sector west of the Escaut River, because Reichenau was already threatening to cut them off from the south. In giving this order, Billotte effectively wrote off the Netherlands; but he really had little choice, because of the speed of the 6th Army's advance.[37] The Dutch Army was finished off by Army Group B's other army, Georg von Kuechler's 18th. It capitulated on May 15.

Reichenau had now completed his primary mission in the western campaign. The Allies had committed the bulk of their best troops against the 6th Army, including most of their mobile reserves, but this was not the main attack. The mobile units of Panzer Group Kleist struck second-rate French units at Sedan and Montherme on May 12 and three days later had achieved the decisive breakthrough. Soon Guderian was racing for the Channel against weak and sporadic resistance. Reichenau, however, was outnumbered two to one by May 15, and his progress was much slower. He probably would not have gained ground at all, except for his superior armored tactics and the German command of the air, both of which he used to full advantage. On May 15 he smashed the 1st Moroccan Division on the Gembloux Plain, and the French 1st Army prevented another German breakthrough only with the greatest difficulty.[38]

That night General Gamelin, the French Commander-in-Chief, decided to order a general withdrawal of Allied forces in Belgium, but it was already too late for that. Guderian was already around their right flank, and Reichenau continued to hammer at their front, pinning them down and making a general withdrawal impossible. Reichenau was driving on Brussels when, much to his disgust, the Army High Command took XVI Motorized Corps from him and gave it to Army Group A. Reichenau nevertheless took the Belgian capital the next day, May 17, and overran the French frontier positions south of Maubeuge, forcing his way into the rear of the French 1st Army and threatening its lines of communications.[39]

William L. Shirer, an American correspondent, interviewed Reichenau about this time. He wrote:

Reichenau, whom I had seen occasionally in Berlin before the war, greeted us on the porch. He was tanned and springy as ever, his invariable monocle squeezed over one eye. With typical German thoroughness and with an apparent frankness that surprised me, he went over the operations thus far, stopping to answer questions now and then. . . .

The general is in an almost jovial mood. He is not tense. He is not worried. He is not rushed. You wonder: "Have these German generals no nerves?" Because, after all, he is directing a large army in an important battle. A few miles down the road two million men are trying to slaughter one another. He bosses almost a million of them. The general smiles and, jauntily, says good-bye.

"I've just given permission for you to go to the front," he says. His eyes light up. "You may be under fire. But you'll have to take your chances. We all do."[40]

The absence of his panzers prevented Reichenau from scoring a major breakthrough on May 17, 18, or 19, and allowed the British to stabilize their line in the vicinity of Escaut and to assemble a mobile reserve, which they used for their counterattack at Arras on May 21. Reichenau continued to hammer against the BEF and the Belgians but managed to achieve only local successes.

No doubt sensing that the Belgians were nearing the end of their powers of resistance, Reichenau struck at their extreme right flank on the morning of May 24 with five divisions. He broke through the Lys line on either side of Courtrai in fierce fighting. The Belgians quickly committed their reserves (the 9th and 10th divisions) and temporarily sealed off the breakthrough, but were pulverized by Stuka dive-bombers. The Belgians abandoned the Lys and retreated under heavy pressure toward Ypres and Roules pursued by the 6th Army's 18th and 311th Infantry divisions. The BEF also retreated and had to be reinforced with the French 2nd Light Mechanized Division.[41] King Leopold of Belgium was already openly considering surrender.

The next morning Reichenau's troops stormed Audenarde, but the main attack of the day came at 5 P.M., when he struck the Belgians with the IX and VI corps, driving a gap between Gheluwe and Lys, which the Belgians were unable to close, even with their last reserves. Lord Gort only barely managed to plug the gap by quickly throwing the British 5th and 50th Infantry divisions, but the Belgians were clearly wavering. That night Fedor von Bock reinforced Reichenau with X Corps, and also sent the 61st Infantry Division to Reichenau's IV Corps.[42]

May 26 saw violent fighting between the British II Corps (5th and 50th Infantry divisions) and the German 18th, 311th, and 61st Infantry Divisions. That afternoon, with the British pinned down, Reichenau struck the Belgians "with extreme violence," according to General Michiels, the Belgian Chief of Staff. Soon a gap developed between the British 5th Division at Ypres and the Belgian Army in the Zonnebeke sector. Neither the British nor the Belgians had any reserves left. By nightfall Reichenau had expanded the gap to eight miles.[43]

As dawn broke on May 27, the German 14th and 19th Infantry divisions continued their advance through the gap in the Belgian line. By nightfall the Belgian Army was in danger of annihilation, and their king was suing for peace. At 11 P.M. that evening, he agreed to an unconditional capitulation. At Château Anvaing, at 12:20 A.M. the following morning, General Desrousseaux surrendered the Belgian Army to Colonel General von Reichenau. It was perhaps the high point of Reichenau's career. The loss of the Belgian Army rendered the position of the French 1st Army hopeless. Reichenau quickly cut across its rear and linked up with Kluge's 4th Army north of Lille. Only the French 12th and 32nd Infantry divisions, plus the remnants of the French Cavalry Corps, managed to cross the Lys and escape. Six other divisions were caught in the trap and surrendered on May 30.[44]

The surrender of the French 1st Army ended the first phase of the western campaign for Reichenau. He quickly redeployed his men to the south, where the remnants of the French Army awaited the final onslaught.

In the final operation of the campaign, Reichenau directed eight infantry divisions, a mountain division, and Panzer Group Kleist (four panzer and two motorized divisions, plus two SS motorized divisions and the Grossdeutschland Motorized Regiment.)[45] The advance began on June 5 against spirited opposition, which soon deteriorated and then collapsed altogether. Reichenau drove from Péronne, crossed the Marne and the Cher, took Orléans, and collected thousands of prisoners.[46] The campaign was not a true test of his abilities, however, since it was essentially a mopping-up operation. The French had no real chance of holding out after the collapse of the Dunkirk Pocket. On July 19, 1940, after the French surrender, Reichenau was promoted to field marshal, along with eleven other generals. He was only fifty-five years old, a relatively young age for a marshal.

LIKE MANY OF Hitler's other field marshals, Reichenau fought his last battles on the Eastern Front. Once again his 6th Army was primarily an infantry force. As of September 3, for example, he directed seventeen infantry divisions, one light, and one panzer division.[47] He performed quite creditably, breaching the Stalin Line, taking Kiev, Belgorod, Kharkov, and Kursk, and playing a role (though not the major one) in several battles of encirclement. The major noticeable change in Reichenau, however, was not the quality of his operations, which was always sound, but rather his changed attitude toward the Jews.

He had never disagreed with what Hitler had stood for on what he considered the major issues (nationalism, rearmament, and military expansion, renouncing the Treaty of Versailles, smashing the Polish menace, and the like); rather, he questioned the Fuehrer's judgment on strategic matters, such as the proposal to attack France in winter, and on Hitler's plans to ally with Italy instead of his beloved Britain in 1936.[48] In earlier years, Reichenau had displayed a friendly attitude toward the Jews, even to the point of attending dinners for Jewish front-line veterans of World War I, in uniform, to the great displeasure of the Nazi Party. Later, in the winter of 1939/40, he officially protested against SS atrocities in Poland. In 1941, however, he issued an order stating: "We have to exact a harsh but just retribution on the Jewish subhumans. This serves the added purpose of stifling at birth uprisings in the rear of the Wehrmacht, since experience shows that these are always conceived by Jews."[49] He also stated that the German soldier was the carrier of an "inexorable racial idea," which transcended all previously accepted codes of military honor. He endorsed the SS massacre of Jews at Kiev in September, and called on his men to cooperate with the *Einsatzgruppen*, the notorious SS death squads.[50]

Despite his newfound anti-Semitism, Reichenau continued to speak his mind on strategic issues, much to Hitler's distaste. In the spring of 1941, Reichenau prepared a detailed and independent study on why Germany should not attack Russia, and sent it directly to Hitler. After Hitler rejected it, Reichenau became generally critical of the Fuehrer, according to Generals Roehrricht, Foertsch, von Vietinghoff, and Speidel.[51] At the end of August or early September 1941, Reichenau suggested to Hitler that White Russian and Ukrainian divisions be formed to fight the Communists. Hitler rejected the idea, saying: "Let Reichenau mind his own military problems and leave the rest to me!"[52]

Typically, Reichenau did not let the matter lie. In fact, his last dispatch to Hitler complained that Germany was losing the opportunity of converting the traditionally anti-Soviet Ukrainians to the Nazi cause. He saw clearly, as did Goebbels and Alfred Rosenberg, that Hitler's racial ideas and anti-Slavic policies would lead to large-scale partisan warfare. Hitler, however, preferred to be guided by Himmler, Erich Koch (Reich Commissioner of the Ukraine), and Fritz Sauckel (his plenipotentiary in charge of labor procurement).[53] As a result, large-scale and costly guerrilla warfare did break out in the rear areas of the Eastern Front, especially after 1941.

In November 1941, Field Marshal von Brauchitsch, sick in body and spirit, was clearly on his way out as Commander-in-Chief of the Army. Once again Reichenau's name was brought up as a potential C-in-C. Once again he was blocked, this time by Hitler. That officer is "too political" for me, the dictator said, observing that when the cat was away the mouse would play. It was Reichenau's third and final rejection. A few days later, Hitler assumed the post himself.

Meanwhile, Kleist's 1st Panzer Army took Rostov but could not hold it. Gerd von Rundstedt, the commander of Army Group South, begged Hitler to consent to a retreat to the Mius River, but the Fuehrer refused to allow it. In desperation, Rundstedt submitted his resignation and gave the order on his own initiative. On the night of November 30 Hitler relieved Rundstedt of his command and replaced him with Reichenau, who initially agreed with the Fuehrer and ordered the retreat halted.[54]

It took Reichenau less than twenty-four hours to change his mind. On his own responsibility he ordered 1st Panzer Army to complete the withdrawal to the Mius and informed Hitler of his decision with a dispatch beginning with the words: "In anticipation of your concurrence . . ." Hitler accepted this *fait accompli*.[55]

On the mainland, Army Group South included the 1st Panzer, 17th and 6th armies, as well as an Italian corps, a Hungarian corps, and two Slovak divisions. It faced nine Soviet armies; nevertheless Reichenau halted the Soviet winter offensive on the Mius. The Germans would stay on this line until the summer of 1942.[56]

On the Crimean Peninsula to the south, Manstein's 11th Army was also attacked. Reichenau left the brilliant Manstein to fight his own battle with his own resources. When the 46th Infantry Division retreated without orders, however, Reichenau declared that it had forfeited its honor by its "precipitate withdrawal." He stripped it of its banners and suspended all of its promotions and decorations until further notice[57] – a cruel verdict indeed for a unit that had been under attack by two Soviet armies and had fought well in Poland, France, the Ukraine, and in the breaching of the Perekop Isthmus.[58] Reichenau also played a discreditable part in the arrest and subsequent imprisonment of Count Hans von Sponeck, the commander of XLII Corps.*

ON JANUARY 12, 1942, Walter von Reichenau went on his usual cross-country run of several miles in temperatures well below minus 20 degrees Fahrenheit. He looked ill later when he appeared at the mess for lunch. He ate a little, signed a few papers, and got up to leave. Before he reached the door he collapsed with a severe heart attack. His Medical Officer, Dr. Flade, happened to be in Dresden at the time. Army Group South signaled for Flade to return immediately. Hitler was also alarmed. He arranged for Reichenau's family doctor, Professor Hochrein, who was serving with Army Group North, to be flown by special aircraft to Reichenau's HQ at Poltava. The physicians did what they could, but five days later the field marshal had still not regained consciousness and was near death. On January 17 they strapped him into an armchair aboard an airplane to fly him to Leipzig, where a team of surgeons stood by. En route, the airplane crash-landed and von Reichenau suffered severe head injuries. It is open to question

---

*See chapter 12 for the details of this incident.

whether he died of heart failure or as a result of his head injuries. What is known is that Field Marshal Walter von Reichenau was declared dead on arrival in Leipzig on the evening of January 17, 1942.[59] He was fifty-seven years old.

OF ALL HITLER's field marshals, Reichenau is the most difficult to evaluate, with the exception of Witzleben. As an army commander and as a strategist he was certainly gifted, but he only commanded at the highest level (army group) for six weeks, and in a secondary sector at that: hardly enough time for us to judge him. His personal characteristics are easier to evaluate: he was cold, intelligent, independent, ambitious, and ruthless. Had he lived, Adolf Hitler would have had a great deal of trouble with him, for "obey without question" was certainly not the cornerstone of Reichenau's personal philosophy. Certainly one cannot imagine him leaving 6th Army to perish at Stalingrad just because Hitler decreed it. Matthew Cooper gave an excellent postmortem to his career when he wrote: "For the Army, it was a tragedy that he never fulfilled his erstwhile ambition to become its Commander-in-Chief; although not recognized at the time, he, alone among the generals, possessed the combination of political insight, courage, drive, and conviction necessary to halt the progress of the later years of Hitler's dictatorship."[60]

5

Ritter Wilhelm von Leeb

"IF VON LEEB ever tried to smile, it would crack his face," Field Marshal Siegmund Wilhelm List said of him.[1] Known for his austerity and forbidding personality, as well as for his high moral code, Wilhelm Joseph Franz von Leeb was born in Landsberg-am-Lech, Bavaria, on September 5, 1876, a descendant of an old Bavarian military family.[2] He entered the Imperial Army as a *Fahnenjunker* (officer-cadet) with the Bavarian 4th Field Artillery Regiment in 1895, as a matter of course.[3] This family tradition was also upheld by his younger brother, Emil, who was a general of artillery and commander of IX Corps during the Polish campaign. Later Emil was Chief of the Army Ordnance Office. Wilhelm's son, Alfred, was later killed in action in the Polish campaign.[4]

Wilhelm von Leeb was commissioned a lieutenant in the 4th Field Artillery, based at Augsburg, in 1897.[5] He attended the artillery and engineer schools from 1897 to 1899, and first saw action in 1900 at Peking, China, during the Boxer Rebellion. After returning to Europe, he attended the Bavarian War Academy in Munich and served on the Bavarian General Staff in Munich (1907–09) and on the Greater General Staff in Berlin (1909–11). Promoted to first lieutenant in 1905 and captain in 1911, he was assigned to the Field Artillery School at Jueterbog (1911–12) and did a tour of troop duty as a battery commander in the Bavarian 10th Field Artillery Regiment at Erlangen (1912–13). He was on the General Staff of the 1 Bavarian Army Corps in Munich in 1914, when World War I broke out.[6]

Captain Leeb served on the Western Front primarily as Ia (Operation's Officer) of the Bavarian 11th Infantry Division, during the first two years of the war. His division was transferred to the east in 1916, and during operations in Galicia and Serbia Leeb won the Bavarian Military Order of Max Joseph for exceptional bravery. This decoration carried with it an honorary, nonhereditary knighthood – hence he held the title "Ritter," but could not pass it on to his descendants.[7]

Leeb was promoted to major in the summer of 1916 and fought with the 11th Infantry against the Russians in the Battle of Kovel; later he took part in the conquest of Rumania. In May 1917 he was transferred back to the Western Front, as the second General Staff Officer (Ib) on the staff of Crown Prince Rupprecht of Bavaria, and remained there until the end of the war.[8] According to one source, he served briefly with the Freikorps in 1919.[9] In any event he was the chief of a department in the Reich Defense Ministry in Berlin in October 1919. Selected for retention in the 100,000-man Army, he rose rapidly in the Reichsheer, especially after 1924. On October 1, 1920, he was promoted to lieutenant colonel. The following year he became chief of staff of Wehrkreis II, headquartered in Stettin, and in February 1922 returned to Munich as Chief of Staff of Wehrkreis VII. He spent a year at Landsberg as commander of the 2nd Mountain Artillery Battalion of the 7th Artillery Regiment (1924), before being promoted to colonel in February 1925. In 1926 he was commander of the 7th Artillery Regiment, then stationed at Nuremberg. Two years later Wilhelm von Leeb was named Artillerie fuehrer V (Artillery Leader V) and one of the two deputy commanders of the 5th Infantry Division at Stuttgart. He was promoted to major general and named Artilleriefuehrer VII and deputy commander of the 7th Infantry Division in Munich in 1929. On December 1, 1929, while serving as commander of the 7th Infantry Division at Munich, Leeb was promoted to lieutenant general, and in 1930 became commander of Wehrkreis VII.[10] He had been promoted from lieutenant colonel to lieutenant general in five years. This rapid advancement might have caused jealousy among his peers had it been another officer; however, Leeb was highly respected in the tight-knit Officer Corps, and his promotions evoked little or no resentment. He was considered an authority on defensive warfare and authored a number of works on the topic; in fact, he had a worldwide reputation as an expert on the subject.[11]

Future Field Marshals Erwin Rommel and Walter Model were also authors, but, of the three, Leeb's work commanded the most respect within his profession prior to 1940. Leeb's book *Defense* was published by the German War Ministry in the *Militarwissenschaftliche Rundschau (The Scientific Military Review)* in 1938 and was later translated into English. Some of his earlier works were translated into Russian and incorporated into the Soviet Field Service regulations of 1936. *Defense* was hailed by experts in the late 1930s as probably "the most important piece of research in the field of strategy and tactics in modern warfare that has appeared in a decade."[12]

Leeb felt that "Defense is mostly the necessary recourse of distress; the defenders are nearly always in a critical position."[13] He carried Clausewitz one step further when he wrote:

Clausewitz depicts defense as "the stronger form," offense as "the weaker one." This interpretation can best be understood, from the point of view of actually conducting a combat, in the following manner: The activities of the attacker mainly are those of movement and fire. During his advance the attacker generally can make no use of his own arms. While advancing he becomes an open target for the fire of the defender, whose activity consists of fire, not of movement. The defender finds a favorable terrain, digs in, hides, and protects himself from losses. These advantages of tactical defense are transferred to the strategic defense.

The aim of the defensive is to hold; that of the offensive, to win. It is easier to hold than to win.[14]

General Leeb felt that Germany should initially maintain a posture of strategic defense in World War II, force the numerically superior enemy to attack, let the German forces bleed them white, and only then should Germany go over to the offensive with its armor. Clearly he did not fully grasp the strategic possibilities of the emerging panzer branch. Unlike the French, however, Leeb placed little stock in the value of fixed fortifications. Instead he advocated the development of strong anti-tank and reconnaissance forces, along with panzer and aviation units.[15]

Besides his writings on defensive warfare, Leeb also wrote *The Chronicle of the von Leeb Family* and earned the nickname "the Family-Tree General."[16]

In his private life, Leeb was described as "simple, direct and uncompromising in matters of principle." He was a practising Catholic who openly went to church with his family even after the Nazis took power. From the beginning he was considered suspect by Hitler and his followers, whose politics he openly rejected.[17]

Unlike most of his contemporaries, Ritter von Leeb was not fooled for a moment by Adolf Hitler. On January 23, 1933, three days after he became Chancellor, Hitler addressed the senior generals after a dinner held at General von Hammerstein's apartment. The would-be Fuehrer declared that the Army was "the sole bearer of arms" for the German nation and called for the eradication of pacifism, Marxism, and democracy. Germany must rearm, he cried, and then conquer "the land to the East," which the generals no doubt took to mean Poland, their traditional and hated enemy. Most of the Army officers were impressed by the Nazi chieftain's speech and policies, but not Leeb. "A businessman whose wares are good does not need to boost them in the loudest tones of a market crier," he commented, adding that he thought Hitler was trying to bribe them.[18]

For his part, Hitler found Ritter von Leeb "an incorrigible anti-Nazi." Leeb had the dubious distinction of being one of the first generals placed under Gestapo surveillance.[19] Leeb, however, was an intellectual and a thinker, rather than a catalyst and a man of action. He did not take an active part in the anti-Hitler conspiracy and was not courted by the German resistance after 1941. He did not even know of the existence of the Stauffenberg assassination plot of July 20, 1944, until after it had failed.[20]

Being a Nazi was not a prerequisite for promotion in the German Army until 1942, so Leeb continued his climb up the professional ladder. He directed Military District VII in southern Germany until 1934, when he was promoted to general of artillery and received a prize appointment: he was named Commander of Army Group 2 at Kassel. At the time there were only two Army groups in Germany. (Later this number was increased to six.)

Leeb's command initially consisted of Wehrkreise V, VI, and VII, which directed the 5th, 6th, and 7th Infantry divisions, respectively. Leeb also controlled the 3rd Cavalry Division at Weimar. Army Group 2 was considerably enlarged during Hitler's military expansion. By October 1937 it included Wehrkreise V, VI, IX, and XII (headquartered at Stuttgart, Muenster, Kassel, and Wiesbaden, respectively). It controlled eleven infantry divisions and four frontier-area commands.[21]

Colonel General Walter von Brauchitsch succeeded Werner von Fritsch as Commander-in-Chief of the Army on February 4, 1938, largely because he agreed to remove a number of commanders whom Hitler considered hostile to National Socialism. Ritter Wilhelm von Leeb was at the head of this list. He was involuntarily retired on March 1 with the honorary (*charakterisierte*) rank of colonel general and was replaced by General Siegmund Wilhelm List.[22]

Leeb was recalled to active duty in August 1938, when it seemed certain that Hitler would settle the Sudetenland crisis by force. He was given command of the newly created 12th Army, which had the mission of supporting the attack of List's 14th Army from Austria into Bohemia. Hitler did not have to resort to combat in this case, however, because the British and French signed the Munich Accords on September 29, forcing Czechoslovakia to surrender its critical frontier zones without a fight. From October 1–10, Leeb's forces occupied much of southern Bohemia.[23] Soon after, Leeb returned to Bavaria and went back into retirement.

During the Polish crisis the following year, Hitler recalled Leeb once again and gave him command of Army Group C. Leeb's new headquarters evolved from his old command (HQ, Army Group 2) and included the 1st, 5th, and 7th armies. Seventh Army (General Friedrich Dollmann) was posted on the southern flank, along the Rhine; 1st Army (General Erwin von Witzleben) held the center, in the Rhineland; and 5th Army (General Curt Liebmann) defended the northern border, facing Luxemburg and the Low Countries. They were supported in the north by 2nd Air Fleet (General Hellmuth Felmy) and in the south by General Hugo Sperrle's 3rd

Air Fleet. Leeb's Chief of Staff was Major General Georg von Sodenstern.[24]

Leeb's forces were not as strong as they appeared on paper. Of the eighteen peacetime corps headquarters, all but four (V, VI, IX, and XII) were assigned to Poland. Leeb had only twelve of the fifty-one regular peacetime divisions, and none of these were armored. Leeb was given only ten reserve and fifteen Landwehr (older-age) divisions to hold the West Wall and the Belgian-Dutch frontiers, and several of these were under strength. With the equivalent of thirty-one infantry divisions, Leeb faced 106 French divisions. Discounting fifteen divisions on the Italian frontier, France had roughly ninety-one divisions, with 10,000 guns and 2,500 tanks, available for use against Army Group C.[25] Leeb did not have a single panzer on the entire Western Front. His infantry units had enough ammunition for only three days of fighting.

Elements of the French 3rd and 4th armies attacked in the Saar sector on September 9, and, after some skirmishing, Leeb fell back to his main defensive positions on the Siegfried Line. By September 13 the French had advanced along a sixteen-mile front to a depth of five miles, taking about twenty abandoned villages. Here they halted, never to advance again.[26]

Considering the odds, Leeb was not too nervous about his position; he considered a rapid Allied reaction unlikely, although he did resist (successfully) an attempt to further weaken his forces. He was more concerned with the remote possibility of an Allied offensive through the Low Countries. While the bulk of the Wehrmacht overran Poland, Leeb busied himself mainly with calling up new reserve formations to bolster this sector, which he placed under the *ad hoc* Army Detachment A, under Colonel General von Hammerstein. By September 20 the Polish Army was in remnants, Leeb had already received substantial reinforcements, and the Dutch and Belgians were engaged in defensive flooding.[27] The Allies had passed up the only real opportunity they would have to invade western Germany until 1944.

Leeb counterattacked in the Saar sector on October 16 and by October 24 had regained all of the ground he had lost in September, at a cost of fewer than two hundred dead.[28] Following this "offensive," stalemate set in on the Western Front.

Colonel General Leeb opposed the western campaign from the

beginning. He was particularly distressed over the proposed invasion of Belgium, which he opposed on moral grounds. The death of his son, Lieutenant Alfred von Leeb of the 99th Mountain Infantry Regiment, was a contributing factor to his father's outspoken opposition to this invasion. Lieutenant von Leeb was killed in the Battle of Lvov, the day before the city fell. Wilhelm von Leeb considered his son's death unnecessary, as the Russians had already entered Poland from the east, and Hitler turned Lvov over to the Soviets a few days later.[29]

In October 1939, Leeb correctly branded Hitler's peace proposals to the West as a hoax and circulated a memorandum among his generals predicting that the entire world would turn against Germany if she violated Belgian neutrality for the second time in twenty-five years.[30] He wanted the Commander-in-Chief of the Army to defy Hitler on this issue, but he realized that no one man could convince the weak-willed von Brauchitsch to stand up to the Fuehrer. Therefore, on November 9, he met with Colonel Generals Gerd von Rundstedt and Fedor von Bock at Koblenz. He proposed that all three of them resign if Hitler continued to push for an offensive in the West. Faced with a united front of his army group commanders, Leeb felt Hitler might be compelled to change his plans. Rundstedt and Bock, however, were anything but pleased by Leeb's proposal. Author Telford Taylor speculates that Leeb's memo had little influence on his fellow officers because many of them regarded him as "overcautious and behind the times, especially in his evaluation of tanks and airplanes in modern warfare."[31] Leeb returned to his headquarters in disgust and even talked to General Sodenstern about unilaterally resigning his command.[32]

Army Group C, which now consisted of only the 1st and 7th armies, played a minor role in the western invasion, which began on May 10, 1940. Leeb had only seventeen divisions (all infantry), but his feints against the Maginot Line were so successful that the French did not begin withdrawing divisions from his sector until after the German mobile forces had scored their decisive breakthrough to the north. By this time the Luftwaffe had cut the French rail lines, making a rapid troop transfer impossible.[33]

After Dunkirk, with the French Army in remnants and the panzers plowing into the rear of the Maginot Line, Panzer Group Guderian was placed under Leeb's control. With these reinforcements, he encircled the French Army Group 2 (2nd, 3rd, 5th, and 8th armies) in the Epinal-Moselle sector on June 18. French General Daille led his XLV Corps into Switzerland – and internment – on June 20,[34] but the bulk of General Pretelat's Army group surrendered to Leeb shortly thereafter. His total haul amounted to approximately 250,000 prisoners.

Along with eleven other Army generals, Ritter von Leeb received his field marshal's baton at the Reichstag on July 19, 1940. He remained in southern France on occupation duty until October 25, when Army Group C was transferred to Dresden to begin preparation for the invasion of Russia. Characteristically, Leeb protested against this new adventure. He foresaw the possible consequences, including the entry of the United States into the war. Hitler and Field Marshal von Brauchitsch ignored his protests.[35]

FOR THE INVASION of Russia, Army Group C was redesignated Army Group North and given the 18th Army (Colonel General Georg von Kuechler), 16th Army (Colonel General Ernst Busch), and 4th Panzer Group (General Erich Hoepner). Leeb was charged with attacking from central East Prussia through Kovno and Dvinsk toward the area south of Pskov, with the objective of cutting off the main Soviet forces in the Baltic States and destroying them before they could escape to the interior. Army Group North was then to clear the Baltic States, assemble in the vicinity of Lake Ilmen, and advance on Leningrad.[36] Colonel General Karl Koller's 1st Air Fleet was to support the advance.

Leeb's problems in this campaign were mammoth. First of all, the terrain in the Baltic States was difficult: flat, thickly forested, and sandy, with much marshland and many swamps, lakes, and streams. The roads were dirt: poor, narrow, and badly maintained, totally unsuitable for rapid motorized advances. The main barrier, the Dvina River, running through Vitebsk and Riga, was more than two hundred miles beyond the Prussian border. Second, Leeb had been assigned no priority of objectives. Was he to clear the Baltic States before seizing Leningrad, or vice versa? This vital question was still unanswered when the campaign began. Finally, Leeb had insufficient forces to carry out his task of cutting off the Soviets in the Baltic States. Army Group North had twenty-six divisions, of which three were panzer and three were motorized. It was much smaller than either of the other two German army groups. It initially faced General Fedor I. Kuznetsov's North-West Front (8th and 11th armies), which had some thirty divisions, including two mechanized corps (four armored and two motorized divisions), as well as a few independent armored brigades. To the Soviet rear lay General M. M. Popov's Leningrad Military District (later North Front), which had the 7th, 10th, and 23rd armies, and X Mechanized Corps – another twenty divisions.[37]

Besides his other difficulties, Leeb himself was neither trained nor suited for directing large panzer formations, which he handled here for the first time in his long career. His tank commander, Hoepner, was a very capable armor leader, but was independent-minded and difficult to direct. Friction soon developed between him and Leeb, whom Hoepner considered too slow. Leeb, on the other hand, became nervous when the panzer general's tactics placed them dozens of miles in front of the infantry, with nothing left behind to cover their rear.

Leeb attacked at 3:05 A.M. on June 22, 1941, with Kuechler on the left, Hoepner in the center, and Busch on the right. He achieved complete surprise all along the frontier and soon smashed the bulk of the advance forces of the Soviet 8th and 11th armies. By the morning of June 23, the vanguard of the 18th Army (Lieutenant General Kurt Herzog's 291st Infantry Division) had already advanced more than forty miles, through Lithuania and into Latvia. Meanwhile, Hoepner split the two corps of his panzer group. He sent Manstein's LVI Panzer Corps through forested country toward the Dvina River bridge at Daugavpils – 220 miles behind the front lines – while General Hans-Georg Reinhardt's XLI Panzer Corps dealt with the Soviet III and XII Tank corps.[38]

On June 23 the first crisis occurred, when Reinhardt engaged three Russian tank divisions (about three hundred tanks) near Rossizny. The Russian tanks were mainly KV-1s and KV-2s – superheavy models of forty-three and fifty-two tons respectively. They were superior to any of the panzers and more than a match for the German anti-tank guns, whose shells simply bounced off – a very unpleasant surprise for both Leeb and the gunners. Fortunately for Reinhardt, the Soviets simply attacked frontally, without skill. Reinhardt halted their advance with his artillery, then counterattacked with the 1st Panzer, 6th Panzer, 36th Motorized, and 269th Infantry divisions, forcing III Tank Corps back against a bog. When the battle ended the next day, more than one hundred and eight Soviet tanks and one hundred pieces of artillery had been destroyed or captured. By June 28, Leeb's forces had destroyed or captured four hundred tanks and armored vehicles, two hundred guns, several hundred aircraft, and several warships along the Baltic coast, but had taken only six thousand prisoners. The Communists were in full retreat, but had not been destroyed.[39]

Meanwhile, elements of the Brandenburger Division took the bridge at Daugavpils, and soon Manstein had the 8th Panzer and 3rd Motorized divisions across the river. He was quickly counter-attacked by the Soviet XXI Mechanized Corps (up from the Leningrad Military District), which he defeated. Manstein wanted to continue the advance, but Hitler ordered him to halt because he was sixty miles in front of the nearest elements of the 16th Army and the only German unit across the Dvina. The conservative Leeb did not object and seemed perfectly satisfied with this timid order. Manstein remained stationary for almost a week, giving the Soviets time to organize their resistance in the Stalin Line, on the old Russo-Estonian frontier. At the same time, Soviet resistance on the German left stiffened at Liepaja, which finally fell to the 18th Army on June 29 after five days of bitter fighting.[40]

On July 1, Leeb met with Hoepner and proposed that 16th Army (on the southern flank of the army group) wheel north and seal off the Baltic States, while 4th Panzer Group protected its eastern flank from Soviet counterattacks. Hoepner objected: he wanted his tanks to advance between Lakes Peipus and Ilmen, on the direct route to Leningrad. Hoepner was surprised that Leeb was so indecisive as to whether the objective was Leningrad or the Baltic States; but clearly the army group commander was leaning toward the more conventional, conservative solution of securing his left flank before proceeding. In doing so he was losing valuable time, for it was vital that Stalin be defeated decisively before the Russian winter came to his rescue.

Due to Hoepner's objections, Leeb proposed a compromise: Manstein was to drive on Novorzhev (in the direction of Lake Ilmen) with 16th Army, while Reinhardt advanced on Ostrov, in the direction of Leningrad. Hoepner was dissatisfied with this broad front approach and argued for the bolder, quick-thrust advance; but he was overruled.[41]

Reinhardt's XLI Panzer Corps, spearheaded by the 1st Panzer Division, took Ostrov against weak opposition on July 4. General Sobennikov, who had replaced Kuznetsov as commander of the North-West Front, desperately tried to build a new front south of Lake Peipus, using the 1st Mechanized Corps and two reserve rifle corps. Reinhardt, with the 1st Panzer, 6th Panzer, and 36th Motorized divisions, pressed on and took Pskov on the southern shore of Lake Peipus despite heavy Soviet armored counterattacks, thus securing a jump-off position for the drive on Leningrad. Meanwhile Manstein, advancing in accordance with Leeb's orders, ran headlong into XXI Mechanized Corps in the Novorzhev sector. Here the dirt roads ran through swamps and thick forests and were jammed with abandoned Russian tanks, vehicles, and guns. Manstein was halted for the first time in the campaign. Hoepner was forced to withdraw LVI Panzer Corps and send it after Reinhardt. Hoepner wanted to send both panzer corps north-northeast, directly toward Leningrad, but Leeb again insisted that it be sent eastward, toward Novgorod and Lake Ilmen, despite the forested and swampy terrain.[42]

On July 7 the campaign-by-compromise continued, when Leeb and Hoepner met with Army C-in-C Brauchitsch at Leeb's headquarters. Brauchitsch approved Hoepner's plan for an advance on Leningrad. Reinhardt's XLI Panzer Corps would advance along the Pskov-Luga-Leningrad road, while Manstein's LVI Panzer drove on to Novgorod and then to Leningrad. These were the only two routes to Leningrad, which meant that the element of surprise would be lacking and the two panzer corps would be separated by more than one hundred miles of forests and swampland, well in front of the infantry of the 18th and 16th armies to the north and south, respectively.[43]

The advance began on July 10, but Reinhardt faced stiff resistance and very difficult terrain. He had gained only a few miles when he was halted on July 12. Two days later Manstein was attacked by the reinforced Soviet 11th Army and at one point was completely cut off from the rest of Army Group North. Hoepner, meanwhile, made a bold move: he sent Manstein's entire corps to the north, to turn the flank of the Russian units barring Reinhardt's progress. The maneuver worked, and by July 17 the Luga obstacle had been overcome and the panzer spearhead was only eighty miles from Leningrad. But Hitler and the High Command had been frightened. They ordered Hoepner to halt Manstein's corps until the foot soldiers of the 16th Army could come up and secure his right flank. This order entailed a delay of three weeks. Leeb appealed to OKW to rescind the order, but without success. He considered giving Reinhardt permission to proceed alone, but did not. The delay once again gave the Russians time to rally their forces and prepare their defenses.[44]

To date, Leeb had made impressive but not spectacular progress. His spearheads had gained 430 miles and were within 80 miles of Leningrad. He had cleared most of the Baltic States region, but both the Russian 8th and 11th armies had escaped encirclement; he had not linked up with the Finns; and he was at the end of a 400+-mile supply line that was subject to attack by Russian stragglers, partisans, and bypassed units. Also, as one moves east, European Russia opens up to the north. Leeb's frontage increased with every step his soldiers advanced. In addition, Hitler finally decided that 18th Army was to finish the conquest of the Baltic States, complete with ports and islands, before Leeb attempted to take Leningrad. Finally, the Fuehrer required Busch to cover the left flank of Army Group Center, to the extent that sixty percent of 16th Army's infantry was employed in this task. General Albrecht Schubert's entire XXIII Corps was actually transferred to Army Group Center. As a result, both flanks of the infantry-poor 4th Panzer Group were exposed to probing attacks by the Soviet 27th Army and elements of the 11th Army, while yet another new Soviet Army – the 22nd – was committed to the front, this one against Busch. Leeb's rate of advance, which had averaged seventeen miles a day prior to July 10, slowed to barely one mile a day in August.[45]

Leeb must personally bear a large share of the responsibility for this dismal lack of progress because of his poor handling of his panzer formations. For example, on August 5 he committed the entire 8th Panzer Division to the task of clearing his lines of communication, a terrible waste of valuable armor and a mission for which it was absolutely unsuited. The 8th Panzer was engaged in this futile duty for more than a month.[46]

Meanwhile, Hoepner's reduced 4th Panzer Group resumed its advance on Leningrad on August 8, with Reinhardt on the left and Manstein on the right. The terrain was swampy and forested, utterly unsuited for armor, and Soviet resistance was both well prepared and stiff. Reinhardt's divisions, the 1st Panzer, 6th Panzer, and 36th Motorized, suffered such heavy casualties that Hoepner considered abandoning the offensive. Then, on August 14, Hoepner broke out and made it beyond the swamps; Leeb, however, had to take away half of his panzer group almost immediately, for a major crisis had developed to the south.

On August 1, General Christian Hansen's X Corps, on the left flank of the 16th Army, had begun an advance on Staraya Russa, an important transportation center south of Lake Ilmen, in order to cover the deep right flank of Army Group North for the final advance on Leningrad. The Soviets realized the importance of Staraya Russa and were fully prepared for Hansen's attack. Ten Corps met the Soviet 11th Army, which was protected by deep minefields (including undetectable, wood-encased mines), dug-in tanks, bunkers, and extensive field fortifications. It took the 30th, 126th, and 290th Infantry Divisions a week of heavy fighting to penetrate the nine miles to Staraya Russa, where they were engaged in bitter house-to-house fighting.[47]

On August 12 Soviet Marshal Voroshilov, the latest commander of the North-West Front, threw his newly activated 34th Army (eight infantry divisions, a tank corps, and a cavalry corps) into an attack on Staraya Russa, with the objective of pinning X Corps against the southern shore of Lake Ilmen and destroying it. Leeb had to transfer LVI Panzer Corps from 4th Panzer Group to the 16th Army on August 15 to save Hansen. On August 19, after a forced march of over a hundred miles, Manstein hurled his two divisions (the 3rd Motorized and the 3rd SS Motorized Division "Totenkopf") into the rear of the Soviet 34th Army, trapping it between himself and X Corps. By August 23 the Soviet army had been destroyed, and 246 guns had been captured. Manstein, however, could not return to the north, because Voroshilov threw three more armies into the attack in the land neck between Lakes Peipus and Ilmen, pinning down both 16th Army and LVI Panzer Corps.[48]

On August 15, the same day he lost Manstein, Hoepner asked

Leeb to immediately switch Kuechler's 18th Army from Estonia to the left flank of 4th Panzer Group, in order to secure his northern flank for a push on Leningrad. After a heated argument, Leeb overruled Hoepner and ordered Kuechler to destroy the Soviet 8th Army on the Baltic, clear the coast, and then capture the Russian fortifications along the southern shore of the Gulf of Finland – all before coming to Hoepner's aid. This was a serious mistake, for it tied down the available German infantry on secondary operations while the Soviets prepared for a decisive Battle of Leningrad. Even though it was now reinforced with General von Richthofen's VIII Air Corps, it would take 18th Army three weeks to complete these missions. Hoepner's panzer group, which now consisted of only one corps, had no choice but to pass up its breakthrough opportunity and go over to the defensive.[49]

Lieutenant General Walter de Beaulieu, the Chief of Staff of 4th Panzer Group, later charged that Leeb made his dispositions in this manner so that General von Kuechler – his personal friend – could play a prominent role in the capture of Leningrad, and historian Paul Carell agrees.[50] This author, however, doubts these conclusions. More probably, in my opinion, Leeb was guilty of overcaution and wanted to remove a possible threat to his left flank before proceeding. This explanation would be in keeping with Leeb's previously established broad-front policy (as opposed to the "panzer thrust" ideas of Hoepner) and is consistent with his demonstrably conservative methods of employing armor. In any event, by September 4 Estonia was finally cleared, and the whole southern coast of the Gulf of Finland was in German hands – except for the Oranienbaum bridgehead, where the Soviet 8th Army was besieged by the German XXVI Corps. On September 7, Leeb was at last ready to begin the final push to Leningrad. Meanwhile, Stalin had rushed his newly formed 52nd, 54th, and 55th armies to the threatened sector.[51] In addition, Marshal Voroshilov, Political Commissar Zhdanov, and General Zakharov, the commandant of the city, had formed twenty Red Militia divisions from Leningrad's 300,000 factory workers. Two major rings of fortifications had also been constructed around the city, mostly by Leningrad's women and children. The inner ring focused on the Duderhof Hills, the key point in the defensive line.[52]

When Leeb's offensive finally began on September 8, Leningrad was already within range of the German 240 mm guns.[53] This city, formerly St. Petersburg, the capital of the czars, had a population of 3,000,000 in 1941 and was the second city of Russia. It contained major munition plants, tank factories, textile mills, shipyards, and was the home port of the Soviet Baltic Fleet.[54] It was of major, perhaps decisive, importance to the Soviet war effort.

In the first week of September 1941, Leeb had received the loan of General Hoth's 3rd Panzer Group (LVII Panzer and XXXIX Panzer corps) from Army Group Center, which he used to defeat the Soviet 2nd, 27th, and 34th armies between Staraya Russa and Kholm. This victory enabled him to anchor his right flank and bring up both the XXVIII and XXXIX Panzer corps under HQ, 16th Army, for the decisive attack.[55]

The fighting was bitter. Leeb's main thrust was from the center of his line, where XLI Panzer Corps, spearheaded by the 36th Motorized Division and supported by the 1st Panzer and 6th Panzer divisions, attacked into the Duderhof Hills. The main advance was covered on the right by L Corps (4th SS Motorized and 269th Infantry Divisions) of 4th Panzer Group, and on the left by XXXVIII Corps (1st, 58th, and 291st Infantry divisions) of 18th Army. On the German right wing, XXVIII Corps of the 16th Army (96th, 121st, and 122nd Infantry divisions) advanced, while on the extreme eastern flank General Rudolf Schmidt's XXXIX Panzer Corps, spearheaded by the reinforced 20th Motorized Division, struck towards Schluesselburg on the southern edge of Lake Ladoga, with the objective of sealing off the city. Map 9 shows Leeb's attacks on the city.

For the first three days Reinhardt's progress could be measured by the yard, despite excellent tactical close air support from the Stukas of VIII Air Corps. Casualties were very heavy on both sides; but at last, at 11:30 A.M. on September 11, Hill 167 – the famous "General's Hill" of the czars – fell. Second Lieutenant Darius of the 6th Panzer Division signaled: "I can see St. Petersburg and the sea." Meanwhile, the 291st Infantry Division knocked out more than one hundred and fifty concrete pillboxes in a single day, while the 58th Infantry Division captured a Leningrad tram-car in the suburb of Uritsk, only six miles from the center of the city. Schleusselburg also fell, captured by Colonel Harry Hoppe's 124th Infantry Regiment, 126th Infantry Division. Its fall blocked the

Map 9

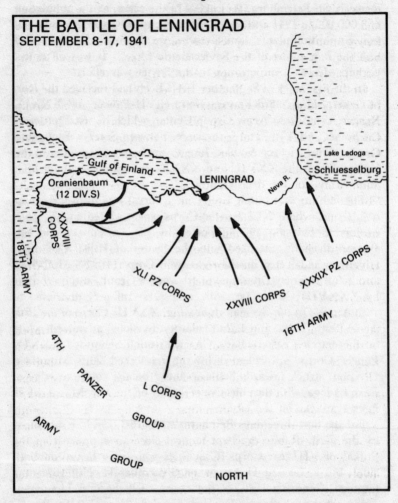

THE BATTLE OF LENINGRAD
SEPTEMBER 8-17, 1941

Gulf of Finland

Oranienbaum
(12 DIV.S)

LENINGRAD

Lake Ladoga

Schluesselburg

Neva R.

XXXVIII
CORPS

18TH ARMY

XLI PZ CORPS

XXVIII CORPS

XXXIX PZ CORPS

16TH ARMY

4TH

PANZER

ARMY

L CORPS

GROUP

GROUP

NORTH

THE BATTLE OF LENINGRAD, SEPTEMBER 1941. Well
supported by the Luftwaffe, Field Marshal Ritter Wilhelm von
Leeb's Army Group North drove to the outskirts of Leningrad and
penetrated the main defenses of the city, only to be halted by the
orders of Adolf Hitler. The Fuehrer had decided to starve it into
submission. This fatal decision resulted in an epic siege, which was
not broken until January 1944. Leningrad never fell.

Neva, the waterway between the Baltic and Lake Ladoga, thus closing the system of canals linking Leningrad with the White Sea and Arctic Ocean, sealing off the city to the east. By now the forward tank crews could see the golden spires of the Admiralty building.[56] Leningrad seemed doomed – when it was saved at the last moment by, of all people, Adolf Hitler.

On September 12, the Fuehrer ordered Leeb not to take the city, but merely to seal it off and starve it into submission. Army Group North was ordered to give up XLI Panzer Corps, LVII Panzer Corps, and VIII Air Corps, as well as Headquarters, 4th Panzer Group – a total of five panzer and two motorized divisions, and the bulk of its air support. In return, Leeb was promised a German infantry division then in France, as well as the 250th (Spanish) "Blue" Infantry Division, and two parachute regiments.[57]

Leeb immediately protested Hitler's strategically ridiculous decision to forgo taking Leningrad, but to no avail. When Leeb objected to the loss of the 4th Panzer Group and VIII Air Corps, Hitler responded that these forces would aid in the success of Army Group Center at Moscow, which would make Leeb's task that much easier.[58]

The decision to besiege Leningrad was one of the greatest tactical blunders of the war. Thirty Soviet divisions were trapped in the city, but not destroyed. As winter descended on northern Russia, the rivers and lakes froze, allowing the Soviets to build a "Road of Life" across the ice of Lake Ladoga. They even constructed a railroad over it, connecting the city with Murmansk,[59] the focal point of American military aid shipments. Eighteenth Army was tied down outside Leningrad until January 1944, when its veteran units were desperately needed elsewhere. As of January 1, 1943, twenty-two full divisions and elements of two more were involved in the siege.[60] In the end, the siege was broken after twenty-eight months. Leningrad was never taken.

FIELD MARSHAL VON Leeb was frustrated by Hitler's amateur generalship, but there was very little he could do about it. He limited himself to local attacks over the next three weeks, and on September 27 managed to take the industrial suburb of Pulkovo, which housed an important tank factory. Meanwhile, desperate Soviet counterattacks failed to retake Schluesselburg.[61]

Winter comes early to northern Russia, and Leeb wanted to make use of the few remaining days of good weather to strengthen his grip on the Lake Ladoga sector. Hitler, however, ordered him to seize the bauxite-producing area of Tikhvin and then to strike northward, linking up with the Finns on the Svir River, on the eastern shore of Lake Ladoga. To do this, Leeb's men would have to cover two hundred and fifty miles – in winter.[62]

On October 15 Leeb's assault force, XXXIX Panzer Corps, moved out from the Volkhov bridgehead and advanced on Tikhvin. General Rudolf Schmidt's command included the 8th Panzer, 12th Panzer, 18th Motorized, and 20th Motorized divisions. In early November Schmidt was named acting commander of 2nd Army, Army Group Center. He was replaced by General Juergen von Arnim, who took Tikhvin on November 8. The Soviet 4th Army was wrecked and the rear of the 7th Independent Army (facing the Finns) was threatened. Stalin responded by counterattacking with his Siberian reserves. The mobile German troops bled the Eastern divisions white, but were themselves threatened with annihilation. On November 15 von Armin was finally forced to retreat. By November 25, XXXIX Panzer and its supporting I Corps held a 230-mile salient to Tikhvin and were under attack by the Soviet 4th and 54th armies, as well as elements of the 7th and 52nd armies.[63]

From the middle of November, Leeb was very nervous over the situation in the Tikhvin salient, but he hoped Field Marshal Bock's Moscow offensive would take some of the pressure off his own army group, as Hitler had assured him it would. It did not, for Stalin was attacking wherever he thought he detected a weakness. On December 8, with Army Group Center at last checked, Leeb finally convinced Hitler to allow him to retreat. On December 22, 1941, in temperatures of minus 61 degrees Fahrenheit, XXXIX Panzer Corps at last limped back through the ice and snow into Volkhov. It had been badly hurt. The 18th Motorized Division alone lost 9,000 men in the Tikhvin operation and was reduced to a strength of 741 – the size of a peacetime battalion.[64]

By now, Ritter von Leeb was wondering aloud if Hitler was secretly allied with Stalin against the German Army.[65] Word of his comments no doubt reached Hitler, who had never been fond of the anti-Nazi marshal. Leeb had also annoyed the Nazis by protesting the massacre of Soviet Jews by the SS and Lithuanian "irregulars."

Colonel Rudolf Schmundt had relayed an order from the Fuehrer, telling Leeb not to interfere in these "political questions."[66] Leeb further aggravated Hitler on November 15 by requesting, through his Chief of Staff, Lieutenant General Kurt Brennecke, to go into winter quarters. On December 14 he sought authorization to pull back behind the Volkhov River. Hitler refused to allow it, as it would weaken his grip on Leningrad.[67] Hitler continued to respect Leeb's technical competence, however, and there is no evidence that he planned to sack Leeb, as he had done with Bock and Rundstedt, the other army group commanders in Russia. It is indeed ironic that Leeb, the most religious and anti-Nazi of the original army group commanders, should retain command longer than his two peers during the winter crisis of 1941/42. In the end it was Leeb's own growing frustration, rather than a Fuehrer order, that led to his dismissal.

Another massive Soviet offensive began on January 7, 1942. Army Group North was under attack by eleven Soviet armies. Leeb met it with thirty-one exhausted divisions. By January 13, the Soviet 2nd Strike Army had broken through 16th Army on a twenty-mile front between Novgorod and Chudovo and had crossed the Volkhov. By now the army group was suffering thousands of casualties due to frostbite, including hundreds of double amputations. Wounded men were freezing to death by the score due to a shortage of blankets. Leeb had already committed his last reserves and had resorted to sending service personnel into combat as *ad hoc* formations, where they suffered appalling casualties. Nevertheless the Soviets continued to gain ground.[68] Headquarters, 281st Security Division (Lieutenant General Theodor Scherer), was surrounded at Kholm with 5,500 men, and II Corps (General Count Walter von Brockdorff-Ahlefeldt) was threatened with encirclement at Demyansk. On January 12 Leeb asked permission to pull II Corps back and proposed a general retreat to the Lovat River, in order to restore his line. Hitler refused to abandon Demyansk, because he believed that such salients tied down more Russian than German troops. Leeb did not accept this reasoning. As a result of Hitler's interference in tactical detail, II Corps, with 100,000 men, was soon surrounded. By January 16 Leeb had had enough, and asked to be relieved of his command. He was replaced the next day by Colonel General von Kuechler.[69]

Leeb retired to Bavaria and was never re-employed. In the autumn of 1944, with the Western Front on the verge of collapse, Field Marshal von Rundstedt asked that this defensive expert be taken out of retirement and given a command in the West, but Hitler rejected his request.[70]

Field Marshal von Leeb was arrested by the Western Allies at the end of the war. In October 1948, at the age of seventy-two, he was sentenced to three years' imprisonment as a minor war criminal,[71] a sentence that seems to be severe in view of his record.

Following his release from prison, Ritter von Leeb retired quietly to the town of Hohenschwangau in his native Bavaria, where he died on April 29, 1956.[76] He was seventy-nine years old.

THERE CAN BE no doubt that Wilhelm von Leeb's talents were misused during the Second World War. A recognized authority on defensive warfare, he was called upon to direct major panzer forces in 1941, an assignment for which he was unqualified and that he mishandled; nevertheless, in justice to Leeb, it must be pointed out that he would have captured Leningrad in September 1941 had he been left to his own devices. Ironically, during the great defensive battles in Russia, Italy, and France during the last half of the conflict, one of the Third Reich's most respected and able defensive commanders sat out the war in professional seclusion. Field Marshal Leeb emerges from history as a decent human being with a rather mediocre record as a military commander. He deserved a better fate.

6

Fedor von Bock

LIKE WALTER VON Reichenau and Ewald von Kleist, Fedor von Bock was the son of a distinguished Prussian general. He was born in the province of Brandenburg on December 3, 1880, and, even as a child, yearned for a career in the Army. He spent much of his youth in the cadet schools of Gross Lichterfelde and Potsdam and entered the Army in 1898 as a second lieutenant in the 5th Prussian Foot Guards Regiment.[1]

Even as a young man, von Bock was noted for his serious, purposeful, and aristocratic bearing. Tall and thin, he was a humorless, ambitious, arrogant, opinionated, and energetic zealot. It was these qualities, plus his undeniable physical courage, that propelled him to the top rank in the Army, rather than any mark of genius. Like many who did not rise so high, Bock was capable but not brilliant. It was his drive and ambition that earned him his nickname with the Army: "The Holy Fire of Kuestrin."

Bock became a member of the General Staff in 1910 and was promoted to captain in 1912. Although he burned for action, he was forced to spend the first two years of World War I on the General Staff of Crown Prince Rupprecht of Bavaria. At last, in 1917, he obtained command of a battalion in the 4th Prussian Foot

145

Guards Regiment, which he led with fanatical courage on the Somme and at Cambrai. He was decorated with the *Pour le Mérite*,[2] and was promoted to major in 1918.[3]

After the war, Fedor von Bock became an associate of General von Seeckt, the Commander-in-Chief of the Reichsheer. During this period Poland became aggressive, invading the Ukraine and making incursions into Upper Silesia and Prussia. The 100,000-man Army allowed Germany under the terms of the Treaty of Versailles was too small to guard her frontiers and provide for internal security during this period of civil unrest, so the "Black Reichswehr," a secret organization of illicit military units, was formed. Major von Bock, now Chief of Staff of Wehrkreis III in Berlin, was deeply involved in the recruiting and arming of these illegal formations. These troops operated under the cover name of the *Arbeits-Kommandos* (AK). They were, officially, volunteer civilian laborers employed on short-term government contracts, but they wore Army uniforms, lived in Army barracks, ate Army food, and were given Army training. By 1923, 20,000 of these men were billeted in the Wehrkreis III fortress of Kuestrin alone. Their commander was Major Bruno Buchrucker, formerly a member of the General Staff.

The right-wing officers revived the *Femegerichte*, or Secret Courts of the Middle Ages, to deal with people who informed to the Allied Control Commission or to the Reich Disarmament Authority about the activities of the Black Reichswehr. Several murders were committed by the Secret Court, and the left-wing press freely charged that Major Bock was involved in them. There seems little doubt that their reports were correct, although von Bock would not have considered them murders. To him, the Black Reichswehr was acting in the interests of the state; to act against that organization was to act against the state, and was therefore an act of treason. The punishment for treason was death.

Later, on the witness stand, recently promoted Lieutenant Colonel Fedor von Bock, as well as Kurt von Schleicher and Baron Kurt von Hammerstein, denied any knowledge of the Black Reichswehr. They were lying, of course, but to Bock a lie in the defense of the nation was an act of patriotism. His guilt was never proven, and his exact role in the Black Reichswehr has never emerged from the shadows of history because, sensibly enough, the Black Reichswehr never recorded its activities on paper.

The Black Reichswehr's end began on September 27, 1923, when, against the advice of von Bock, Major Buchrucker mobilized the AK for a revolt against the democratic Weimar government. General Seeckt, aided by Bock, quickly suppressed it in a two-day siege at Kuestrin. Seeckt then dissolved the Black Reichswehr in early October 1923.[4]

IN 1924, BOCK became commander of II Battalion, 4th Infantry Regiment, at Kolberg. After his troop duty was completed (probably in 1925), he was promoted to full colonel and assigned to the staff of the Defense Ministry. He was promoted to major general in late 1928 and given command of the 1st Cavalry Division at Frankfurt-am-Oder. He was only forty-eight years old.

Bock's rise continued throughout the 1930s. In 1930 he was given command of the 1st Infantry Division in East Prussia. Promoted to lieutenant general in 1931, he assumed command of Wehrkreis II at Stettin, a post he held until 1935. Advanced to general of infantry that year, he commanded Army Group 3 at Dresden from 1935 to 1938, during Hitler's military expansion. In October 1935 this force included Wehrkreise IV, VII, and X, a total of eight infantry divisions and three frontier commands. By October 1937 Wehrkreise XI and XIII had been added, increasing Bock's strength by three infantry divisions, with more on the drawing boards or in the early stages of formation.[5]

Bock was a non-Nazi (as opposed to anti-Nazi), but he wholeheartedly supported Hitler's military policies. The Fuehrer's domestic and foreign policies did not concern him, nor did Hitler's retirement of numerous senior generals in 1938 seem to interest von Bock, except insofar as it concerned his personal advancement. After commanding the German forces in the occupation of Austria (during which his army group was temporarily designated 8th Army), Bock replaced Gerd von Rundstedt as commander of Army Group 1 in Berlin. He was promoted to colonel general on March 1, 1938.[6]

Of Fedor von Bock, Taylor wrote: "His mind was closed to everything but the most immediate consequences of 'soldiering for the King.' . . . Frederican Prussianism was deeply ingrained in his character; he was a violent nationalist, a stern disciplinarian, and intent only upon strengthening the Army and advancing his own military career, in which he was distinguished by industry and determination more than brilliance."[77] Arrogant and cold-blooded, Bock's humorless, vain, inflexible, and irritating personality earned him many enemies, both in the Army and in the Party. He had nothing but contempt for all civilians and did not get along well with his subordinates, especially Heinz Guderian, the brilliant panzer leader whom he commanded in Austria and later in Poland and Russia. Bock also disliked General von Brauchitsch, who was junior to him but who nevertheless was promoted over Bock when he was named Commander-in-Chief of the Army on February 4, 1938.[8] Hitler, however, appreciated the tall Prussian from Kuestrin in whom he found a willing tool.

FOR THE INVASION of Poland, Bock's headquarters was redesignated Army Group North. It consisted of General Guenther von Kluge's 4th Army in Pomerania and General Georg von Kuechler's 3rd Army in East Prussia. They were separated by the Polish Corridor, which was held by Major General W. Bortnowski's Pomorze Army (five infantry divisions and one cavalry brigade, plus four naval battalions and miscellaneous coastal defense troops). Kluge would control five infantry divisions, plus two motorized divisions and the 3rd Panzer Division under Guderian's XIX Corps. Kuechler would have seven infantry divisions, two *ad hoc* infantry brigades, the 1st Cavalry Brigade, and Panzer Division Kempf, another provisional formation. Bock initially kept four divisions in army group reserve, including the 10th Panzer. Of the 1,516,000 men the Army would commit to the invasion, Bock would direct 630,000 (320,000 in the 3rd Army, 230,000 in the 4th, and 80,000 in army group reserve). The rest came under Rundstedt's Army Group South. They faced about the same number of Poles.[9]

The initial plan called for Rundstedt to deliver the main blow, taking Warsaw from the southwest. Third Army's main attack would be to the south, against the Polish Modlin Army (two infantry divisions and two cavalry brigades). Third Army was to launch a secondary attack to the southwest, to link up with 4th Army. Fourth Army's mission was to attack to the east and south, sealing off and then destroying the Pomorze Army in the Corridor.

Bock pointed out to OKH that its plan would leave the Free City of Danzig exposed to Polish capture for several days. He recommended that a secret brigade be raised from the 120,000 Germans in Danzig with military experience, including Army reservists, discharged veterans, SA men, some SS troops, and city policemen. The Navy could also disembark a battalion on the day of the invasion to help defend the city. Hitler approved the plan and sent Major General Friedrich-Georg Eberhardt, in plain clothes, to Danzig to organize the "Freikorps."[10] It would be called Brigade Eberhardt when the invasion started and would later be expanded into the 60th Motorized Infantry Division.[11]

The war began on September 1, 1939. Brigade Eberhard took Danzig with little trouble. Third Army, attacking south with I Corps and Corps Wodrig, made unexpectedly rapid progress toward Warsaw, while Lieutenant General Nikolaus von Falkenhorst's XXI Corps pushed to the southwest, toward its link-up with 4th Army. Kluge also made rapid progress, and by nightfall on September 2 the Polish 9th and 27th Infantry divisions and the Pomorska Cavalry Brigade were virtually cut off in the Corridor. The 3rd and 4th armies linked up the next day at Neuenburg (Nowe Swiecie). Although Polish garrisons at Westerplatte (in Danzig harbor) and the Hela peninsula would hold out for some time, the Corridor was effectively eliminated, and the bulk of the Pomorze Army had been destroyed, with a haul of 15,000 prisoners and 90 guns.[12]

Bock had accomplished his primary mission of overrunning the Corridor and establishing ground contact with East Prussia by September 4. Kuechler continued to push southward on Warsaw against stiffening resistance, while Bock saw to the rest of the army group. He sent Guderian's corps to the far left wing of 3rd Army and ordered General Leonhard Kaupisch's Frontier Zone Command I (207th Infantry Division and Brigade Eberhard, plus some security units) to reduce the Westerplatte, Gdynia, and the Hela peninsula, while the rest of 4th Army (General Adolf Strauss's II Corps and General Curt Haase's III Corps) advanced southeast along the Vistula. Bock planned for Guderian to sweep behind the Polish deep right flank and envelop the Polish forces defending north of Warsaw. On Guderian's suggestion, however, the maneuver was changed to a panzer thrust on Brest-Litovsk in eastern

Poland, in order to prevent the Poles from retreating eastward and establishing a new defensive line.[13]

This operation, too, went according to plan. Brest fell on September 17, after a three-day battle. That same day the Russians entered the war by invading eastern Poland and linked up with Army Group North the next day. The 3rd Army closed in on Warsaw from the east, while 4th Army cleared the Bialystok area, north of Guderian's corps. Except for the Warsaw sector, Army Group North faced only minor resistance after mid-September 1939. By early October Bock was on his way to the Western Front.

Initially, Fedor von Bock was slated to command the major attack in the West, despite his view that the Army was not ready for the campaign. His forces, now redesignated Army Group B, formed on the German right (northern) flank, and were to advance through the Netherlands and Belgium into northern France, defeating the Dutch, Belgian, British, and French armies on the way. Bock, however, wrote a pessimistic memorandum to the War Ministry and Hitler, expressing his belief that the British would land at Antwerp before he could take it and that the war would deteriorate into a long and bloody battle of attrition in Belgium.

Hitler was not particularly satisfied with the OKH plan either, and when the Manstein Plan reached him he promptly embraced it (see chapter 2). This plan reduced Bock's role to a secondary one. During the first phase of the French campaign, Bock directed only the 6th and 18th armies (Reichenau and Kuechler, respectively). His mission was to drive into the Low Countries with enough vigor to convince the French and British that his was the main attack. This mission he accomplished beyond question. His men overran Holland and Belgium and finished off the French forces at Dunkirk on June 4, taking 40,000 prisoners.[14]

During the second phase of operations, Bock directed the 4th, 6th and 9th armies, as well as Panzer Groups Hoth and Kleist, and overran western France.[15] After France capitulated, Bock was assigned the task of guarding the Atlantic coast from Brest to the Spanish frontier. He was promoted to field marshal on July 19, 1940.[16]

Bock was dissatisfied with his new assignment. He commented caustically that all he had to do was make sure that neither the seacoast nor the demarcation line was stolen.[17] Perhaps as a result of his acid comments, he was named Commander-in-Chief, East (OB East), in the fall of 1940. Headquartered at Posen, he initially controlled the 18th Army, with the 2nd and 4th armies on the way.[18] For much of the winter of 1940/41 he was absent from duty due to severe stomach ulcers.[19]

BOCK WAS OPPOSED to invading Russia in 1941 and even refused to issue the infamous Commissars' Order to his army group.[20] His HQ was a hotbed of the anti-Hitler conspiracy after Colonel Henning von Treschow became his Ia (Chief of Operations) in 1941. Bock's personal aides – Count Heinrich von Hardenberg (a descendant of Bismarck) and Count Heinrich von Lehndorff-Steinort (grandson of a favorite of Wilhelm I) – were both involved, as were several others, including Lieutenant Fabian von Schlabrendorff, who was one of the few conspirators to survive the war. The conspirators hoped to convince Bock to lead a coup against Hitler, but the man who had helped suppress the Black Reichswehr would not join a conspiracy now. Of Bock, John Wheeler-Bennett wrote: "Though he despised National Socialism and found repellent its increasing blood-lust, he was consumed with vanity and egotism, and the insignificance of his character prevented him from lifting a finger to overthrow a system for which he felt nothing but contempt. He was among those many whose response to the approaches of the conspirators was: 'If it succeeds, I'll support you, but I won't take the consequences of failure.'"[21]

Bock's headquarters was designated Army Group Center for the invasion of Russia. It had the most important mission of the Russo-German war: take Moscow. It's initial objective was to destroy the strong Soviet forces in the Brest-Vilna-Smolensk triangle. For this task, Bock was given two of the four panzer groups (the 2nd and 3rd) and the 4th and 9th armies, a total of nine panzer, seven motorized, 31 infantry, and three security divisions, plus the 1st Cavalry Division: a total of 51 of the 149 German divisions committed to Operation Barbarossa.[22] He was supported by Field Marshal Albert Kesselring's 2nd Air Fleet, which included the bulk of the Luftwaffe's Stuka dive-bombers.

On the evening of June 21, Kesselring visited Bock at his headquarters and found him "very dispirited," in contrast to his attitude in previous campaigns.[23] Bock nevertheless performed remarkably well in the first stage of the invasion, closing in on Minsk, 170 miles behind the frontier, with his two panzer groups. Hitler grew nervous over this ambitious maneuver and, bypassing Brauchitsch, suggested to von Bock that it be abandoned in favor of a much shorter envelopment. Bock argued strongly and successfully against this timidity. As a result, the majority of three Soviet armies and parts of two others were encircled in and around the Belorussian capital by June 29. After the pocket collapsed on July 3,[24] Army Group Center reported the capture or destruction of 324,000 men, 3,332 tanks, and 1,809 guns.[25]

Bock's next target was Smolensk, a city on the Moscow Highway at the head of navigation on the Dnieper River. It was taken by the 29th Motorized Division on July 16 after another double envelopment. The pocket was cleared on August 5, yielding 310,000 more prisoners, 3,205 tanks, and 3,120 guns.[26] Three days later Guderian completed another battle of encirclement at Roslavl, southeast of Smolensk. He took another 38,000 prisoners and captured or destroyed 250 tanks and 359 guns.[27] Next, Bock sent General Baron Leo von Geyr von Schweppenburg's XXIV Panzer Corps southward, into the rear of the newly formed Soviet Central Front, while Baron von Weichs's newly committed 2nd Army attacked it from the west. The result was another pocket at Gomel, where another 84,000 Russians, with 144 tanks and 848 guns, had been captured or destroyed by August 24.[28]

By the last week in August, Army Group Center had advanced more than 500 miles and was only about 185 miles from Moscow.[29] Fedor von Bock had performed brilliantly. He had inflicted well over three quarters of a million casualties on the Russians and had captured or destroyed some 7,000 tanks and over 6,000 guns, while suffering fewer than 100,000 casualties himself.[30] Now he expected to launch the decisive drive on Moscow, but it was not to be. On August 4 Hitler ordered the transfer of the 3rd Panzer Group to Army Group North and dispatched 2nd Panzer Group and 2nd Army to the south, against Kiev. Bock, much to his disgust, lost four of his five panzer corps and three infantry corps, plus much of the 2nd Air Fleet. He had no choice but to go over to the defensive in the Yelnya Bend, 47 miles east of Smolensk, with the 4th and 9th armies, while Hitler dispersed his strength elsewhere. Meanwhile, the sunny campaigning weather of summer merged imperceptibly with the shorter days of fall. The much-feared Russian winter was not far off.

When Hitler deprived Bock of his tank units, the road to Moscow was almost clear. Now Stalin rushed reinforcements to this critical sector and hurled all or part of four armies against the Yelnya Bend, which was an obvious springboard for an attack on the Soviet capital. At no time did Bock have more than four divisions in the sector. He was eventually forced to abandon the Yelnya salient in early September, but he held his line despite heavy Russian attacks.[31] By the end of September, Bock was facing 1,500,000 to 2,000,000 men.

After Kiev fell in early September, Hitler considered going into winter quarters, but Bock felt his position was unsuited for a winter line. Bock, Kesselring, Brauchitsch, and others convinced Hitler to launch a drive on the Soviet capital, despite the questionable campaign weather. Hitler transferred 4th Panzer Group (redesignated Panzer Army on October 6) back to Army Group Center, with five panzer and two motorized divisions, as well as VIII Air Corps. He returned 2nd Panzer Group and 2nd Army to Bock's control, and transferred nine divisions from Army Group South to Army Group Center. Two of these were motorized, and two more were panzer units. OKH decided not to return 2nd Panzer, 3rd Panzer, and 2nd armies to the Smolensk sector; they were ordered to attack from where they were. Bock's frontage thus extended more than four hundred miles, and he had less than two divisions in reserve. He protested this dispersal of forces, but to no avail.[32]

On the morning of September 30, Bock began his offensive with pincer movements on Vyazma and Bryansk, a double battle that Carell called "the most perfect battle of encirclement in military history."[33] From north to south, his forces included 3rd Panzer Army (Hoth), 9th Army (Strauss), 4th Army (Kluge), 4th Panzer Army (Hoepner), 2nd Army (Weichs) and 2nd Panzer Army (Guderian). Bock ordered Hoepner to attack frontally through the Russian center to Meschovsk; then he was to wheel north, to Vyazma, which Hoth was to approach from the east. Meanwhile, Strauss and Kluge were to attack the Soviets frontally and pin down their main forces north of the Smolensk-Yelnya line.[34] To the

Map 10

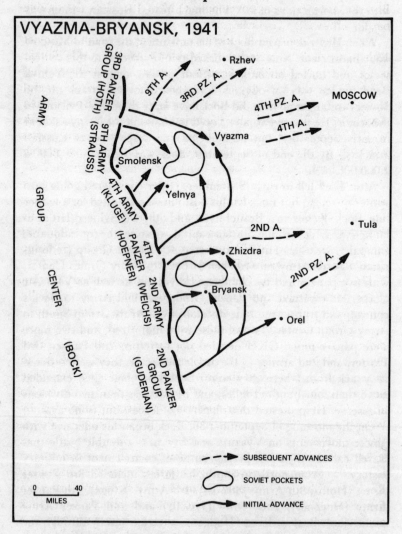

VYAZMA-BRYANSK, 1941

- Rzhev
- 9TH A.
- 3RD PANZER GROUP (HOTH)
- 3RD PZ. A.
- MOSCOW
- 4TH PZ. A.
- 4TH A.
- ARMY
- 9TH ARMY (STRAUSS)
- Vyazma
- Smolensk
- Yelnya
- 4TH ARMY (KLUGE)
- GROUP
- 4TH PANZER (HOEPNER)
- 2ND A.
- Tula
- Zhizdra
- 2ND PZ. A.
- CENTER
- 2ND ARMY (WEICHS)
- Bryansk
- Orel
- (BOCK)
- 2ND PANZER GROUP (GUDERIAN)

- - - → SUBSEQUENT ADVANCES

◯ SOVIET POCKETS

——→ INITIAL ADVANCE

0   40
MILES

THE DOUBLE ENVELOPMENT OF VYAZMA-BRYANSK,
SEPTEMBER–OCTOBER 1941. This operation, directed by Field
Marshal Fedor von Bock, resulted in the destruction of several
Soviet armies and almost resulted in the capture of Moscow. It was
a masterpiece of mobile warfare.

south, Weichs and Guderian were to converge on Zhizdra and Bryansk, in a separate envelopment. Map 10 shows the double battles of Vyazma-Bryansk.

To everyone's surprise, Guderian easily broke through the Soviet 13th Army, and his spearhead – Major General Baron Willibald von Langermann und Erlenkamp's 4th Panzer Division – covered eighty miles the first day. On October 6, Lieutenant General Hans-Juergen von Arnim's 17th Panzer Division took Bryansk in a surprise coup. Later that day Guderian's vanguard linked up with Weich's 2nd Army, encircling twenty-six divisions of the Soviet 3rd, 13th, and 15th armies. The next day Major General Wolfgang Fischer's 10th Panzer Division of Hoepner's 4th Panzer Army took Vyazma and linked up with Hoth's spearheads, thus encircling six more Soviet armies and dooming fifty-five more enemy divisions. The fighting continued until October 17, and several Russian units succeeded in breaking out and escaping; nevertheless some 663,000 men, 1,242 tanks, and 5,412 guns were destroyed or captured in the double battle of Vyazma-Bryansk.[35]

The first snow fell on October 7, but it quickly melted. Russian roads immediately turned into rivers of mud. It was virtually impossible to bring up fuel, ammunition, food, or replacements – or winter clothing, of which there was very little. Bock also lost most of his mobility, the key to his earlier victories. To make matters worse, Hitler sent II Air Corps and HQ, 2nd Air Fleet, to Sicily; and OKH ordered the 3rd Panzer and 9th armies to strike northeast, away from the Soviet capital.[36] Bock continued to advance eastward, however, ordering Guderian (supported by Weichs) to take Tula, an industrial city south of Moscow, while 4th Panzer, 4th and 9th armies continued on to Moscow. The mud was so bad that the 292nd Infantry Division reported a team of sixteen horses was not able to move a single howitzer of the 292nd Artillery Regiment. Motorized supply columns were averaging less than five miles a day, and more than two thousand vehicles were stuck on the unpaved Moscow Highway alone.[37] The Luftwaffe was grounded, the artillery and panzers stuck in the mud. Bock, only about seventy miles from Moscow, halted the offensive on October 30, to await freezing weather when the ground would again be hard enough to bring up food and ammunition.

Leeb and Rundstedt now wanted to call off the offensive and

Hitler seemed inclined to agree with them, but not Bock. Supported by Brauchitsch and Halder, he insisted on returning to the attack. Hitler therefore ordered the final advance to begin on November 15.[38]

The temperature was below zero when the attack resumed. The artillery was now useless, since the German Army lacked the cold-weather lubricants to protect the moving parts on the guns; only about 30 percent of the vehicles were operative; and the panzers were also neutralized, because their optical sights gave off a bloom in such low temperatures.[39] The infantry, without winter clothing and inadequately supplied, struggled forward, despite thousands of cases of frostbite. Many units lived mainly on a diet of horsemeat. They still managed to push through heavy resistance to within six miles of the Kremlin, to the very suburbs of Moscow. Bock, in a display of nervous energy, personally directed the final thrusts from an advanced command post, but by December 1 even he realized that Moscow could not be taken. The next day he finally gave the order to disengage.[40]

Stalin launched his counteroffensive on December 6. Hitler commanded all units to hold where they were – an order that doubtlessly caused heavy losses in men and *matériel*, but also averted panic and may have saved the German Army. Army Group Center was nevertheless slowly pushed back by the Soviets with appalling casualties. Several divisions had to leave most or all of their artillery behind.

Meanwhile, Field Marshal von Bock poured his heart out to Colonel Rudolf Schmundt, Hitler's personal adjutant, on December 16. He described his own health as precarious (his ulcers were acting up again) and asked Schmundt to relay the details of his condition to Hitler, which Schmundt no doubt did. Two days later Bock received a telephone call from Field Marshal Keitel, who informed him that the Fuehrer suggested he take an extended leave to restore his health. Bock quickly did so. He was replaced the same day by Field Marshal Guenther von Kluge.[41] Hitler sent Bock word that he did not hold him responsible for the failure to take Moscow.[42]

One month later, on January 17, 1942, Field Marshal von Reichenau died, probably from a heart attack. The next day Hitler summoned Bock to Fuehrer Headquarters and appointed him

Commander-in-Chief of Army Group South. Bock's command included Manstein's 11th Army in the Crimea and the 6th, 17th, 1st Panzer and 2nd armies in southern Russia (led by Colonel Generals Friedrich Paulus, Hermann Hoth, Ewald von Kleist, and Baron Maximilian von Weichs, respectively). His first task was to halt the first Soviet winter offensive on the southern sector.

In mid-January 1942, Soviet Marshal Semën Konstantinovich Timoshenko had achieved a deep breakthrough on both sides of the Izyum. By January 28 he was only twelve miles east of Dnepropetrovsk, threatening the communications routes of the 6th and 17th, and 1st Panzer armies.[43] Soviet troops cut the Dnepropetrovsk-Stalino railroad, the main supply artery of 1st Panzer Army, took the 17th Army's main supply base at Lozovaya, and established a huge bridgehead over the northern Donets at Izyum, which threatened both Kharkov and the Dnieper crossings. At one point, seven German divisions were fighting thirty-two Soviet infantry and cavalry divisions, supported by ten tank brigades.[44]

The Soviet offensive was halted more by Russian troop exhaustion, deep snow, and supply difficulties than by anything von Bock did. As soon as it had halted, the field marshal began building up his forces for a counterattack against the Izyum salient. On the other side, Marshal Timoshenko began building up for a resumption of the attack.

Hitler planned for his major offensive of 1942 to be conducted on the southern sector; accordingly, Bock received priority in supplies and reinforcements. Hitler ordered that Bock's infantry divisions be brought up to full strength, while those of Army Groups North and Center were to remain at 50 to 55 percent of their establishments. Bock's panzer divisions were to be brought up to a strength of three panzer battalions, while those in the other sectors remained at one. Units on the southern sector were to have 85 percent of their motor transportation, while the rest would have to get by with far less.[45]

Bock planned to attack the Izyum salient on May 18, but Timoshenko struck six days earlier, with 640,000 men and 1,200 tanks, pushing back 6th Army. By May 17 the Soviets were within twelve miles of Kharkov, the critical supply and communications center in the rear of Army Group South.

Hitler boldly refused to commit his reserves and allowed the

Soviets to advance, despite several nervous requests from Field Marshal Bock.[46] Then, on May 17, he struck the southern flank of the Red advance with his fresh 1st Panzer and 17th armies (both operating under von Kleist). The Russian drive was halted, and by May 19 Timoshenko was counterattacking Kleist with all the forces he could muster. The next day 6th Army joined the battle, and on May 24 Paulus and Kleist linked up west of Izyum, trapping the entire Soviet strike force. Only remnants managed to escape. By the time the fighting ended on May 29, Bock had taken 240,000 prisoners, along with more than 1,200 tanks and 2,000 guns. He had suffered only 20,000 casualties himself.[47] Hitler, however, was not satisfied with Bock's lack of nerve before Kharkov.

Hitler now began the second phase of his summer offensive (Operation Blue) by ordering Bock to clear the west bank of the Don and to take the city of Voronezh, if the cost was not too high; otherwise, he was to bypass it. Then Army Group South would be split in two. Newly formed HQ, Army Group A (1st Panzer and 17th armies), under Field Marshal List, was then to cross the lower Don, take Rostov, and advance southeast, seizing the Caucasus oil fields. Army Group B under von Bock (2nd, 4th Panzer, and 6th armies, plus the 2nd Hungarian Army) was to cover his northern flank and advance eastward to the Volga.[48]

Bock attacked on June 28 with more than a million men. The Russians quickly retreated before his advance and the expected large haul of prisoners from west of the Don was not realized. Bock then committed 2nd Army to combat at Voronezh, a decision that delayed Blue several days.[49] Hitler was very angry, both over the delay and because Bock was slow in sending the 4th Panzer Army south, thereby allowing a number of large Soviet units to escape across the Don. Actually, Bock did not want to release his armor until the situation at Voronezh was taken care of and his left flank secured. Hitler signaled Bock to break off the battle, but the field marshal ignored his order.

Bock was indeed preoccupied with his left and was openly critical of Hitler's plan, which called for unreliable foreign armies (Rumanians, Hungarians, and Italians) to guard the flanks of the advance to the Volga and Stalingrad, while Army Group A moved off in a divergent direction. Army Group B was scheduled for activation on July 13. That afternoon, Keitel telephoned Bock and told him that Hitler had decided to give this command to Colonel General von Weichs and strongly advised him to ask to be relieved of his command on the grounds of illness. After some argument, Bock acquiesced.[50] Hitler told Major General Schmundt that he still admired Bock but could work only with commanders who followed his orders to the letter.[51] Bock was placed in Fuehrer Reserve on July 15 and was never re-employed.[52]

BOCK'S PRESTIGE WITH the German people was such that the fiction that he was still in command in southern Russia was kept up for some months, and his name was frequently mentioned in propaganda bulletins. This embittered Bock, who felt that he was being made a scapegoat for the Stalingrad débâcle.[53] He was approached by the anti-Hitler conspirator Professor Dr. Johannes Popitz in July 1943, but refused to join any coup that did not include Reichsfuehrer Himmler, because, he said, no putsch could succeed without the support of the Waffen-SS. He also correctly warned Popitz not to depend on Colonel General Friedrich Fromm, the Commander of the Replacement Army, whom he considered unreliable.[54]

"Although Bock detested National Socialism," Lieutenant Fabian von Schlabrendorff wrote later, "he was never willing to lift a hand against Hitler. Much of his character was already mortgaged to vanity and egotism, and what remained was diminutive."[55]

In 1945, with the Russians already on the outskirts of Berlin, Bock received a telegram from Manstein, telling him that Grand Admiral Karl Doenitz was forming a new government at Hamburg. Bock left for that city at once. He was probably even then hoping for a new command. On May 4, with Hitler already dead and the war's end less than a week away, his car was attacked on the Kiel Road by a British fighter-bomber. British soldiers found his bullet-riddled body several days later.[56] His wife and daughter were also killed in the attack.[57] Fedor von Bock thus became the only one of Hitler's field marshals to actually be killed by enemy bullets. He was sixty-four years old.

IT IS GENERALLY accepted that Field Marshal von Bock was not a pleasant person. He was humorless, difficult to deal with or to work for, and highly arrogant and egotistical. He was loyal to Hitler, but whether this loyalty was due to personal ambition or belief in the principle that a soldier cannot act against the head of state without committing treason is a matter of opinion. Perhaps it was both. Evaluations of his generalship also differ. He performed well in Poland, the Low Countries, and in the initial advance on Moscow, smashing over a dozen enemy armies in the process. Had Hitler listened to him, Moscow would have fallen in 1941 and Stalingrad would never have happened. On the other hand, he continued attacking toward Moscow far too long and showed timidity at Kharkov and Voronezh. In this author's opinion, he was not a military genius of the caliber of Manstein, but he was a capable commander who led his armies with considerable success during the first three years of the war.

7

Wilhelm Keitel

WILHELM BODEWIN JOHANN Gustav Keitel was born on his father's six-hundred-acre farmstead, "Helmscherode," near Gandersheim in western Brunswick, on September 22, 1882. He had a cheerful childhood, in the course of which he showed the qualities that would stamp his future career: obedience and no more than average intelligence. He wanted, above all, to be a farmer, like his ancestors. His father, however, remarried after Keitel's mother died, and "Helmscherode" was not prosperous enough to support two families, so the elder Kietel packed his son off to the Army as an officer-candidate. Wilhelm obediently joined the 46th Field Artillery Regiment, his father's old unit, at Wolfenbuettel, Brunswick, in 1901. He would have preferred a cavalry appointment, but his father could not afford to buy him a horse.[1]

After the war, Allied psychologists and journalists attempted to portray Kietel as the typical Prussian junker. He was not. His family was Hanoverian and his grandfather, who was closely connected with the Hanoverian royal family that Bismark overthrew in 1866, would not allow his son to enter the house in his Army uniform.[2]

Keitel was commissioned second lieutenant on August 18, 1902. He was a good, energetic, though not outstanding, junior officer, who seemed to get along with everybody. He loved eating, drinking, hunting, riding, socializing, and the outdoor life. He did a tour at the Military Riding Academy in 1906 and was a good horse jumper. He became regimental adjutant in 1908, was promoted to first lieutenant in 1910, and became captain on October 8, 1914.[3]

Lieutenant Keitel married Lisa Fontaine, the daughter of a Hanoverian brewer and estate owner, on April 18, 1909. Lisa was beautiful, intelligent, and ambitious for her husband. She gave him three sons (all of whom became officers) and three daughters, one of whom died in childhood. Definitely a stronger personality than her husband, she was an admirer of Hitler and a major influence in propelling Keitel upward.[4]

Keitel attended X Corps course for current or future General Staff officers in the spring of 1914, but went to war in Belgium and France with his regiment, and in September was seriously wounded in the right forearm by a shell splinter. Upon recovering, he returned to the 46th Field Artillery where he became a battery commander in November. In March 1915 he was appointed to the General Staff and transferred to XV Reserve Corps. He later served as a General Staff officer with XIX Reserve Corps (1916–17) and the 199th Infantry Division (1917), before being transferred to the General Staff of the Army in Berlin (December 1917).[5] He served in the Freikorps on the Polish frontier in 1919.[6]

Keitel's career in the early days of the Reichsheer was not remarkable. He spent three years as an instructor (i.e., lecturer) at the School of Cavalry at Hanover (1920–23), before joining the regimental staff of the 6th Artillery Regiment. His career got a major boost in 1925 when Colonel von dem Bussche-Ippenburg, the Chief of the Army Personnel Office, assigned him to the organizational branch of the *Truppenamt* (Troop Office), as the clandestine General Staff was then called. Bussche-Ippenburg and Keitel had been friends prior to the First World War and had attended the X Corps school together in the spring of 1914. Keitel's job involved creating modest reserve forces, which was an illegal activity under the Treaty of Versailles. Keitel did not owe his appointment to any talent, but he performed his duty in a solid, dependable manner and made or renewed some important friendships. His circle included Werner von Blomberg, Werner von

Fritsch, Wilhelm Adam, and Walter von Brauchitsch. Keitel served on the General Staff from February 1, 1925, to November 1, 1927, and then returned to Muenster as commander of II Battalion, 6th Artillery Regiment. He was promoted to major in 1923 and lieutenant colonel on February 1, 1929.[7]

Keitel returned to the General Staff in October 1929 as head of the Organizations Department. Even his bitter enemy, Field Marshal Erich von Manstein, later admitted that he did excellent work in this job. He was involved in secret preparations to triple the size of the Army from ten to thirty divisions in case of national emergency, and made at least one trip to the Soviet Union with General Adam and Colonel von Brauchitsch in 1931, in connection with the Reichsheer's secret training. He was highly impressed with Russia – with its immense space, its disciplined army, and its controlled economy.[8]

Despite his impressive physique and bearlike appearance, Keitel was a very nervous man, especially after 1929. He smoked too much and overworked himself; perhaps he had an inkling that he was being promoted above his ceiling. His health cracked under the strain. He developed severe phlebitis in his right leg but ignored it, and even continued to walk to work from his home in west Berlin to his office in the Defense Ministry on the Bendlerstrasse. The physical and mental strain finally led to a heart attack, complicated by double pneumonia. He was recovering at a clinic in the High Tara Mountains of Czechoslovakia on January 30, 1933, when Adolf Hitler took power in Berlin.[9] Keitel's old friend Werner von Blomberg became Minister of Defense the same day.

Upon regaining his health, Keitel (a full colonel since late 1931) returned to his old job in Berlin and, in July, 1933, met Adolf Hitler for the first time at Bad Reichenhall. Keitel was immediately taken with the Fuehrer, whom he would idolize until the day that he died.[10]

Wilhelm Keitel began a year's tour of troop duty in October 1933, when he became Infantry Commander III. In this post he served as one of the two deputy commanders of the 3rd Infantry Division and directed the infantry units assigned to that formation, which was headquartered in Berlin. He was promoted to major general on April 1, 1934.[11]

That spring Keitel's father died, and Wilhelm inherited the

family estate at Helmscherode. At last Keitel felt that he could realize his ambition to become a farmer. He accordingly submitted his resignation, to become effective October 1, 1934. He was, however, called before General Victor von Schwelder, the chief of the Army Personnel Office, at the behest of Keitel's old friend, Werner von Fritsch, who was now Commander-in-Chief of the Army. Fritsch, Schwelder said, was prepared to offer him command of one of the new divisions that would be formed very soon, when Hitler publicly announced his initial military expansion. Keitel could choose his own command if he would withdraw his resignation. Keitel could not resist the opportunity and chose the 22nd Infantry Division at Bremen. "Such," he wrote later, "is the force of human destiny."[12]

Keitel directed the 22nd Infantry for less than a year. In August 1935, Defense Minister General von Blomberg offered him the post of chief of the *Wehrmachtamt*, the Armed Forces Office of the Defense Ministry, to replace Walter von Reichenau, who had been appointed commander of Wehrkreis VII. Keitel had been recommended by General von Fritsch. The other candidate, Major General Heinrich von Vietinghoff, said he did not want the job. Neither did Keitel, who initially begged his immediate superior, General Guenther von Kluge, commander of Wehrkreis VI, to "move heaven and earth" to prevent his appointment. "I had never been so happy as I was now as a divisional commander in Bremen," he wrote later, and "I wanted nothing to do with politics."[13] However, the ambitious Lisa Keitel urged her husband to accept the offer, which he finally did. He took office on September 9, 1935. The new position carried promotions with it, and he was advanced to lieutenant general effective January 1, 1936, and general of artillery on August 1, 1937.[14]

Keitel's new office included a strategic planning department, a military command department, and a national defense department; it was responsible for handling all the signal, military intelligence, and administrative functions of the ministry. It also had a joint services command function. Keitel worked efficiently for Blomberg, with whom he never disagreed, but their relationship was largely impersonal, even after Blomberg's daughter Dorothea became engaged to Lieutenant Karl Heinz Keitel, Wilhelm's son. Keitel was absolutely obedient to Blomberg and was a "yes-man" to the

War Minister, just as he became a yes-man to Hitler later on.[15] When Blomberg married a prostitute in January 1938, however, Keitel did nothing to protect him; on the contrary, when the incriminating evidence fell into his hands he did not destroy it, as he could have done, but rather forwarded it to Hermann Goering, who coveted Blomberg's job, as Keitel must have known. It was Goering who engineered Blomberg's fall from power on January 24, 1938. In fact, Telford Taylor later wrote, Keitel "actually betrayed Blomberg, whether by design or ineptitude."[16]

On January 27 Hitler took final leave of Blomberg at the Chancellery. The departing field marshal recommended that Hitler assume the post of Minister of War himself. Hitler did not reply to this suggestion, but asked who would be suitable to direct the Armed Forces staff under himself. Blomberg had no idea. Hitler then asked who was in charge of Blomberg's staff. Keitel, Blomberg answered, but there was no question of using him, because "he's nothing but the man who runs my office."

"That's exactly the man I am looking for!" Hitler exclaimed. He set up an appointment with Keitel for that very afternoon.[17]

In Keitel, Hitler found exactly the type of officer he was seeking: someone who would carry out his commands to the letter and without question, a yes-man who would be content to be merely a glorified executive officer, without independent command prerogatives. He appointed Keitel Commander-in-Chief of the High Command of the Armed Forces (Oberkommando des Wehrmacht, or OKW), to date from February 4, 1938.

Keitel organized his new command into four sections: the Armed Forces Operations Staff (*Fuehrungstab*, or WFA), the *Abwehr* (Intelligence and Counterespionage Office) the Armed Forces Central Office, and the Armed Forces Economic Office. The Operations Staff was the most important section, and Keitel chose Lieutenant General Max von Viebahn, Leeb's former Chief of Staff at Army Group 2 and the former commander of the 34th Infantry Division, to head it. Viebahn and Keitel did not get along, however, so Viebahn was replaced within two months by Major General Alfred Jodl. The Abwehr was headed by Admiral Wilhelm Canaris until February 1944, when it was dissolved. Keitel had no idea that Canaris had been engaged in anti-Nazi activities for years. (Canaris was not caught until after the July 20, 1944, assassination attempt failed. He was executed in April 1945). The General Office was directed by Colonel Hermann Reinecke, and Major General Georg Thomas supervised the economic office.

Jodl was by far the most important OKW officer after Kietel and was regarded as his twin by the prosecutors at Nuremberg. Colonel (later General of Artillery) Walter Warlimont, who became Chief of the National Defense Branch, was the third most important man at OKW, after Keitel and Jodl. Both Jodl and Warlimont were quite intelligent, despite their obedience to the Nazi régime. Keitel was not, but this enhanced his standing with Hitler, rather than detracted from it.

Keitel never felt adequate to his high position (he was, in fact, not), so he trusted blindly in the genius of the Fuehrer. His influence with Hitler was highest just after he was appointed. Colonel General von Fritsch was relieved on trumped-up charges of homosexuality the week after Blomberg departed, and Hitler wanted to replace him as C-in-C of the Army with Walter von Reichenau, a choice unpalatable to most of the senior officers of the Army and to Keitel personally. Perhaps Keitel hated Reichenau because of his independent mind. In any event Keitel led the opposition, telling Hitler that Reichenau was "not thorough enough, not a hard worker, a busybody, too superficial, little-loved and a soldier who sought satisfaction for his ambitions more in the political than in the purely military sphere."[18] Keitel succeeded in getting his own nominee, Walter von Brauchitsch, appointed instead. He also managed to get his brother, Bodewin Keitel, named chief of the Army Personnel Office, and pro-Nazi Major Rudolf Schmundt installed as the Fuehrer's Army adjutant. He also succeeded in securing his own promotion to colonel general on November 1, 1938.[19]

Keitel had dreams of setting up a *real* Armed Forces High Command, with operational command over the Army, Air Force, and Navy, but the other two branches of the service refused to co-operate. Goering, for example, wrote to Keitel personally: "Whether (and it is in regard to this point that I would like to put it most emphatically) these orders are signed 'In the name of the Fuehrer, Keitel, Colonel General' or 'In the name of the Fuehrer, Maier, Staff Sergeant' is completely irrelevant as far as I am concerned."[20] The Reichsmarschall would take orders only from

Hitler. Grand Admiral Raeder felt the same way, although he avoided expressing himself in such outspoken terms.

KEITEL WAS TEMPERAMENTALLY unequipped to deal with Hitler. His lifelong habit of unconditional and unquestioning obedience to authority, which had served him so well in the Weimar Republic, transferred automatically to the Fuehrer, who used it for his own ends – with disastrous consequences to Keitel, the Army, Germany, and to much of the world. To Keitel, any expression of criticism of Hitler or his orders was an act of disloyalty bordering on treason. An order from the Fuehrer was like a commandment from the Almighty: it was to be obeyed at once, no matter what it stipulated. After the war, Keitel told his interrogator: "At the bottom of my heart I was a loyal shield-bearer for Adolf Hitler; my political conviction would have been National Socialist."[21]

Since Keitel never really exercised command, there are no battles to discuss in this chapter. It only remains to list his war crimes. They were not even Keitel's crimes in the purest sense, for they did not originate with him; he was merely an accomplice. Sometimes this only involved signing an order.

In February 1938, Keitel was a supporting actor in Hitler's brow-beating of Austrian Chancellor Dr. Kurt von Schuschnigg at Berchtesgaden. This session led to the Anschluss – the incorporation of Austria into the Reich.

In March 1939 he played a similar supporting role in the mental subjugation of the Czechoslovakian President, Dr. Emil Hacha, who signed a document placing his country under Nazi "protection."

In September 1939 he echoed Hitler's sentiments, calling for the extermination of Polish Jews, intellectuals, pastors, priests, and nobles, in order to break the will of the Polish people.[22] He later issued orders assisting the SS and Gestapo in the implementation of this policy and condoned measures leading to mass murder in Poland.[23]

In October 1939 Keitel returned from Zossen, impressed by the arguments of Brauchitsch and Halder against launching the invasion of France during winter weather. When he agreed with the sober military logic of these two officers, Hitler flew into a rage, bitterly accusing Keitel of joining the generals' conspiracy against him. Keitel was so shocked that he offered his resignation, which Hitler refused to accept. Don't be so touchy, he said, or words to that effect. Keitel privately promised to obey orders without question in the future.[24]

Wilhelm Keitel certainly looked the part of a tough Prussian general (although he did not have the backbone for it) and made a good physical impression. He conducted the French surrender negotiations with some dignity. A month later, on July 19, 1940, he was promoted to field marshal. He had never dreamed of advancing this far.

At the end of July, Keitel took ten days' leave and went hunting deer and wild boar with friends in Pomerania. Then he visited Helmscherode for a few days and purchased some farm implements for it, thoroughly enjoying his role as the gentleman-farmer – for the last time in his life.[25] Back on duty in August, he was greatly disturbed when Hitler announced that he was considering invading Russia. Rather than risk another rebuke, Keitel submitted his objections to the war in a handwritten memorandum to the Fuehrer. Hitler summoned him and gave him a scathing reprimand. Keitel, deeply wounded, suggested Hitler find a OKW chief whose judgment he trusted more. Hitler flew into a rage and denied him the right to resign. He would serve, the dictator shouted, until the Fuehrer had no further need of him. Keitel left the room without a word.[26] He was humiliated – and trapped in a gilded cage. Perhaps he now saw clearly part of the price he would have to pay for accepting promotions he did not deserve and a position for which he was not intellectually qualified. His reaction to this impossible situation was to submit completely to the will of the Fuehrer.

In May 1941 Keitel signed the infamous Commissar Order, in which German field commanders were ordered to shoot Communist Party officials immediately after they were captured in battle, without court-martial or trials of any kind.[27] A great many generals protested against this criminal order, but Keitel never questioned it in the slightest and insisted it be obeyed to the letter. It was an order from the Fuehrer, after all . . .

On July 27, Keitel signed an order giving Reichsfuehrer Himmler of the SS absolute power in implementing his racial program in Russia.[28] This order was tantamount to endorsing mass murder.

On December 16, 1942, Keitel issued another order to the Armed Forces. It read in part: "It is not only justified, therefore, but the duty of the troops to use every method without restriction, even against women and children, provided it ensures success. Any act of mercy is a crime against the German people."[29]

By September 1942, Keitel's prestige had fallen to a new low. Hitler sent Jodl to the Caucasus to investigate Field Marshal List's operations, and Jodl reported back that List had done all he could with the resources at hand. Hitler began to verbally abuse Jodl (now a colonel general), but the Bavarian staff officer turned on him and sharply defended both himself and List.

Hitler was shocked by this outburst – even his most loyal generals were showing disloyalty! He refused to shake hands with Jodl or Keitel for months after this and henceforth took his meals alone. He told Jodl that he would be replaced by Colonel General Friedrich Paulus as soon as the Battle of Stalingrad was over. He considered replacing Keitel with Kesselring, because Jodl was Keitel's deputy and Keitel had advocated List's appointment three months before. List, of course, was sacked, as was Franz Halder, the chief of the Army General Staff, who had also recommended List for the command of Army Group A. Keitel suggested Manstein or Paulus be named chief of the Army General Staff, but was ignored. Hitler selected General Kurt Zeitzler.[30] At the same time, General Bodewin Keitel was sacked as chief of the personnel office and replaced by Major General Rudolf Schmundt.[31]

A month later, Hitler was again heaping abuse on the Army. "My field marshals are great tacticians," he sneered. "By tactics, of course, they mean retreating!" Then he added: "My field marshals' horizon is the size of a lavatory lid!" Keitel said nothing; he was becoming accustomed to swallowing the most outrageous insults without comment. Zeitzler, however, was not. He asked for a private conference with the Fuehrer and categorically demanded that Hitler not make such embarrassing remarks in his presence again. Hitler, dumbfounded at first, agreed. Keitel did nothing.[32]

Keitel had seen as early as December 1941 that the summer offensive of 1942 might fail, and said so privately, but never dared mention his real opinions to the Fuehrer. When the 6th Army was surrounded at Stalingrad, Hitler refused to allow it to break out. Keitel obediently echoed Hitler's views and supported the Fuehrer against the protests of Weichs, Manstein, Richthofen, and every corps commander in the 6th Army. Keitel thus protected his position, although he must have known how dangerous this decision was. On January 31, 1943, Paulus surrendered the remnants of 6th Army. Germany lost 230,000 men it could not replace.

From this point on, Keitel supported every single "hold at all costs" order that Hitler gave. By reinforcing Hitler's decisions he kept his post, but the effect in the field was disastrous: Army Group Afrika was destroyed in Tunisia; 17th Army was destroyed in the Crimea; 1st Panzer Army was surrounded in Galicia; Army Group South was mauled in the Ukraine; Army Group North was cut off in Courland; Army Group Center was virtually annihilated in Belorussia; and Army Group B was smashed in Normandy, with the resultant loss of France. This list is by no means complete, as it includes only the major disasters. Keitel had no part in making these decisions; he merely endorsed them blindly after Hitler made them. The results were catastrophic nevertheless, for Hitler consistently refused to change his mind and reverse his decisions. At critical points in arguments with field marshals other than Keitel, Hitler would turn to his OKW chief and ask his opinion, confident that it would be a duplicate of his own. Thus reinforced, Hitler would win every argument – and lose every battle.

Keitel had virtually no input into Hitler's strategic decisions. When General Friedrich Olbricht of the Replacement Army asked him how matters stood between Hitler and OKW, Keitel replied bitterly: "I don't know. He tells me nothing. He only spits at me!"[33] Keitel accepted such abuse as part of the price of his position. Formerly a respected member of the Officer Corps, Keitel was now thoroughly detested by his peers. Even junior generals referred to him as *Lakaitel* – lackey – and "the nodding ass."

Keitel signed Hitler's Night and Fog (*Nacht und Nebel*) decree, which was designed to terrorize the occupied countries, especially France and the Low Countries. Under it, people suspected of resisting the Nazis would simply disappear into the night and fog, as if they never existed. Actually, they were turned over to the Gestapo, who murdered them. Keitel justified the decree with the comment: "It is the will of the Fuehrer!"[34]

Wilhelm Keitel approved the execution of striking railroad workers in Holland, the murder of Jews in Russia, and the killing of suspected partisans everywhere. He went along with a proposal to encourage German civilians to lynch captured Allied airmen, saying: "I am against legal procedure. It does not work out."[35] He did, however, unsuccessfully oppose the execution of fifty RAF officers who escaped from the Sagan prison camp in Silesia and were recaptured. Fifteen others were quickly captured in the immediate vicinity of Sagan within hours of the breakout. Keitel ordered these returned to prison, instead of being turned over to the Gestapo, and must be given credit for saving their lives.[36] Such acts of decency were extremely rare in the career of the OKW chieftain, however. More typical was his order that Allied paratroopers captured in places not within or near the immediate combat zone be executed as spies or turned over to the SD, which was the same thing. He did not even object when German generals were imprisoned or shot without trial for failing to carry out impossible orders. Keitel ordered the execution of commandos captured behind German lines and even considered tattooing Russian prisoners on the buttocks, despite the opposition of Foreign Minister Joachim von Ribbentrop, who pointed out that such a measure was a clear violation of international law. He was dissuaded only when a camp commandant pointed out that the Russians would probably retaliate by branding German POWs on the forehead.[37]

WHEN COLONEL VON Stauffenberg's bomb exploded in the Fuehrer's conference room on July 20, 1944, Keitel was in his usual place: slightly behind the Fuehrer and to his left. He physically supported the wounded dictator and half-carried him to the medical station. Keitel suspected Stauffenberg long before anyone else did and took immediate steps against a possible coup.[38] Irving wrote that Keitel's "energetic countermeasures crushed the putsch in the provinces before it had even begun."[39] He arrested his own signals chief, General Erich Fellgiebel, whom he suspected of deliberately isolating the Wolf's Lair (Fuehrer HQ) just after the bomb exploded. (He was right. Fellgiebel was executed in August 1944 for his part in the conspiracy.) Keitel also ordered the arrest of Colonel General Friedrich Fromm, C-in-C of the Replacement Army, and Field Marshal Erwin von Witzleben. He was later president of the Court of Honor, which paved the way for the executions of dozens of officers. In October he played a role in the suicide of Field Marshal Erwin Rommel, offering him the choice of death or trial by the Peoples' Court. Rommel chose death.

When the Allies invaded Germany, Keitel issued an order (also signed by Himmler) demanding that cities that were traffic centers be defended to the last man. Any commander who failed in this duty was to be executed.[40]

During the Battle of Berlin, Keitel wanted to remain in the capital with the Fuehrer, but was ordered out. He tried desperately to relieve the city. "History and the German people will despise everyone who does not do his utmost to save the situation and the Fuehrer," he said.[41] He sacked Colonel General Gotthard Heinrici, the Commander of Army Group Vistula, and his Chief of Staff, Lieutenant General Ivo-Thilo von Trotha, for retreating without orders, but had trouble finding anyone who would fill the vacated posts. In the end he appointed Colonel General Kurt Student, but Hitler was dead by the time Student arrived at his new headquarters.

On May 8, 1945, Keitel signed the final act of surrender at Berlin. Admiral von Friedeburg signed for the Navy and Colonel General Stumpf for the Luftwaffe.

Tried at Nuremberg as a major war criminal, Keitel still maintained his loyalty to the Fuehrer. "Even today," he said, "I am a convinced adherent of Adolf Hitler. This does not exclude my rejecting some items of the Party program," he added. In his defense, he held that he was merely obeying orders. "I was never permitted to make decisions," he said, truthfully enough. "The Fuehrer reserved that right to himself, even in seemingly trivial matters."[42]

Keitel was found guilty of committing crimes against peace, of war crimes, and of crimes against humanity. "There is nothing in mitigation," his judge said. "Superior orders, even to a soldier, cannot be considered in mitigation where crimes as shocking and extensive [as these] have been committed consciously, ruthlessly."[43]

During the trial, Keitel wrote his *Memoirs*, which were designed more to save his face than his neck. He had got as far as the Stalingrad campaign when he was sentenced to death, so he spent the last ten days of his life describing the events in and around Berlin from April 20, 1945, until his arrest by the Americans on

May 12; thus the period between early 1943 and April 19, 1945, is missing. It is a shame that he did not have time to complete these memoirs, for they make interesting, if distorted, reading. He made one really excellent point when he wrote: "Why did the generals who have been so ready to term me a complaisant and incompetent yes-man fail to secure my removal? Was that all that difficult? No, that wasn't it; the truth was that nobody would have been ready to replace me, because each one knew that he would end up just as much a wreck as I."[44]

Keitel was certainly correct on this point. Despite their hatred of him and their fervent wishes to see him replaced, not one of the generals wanted his thankless job himself. Who in his right mind would have? Only a mediocre and subservient personality like Keitel could have held it as long as he did. Wilhelm Keitel paid the final price for his subservience on October 16, 1946, when he was hanged at Nuremberg. He was sixty-four years old.

LIKE THE JUDGMENT at Nuremberg, the verdict of history has gone against Wilhelm Keitel. John Wheeler-Bennett put it well when he wrote: "He had ambition but no talent, loyalty but no character, a certain native shrewdness and charm but neither intelligence nor personality. Under [Gen. Hans] von Seeckt it is doubtful whether he would have gone beyond his majority."[45]

8

Erwin Rommel

ERWIN JOHANNES EUGEN Rommel, the famous "Desert Fox," was born at Heidenheim in Swabia, a district of Wuerttemberg, in southern Germany, on November 15, 1891. Even as a child he was tough, serious, innovative, daring, and self-reliant, almost to the point of pigheadedness. There was little military background in his family, and his father opposed his career choice, but a military career it would be. He joined the 124th (6th Wuerttemberg) Infantry Regiment as an officer-cadet on July 19, 1910, at the age of eighteen. He was promoted to corporal three months later, and was a sergeant by early 1911. In March 1911 he was admitted to the War Academy at Danzig, and received his commission as second lieutenant in January 1912.[1]

Rommel was attached to the 19th Field Artillery Regiment in 1914 when World War I broke out. Until this point, Rommel's career had been perfectly average and absolutely undistinguished. The battlefield, however, transformed him into a warrior of the first class. Historian Brigadier Desmond Young wrote: "From the moment that he first came under fire he stood out as the perfect fighting animal: cold, cunning, ruthless, untiring, quick of decision [and] incredibly brave."[2] A fellow officer remembered: "He was the body and soul of war."[3]

Rommel quickly rejoined the 124th Infantry and fought in Belgium and France, at Verdun and the Argonne. He was wounded in late 1914 but returned to the trenches in early 1915 as commander of the 4th Company. Then, in September 1915, he was promoted to first lieutenant and named CO 2nd Company, in the élite Wuerttemberg Mountain Battalion, which was then forming. He led this company in Rumania and Italy in 1917, with what one of his platoon leaders called "a holy zeal."[4] He proved to have an uncanny instinct for fighting and improvisation. In the October 1917 struggle for Monte Matajur in the Italian Alps, he captured 9,000 Italians and 81 guns in three separate actions over a 48-hour period.[5] For this incredible feat he was promoted to captain and awarded the coveted *Pour le Mérite*. He spent the rest of the war in Germany in staff assignments.

Rommel went on leave in the winter of 1916/17 and married Lucie Mollin, a language student he met in Danzig in 1912. They remained together happily married, until his death twenty-eight years later. They had one child, a son named Manfred, who was born on Christmas Eve, 1928.

Rommel's career in the Reichsheer era was not extraordinary. He commanded the 32nd Internal Security Company in Muensterland and Westphalia during the civil disturbances of 1919–20, and then the 2nd Company, 13th Infantry Regiment, at Stuttgart. He remained there until 1929, when he was sent to the Infantry School at Dresden as an instructor. He was not promoted to major until after 1930.[6]

In 1933, Rommel was named CO, III Battalion, 17th (Mountain) Infantry Regiment, at Goslar. After this successful command, he was promoted to lieutenant colonel and sent to the War Academy at Potsdam in 1935 as an instructor. Here he was attached to the Hitler Youth as a military adviser, until he clashed with Hitler Youth leader Baldur von Schirach over the latter's efforts to militarize Germany's young people. In one argument, Rommel bluntly told the lifelong civilian that if he were determined to train soldiers, he should first learn to be a soldier himself! Tact was never Rommel's strong suit. Schirach arranged for Rommel's immediate return to the War Academy.[7]

Rommel, the son and grandson of teachers, was an excellent instructor. While at Dresden he wrote *Infantry in the Attack*, based on his lectures about his World War I experiences.[8] To his astonishment, it was a bestseller in Nazi Germany, and the Swiss Army even adopted it as a training manual. Chancellor Hitler also read it and was impressed. He had Rommel attached to his escort during the Nuremberg Party Rallies of 1936, and the two hit it off well. Rommel, who was always politically naive, supported the Fuehrer until 1943, when he learned of the atrocities the Nazis were committing and of Hitler's personal involvement in them, but this is getting ahead of our story.

In 1938, Rommel was named commander of the Infantry School at Wiener Neustadt, south of Vienna, in what was formerly Austria. This was the happiest period of his military career, he later declared. The duty was both challenging and rewarding, and the countryside beautiful. He dearly loved to go on outings with his wife and son and took up a new hobby: photography. His tenure here, however, was interrupted by temporary duty assignments as commander of the Fuehrergleitbataillon, Hitler's personal bodyguard, during the Sudeten and Czech crises. Hitler promoted him to major general on August 23, 1939.[9] Nine days later the panzers crossed the Polish frontier, and the Second World War began.

As commander of the Fuehrer's bodyguard battalion in Poland, Erwin Rommel observed the blitzkrieg firsthand. He saw that mechanized warfare was the wave of the future. Although he had spent his entire twenty-nine-year career in the infantry, he decided his future lay in the armored branch. He asked Hitler for a command. Hitler, in turn, asked him what type of command he wanted. Rommel asked for a panzer division.

"That was an immoderate request on my part," Rommel recalled later. "I did not belong to the armored branch of the service, and there were many generals who had a much stronger claim to a command of this nature."[10] Hitler nevertheless gave Rommel command of the 7th Panzer (formerly 2nd Light) Division in February 1940, replacing Lieutenant General Georg Stumme.

Seventh Panzer was one of the worst-equipped armored formations in the Wehrmacht. It had only three tank battalions (as opposed to the normal 1940 contingent of four battalions per panzer division) and was outfitted mainly with captured Czech T-38 tanks, which weighed only about nine tons, against the twenty-three-ton PzKw III, the standard main battle panzer. The

T-38s were virtually useless against the much heavier British and French tanks. Rommel's men were in little better shape than his armor. They were from Thuringia, a province not noted for producing good soldiers. "Most of my officers are very comfortably inclined," Rommel wrote to his wife, "and some are downright flabby."[11] Rommel set about correcting the sorry state of his new command. Training intensified, discipline improved, and combat efficiency increased remarkably. When the 7th Panzer crossed into Belgium on May 10, 1940, it was ready for what lay ahead.

In the West, Rommel pushed his men forward ruthlessly. The 7th Panzer suffered a higher rate of casualties than any other German division in the campaign. It breached the Meuse, penetrated the Belgian frontier extension of the Maginot Line, overran the 1st French Armored and 4th North African divisions, repulsed the major British counterattack of the campaign at Arras, smashed the 31st French Motorized Division at Fécamp, and captured the ports of St. Valery and Cherbourg, including the bulk of the 51st British Infantry Division and its commander. In six weeks, Rommel lost 2,594 men killed, wounded, and captured. During the same period he took 97,468 prisoners, shot down fifty-two aircraft, destroyed fifteen on the ground and captured a dozen more. He captured the commander of the French Atlantic Fleet, four other admirals, at least seventeen generals, 277 guns, sixty-four antitank guns, 458 tanks and armored cars, 4,000 to 5,000 trucks, 1,500 to 2,000 cars, at least 1,500 horse-drawn vehicles, and tons of supplies and equipment.[12] Erwin Rommel had indeed distinguished himself and proved that he was a master of the blitzkrieg. He has also convinced the Fuehrer that he was capable of handling an independent command.

IN DECEMBER 1940, British Lieutenant General Sir Richard O'Connor's Western Desert Force (31,000 men) attacked General Mario Berti's 10th Italian Army in western Egypt. The entire Italian Army collapsed like a house of cards. In less than two months O'Connor swept across Egypt into Libya, overran Cyrenaica, captured Bardia, Tobruk, Derna, and Benghazi, and destroyed ten Italian divisions. Mussolini lost 130,000 guns, 400 tanks, and 150 aircraft. All that remained of the Italian Empire in North Africa by February 3, 1941, was a demoralized garrison at Tripoli.[13] This

Map 11

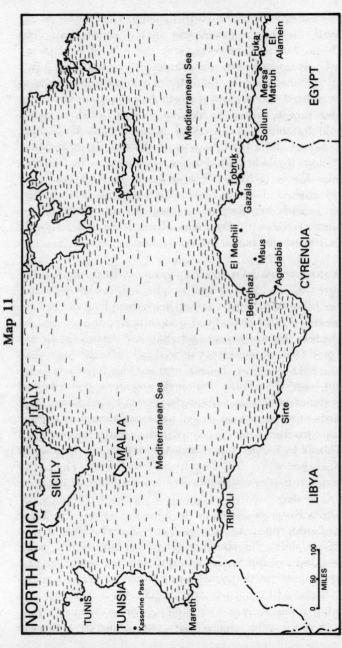

THE NORTH AFRICAN THEATER, 1941–43. This sector was dominated by the leadership of Field Marshal Erwin Rommel until his defeat at El Alamein in early November 1942. Trapped between the British and Americans, the last German unit in North Africa surrendered in Tunisia on May 12, 1943. Rommel had been ordered to return to Germany in March.

would have fallen if Churchill had listened to General Sir Archibald Wavell, the theater commander in the Middle East. The British Prime Minister, however, sent the best of O'Connor's troops to Greece, where they were thoroughly trounced by List's 12th Army two months later. Adolf Hitler also had some moves to make. He realized that the loss of North Africa was not important in itself, but that its capture would free a dozen British divisions, which could destabilize his entire Mediterranean flank. He decided to send a panzer and a light division to Africa to tie them down. These divisions would be placed under a new corps – the Deutschland Afrika Korps (DAK). He summoned one of his military favorites, Lieutenant General Erwin Rommel, to his headquarters at Staaken in early February and named him commander of the DAK. Map 11 shows the locations of the Italians defeats and Rommel's subsequent battles in North Africa.

ROMMEL'S EXPLOITS IN the desert are legendary. Realizing that the British were weak and badly positioned, he went over to the attack even before his second division arrived, even though he violated the direct orders of Field Marshal von Brauchitsch in the process. By doing so he was able to recapture Benghazi and destroy the British 2nd Armored Division piecemeal, as well as isolate the Australian 9th Infantry Division in Tobruk. Among his prisoners were Lieutenant-General Sir Philip Neame, the recently appointed Chief of the Cyrenaican Command (formerly Westen Desert Force), and Sir Richard O'Connor, whom Wavell had sent forward to "advise" Neame when his front began to collapse. Meanwhile, Rommel tried to take Tobruk by *coup de main* in mid-April and failed. Two weeks later he launched a prepared assault and failed again. The rest of the fierce desert battles of 1941 focused around Allied attempts to relieve this fortress.

The Afrika Korps consisted of the 15th Panzer and 5th Light (later 21st Panzer) divisions. In the summer of 1941 it had the dual mission of containing the reinforced Australian 9th Division inside the fortress and defeating relief attempts from the west. The first such effort (Operation Battleaxe) was directed by Major General Sir Noel Beresford-Pierse, with the Indian 4th and British 7th Armoured divisions. Although outnumbered more than two to one, Rommel used the principles of mass and maneuver almost to perfection, and defeated the British in a three-day battle from July 15–17, 1941. Rommel lost about twenty-five tanks, against more than one hundred for the Allies. Hitler was so pleased that he promoted Rommel to general of panzer troops and gave him command of Panzer Group Afrika in July.[14] Unfortunately for Germany, the Fuehrer would not send Rommel any of the reinforcements he requested, save the 164th Infantry (later Light Afrika) Division in the summer of 1942. Hitler was preoccupied with the war in Russia until after it was too late to win the Desert War.

Panzer Group Afrika consisted of the Afrika Korps and the then-organizing 90th Light Division, which was not fully motorized until early 1942. These were all the German forces Rommel had, except for a few miscellaneous GHQ units. The panzer group also included the Italian Ariete Armored Division, two Italian motorized divisions, and four Italian infantry divisions. These units were of marginal value at best, because Italian morale never recovered from the defeats of 1940/41. They still had to be supplied, however, and the British naval and air bases on the island of Malta continually raided Rommel's supply lines. The Desert Fox was never able to build up enough supplies to attack Tobruk again, and at one point the panzer group was threatened with starvation. Rommel faced the Allied winter offensive (Operation Crusader) with only 15 percent of the ammunition and fuel he needed.[15]

Operation Crusader lasted from November 18 to December 7, 1941, and was one of the most confusing battles of the Second World War. The British 8th Army attacked Rommel with five motorized infantry divisions and an armored division, plus three armored and two motorized brigades. They had 748 tanks against his 249 panzers and 146 nearly useless Italian tanks.[16] Rommel still managed to defeat the initial attacks, but lost the battle when he became too impressed with his local successes and led a fruitless raid into Egypt with the Afrika Korps, giving the British time to recover. Allied losses were much heavier until this point, but the Siege of Tobruk was broken on December 5, after 242 days. Three days later Rommel retreated from Cyrenaica, having lost all but twenty-six of his panzers.[17]

The British thought Rommel was finished after Operation Crusader and began building up for the final drive on Tripoli. The Desert Fox, however, had a surprise for them. In early January

1942, a naval convoy carrying fifty-five panzers and tons of other supplies got by Malta, thanks largely to the efforts of Kesselring's 2nd Air Fleet.[18] On January 21 Rommel struck the Allies before they could complete their buildup, swamping the 201st Guards Brigade and half of the British 1st Armoured Division in the British assembly areas. He recaptured Benghazi and pursued the British to the Gazala Line, where he halted due to a lack of supplies. For this success, Hitler promoted Rommel to colonel general in January 1942, having upgraded his command to Panzer Army Afrika a few days before.[19]

After the drive to Gazala, a lull descended on the North African theater, while both sides built up supplies for the next attack. Rommel struck first, as usual. He was outnumbered 333 to 900 in tanks (excluding 228 near-worthless Italian tanks), ten to one in armored cars,[20] eight to five in artillery, and six to five and a half in aircraft.[21] The battle lasted from May 26 to June 12. At one point the Afrika Korps was surrounded because Rommel advanced too rapidly and got himself cut off. Despite the odds, however, Rommel broke through the heavily mined Gazala Line, outmaneuvred and outfought the Allies, and nearly destroyed the 8th Army.[22] Hardly allowing his exhausted men a pause, the Desert Fox pursued his defeated enemies to Tobruk, which he finally captured on June 21, with a bag of 32,000 prisoners. The next day a grateful Fuehrer promoted him to field marshal.

At age fifty, Rommel was the youngest marshal in the Army. He had reached the peak of his military career. He celebrated by eating a tin of pineapple and drinking a well-watered glass of captured whisky. "Hitler has made me a field marshal," Rommel wrote to his wife that night. "I would much rather he had given me one more division."[23]

After Tobruk, Rommel had only forty-four operational panzers left.[24] Despite his weakness, he invaded Egypt. Rommel felt that if he could strike quickly enough he could seize Alexandria and Cairo and win a decisive victory in the desert before the battered British 8th Army could recover. He was almost successful in pulling it off; however, he was halted at El Alamein, only sixty miles from Alexandria.

There were actually two battles of El Alamein. In the first,

Rommel tried to break through to the Nile at full throttle, but failed. Then General Sir Claude Auchinleck, the 8th Army's latest commander, changed British tactics. Instead of concentrating against the Germans as before, Auchinleck struck only at Italian units. Mussolini's new Roman legions broke almost every time, and Rommel was forced to use the Afrika Korps as a fire brigade, rushing from point to point to restore the front. Each time it was left weaker than before. Precious supplies were used up. Rommel was now a thousand miles from his main supply base (the Italian Navy would not use Tobruk because of the risk involved) and his supply lines collapsed almost completely.

By now, the Afrika Korps subsisted almost entirely on supplies captured in the Gazala Line-Tobruk battles. Some 85 percent of Rommel's transport vehicles, for example, had been manufactured in the United Kingdom or in Detroit. The Desert Fox repulsed ten attacks in the period of July 5–27. British losses were heavy, but Rommel had reached the end of his rope. On July 26, his heavy artillery fired its last shell, and the medium artillery only continued firing because it had equipped itself with captured British guns and was using captured British shells. Rommel decided to retreat if the British attacked again, but they were equally exhausted. Stalemate once again set in on the African front.

In the last half of August 1942, the Allies off-loaded 500,000 tons of supplies in North Africa, as opposed to 13,000 for the Axis: a supply imbalance of 38 to one. The Royal Air Force had swept the Luftwaffe from the skies, and Rommel had only enough fuel for a panzer advance of eighty miles. The British had more than seven hundred tanks to range against Rommel's 259 worn panzers, giving them an overall superiority of nearly three to one.[25] Most of Rommel's tanks came from the repair shops and were in need of complete overhauls, but this was not possible in the summer of 1942. The British had won the battle of supplies and were increasing their superiority in all categories every day. Rommel decided to launch one more attack, before the British grew too strong for him to attack at all.

Rommel's new opponent, General Sir Bernard Law Montgomery (the fifth 8th Army commander in less than a year) was waiting for just such an offensive. In the Battle of Alam Halfa Ridge (August

30–September 2), he destroyed forty-nine panzers (and lost sixty-seven tanks himself)[26] and turned back the Desert Fox's last attempt to break the El Alamein line.

Erwin Rommel was now a sick man. Exhausted by a year and a half in the harsh environment of the Sahara Desert, suffering from desert sores, chronic stomach and intestinal catarrh, circulatory problems, and symptoms of exhaustion, as well as liver trouble, he left for Semmering, a mountain resort near Vienna, on September 23.[27] He was replaced by General Georg Stumme.

Apparently Hitler intended to let Rommel recover, then give him a command in Russia. However, when Montgomery began his long-awaited offensive on October 23, Stumme was reported missing in action. The next evening, Hitler telephoned Rommel and asked him to return to Africa. Meanwhile, they found Stumme's body; he had died of a heart attack.

Montgomery's superiority at El Alamein was overwhelming: four to one over the Germans in men, five to one in tanks and artillery, three to one in anti-tank guns and four to one in operational aricraft when the offensive began.[28] Rommel did a magnificent job in holding him up for more than a week of constant combat. Finally, however, the Afrika Korps was down to thirty-five tanks. The once-mighty 15th Panzer Division was all but wiped out, reduced to a strength of zero tanks and seven guns. On the night of November 2/3, Rommel admitted defeat and ordered a general retreat. Much to his surprise, Hitler sent him a dispatch, commanding him to "stand fast, yield not a yard of ground, and throw every gun and every man into the battle."[29]

Rommel was flabbergasted. Hitler had never interfered in his tactical operations before. As a soldier, Rommel felt compelled to obey the Fuehrer's order, a decision that cost him more than half of his remaining panzers, the Ariete Armored Division (which was encircled) and the entire Italian X Infantry Corps. Rommel ordered a retreat without Hitler's permission the next evening.

Until then, Rommel's relationship with Hitler had been good. El Alamein was the turning point. From then on, it deteriorated steadily. At Fuehrer Headquarters, Rommel was treated to the same scenes as Keitel and some of the others: charges of defeatism, screaming fits, temper tantrums, violent outbursts of hatred, and other forms of unreasonable and irrational behavior. Hitler even went so far as to question the courage of the Afrika Korps, whereupon Rommel walked out of the room. Later, he became more outspoken. When Hitler insisted that Rommel's men stand and die rather than retreat from a tactically hopeless situation, Rommel asked him why the Fuehrer or some of his entourage didn't come to the front and show them how to do it.

ROMMEL RETREATED, AGAINST orders, on November 4, a decision that Hitler ratified after the fact. Rommel only got his army out of Egypt because Montgomery pursued him so slowly. After the British and Americans landed in Morocco and Algeria, Rommel wanted to abandon North Africa altogether and use his panzer army to defend Sicily and Italy. Instead, Hitler sent an entire army (the 5th Panzer under Colonel General Juergen von Armin) to Tunisia, even though he could not supply it properly. Hitler could not be seen to support a winning cause nor abandon a lost one.

The Desert Fox conducted a brilliant, one-thousand-mile retreat and got the remnants of the Afrika Korps to Tunisia in early 1943. Here he briefly commanded Army Group Afrika (5th Panzer Army and the 1st German-Italian Panzer Army, as his old command was renamed in early 1943). He turned on the Allies and administered the Americans a startling defeat in a surprise attack at Kasserine Pass in late February 1943. He was less successful when he attacked the prepared defenses of the 8th Army at Medenine on March 6, losing fifty panzers without destroying any British tanks – his worst tactical defeat in North Africa. Hitler then sent him on sick leave, and Erwin Rommel left Africa for the last time on March 9.[30] Hitler decorated him with the Knight's Cross with Oak Leaves, Swords and Diamonds, and sent him off in unofficial disgrace.[31]

Rommel recovered his health in semi-retirement while Army Group Afrika collapsed in early May, just as he had predicted it would. In the end, some units used Tunisian wine for fuel due to the absence of gasoline or diesel. Germany lost 130,000 men in the Tunisian débâcle, including some of its best warriors. Hitler summoned Rommel to Fuehrer Headquarters as the agony neared its end. "I should have listened to you," he confessed.[32] Erwin Rommel was out of the doghouse. Hitler took him out of his semi-retirement and eventually named him C-in-C of Army Group

B in Munich. He was in charge of the German forces in northern Italy and briefly shared German authority in that country with Kesselring, whose Army Group C was stationed in southern Italy and Sicily. This arrangement did not work and, since Kesselring's notions of defense more closely coincided with Hitler's own, the Fuehrer pulled Rommel's HQ out of Italy. While deciding on Rommel's future employment, Hitler sent him on an inspection tour of the Atlantic Wall, as the coastal defenses of Denmark, the Low Countries, and France were called. This zone was part of the responsibility of Field Marshal von Rundstedt, the C-in-C, West (OB West).

Rommel was not at all satisfied with the coastal defenses. He was, however, convinced that the Allied invasion of 1944 would be Germany's last chance of winning the war, and he wanted to command. Rundstedt, on the other hand, feared that Rommel had been sent west to replace him. The two marshals met in late December and reached an agreement. On December 30, Rundstedt proposed that HQ, Army Group B, be placed under OB West, where it would control the 7th and 15th armies and the German Armed Forces Netherlands. Hitler was hardly overjoyed by the idea, for he apparently wanted to use Rommel in the East, but he finally agreed to it. Rommel had received his largest and last command.

Army Group B initially consisted of twenty-four infantry and five Luftwaffe field divisions under eight corps headquarters, extending from the Netherlands to south of Brittany. It did not have a single panzer division, which led to the major strategic debate of the campaign: where to position the ten panzer and panzer grenadier divisions in OB West's reserve. Rommel argued that they must be posted near the coast, where they would be in a position to launch immediate counterattacks against the Allied landings. Rundstedt, backed by his chief armor advisor, General Baron Leo von Geyr von Schweppenburg, wanted to keep his tanks in a central reserve, so they would be in a position to fight the decisive battle somewhere in the interior of France.

Rommel realized that the days of the great panzer victories were over. Of all the top generals in France and Germany, he alone had experienced Anglo-American air power first hand. He knew that if the Allies were allowed to establish themselves in Europe, the Germans would never succeed in dislodging them. If this happened, the fall of the Third Reich was only a matter of time. The only chance Germany had left, therefore, was to attack the Allies on the beachhead while they were still vulnerable. He concluded that the first twenty-four hours of the invasion would be decisive. Much to his frustration, however, Rommel was unable to convince Rundstedt, Geyr von Schweppenburg, or many of his own subordinates of the correctness of his views.

Confronted by these two different schools of thought, Hitler should have chosen between them. Unfortunately for Nazi Germany, he compromised and chose them both. He assigned 2nd, 21st, and 116th Panzer divisions to Army Group B, the 9th, 11th, and 2nd SS Panzer divisions to newly activated Army Group G in southern France, and left the 1st SS Panzer, 12th SS Panzer, 17th SS Panzer Grenadier, and Panzer Lehr divisions under Panzer Group West, in reserve. No one was satisfied with this arrangement: Rommel still did not have enough armor to carry out his defensive designs, and Rundstedt lost six of the ten divisions in his mobile reserve. In other words, Hitler ruined Rundstedt's plans but did not give Rommel the forces he needed to carry out his own.

THE FIRST GERMAN to correctly pick Normandy as the site of the Allied invasion was Adolf Hitler. Rommel also came around to this view for more scientific reasons: he analyzed the pattern of Allied pre-invasion bombing and concluded that they were trying to isolate Normandy. In the month of May 1944 alone, he reinforced the 7th Army in this sector with the 91st Air Landing Division, the 6th Parachute Regiment, the 101st Stellungswerfer (Rocket-Launcher) Regiment, and the 206th Panzer, 100th Panzer Replacement, 17th Machine Gun, and 7th Army Sturm battalions.[33] Rommel also asked OKW to move the Panzer Lehr Division and III Flak Corps to positions between the Orne and the Vire, the 12th SS Panzer Division to the Vire, and a rocket-launching brigade west of the Orne. All of his appeals were opposed by Rundstedt and subsequently rejected by Hitler and the High Command. "They would have been exactly in the right places to counter the invasion," Admiral Ruge moaned later.[34]

Rommel also prepared for the invasion by making the coastal defenses as close to impenetrable as possible. By May 20, his men had lain 4,193,167 mines in less than five months – more than twice the number OB West had lain in the previous three years. He had also erected 517,000 offshore obstacles, thousands of anti-glider obstacles, and thousands of tank traps, dummy positions, strong-points, and machine-gun nests.[35] "About all that was missing from Rommel's medieval arsenal of weapons were crucibles of molten lead to pour down on the attackers," Cornelius Ryan wrote, "and in a way he had the modern equivalent: automatic flame throwers."[36]

The constant work, arguments, and inspection tours had taken their toll on Rommel, and by June 4 he needed a rest. Checking the meteorological forecasts, he learned that the weather in the English Channel for the next several days was anything but favorable for an invasion. He then left his HQ for Germany, where he planned to spend a couple of days at home on leave and then see Hitler, to personally ask for more reinforcements. It was a fatal mistake.

On June 6, 1944, the Allies landed on five separate beaches in Normandy. They attacked with three airborne and six reinforced infantry divisions against two understrength German infantry divisions (the 352nd and 709th). The defenders struggled fiercely to check the Allies at the water's edge and did cause them significant delays, but in the end they were all but destroyed. Without Rommel, command paralysis gripped the German side. Only one panzer division (the rebuilt 21st) managed to counterattack that day, and it was badly directed. Erwin Rommel, at home in Germany, did not learn of the invasion until 10:15 A.M., three hours and forty-five minutes after the landings began. "How stupid of me, how stupid of me," was his only comment.[37] He had missed the most important battle of his military career.

Rommel arrived back in France that night and for the next three days struggled to restore his front. On June 9 – at least two days too late – he launched his counterattack with the 21st Panzer, 12th SS Panzer, and Panzer Lehr divisions, under Headquarters, Panzer Group West. The spearheads came within three miles of the coast, but were halted by four British divisions and overwhelming Allied air and naval support. HQ, Panzer Group West was knocked out by enemy bombers; General Geyr von Schweppenburg was seriously wounded, and his Chief of Staff, Major General Ritter und Elder Sigismund-Hellmut von Dawans, was killed, as was his operations officer and other key personnel.[38] The group headquarters had to be withdrawn from the battle, and Rommel went over to the defensive all along the line. No other major counterattacks were attempted until August (see chapter 16).

For six bloody weeks Rommel contained the Allies in the hedgerow country of Normandy. "The Germans are staying in there just by the guts of their soldiers," US Major General Raymond Barton commented in mid-July. "We outnumbered them ten to one in infantry, fifty to one in artillery, and by an infinite number in the air."[39] Just as in North Africa, Erwin Rommel was getting the maximum effort from his men; just as in Africa, it was not enough.

Until D-Day, Hitler expected the invasion in Normandy. As soon as the Allies touched ground, however, he decided that the Normandy landings were just a diversion, and that the real invasion would come in the Pas de Calais sector, in the zone of the 15th Army. Rommel could not persuade him to release the infantry units of the 15th Army for the Battle of Normandy; meanwhile, the weaker 7th Army and Panzer Group West were bleeding to death in the hedgerow country. On July 15 he sent Hitler what amounted to an ultimatum, calling on him to draw the proper conclusions and strongly implying that he should end the war. "I have given him his last chance," Rommel said. "If he does not take it, we will act!"

Rommel was by now deeply involved in the anti-Hitler conspiracy. Although he naively opposed killing Hitler, he did want to arrest the dictator and put him on trial for his crimes. Alone of the field marshals still in active command, he was ready to play a part in deposing the Nazi régime. He even succeded in getting SS General Sepp Dietrich, the commander of II SS Panzer Corps, to agree to follow only his (Rommel's) orders in case of an anti-Nazi *coup*.

Unfortunately, fate took Army Group B out of Rommel's hands. On July 17 he was critically wounded in the head by shells from an enemy fighter-bomber. Not expected to live through the night, he nevertheless survived and eventually returned home to Herrlingen, a village in his native Swabia, near Ulm, where he had moved his family in late 1943. (The Luftwaffe had built a major aircraft factory at Wiener Neustadt, and Rommel correctly feared that the town would be bombed.)

Meanwhile, the Gestapo (and thus Hitler) had learned of Rommel's involvement in the conspiracy, which ended in the unsuccessful assassination attempt of July 20. On October 14 Army

Personnel Chief Lieutenant General Wilhelm Burgdorf and his deputy, Major General Ernest Maisel, appeared at Rommel's home, after quietly surrounding the place with SS men. They offered the Desert Fox a choice: suicide or a trial before the Peoples' Court. Rommel chose the trial. Then the OKH officers pointed out the consequences to his family, if he chose the trial, under the doctrine of collective family responsibility. If he committed suicide, however, they promised him a state funeral with full honors, plus safety and a pension for his wife and son. They had a poison capsule with them, they said, and his death would be quick and painless. For his family's sake, Rommel chose the poison. After a brief farewell to Lucie and Manfred, Rommel drove off with the generals. He was reported dead on arrival at the Wagnerschule Reserve Hospital in Ulm. The cause of his death was officially listed as a brain seizure.

Hitler kept his end of the bargain, and the surviving Rommels were not molested by the Nazis. The field marshal received his state funeral. His body was cremated to remove all traces of his murder, and his ashes were buried in a corner of the graveyard of the village church at Herrlingen. Rommel was only fifty-two years old at the time of his suicide.

TO CONDENSE THE career of a man I have written three books about into a single chapter is not an easy task. Erwin Rommel was a hero in many respects and always a man of action. He had his share of warts, but certainly it was his own talent that secured him one of the most exciting careers in modern military history. Many people rate him as the best of Hitler's field marshals. Certainly he was brilliant and remarkably courageous (he was wounded no fewer than six times), but he was also impetuous and bullheaded and sometimes too impressed with local successes. His achievements in the face of tremendous odds have become legendary; his attacks were bold and daring and were driven home with reckless abandon. He has been given less credit for his abilities as a defensive commander, but in many ways Normandy was his best battle. Had he been given complete freedom of action, the success of the D-Day invasion becomes questionable. I believe he ranks just behind Manstein as the best German field marshal in the Second World War.

9

Siegmund Wilhelm List

ONE OF THE least famous of Hitler's field marshals is Siegmund Wilhelm List. He was born in Oberkirchberg, Wuerttemburg, a province in southwestern Germany, on May 14, 1880. The son of a doctor, he joined the Army as a *Fahnenjunker* (officer-cadet) in the Bavarian 1st Engineer Battalion on July 15, 1898. Commissioned second lieutenant on March 7, 1900, he attended artillery and engineer schools and later became the adjutant of his parent battalion. In 1908 he was promoted to *Oberleutnant* (first lieutenant) and was sent to the War Academy, where he underwent General Staff training. He did a tour of fortification duty in the early 1910s, and was promoted to captain in 1914. He was on the Bavarian General Staff in Munich when the First World War broke out.[1]

Captain List was assigned to the Bavarian II Corps for the first two years of the war. He fought on the Somme, at Ypres, in Flanders, at La Bassée and Amiens, on the Maas, and in the Battle of Mosel. He did not command Corporal Hitler's regiment on the Western Front, as some sources later believed (that was another List). In the summer of 1916 he was sent to the East, and served several months in the Balkans and with Turkish forces. Here he gained vital experience in southern European affairs – knowledge that would be very useful to him later on. Following this tour of duty he returned to the Western Front in 1917, where he was the First General Staff Officer (Ia, or Operations Officer) of the Bavarian 8th Reserve Infantry Division. In January 1918 he was promoted to major and appointed an instructor with the Bavarian War Ministry, and was still in Munich when the war ended.[2]

Major List served briefly with the Freikorps in 1919 but was selected for the Reichsheer after the Treaty of Versailles was signed. He served on the General Staff of General Ritter Franz von Epp's 7th Infantry Division in Munich (1920–22), as the commander of a mountain infantry battalion (1922–23), on the staff of Wehrkreis VII (1924), and with the 19th Infantry Battalion (1924–25). He was promoted to lieutenant colonel by 1924 and in 1926 was named Chief of the Army Organizations Department in the Reichswehr Ministry. Shortly thereafter he became a full colonel, and on November 1, 1930, he was promoted to major general and named commander of the Infantry School at Dresden.[3]

Siegmund List first ran afoul of the Nazis in 1931. As CG of the Infantry School, he took disciplinary actions against *Fahnenrich* (cadets) who engaged in National Socialist political activities. Goerlitz believes that Hitler's dislike for him dated back to these incidents.[4]

By 1932, List had the reputation of being a calm, cool, rational, methodical General Staff officer. "He was a clever, cool, and sound strategist – not an impulsive charger at closed doors, but a man who believed in sound planning and leadership and detested all military gambles."[5] He was considered a gentleman and even Heinz Guderian, his subordinate in France and a man famous for not getting along with his superiors, later remembered List warmly and spoke of his "chivalrous nature."[6]

List was promoted to lieutenant general in 1932 and given command of the 4th Infantry Division. On October 1, 1935, he was again promoted (to general of infantry) and given his third straight assignment at Dresden: commander of Wehrkreis IV. This military district initially included the 4th, 14th, and 24th Infantry divisions and Frontier Zone Command 5. List was now eighth on the Army's all-important seniority list, behind Blomberg, Fritsch, Rundstedt, Leeb, Bock, Liebmann, and Adam.[7]

General List enhanced his chances for future promotion by

1 Werner von Blomberg

2 Walter von Brauchitsch

3 Ewald von Kleist

4 Walter von Reichenau

5 Ritter Wilhelm von Leeb

6 Fedor von Bock

7 Wilhelm Keitel

8 Erwin Rommel

9 Siegmund Wilhelm List

10 Baron Maximilian von Weichs

11 Friedrich Paulus

12 Erich von Manstein

13 Georg von Kuechler

14 Ernst Busch

15 Gerd von Rundstedt

16 Guenther von Kluge

17 Walter Model

18 Erwin von Witzleben

19 Ferdinand Schoerner

20 Hermann Goering

21 *Left:* Erhard Milch

22 *Below left:* Hugo Sperrle

23 *Below right:* Albert Kesselring

24 *Right:* SS Colonel General 'Sepp'
Dietrich

25 *Below:* Hitler observes the bombardment of Warsaw, September, 1939. At
his left is Colonel General (later Field
Marshal) Walter von Reichenau, who
led the 10th Army in Poland and the 6th
Army in Belgium, France and Russia

26 Hitler with Colonel General Johannes Blaskowitz (left) and von Brauchitsch, 1938

27 Paris, 14 June, 1940. German troops in the Place de la Concorde

28 German tanks enter Salonika, 9 April, 1941

29 One of the first pictures to be seen in the West of the German invasion of Russia which began on 22 June, 1941

30 German soldiers hanging Russian partisans, Minsk, October, 1941

31 German troops halt for a rest in the North African desert, July, 1941

32 A PzKw IV on the Russian Front

33 *Left:* This picture gives some idea of what conditions were like for the infantry on the Eastern Front in the winter of 1941/42

34 *Below:* A soldier comforts his horse on the Russian Front, winter 1941/42. For most of Hitler's divisions, the horse carried more supplies than did motorized transport

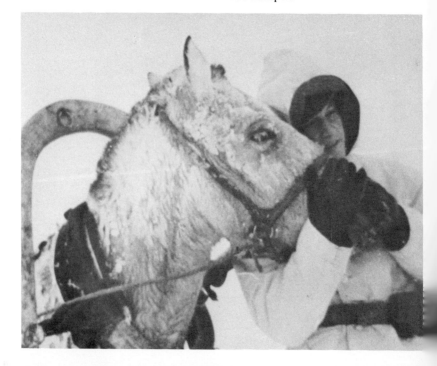

35 *Above:* Stalingrad, February, 1943, the last month of the battle

36 *Below:* Leningrad. The city was under siege from September, 1941 until January, 1944; it never fell

37 A German Panzer IV during the Battle of Kursk, July, 1944

38 An aerial view of the *bocage* country in Normandy which shows why it was ill-suited for armoured warfare

39 The Fuehrer Conference Room, 20 July, 1944, after the unsuccessful attempt on Hitler's life

40 The coast of Grandcamp-les-Bains showing German teller mines fixed to posts planted several hundred feet from the beach. At high tide these were covered by the sea, causing much damage to landing craft

41 Rommel inspecting a panzer artillery unit, France, 1944

42 Falaise, where Field Marshal Model's Army Group B was nearly annihilated in August, 1944

coming down solidly on Hitler's side during the Blomberg-Fritsch crisis. He thus escaped the Brauchitsch purge of 1938 and was in line for a higher post. He assumed command of Army Group 2 at Kassel in February, replacing Ritter von Leeb, who had been forced into retirement.[8]

List was not destined to hold his new post for long. The Anschluss took place on March 12, 1938, and Austria was incorporated into the Third Reich. The occupation forces were commanded by General Fedor von Bock, an arrogant Prussian who quickly offended Austrian sensibilities. A change in command was definitely in order. List, a man with experience in East European affairs and with considerable diplomatic talent, was selected to set up the new Army Group 5, headquartered in Vienna.

From Hitler's point of view, List was a happy choice. He organized Austria into two military districts (XVII and XVIII, at Vienna and Salzburg, respectively). Wehrkreis XVII controlled the two Austrian infantry divisions (the 44th and 45th), while Wehrkreis XVII directed the 2nd and 3rd Mountain divisions. The 4th Light was created from Austrian cavalry units, and the 2nd Panzer – which had accompanied Bock to Austria – remained in Vienna. Like the 4th Light, it came directly under army group control.[9]

List's HQ was temporarily designated 14th Army and earmarked for the invasion of Czechoslovakia in the fall of 1938. After the Munich Accords, he directed the occupation of southern Moravia. By now looked upon as definitely pro-Nazi, he was promoted to colonel general on April 1, 1939, at the age of fifty-nine.[10]

For the invasion of Poland, List's 14th Army occupied the southern flank of the German Army. His four corps (VIII, XVII, XVIII, and XXII) controlled an odd assortment of divisions: 2nd and 5th Panzer, 4th Light, 7th, 8th, 28th, 44th, and 45th Infantry, and 1st, 2nd, and 3rd Mountain – eleven divisions in all. List did a good job of overcoming Polish defenses in the mountains, taking Krakow and Lvov and covering the right flank of the main attack force under Reichenau. After the invasion his HQ was redesignated Frontier Army Command South, and List was simultaneously named Military Government Commander, Krakow.[11] He was relieved of this assignment about a month later, and given command of the newly formed 12th Army for the upcoming invasion of France.

For that invasion, List has six infantry divisions, 1st Mountain Division, and Panzer Group Kleist – five tank divisions under Guderian's XIX and Reinhardt's XLI Motorized Corps.[12] List left the direction of the main armored thrust to Kleist, Guderian, and Reinhardt, and concentrated his energies on bringing up his infantry to secure the "Panzer Corridor" to the English Channel. He moved his forces with such speed that he once more advanced his reputation within the Army.[13] His most famous success in the campaign, however, was a diplomatic one. Hitler, fearful of his too-quick victory, ordered his armored spearhead to halt just after it scored the decisive breakthrough at Sedan, to await the arrival of the infantry. Guderian ignored the order, which led to an angry clash with Kleist on May 17, 1940, during which Guderian resigned his command. He turned his corps over to his senior divisional commander (Lieutenant General Rudolf Veiel of the 2nd Panzer) and was on the point of flying to Army Group A Headquarters when Colonel General von Rundstedt sent him a dispatch. He was to remain where he was; General List was en route to XIX Corps to settle the dispute.

List's solution to the problem was to evade the Fuehrer's order. Corps Headquarters was to remain where it was, he said, but Guderian was allowed to conduct "reconnaissances-in-force" if he wanted to. List knew that Guderian would interpret this order in his own way: it was tantamont to resuming the advance.[14] Guderian kept his command and reached the English Channel on May 20, trapping the main British, French, and Belgian forces to the north.

While the Dunkirk Pocket was being eliminated, List faced the French armies to the south, guarding the Panzer Corridor against a counteroffensive that never came and securing important bridgeheads for the second phase of the operation. For 12th Army, this phase began on June 9. List now controlled III, XIII, XXIII, and XVII Corps plus Panzer Group Guderian (XXXIX Motorized and XLI Motorized Corps) – twelve infantry, four panzer, and three motorized divisions in all.[15]

List had been criticized – and rightly so – for insisting that his infantry divisions secure the bridgeheads across the Aisne River on June 9, before committing the panzer forces. His plan, although successful, led to unnecessary confusion and road congestion and

would have been dangerous had not France already been on the
verge of collapse.[16] Despite his poor initial handling of his armor,
List's men broke the Weygand Line, enveloped the Maginot Line,
and advanced all the way to the Swiss frontier. On July 19, less
than a month after the French capitulated, Siegmund Wilhelm List
was promoted to field marshal.

LIST'S NEXT ASSIGNMENT was in the Balkans, where Greece was at
war with Italy and Mussolini needed help from his German ally. In
February 1941, List skillfully drew up an agreement with the
Bulgarians, allowing German troops to attack Greece's northern
flank from their territory. The Germans were about to launch their
offensive when, during the night of March 26/27, a coup took place
in Yugoslavia. Prince Paul was deposed and replaced by an
anti-Nazi junta under General Richard D. Simovic, the former
commander of the Yugoslav Air Force. List had to quickly revise
his plans to secure his right flank and assist General Baron von
Weichs's 2nd Army in the invasion of Yugoslavia.

In Operation Marita, as the Greek invasion was called, List
faced the Greek 2nd Army (70,000 men) which concentrated in the
strongly fortified 125-mile long Metaxas Line, north and east of
Salonika. Its eastern flank was covered by the Yugoslav 5th Army
and the Greek 20th Infantry Division, screening the Greco-
Yugoslav frontier. Meanwhile, the British were rushing reinforcements to Greece from North Africa. Assembling north of Mount
Olympus, the Australian I Corps consisted of the Australian 6th
and New Zealand 2nd divisions and the 1st Tank Brigade of the
British 2nd Armoured Division, all of which were initially in
reserve. It was in a position to block a German thrust down the
Aliakmon Valley west of Mount Olympus should List succeed in
outflanking the Metaxas Line. To the west of the British, the bulk
of the Greek forces (fourteen divisions) were concentrating against
the Italian 11th Army in Albania. The Yugoslav 3rd Army (four
divisions) was also concentrating on the Albanian border for a joint
Greek-Yugoslav offensive against the Italians.[17] Map 12 shows the
Allied dispositions and List's subsequent attack.

For the invasion of Greece, List had only XL Panzer Corps
(General Georg Stumme), with the 9th Panzer and 73rd Infantry
divisions, plus the reinforced 1st SS Motorized Regiment "Leib-

Map 12

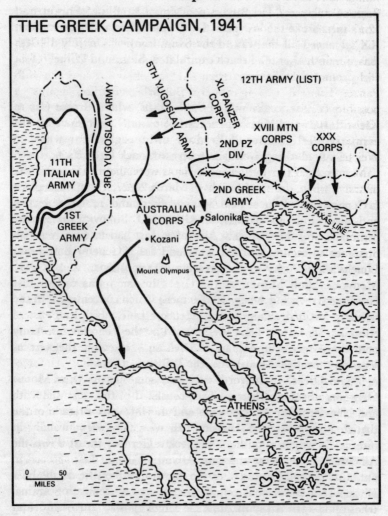

THE GREEK CAMPAIGN, 1941. Breaking through the Yugoslav 5th Army on April 6, Field Marshal Siegmund Wilhelm List was able to outflank the Australian I Corps, cut off the Greek 1st Army, and drive on Athens. Meanwhile, his infantry units took Salonika and compelled the Greek 2nd Army to surrender. By the end of the month Greece had been cleared of Allied forces.

standarte Adolf Hitler"; XVIII Mountain Corps (General Franz Boehme), with the 2nd Panzer, 5th Mountain, 6th Mountain, and 72nd Infantry divisions, plus the 125th Infantry Regiment; and XXX Corps (General Otto Hartmann), with the 50th and 164th Infantry divisions. General Georg Lindemann's L Corps (46th, 76th, and 198th Infantry divisions) was en route, and the 16th Panzer Division was in eastern Bulgaria, guarding against a possible Turkish intervention on the Allies' behalf. Panzer Group Kleist also came under List's control initially, but since it was earmarked for the drive on Belgrade and was soon transferred to Weichs's 2nd Army, it will not be considered here.[18]

Marita was List's masterpiece. He saw at a glance the weak link in the Allied plan was the Yugoslav 5th Army. Not waiting for L Corps to arrive, he struck the Yugoslavs on April 6, before they had time to complete their mobilization. Striking through the Strimon Valley against weak resistance, 2nd Panzer Division took Strumica by nightfall. It then wheeled south, flanking the Metaxas Line while XXX Corps overran western Thrace and XVIII Mountain Corps (minus 2nd Panzer Division) pinned down the Greek 2nd Army and penetrated the Metaxas Line in heavy fighting. When Salonika fell on April 9, the Greek 2nd Army was effectively surrounded. It surrendered the next day. Not wishing to be delayed by prisoners, List released all of the Greek soldiers as soon as they had been disarmed.[19]

Meanwhile, XL Panzer Corps had also broken through the Yugolsav 5th Army. Instead of heading for the Aliakmon Valley, as the Allies anticipated, List ordered XL Panzer to attack through the Monastir Gap for Kozani, further west. This move would put him in a position to outflank the Australian I Corps and encircle the Greek 1st Army in southern Albania. To execute this maneuver, List demanded and received the transfer of the 5th Panzer Division from Panzer Group Kleist. It was assigned to Stumme, whose corps pivoted south, took the Monastir Gap on April 10, and headed for Kozani. The Allies tried to stop them in the hilly terrain near the village of Ptolemais, but were defeated by the 9th Panzer, losing thirty-two tanks and anti-tank guns and several trucks in the process. The Germans lost only two PzKw IVs, a PzKw I, and a PzKw II. Kozani fell the next morning, but the Allies retreated in an orderly manner.[20]

The Greek 1st Army realized its danger as early as April 13 and began evacuating southern Albania, with the Italian 11th Army pursuing them in a very hesitant manner. List was too fast for the Greek infantry, however. The 73rd Infantry Division cut off their retreat through the Pindus Mountains on April 15, and their encirclement was completed on April 20, when the 1st SS Motorized Regiment seized the Metsovon Pass in heavy fighting. The Greek 1st Army surrendered the next day. In recognition of their valor, List ordered that they not be treated as prisoners of war. Officers were permitted to keep their side arms, and the Greek soldiers were allowed to return to their homes as soon as they were disarmed and their units demobilized.[21]

List's terms created an international incident, for he had deliberately acted independently of the Italians. On April 21, an enraged Mussolini contacted Hitler and demanded, in blunt language, that the Greeks be forced to surrender to the Italians also. Mussolini had, after all, lost 63,000 men in his six-month war with the Greeks in Albania and still had 500,000 men in the field. Hitler reluctantly backed down and ordered Jodl to renounce List's actions. The Greeks had to undergo the humiliation of a second surrender ceremony at Salonika on April 23, in which they capitulated to the commander of the Italian 11th Army. Even then the Greek officers were allowed to retain their swords and daggers, despite the objections of the Italians.[22]

The Army was furious at Hitler for renouncing List's terms to save the faces of the Italians. Even Keitel opposed Hitler on this matter, although Foreign Minister von Ribbentrop supported the Fuehrer.[23] Meanwhile, 12th Army fought the battle of Greece to its logical conclusion.

List, operating mainly on captured supplies, quickly regrouped his forces in an attempt to head off and destroy the only major Allied force still intact: the Australian I Corps. General Maitland Wilson, the commander of the British Expeditionary Force in Greece, had recognized his hopeless position, of course, and ordered the evacuation of Greece to begin on April 13. List attempted to cut off their retreat via a panzer thrust at Thermopylae, and an airborne drop of elements of the 2nd Parachute Regiment at the Isthmus of Corinth on April 26, but only succeeded in cutting off rear-guard units. Fifty thousand of the

62,500-man BEF made good their escape to the island of Crete in the eastern Mediteranean. They were, however, compelled to destroy most of their heavy equipment and the tanks of the 1st Tank Brigade, along with some 8,000 vehicles,[24] actions that enabled the German paratroopers to successfully launch an airborne attack on Crete the following month. Meanwhile, Athens fell on April 27, and the fighting ended on April 30.

During the conquest of Greece, List captured 90,000 Yugoslavs, 270,000 Greeks, and more than 12,000 British, Australian, and New Zealand soldiers.[25] His own casualties were 1,100 killed and 4,000 wounded or missing.[26]

After the fall of Athens, 12th Army remained in Greece on occupation duty. Hitler appointed List Commander-in-Chief, South-east, on June 10, 1941, a post he held until October 15, when he apparently fell ill and was replaced by General of Engineers Walter Kuntze,[27] who was later succeeded by Colonel General Alexander Loehr (1942–43) and Field Marshal von Weichs (1943–45). Field Marshal List was without a command for nine months. During that period he investigated the situation on the German Arctic front in Lapland, Finland, and Norway, and made a number of far-reaching recommendations concerning coastal defense construction, the strengthening of the coastal artillery defenses, and the improvement of inter-service communications.[28]

LIST'S FINAL CAMPAIGN began in late June 1942 when, as we have seen (chapter 6) Hitler divided Army Group South into Army Groups A and B, and sent them off in divergent directions. List took over the newly formed Headquarters, Army Group A, on June 26, two weeks before it became operational on July 9. Initially it consisted of 11th Army (Colonel General von Manstein), 4th Panzer Army (Colonel General Hoth), 1st Panzer Army (Colonel General von Kleist), and 17th Army (Colonel General Richard Ruoff). List's first mission was to seize Rostov, after which he was instructed to occupy the entire eastern coast of the Black Sea (thus eliminating the Soviet Black Sea Fleet), seize the Caucasus oil fields (especially Maikop and Grozny), and advance to Baku, the oil city on the western coast of the Caspian Sea.[29] Meanwhile, 11th Army was to capture Sevastopol, the Soviet naval fortress on the southwestern tip of the Crimean peninsula that had been under siege since October 1941, while Army Group B (under Colonel General von Weichs) was to advance on the Volga and Stalingrad.

List's forces were not as impressive as they initially appear, for he had to contend with both the vast spaces of Russia and Hitler's strategy, which had no focus anywhere. Sevastopol fell on July 2, but rather than reinforce List or Weichs, the Fuehrer sent 11th Army to Army Group North, with the idea of attacking Leningrad. List stormed Rostov on July 23 and took 240,000 prisoners,[30] but a week later had to hand 4th Panzer Army (minus General Baron Geyr von Schweppenburg's XL Panzer Corps) over to Army Group B for its thrust on the Volga.[31] Table 3 shows List's Order of Battle as of August 12.

Table 3

ORDER OF BATTLE ARMY GROUP A

Army Detachment Ruoff (HQ, 17th Army)
> 3rd Rumanian Army (General Dumitrescu): three Rumanian cavalry divisions and 298th German Infantry division
> V Corps: 9th, 73rd, 125th, 198th, Infantry divisions

1st Panzer Army (Kleist)
> XLIX Mountain Corps: 1st and 4th Mountain divisions and 2nd Rumanian Mountain division
> LVII Panzer Corps: 5th SS Motorized division and the Slovak Security division
> III Panzer Corps: 16th Motorized and 19th Panzer divisions
> XLIV Corps: 97th and 101st Jaeger divisions
> XL Panzer Corps: 3rd and 23rd Panzer divisions
> LII Corps: 111th and 370th Infantry divisions

Rear Area Command A: 444th and 454th Security divisions and 4th Security Regiment

Army Group Reserve: Grossdeutschland Motorized division and the Italian Tridentina Infantry division

En Route to Army Group A: Italian Alpine Corps (two divisions) and 13th Rumanian Infantry division

TOTAL STRENGTH: nineteen German divisions (six of them mobile) plus nine foreign divisions.

SOURCE: *Kriegstagebuch des OKW,* Volume II, p. 1378.

List was "unenthusiastic" about his mission. He had fewer than four hundred tanks and faced two full Soviet fronts (army groups), with two more in reserve. It was more than seven hundred miles from Rostov to Baku, and List's frontage was eight hundred miles long. Several rivers lay in his path, the steppe beyond them was virtually waterless, the terrain was difficult, the Russians had air superiority, and his vehicles were short on fuel before the advance began. To make matters worse, the Soviet leadership had abandoned its 1941 practice of trying to hold everywhere; after Rostov, the Soviets continued to resist fiercely, but fell back quickly when threatened with encirclement.[32]

The Caucasus offensive began on July 25, 1942. Army Group A, with Ruoff on the left and Kleist on the right, crossed the lower reaches of the Don and advanced swiftly to the northern edge of the mountains. In temperatures of 100 degrees Fahrenheit, the infantry covered up to thirty miles a day at what General Plocher called "an incredibly fast pace," and soon established a bridgehead across the Kuban River. On August 10 they took Krasnodar, the capital of the Kuban region. That same day the panzers rolled into Maikop, the center of the western Caucasus oil district, only to find the oil installations in flames. They were now in Asia. On August 22, a mountain detachment raised the Reich battle flag over the 18,481-foot summit of Mount Elbrus in the Caucasus. The Novorrossiysk naval base and the Taman peninsula fell on September 6, the same day 1st Panzer Army crossed the Terek River in heavy fighting and advanced along the northern foothills of the Caucasus toward the Groznyy oil center.[33]

Army Group A, however, had to slow its advance considerably in late August and was forced to go over to the defensive in early September due to heavy Soviet resistance and a lack of supplies. General Kurt von Tippelskirch later wrote: "Supply routes had become so long that the supply columns used up virtually all the fuel they could carry in order to cover the long distances. Finally, the paradoxical situation came about that camel caravans had to be pressed into service for transportation of fuel supplies."[34]

Hitler summoned List to Vinnitsa on August 31 and was very upset when he discovered that List had brought only an unmarked small-scale map (1:1,000,000 scale) with him. Hitler ignored the fact that he himself had expressly forbidden generals to carry marked maps with them on airplane flights. Hitler maintained a façade of friendliness and understanding in front of List, and even approved his plans to continue the advance across the Terek to the Groznyy oilfields; but as soon as the field marshal left he flew into a tirade against him. He also violently reprimanded Keitel and Halder for suggesting List's appointment in the first place.[35]

Hitler had been reluctant to give List the army group from the outset, because he had never liked him. In early September he sent Jodl to the Caucasus sector to investigate List's conduct of operations. When Jodl returned on September 7 and said, in effect, that the field marshal was doing all that could be done, Hitler turned on him violently. Much to the Fuehrer's surprise, Jodl replied in the same vein. Hitler was so furious that he decided to replace Jodl with Paulus as soon as the Battle of Stalingrad ended, and even considered court-martialling him. He also considered replacing Keitel with Kesselring, refused to eat with Jodl or Keitel again, as noted earlier, and would not shake hands with either of them for months. Because of his support for List, Colonel General Franz Halder, the Chief of the General Staff of the Army, was sacked and ended the war in a concentration camp.

Nothing, of course, could save List. Hitler sent Keitel to his HQ to obtain his resignation, which was dated September 9, 1942. Hitler temporarily assumed the role of Commander-in-Chief of Army Group A himself. Lieutenant General Hans von Greiffenberg, List's Chief of Staff since the Balkans campaign, remained in the field as Hitler's executive officer.[36] Eventually Kleist was given the vacant command.

List retired into obscurity and was never re-employed. Arrested in 1945, he was tried by the American Military Tribunal at Nuremberg as a minor war criminal and, in February 1948, was sentenced to life imprisonment, chiefly for offenses committed in the Balkans and Greece. He was pardoned and released at Christmas 1952 and retired quietly. He died at Garminsch on June 18, 1971, at the age of ninety-one.[37]

ALTHOUGH ONE OF the least famous of Hitler's military leaders, Field Marshal Siegmund Wilhelm List must be rated very highly by any impartial military observer. Although an infantryman, he handled panzer formations very well, except for his attack on the Aisne on

June 9, 1940. He performed very well in Poland and France and brilliantly in Yugoslavia and Greece. He was admired by even the most difficult subordinates, including Guderian and Rommel, both of whom spoke highly of him. He undoubtedly had a talent for diplomacy, and no one exceeded his ability for getting the maximum amount of speed out of his infantry formations, as he proved in all of his campaigns but especially in covering the Panzer Corridor in 1940 and in the Caucasus campaign. We do not know how effectively he would have performed in defensive operations, because he never conducted a retreat. It is my opinion that this capable Bavarian is perhaps the most neglected and underrated of all of Hitler's field marshals.

10

Baron Maximilian von Weichs

BORN AT DESSAU, Anhalt, on November 12, 1881, Baron von Weichs zur Glon was a devout south German Catholic his entire life. At the age of eighteen he joined the 2nd Bavarian Heavy Cavalry Regiment as a *Fahnenjunker* on July 15, 1900, and was associated with the cavalry for most of his career. Commissioned second lieutenant on March 9, 1902, he was named adjutant of his regiment in early 1908. He spent two years on the staff of the School of Cavalry (1908–10), before being assigned to the War Academy in 1910, where he did his General Staff training. Weichs was promoted to first lieutenant in 1911 and captain of cavalry (*Rittmeister*) in early 1914. He was with the Bavarian Cavalry Division when the war broke out and served as a brigade adjutant. Later he served as a General Staff officer with the 5th Infantry Division (1915–17) and with II Corps (1917–20).[1]

Weichs was selected for the 4,000-man Officer Corps in the Reichsheer following World War I. He returned to the cavalry in 1920, working as Operations Officer of the 3rd Cavalry Division at Weimar (1920–22) and later joined the 18th Cavalry Regiment, probably as a squadron commander (1922–25). From February 1925 to October 1927, he was on the staff of the Infantry School, after which he returned to the 18th Cavalry as second-in-command. He was regimental commander from February 1, 1928, to March 1, 1930, after which he was General Staff Officer to the 1st Cavalry Division at Frankfurt an der Oder. He was promoted to major in 1923, lieutenant colonel in 1928, and full colonel in 1930.[2]

Baron von Weichs was married on July 28, 1928, at the relatively advanced age of forty-six. It seems to have made little impact on his habits or his career. He was a solid professional soldier who opposed the introduction of politics into the service, but was certainly not the stuff of which coups are made. Colonel von Weichs was Ia (Operations Officer) to another Catholic, Ritter Wilhelm von Leeb, the commander of Army Group 2 at Kassel, when Hitler rose to power in January 1933.[3] Unlike Leeb, Weichs was a non-Nazi, rather than an anti-Nazi, and he seems to have got along well enough with Hitler and the Party; in fact, he gradually became something of a Nazi sympathizer, despite his professionalism and his aristocratic and religious background, because he approved of Hitler's successful programs for ending unemployment and expanding the Army.

Meanwhile, Weich's advancement continued. He was named Infantry Commander III and Deputy Commander of the 3rd Infantry Division in Berlin in February 1933 and was promoted to major general effective April 1, 1933. In December 1933 he received what, for him, must have been a dream-fulfilling assignment: he was appointed commander of the 3rd Cavalry Division at Weimar. He held this post until October 15, 1935, when he was named commander of the 1st Panzer Division at Weimar. Baron von Weichs was acting commander of Wehrkreis VII in 1936, while Reichenau was away in China, and on October 12, 1937, was named commander of Wehrkreis XIII at Nuremberg. Here he was involved in staging the Nuremberg Rallies of the Nazi Party, where he described himself as a cross between a drill sergeant and a film director. Perhaps because of this service he escaped the Brauchitsch purges of 1938. He was promoted to lieutenant general in 1935 and general of cavalry on October 1, 1936.[4]

General Maximilian von Weichs took the primary component of Wehrkreis XIII to the field in August 1939, as XIII Corps (the deputy component remained in Nuremberg as Wehrkreis XIII under the command of General Franz Kress von Kressenstein). In Poland, Weichs controlled the 10th and 17th Infantry divisions under 8th Army, Army Group South, and played a minor role in the conquest of the Polish Plain, in the encirclement of the Poznan, Lodz, and Pomorze armies at Kutno, and in the subsequent 8th Army advance on Warsaw.[5] By September 25 he was already inside the outer fortifications on the southwestern side of the Polish capital. The next day, supported by a heavy artillery bombardment, his attacks so shook the Poles that the garrison commander, General Rommel, asked for an armistice. Warsaw surrendered the following morning.[6]

After his successes in Poland, Weichs returned to Germany and was given command of the 2nd (formerly 8th) Army on October 29, 1939, replacing Colonel General Johannes Blaskowitz, who remained in Poland as Commander-in-Chief, East.[7] Initially in Army Group A's reserve, Weichs's army did not take part in the first phase of the French campaign, which ended with the fall of Dunkirk on June 4, 1940.[8] During the second phase, which was essentially a mopping-up operation, he directed the nine infantry divisions of VI, XXVI, and IX Corps, again in a secondary role.[9] After the French surrendered, Weichs received his Knights' Cross and was promoted to colonel general in the omnibus promotions of July 19, 1940.[10] His HQ was then transferred to Munich, where it was responsible for training divisions stationed in southern Germany and the Protectorate of Bohemia and Moravia (most of what was once Czechoslovakia).[11]

Early in the spring of 1941, Weichs received his first independent command: he and his headquarters were sent to Graz, Austria, to direct the invasion of northern Yugoslavia, following the ousting of pro-Nazi Prince Paul in a surprise coup on the night of March 26/27. For this operation he controlled four corps, consisting of four infantry and two panzer divisions, plus one frontier guard, one mountain, one light, and one motorized division. His order of battle is shown in Table 4.[12]

Since the invasion was a hasty operation, the infantry divisions of LII Corps did not arrive in time for the initial assault. Weichs did not need them in any case. His XLIX Mountain and LI corps quickly broke through the Yugoslav frontier defenses on April 6, 1941 – the first day of the invasion – and converged on the Croatian capital of Zagreb, which fell on April 11. The Yugoslav 4th Army, which consisted largely of Croats who felt no loyalty to the

Table 4

ORDER OF BATTLE, 2nd ARMY YUGOSLAVIA, 1941

2nd Army: Colonel General Baron Maximilian von Weichs
XLIX Mountain Corps: General Ludwig Kuebler
    1st Mountain Division
    538th Frontier Guard Division
LI Corps: General Hans Reinhardt
    101st Light Division
    132nd Infantry Division
    183rd Infantry Division
LII Corps: General Kurt von Briesen
    79th Infantry Division
    125th Infantry Division
XLVI Panzer Corps: General Heinrich von Vietinghoff
    8th Panzer Division
    14th Panzer Division
    16th Motorized Division
1st Panzer Group: Colonel General Ewald von Kleist*
    XIV Panzer Corps: General Gustav von Wietersheim
        5th Panzer Division
        11th Panzer Division
        294th Infantry Division
        4th Mountain Division
    XI Corps: General Joachim von Kortzfleisch
        60th Motorized Infantry Division
        Miscellaneous units

SOURCE: DA *Pam 20–260*, pp. 39–41

Belgrade government, disintegrated quickly. The German infantry was delayed more by high water and snowstorms than by the Yugoslavs. Weichs then moved his HQ to Zagreb and directed the pursuit to Sarajevo, where the Yugoslav 2nd Army surrendered to him on April 15. Meanwhile, his XLVI Panzer Corps wheeled

---

*Attached to 2nd Army on April 13.

southwest down the Sava River Valley and, along with the independent XLI Panzer Corps and the XIV Panzer Corps of Panzer
Group Kleist (part of List's 12th Army), converged on Belgrade,
which fell on April 13. Panzer Group Kleist was then placed under
Weichs's control for the rest of the campaign (see Map 8).[13]

The Yugoslavs asked for an armistice late on April 14, and OKH
deputized Weichs to conduct the surrender negotiations. The
Yugoslavs capitulated unconditionally at noon at April 18, just
twelve days after the campaign began. During the offensive, the
Germans (mainly 2nd Army) suffered a total of only 558 casualties,
of which 151 were killed. They took 254,000 prisoners, excluding
Croatians, Volksdeutsch, Hungarians, and Bulgarians living in
Yugoslavia. These were quickly released.[14]

SECOND ARMY HEADQUARTERS was earmarked for the invasion of
the Soviet Union but did not take part in the initial attack on June
22, 1941. As of July 4, part of it was still en route to Russia,
although it was officially part of Army Group Center's reserve as
early as June 27.[15] On June 30, Kluge's 4th Army Headquarters
temporarily took over the direction of the 3rd and 4th Panzer
groups then advancing on the Dnieper and Weichs's HQ assumed
control of the infantry divisions formerly belonging to 4th Army.[16]
He took part in the clearing of the Bialystok Pocket (along with
Strauss's 9th Army). The Pocket was surrounded on July 3. By July
8 it had yielded 290,000 prisoners, 2,500 tanks, and 1,500 guns –
the equivalent of twenty-two rifle divisions, seven tank divisions,
and six mechanized brigades.[17]

Weichs hurried his infantry forward after the panzers and, in the
latter part of August, attacked the Soviet Central Front at Gomel,
in conjunction with Geyr von Schweppenburg's XXIV Panzer
Corps of Guderian's 2nd Panzer Group. When this battle ended on
August 24, another 84,000 Soviet troops marched off to prisoner-
of-war camps.[18] Thereafter, Weichs remained on the southern
flank of Army Group Center. With XIII and XLIII corps and
Corps Command XXXV (seven infantry divisions), he supported
Guderian's thrust behind the Russian armies defending Kiev,
where another 667,000 prisoners were taken.[19] Again teamed with
Guderian, Weichs played a major role in the destruction of the
Soviet 3rd, 13th, and 15th armies at Bryansk, a battle of encirclement that lasted from September 30 to October 17.[20]

Maximilian von Weichs was now sixty years old and the strain of command began to tell on him. He fell ill in November 1941, shortly after the Russian winter began, and was temporarily replaced by General Rudolf Schmidt. When he returned to duty in mid-January 1942, his 2nd Army was on the northern wing of Army Group South. He helped turn back the Russian winter offensive between Orel and Kursk, although his forces certainly did not bear the brunt of the fighting.[21]

In late June 1942, when Hitler launched his summer offensive, the Baron was in command of Group Weichs, a temporary force that included his own 2nd Army, as well as 4th Panzer Army (Hoth) and the Hungarian 2nd Army (General Jany). As such, he delivered Field Marshal von Bock's ill-fated attack on Voronezh in early July. Although he eventually took the city (on July 8, along with 28,000 prisoners and 1,000 tanks),[22] the delay so infuriated Hitler that he relieved Bock of his command. Army Group South was divided at this time, and Weichs was given command of Army Group B. It was to be his most important and fateful assignment.

WEICHS'S ARMY GROUP B initially included the German 2nd and 6th armies, as well as the Hungarian 2nd, Italian 8th, and Rumanian 3rd armies, the latter of which was still in the process of forming.[23] Second Army, without any motorized divisions, had to be left in the Voronezh sector. As a result of his shortage of reliable German troops, Weichs could not clear the Don until the end of July, and even then the Soviets still held three bridgeheads. Hitler had tremendously complicated his problems by sending Army Group A (4th Panzer, 17th, and 1st Panzer armies) off to the south, toward Rostov and the Caucasus. The German supply and transport echelons simply could not provide for both, so Hitler gave priority to Army Group A and even stripped Weichs of half of his motorized transport. Short of fuel and ammunition, Weichs could not send 6th Army against the Kalach bridgehead until August 7. This battle ended on August 11 with the destruction of most of the Soviet 1st Tank and 62nd armies. By August 18 Paulus's 6th Army had bridgeheads across the Don, but was too exhausted and did not have the fuel to make the thirty-five-mile thrust to Stalingrad.[24]

By dividing his offensive into two wings. Hitler deprived both of them of the strength necessary to succeed. Now he further dissipated his strength by breaking up 4th Panzer Army. He transferred XXIV Panzer Corps to 6th Army, XL Panzer Corps to Army Group A, and the Grossdeutschland Motorized Division to France, leaving General Hoth with only the XLVIII Panzer Corps (one panzer and one motorized division), IV Corps (two infantry divisions), and the Rumanian VI Corps (two Rumanian divisions). Hitler then ordered 6th Army (with VIII, XIV Panzer, XVII, XXIV Panzer and LI corps) to advance on the Volga and Stalingrad.[25] Meanwhile Hoth, with what was left of 4th Panzer Army, was assigned to Army Group B and ordered to advance on the city from the south.

The XIV Panzer Corps reached the outskirts of Stalingrad on August 23, 1942, and the battle for the city began. It attracted units like a magnet. Hitler, changing his focus once again, became obsessed with taking the city. Stalin, on the other hand, was perfectly content to fight a battle of attrition. His recruiting class of 1925 was 1,400,000 men; Hitler could muster only about 500,000 replacements from that class.[26]

While the 6th Army exhausted itself in heavy street fighting, Weichs had the task of protecting its exposed flanks. To do this, he committed his foreign armies, despite the fact that he was concerned about their ability to withstand a determined Soviet attack. From north to south, along the Don and Volga, his order of battle was 2nd Army, Hungarian 2nd Army, Italian 8th Army, Rumanian 3rd Army, 6th Army, 4th Panzer Army, and Rumanian 4th Army. As early as October 29, Weichs was calling attention to the threat on his southern flank.[27]

OKH was not concerned about Weichs's position, for its Eastern Intelligence Branch was predicting that the Russians would eventually attempt an offensive – but the focus would be against Kluge's Army Group Center, not Army Group B. Weichs disagreed and was especially worried about the Soviet bridgehead across the Don at Serafimovich, but on October 31 the Intelligence Branch predicted local attacks only. Hitler, for once, was more realistic. On October 26 he ordered some of the newly formed Luftwaffe Field divisions to the Don above Stalingrad, to stiffen the defenses of the Italians, Hungarians, and Rumanians. He became more worried on November 2, when aerial reconnaissance photographs revealed several new bridges over the Don near Serafimovich. Two days

Map 13

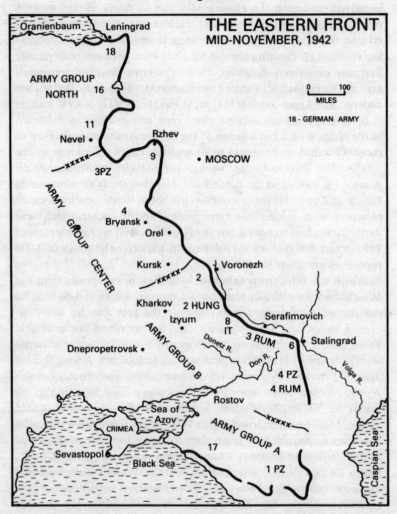

THE EASTERN FRONT, MID-NOVEMBER 1942. On the eve of the Stalingrad encirclement, Germany's armies in Russia held an over-extended line tailing off to the east. Hitler had to depend on unreliable and ill-equipped foreign armies to hold critical sectors, and some sectors were not occupied at all. Neither Army Group B, OKH, or OKW had significant reserves.

later he ordered the 6th Panzer Division and two infantry divisions be transferred from the English Channel to Army Group B, as a reserve behind the Italian 8th and Rumanian 3rd armies. It would take them approximately five weeks to complete their refitting and arrive in southern Russia. Hitler, however, did not expect the Russians to attack until early December; the reinforcements should arrive just in time.[28] Map 13 shows the German situation on the Eastern Front in mid-November, 1942.

By the second week in November, Weichs had identified elements of the Russian 5th Tank Army at the Serafimovich bridgehead and concluded that there would definitely be a major offensive in the zone of the Rumanian 3rd Army and probably against the 4th Panzer Army as well. All of his German reserves had been committed at Stalingrad, so he decided to create a new one under Headquarters, XLVIII Panzer Corps (Lieutenant General Ferdinand Heim). He shifted the weak 22nd Panzer Division from behind the Italian 8th Army to the XLVIII Panzer, which he posted behind the Rumanian 3rd Army. He also gave Heim the Rumanian 1st Armored Division and considered transferring the 4th Panzer Army's 29th Motorized Division to him as well but did not, because he expected an offensive in Hoth's sector also.[29]

Weichs's efforts were really inadequate, because Army Group B seemed more concerned with building up 6th Army for a last push in Stalingrad than with strengthening its endangered flanks. This "push" began on November 11 and had failed with heavy casualties by November 18. Meanwhile, the Soviets concentrated the 5th Tank, 1st Guards, and 21st armies against the Rumanian 3rd Army. Fifth Tank alone had six rifle divisions, two tank corps, and a cavalry corps, plus hundreds of artillery, anti-aircraft, mortar and rocket-launcher regiments.[30] On the forty-mile sector they had over half a million men, supported by 900 new T-34 tanks, 230 field artillery regiments, and 115 rocket-launcher regiments – the greatest concentration of firepower yet achieved on the Eastern Front. They also concentrated the 57th, 51st, and 64th armies against the weak 4th Panzer and Rumanian 4th armies on Weichs's southern flank.[31] In all, well over a million Soviet troops faced about 250,000 German and 250,000 unreliable Axis troops in the Stalingrad sector.[32]

Behind the Rumanian 3rd Army, the 22nd Panzer Division was

no more than a regiment. It had only forty-six tanks, of which thirty-eight were in running order.[33] The Rumanian 1st Armored Division had only ninety-two tanks and they were obsolete T-38 Czech models weighing about nine tons – absolutely useless against the twenty-six-ton Soviet vehicles.[34] The Russians waited patiently for 6th Army to bleed itself white at Stalingrad, for the ground to freeze solid, and for the British and Americans to land in French North Africa, in Rommel's rear, which they did on November 9. Hitler obligingly committed his strategic reserve here and in Vichy France, just as the Soviets hoped he would. Then, at 7:20 A.M. on November 19, the Russians struck the Rumanian 3rd Army with a massive artillery bombardment. An hour and a half later, the infantry attacked. Showing new sophistication, the ground troops massed on narrow frontages and began opening gaps for the tanks. The 5th Tank Army alone had committed two tank corps and a mechanized corps (approximately 550 tanks and 37,000 men) to the exploitation. The Rumanians quickly collapsed. Weichs had hoped that they would delay the Russians long enough for XLVIII Panzer Corps to arrive and counterattack, but they fell apart immediately.[35]

Hoth, whose 4th Panzer Army (four German divisions) was intermixed with the Rumanian 4th Army, was also in serious trouble. Attacked by three reinforced Soviet armies, he asked permission to retreat. Weichs rejected his appeal, remarking that if the Rumanians started to retreat, no one would be able to stop them.[36] Map 14 shows the encirclement of Stalingrad.

That night Weichs ordered Paulus to halt operations against the last Russian bridgeheads in Stalingrad. He instructed him to take three panzer divisions and an infantry division out of Stalingrad, place them under XIV Panzer Corps, and counterattack. This they did the following day and checked the Soviet inner wing; however, due to fuel shortages and vastly superior Russian strength, they were unable to contest the more important Soviet outer envelopment.

November 20 was the decisive day of the battle. Of the Rumanian 3rd Army, only General Mihail Lascar's division continued to resist, and did so courageously. Heim counterattacked with his panzer corps and saved Lascar and 6,000 of his men; then he, too, was overwhelmed. Soon Heim was not even able to make contact

Map 14

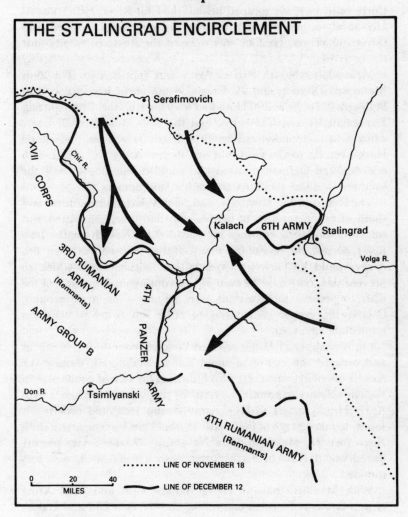

THE STALINGRAD ENCIRCLEMENT

Serafimovich

XVII CORPS

Chir R.

Kalach   6TH ARMY   Stalingrad

Volga R.

3RD RUMANIAN ARMY (Remnants)

4TH PANZER ARMY

ARMY GROUP B

Don R.   Tsimlyanski

4TH RUMANIAN ARMY (Remnants)

0   20   40
MILES

········· LINE OF NOVEMBER 18

▬▬▬ LINE OF DECEMBER 12

THE STALINGRAD ENCIRCLEMENT, NOVEMBER 1942.
Breaking through the 3rd and 4th Rumanian armies and the weak 4th
Panzer Army on November 19 and 20, 1942, the Russians encircled
6th Army in the Stalingrad area on November 22. Field Marshal
Erich von Manstein's newly activated Army Group Don took charge
of the sector from Weichs's Army Group B on November 27.

with his two divisions. In the end, the remnants of XLVIII Panzer Corps only narrowly escaped behind the Chir River. Hitler was so furious at its performance that he ordered Heim arrested and thrown in prison. He had only delayed the Russians twenty-four hours at best.[37]

Meanwhile, the 4th Panzer Army was split in two. The 29th Motorized Division and IV Corps on the north were trapped in Stalingrad. To the south, Hoth had only his HQ, the disintegrating Rumanian VI and VII corps, and the 16th Motorized Division, which was surrounded at Khalkuta. It cut its way out and joined Hoth's retreat to the west, but 4th Panzer Army was reduced to one depleted German division and could do nothing to halt the southern wing of the Russian double envelopment.[38]

The Russians had now broken through Weichs's front north and south of 6th Army. All of his reserves had been committed and smashed. Both Soviet wings now headed for Kalach on the Don River, deep in the rear of 6th Army. If they reached this town, 6th Army would be encircled. Weichs had nothing with which to prevent this, nor could he even form a continuous front west of the Chir to prevent the Russians from gaining even more ground. Clearly the proper course was to order 6th Army to stage an immediate breakout.

On November 21 Hitler rejected Weich's request for a breakout and ordered 6th Army to stand fast at Stalingrad, despite the danger of encirclement. He also indicated his lack of confidence in Weichs's ability to handle the crisis by upgrading Manstein's 11th Army Headquarters to HQ, Army Group Don, and ordering it south, to take charge of the battle. It would not become active until November 27. Meanwhile, on November 22, the Soviet pincers linked up at Kalach. Sixth Army, with 230,000 men, was surrounded.

With Manstein now in charge on the Chir and Don, Army Group B was reduced to controlling the German 2nd and Italian 8th armies, between Army Groups Center and Don. Weichs's force was extremely weak because the Italians were considered even less reliable than the Rumanians had been, and 2nd Army had virtually no mobile units. On December 20, Weichs's right wing was attacked, and the Italian Celere and Sforzesca divisions collapsed, as did the two Rumanian divisions on Manstein's left. OKH transferred XXX Corps (General Maximilian Fretter-Pico) from Army Group North to plug the hole and, significantly, placed it under the command of Manstein.[39] The Russians continued to attack Army Group B for the next seven weeks. The Italian 8th Army disintegrated altogether.

On January 12, 1943, Weichs signaled Hitler that he had only seven divisions left to hold his two-hundred-mile front. He could not stop the Russian advance westward, he said, and 2nd Army was in danger of being encircled.[40] One full-strength division could be expected to hold only six miles of frontage against a determined attack, and Weichs's understrength units were defending an average of twenty-eight miles. By November 21 the gap between Manstein and Weichs was two hundred miles, and the remnants of Army Group B were retreating through deep snow toward the Aydar River forty miles to the west. Brilliantly resupplied by aircraft, the Soviets broke this line on January 25, 1943. Two days later, two of 2nd Army's three corps were surrounded by a Soviet double envelopment west of Voronezh, and the third was smashed but managed to escape to the north, behind Army Group Center's front.[41] General Hans von Salmuth, the commander of 2nd Army, led his men in a breakout from the Voronezh Pocket, and most of them escaped after a 120-mile forced march to Rylsk, in temperatures of minus 13 degrees Fahrenheit. Almost all of their heavy equipment was lost, however.[42] Meanwhile, Weichs continued to do his best to shield the left flank of Army Group Don, but he had only one division left to do it with.[43]

Despite his promotion to field marshal on February 1, 1943 (the day Paulus surrendered), Weichs had clearly failed as an army group commander on the Eastern Front. On February 14 his headquarters was taken out of the chain of command. The remnants of his forces were distributed between Army Groups Center and Don. Weichs's headquarters was finally disbanded on July 10, 1943, and he was transferred to Fuehrer Reserve.[44]

BARON MAXIMILIAN VON Weichs's retirement was extremely short-lived. On July 26, 1943, following the Allied landings in Sicily, he was named Commander-in-Chief, Southeast, and C-in-C, Army Group F, controlling all the Axis forces in the Balkans. Here he had a number of serious problems to deal with: the guerrilla movement;

the possibility of an Italian defection, which was expected any day; and the possibility of Allied landings in the Balkans.[45]

Weichs's forces (as of December 26) consisted of: Army Group E (under Luftwaffe Colonel General Alexander Loehr) in Greece and the offshore islands, with two light divisions, one air landing division, one Luftwaffe Field, one motorized SS Police division and three Bulgarian divisions; the 2nd Panzer Army (General Dr. Lothar Rendulic) in Serbia and Croatia, with nine infantry divisions, three light divisions, two mountain divisions (one of them SS), and the 1st Cossack Cavalry Division; plus four Bulgarian infantry divisions in Serbia, under the Military Commander Southeast.[46] Except for the 1st Mountain and 22nd Air Landing divisions, none of Weichs's divisions was first-rate. Most of them were under-strength and many consisted of older troops or Volksdeutsche.

When Italy defected on September 8, 1943, it had thirty-one divisions (380,000 men) in the Balkans. Some German planners suggested that Hitler abandon the southern Balkans, but he refused and with good reason: all of Germany's chromium, 60 percent of its bauxite, 24 percent of its antimony, more than half of its oil, and 21 percent of its copper came from the Balkans.[47]

Many people feared that the Italian troops would go over to the guerrillas, and some did, but most were more afraid of partisan vengeance than of the Germans. The Brennero Division declared itself available to continue the war on the side of the Third Reich, while most simply surrendered and were incorporated in labor battalions. On the other hand, the entire Firenze Division (its commander included) went over to the guerrillas in Albania. The Acqui Division (General Gandin) held the island of Cephalonia against the Germans until September 22, when it finally ran out of ammunition. Most of its survivors were shot after they surrendered. The Bergamo Division (General Cigala-Fulgosi) held Spalato for nineteen days against the 7th SS Mountain Division "Prinz Eugen", which slaughtered it. Weichs's forces, almost none of which were motorized, did a great deal of marching in September, but they were successful in minimizing the damage caused by the Italian defection. Large sections of the Balkan peninsula's mountainous interior were lost to the guerrillas because Weichs did not have enough troops to post garrisons everywhere with the Italians gone; however, the vital raw materials continued to flow to Germany unabated.[48]

To deal with the partisan movements, Weichs set up mobile armored-car patrols and raiding detachments (*Jagdkommandos*) consisting of younger troops, mostly veterans of the Eastern Front. Weichs was also helped by the C-in-C, South (Field Marshal Kesselring), who turned over most of the tanks and armored vehicles captured in Italy. These were too poor to be used against the well-equipped Western Allies, but were easily a match for Tito's ill-equipped guerrillas in Yugoslavia.[49]

Weichs conducted three major anti-partisan operations in late 1943, killing, wounding, or capturing about 12,000 of Tito's 90,000 men. When the partisans killed 29 German soldiers (including a Knights' Cross holder) on the island of Korcula, Weichs retaliated by executing 220 prisoners. Later, in May 1944, when Major General Krech, the commander of the 41st Fortress Division, was murdered by Greek Communists, Weichs's men shot 325 Communist suspects. Later that month, in Operation Roesselsprung, Weichs's mobile forces routed Tito's forces, inflicting 6,000 casualties on them, and forced the partisan leader himself to flee to the island of Vis, which was held by British troops.[50] Although never able to completely neutralize the guerrillas, Baron von Weichs succeeded in making their lives miserable, and he was certainly more successful in the Balkans than he had been as an army group commander in southern Russia.

THE SOVIETS OVERRAN Rumania in August 1944, and Bulgaria defected to the Russians on August 24. The rear of Army Group F was now thoroughly exposed. Accordingly, Weichs began evacuating the Balkans, except for about 20,000 troops on the Greek islands who could not be evacuated due to a shortage of boats. British forces, including the 2nd Airborne Division, joined the Greek partisans and tried to cut off the retreat of Army Group E in the Peloponnese, but were unsuccessful. General Felmy, the commander of LXVIII Corps, handed Athens over to its mayor on October 4. Weichs's men left Greece with little loss or delay.[51]

Weichs managed to maintain a continuous front as he executed a skilful, step-by-step retreat in the face of partisans, British forces, and the Soviet and Bulgarian armies. The Russians crossed the Danube near Turnu Severin on October 1, pushing back Friedrich Wilhelm Mueller's XXXIV Corps (1st Mountain and 7th SS Mountain divisions), and the Bulgarians took Nis on October 14, cutting Army Group E's best escape route. General Loehr was thus forced to execute a rather tricky detour over difficult terrain near the Adriatic coast. Tito tried to delay him long enough for the Russians to penetrate to the Adriatic and cut him off, but was unsuccessful.[52]

On October 20, the Red Army and a corps of Tito's partisans took Belgrade from the rear-guards of Army Group F's Army Detachment Felber; however, Field Marshal Weichs had already succeeded in extricating almost all of his troops.[53] Army Group F had escaped the Balkan peninsula and, by January 20, 1945 was fighting in Hungary.

Weichs was ordered to transfer 2nd Panzer Army to Army Group South (formerly South Ukraine) in early December 1944.[54] The few second-rate divisions he controlled hardly justified the existence of his two army group headquarters (E and F). Colonel General Heinz Guderian, the Chief of the General Staff of the Army, wanted to transfer both Weichs and his headquarters to eastern Germany – to defend Berlin and to organize the entire German national defense behind the Eastern Front, but Hitler rejected the idea on January 24, 1945, after Colonel General Jodl made a sneering remark about Weichs's deep religious beliefs. The Fuehrer gave both important tasks to an absolutely unqualified commander: Heinrich Himmler.[55] Possibly as a consolation prize, Weichs was awarded the Oak Leaves to the Knights' Cross on February 5. His superfluous headquarters was finally dissolved on March 22, his staff was incorporated into HQ, Army Group Vistula, and he was sent into retirement. After the fall of the Third Reich, Weichs was held for a time as a prisoner of war but fell seriously ill and was released from captivity in 1947. Almost alone of the surviving field marshals, Weichs was never put on trial as a war criminal. After his release he lived quietly in retirement in West Germany. He died in Roesberg-Cologne on September 27, 1954.[56]

TALL AND WIRY, balding, and wearing thick wire-rimmed glasses, with the characteristics and mannerisms of the aristocrat, he was Baron Maxililian von Weichs looked more like a university history professor than a Nazi field marshal. Guderian said he was "as clever as he was upstanding and valiant."[57] The old cavalryman certainly must have walked an ideological tightrope between his deep religious beliefs on one hand and his adherence to Hitler on the other; nevertheless he kept the Fuehrer's respect almost until the end and yet evaded the military tribunals after the war. He distinguished himself as a corps commander in Poland and as an army commander in the Balkans and Russia. The task of commanding Army Group B was too much for him, and he must bear at least part of the responsibility for the Stalingrad débâcle. He redeemed himself later in the Balkans and emerged from the war as a solid and capable – but certainly not brilliant – professional soldier.

11

Friedrich Paulus

HIS NAME WILL forever be associated with Stalingrad: one of the greatest disasters in German military history and the turning point of the Second World War. Germany could have survived El Alamein or the Battle of Britain. It did survive Moscow, Rostov, and Tikhvin in the terrible winter of 1941/42. Dunkirk – the protestations of certain authors to the contrary – can hardly be classified as a German defeat at all, much less a decisive one. Kursk, Normandy, the Crimea, Vitebsk-Minsk, Falaise, the retreat through France, the Ukraine, and Rumania: would these have occurred if the 230,000 tough, experienced veterans of the 6th Army had been available, with their panzers, artillery, combat engineer and anti-tank battalions, instead of lying dead in the snows of Russia or sitting idle, regretting their misfortune in some prison camp in Siberia? The question is rhetorical, of course, but it is certainly conceivable that twenty effective fighting divisions would have made a difference in any one of these, Vitebsk-Minsk excepted. Finally the question must be asked: to what degree was the commander of 6th Army responsible for the catastrophe?

FRIEDRICH WILHELM ERNST Paulus was born on the evening of September 23, 1890, in the parish of Breitenau-Gershagen in the

223

province of Hesse-Nassau. His father was a bookkeeper in the civil service, so his son was considered a man of the people, to use Third Reich jargon. The future marshal was educated at Wilhelms-Gymnasium at Kassel, from which he graduated in 1909. He applied for an officer-cadet's slot in the Navy but was rejected because of his lack of aristocratic blood. He briefly studied law at the University of Munich before joining the 111th (3rd Baden) Infantry Regiment "Markgraf Ludwig Wilhelm" at Rastatt as an officer-cadet on February 18, 1910. He was commissioned second lieutenant on October 18, 1911.[1]

Lieutenant Paulus married Elena "Coca" Rosetti-Solescu, a twenty-one-year-old Rumanian aristocrat, in 1912. She was beautiful, graceful, strong-willed, and ambitious for her husband. She gave him three children: a daughter named Olga, born in 1914, who later married a baron, and twin sons, Friedrich and Alexander, born in 1918. Both became captains in Hitler's army. Friedrich was killed in action at Anzio and Alexander was wounded in the Stalingrad campaign. After his father started working for the Russians in 1944, Alexander was arrested by the Nazis and sent to a detention camp, where he spent the rest of the war.[2]

The outbreak of World War I found Paulus as the adjutant of the III Battalion, 3rd Baden Infantry. One of the company commanders in this battalion was Captain (later Colonel General) Johannes Blaskowitz, who would command armies and army groups in the next world war. Paulus was later assigned to the staff of the 2nd Prussian Jaeger Regiment (1915) and to the operations staff of the Alpine Corps (1917). Promoted to first lieutenant in 1915,[3] he emerged from the war as a captain after serving on both the Eastern and Western fronts and in Rumania. After the armistice he was the General Staff Officer of the 48th Reserve Division and helped organize (and apparently fought with) Freikorps Grenzschutz Ost ("Free Corps Border Guard East") in the Eastern Marchland.[4]

Paulus was selected for the 4,000-man Officer Corps allowed by the Treaty of Versailles. His first assignment was as adjutant of the 14th Infantry Regiment at Konstanz, whose colonel was his old friend, Johannes Blaskowitz. Later, in October 1922, Paulus attended the "R" Course in Berlin, where he received clandestine General Staff training. The following year he was (unofficially) on the General Staff of Army Group 2 at Kassel. From 1924 to 1927 he was a General Staff officer with Wehrkreis V at Stuttgart, before doing his troop duty there (1928-29) as Commander, 2nd Company, 13th Infantry Regiment. Another future field marshal, Erwin Rommel, was the machine-gun company commander in this regiment.

Paulus's efficiency reports during the 1920s are illuminating. One read: "He is . . . at pains to avoid making enemies . . . He is slow, but very methodical . . . displays marked tactical ability, though he is inclined to spend overmuch time on his appreciation, before issuing his orders." This fitness report also commented that Paulus was too fond of working all night, sustaining himself with coffee and cigarettes. Another evaluator complained: "This officer lacks decisiveness."[5] The characteristics he displayed in the Stalingrad campaign were already in evidence.

In 1930 Paulus became a tactics (i.e. General Staff) instructor with the 5th Infantry Division. He was promoted to major soon after. In 1934, as a lieutenant colonel, he received a choice assignment: Commander of Motor Transport Section 3, a unit that was soon transformed into one of Germany's first panzer/reconnaissance battalions. Paulus was promoted to colonel on June 1, 1935, and in September became Chief of Staff to the commander of Mechanized Forces (General Oswald Lutz) in Berlin,[6] replacing Colonel Heinz Guderian, who had assumed command of the 2nd Panzer Division a short time before. It was probably here, for the first time, that he attracted the attention of General Walter von Reichenau, the Chief of the Armed Forces Office in the Ministry of War. Also an advocate of armored warfare, Reichenau was to figure more prominently in Paulus's career than any other man, as we shall see.

Paulus's last prewar assignment was Chief of Staff, XVI Motorized Corps, which directed the training and enlargement of Germany's four original light divisions – mobile forces that included two or three motorized infantry regiments, an organic panzer battalion (except for the 1st Light, which had a panzer regiment), a reconnaissance regiment, and a motorized artillery regiment. Now considered an expert on motorized warfare as well as a very capable General Staff officer, Friedrich Paulus was promoted to major general in 1939.[7]

On August 26, 1939, just five days before the start of the war, Paulus was named Chief of Staff of Reichenau's 10th Army, the main assault force in the German invasion of Poland. The slow, methodical staff officer was perfectly matched with the energetic, dashing Reichenau, who hated paperwork and the details of running a headquarters. Paulus, on the other hand, might have been chained to his desk. The two men formed an effective team in the conquest of Poland, Belgium, and France (10th Army was renamed 6th Army after the fall of Warsaw). After France fell, Paulus was promoted to lieutenant general and, in September, 1940, was named Oberquartiermeister I (O Qu I) – Deputy Chief of the General Staff of the Army.[8]

In his new post, Paulus was responsible for all Army organization and training. He also visited Rommel in North Africa on a fact-finding tour (where he was critical of his former colleague) and conferred with the Hungarian leaders about the invasion of Yugoslavia. His main task, however, was conducting a strategic survey for the invasion of the Soviet Union.[9]

Paulus's survey stated that, to defeat Russia, Germany must not allow Soviet forces to retreat into the interior. It called for the opening of gaps at critical points, battles of encirclement, and a principle thrust north of the Pripyat Marshes toward a single main objective: Moscow. The campaign had to be successfully concluded, he said, by late October, when the Russian rainy season normally began. The survey, however, failed to convince Hitler that the capture of Moscow was particularly important.[10]

WITH THE FIRST Russian winter offensive in full swing, Field Marshal Reichenau was named Commander-in-Chief of Army Group South. On the eve of December 3, 1941, while having a vegetarian dinner with Hitler, Reichenau recommended that Friedrich Paulus replace him as commander of the 6th Army, and Hitler concurred. Paulus, who had been longing for a field command, was delighted with his new assignment.[11] Promoted to general of panzer troops on January 1, 1942, he took up is new post four days later.[12]

The powerful and commanding Reichenau no doubt intended to guide his former Chief of Staff in his new duties, but he suffered a heart attack on January 12 and died on January 17. He was succeeded by the less able Fedor von Bock.

IT WOULD BE difficult to imagine a general less suited to high command than Friedrich Paulus was in 1942. He was a solid, technically proficient staff officer, it is true, but he had never held a command higher than an experimental motorized battalion. He was a desk soldier to his toes. Tall, slim, and fastidious, he habitually wore gloves because he hated dirt. He bathed and changed clothes twice a day and was sarcastically nicknamed "The Noble Lord" and "Our Most Elegant Gentleman" by some of his more combat-experienced peers.[13] (It must be remembered that most Europeans do not bathe daily, as most Americans do.) Worse still, he lacked decisiveness and had convinced himself that Hitler was an infallible military genius – a fatal combination. He probably would have disobeyed the Fuehrer on Reichenau's orders, but he would never do so on his own.

PAULUS FOUGHT HIS first battle as the commander of 6th Army in the Dnepropetrovsk sector, where Army Group South checked Timoshenko's advance on the Dnieper and brought the Soviet winter offensive in the southern sector to a halt. Both sides were exhausted by February 10, 1942, when the Soviet salient at Izyum was sealed off from the west. Now both sides were engaged in a race of supplies. The side that felt it could attack first would have a marked advantage in the spring campaign.

The Russians struck first, at Volchansk on May 9. The main attack came near Aleksujevka on May 12. Timoshenko employed 640,000 men and 1,200 tanks. Sixth Army was hurled back toward Kharkov. By May 15 Soviet pincers threatened to envelop the city from the north and south. General Plocher estimated the Soviet strength as follows: north of the city, six to seven infantry divisions, three or four armored divisions and a cavalry division, with four infantry divisions, a motorized brigade, four to six armored brigades, and eight cavalry divisions in reserve; south of the city, twelve infantry and three armored divisions, with three cavalry divisions, an infantry division, and two motorized brigades in reserve. Paulus had only ten infantry divisions, a Hungarian light division, and a Slovak artillery regiment. His VIII Corps alone was attacked by three Russian armies.[14]

Sixth Army was saved by the prompt intervention of Group Kleist (1st Panzer and 17th armies), which struck Timoshenko's exposed southern flank on May 17. By May 19 the pressure on

Kharkov was eased, as the Russians turned to face Kleist. Paulus counterattacked east of Kharkov on May 20 and four days later linked up with Kleist west of the city, encircling the main Soviet strike force. By May 28 all Soviet resistance had ended. A total of 240,000 men, 2,026 tanks, and 1,249 guns were captured or destroyed in the Kharkov Pocket.[15] Paulus received the Knights' Cross for his part in this victory.[16]

In the summer of 1942, 6th Army took part in the drive to Voronezh and the clearing of the Don. Then Hitler divided Army Group South. He ordered List's Army Group A south, toward Rostov and the Caucasus, while Weichs's Army Group B was to drive east, across the Don to the Volga – and Stalingrad. Sixth Army was to be the spearhead of the eastern thrust. Hitler, however, initially gave supply priority to the forces advancing on the Caucasus.

Paulus advanced toward Stalingrad with 20 divisions: 250,000 men, 500 panzers, 7,000 guns and mortars, and 25,000 horses.[17] His advance was very slow because Hitler had diverted the bulk of the available fuel to Army Group A, which he considered the most important thrust – for the moment, at least.

Hitler's violation of the principle of objective was fatal to the entire summer campaign. Kleist held the opinion that Stalingrad could have been taken without a fight at the end of July, but Paulus ran out of fuel 150 miles west of Kalach and remained immobilized until August 7, when he attacked two Soviet armies west of the Don at Kalach. By August 11 the bulk of the Soviet 1st Tank and 62nd armies had been destroyed, and 50,000 Soviet troops killed or captured, along with about 270 tanks and armored vehicles, and 600 guns.[18]

By August 18 Paulus was within thirty-five miles of Stalingrad, but he was again low on fuel and considered his army exhausted, in no shape to make the final push to the city.[19] He waited five more days and then, ignoring the Soviet Don River bridgeheads at Kremenskaya and Serafimovich to the north, thrust forward again, but with only a single corps: von Wietersheim's XIV Panzer. Wietersheim advanced fifty miles and reached the Volga north of Stalingrad on August 24, but found himself at the end of a corridor thirty miles long and only two miles wide. The Soviets counterattacked all along the corridor, and also from their Serafimovich and

Kremenskaya bridgeheads on Paulus's left flank, using their 63rd, 21st, and 1st Guards armies. Paulus decided he could not spare enough infantry to secure the corridor until Hoth's 4th Panzer Army, advancing on Stalingrad from the south, freed his right flank. As a result, contact with XIV Panzer Corps was lost until, at the end of August, the Soviets fell back into their inner defenses at Stalingrad. A secure corridor to Wietersheim was not opened until September 2.[20]

Hitler's mood had changed again, and Stalingrad was now the focal point of the 1942 summer offensive. It was then a city of 500,000 people, the third largest industrial city in the Soviet Union. It produced more than 25 percent of the Red Army's tanks and armored vehicles, as well as significant quantities of small arms and ammunition. The City of Stalin was constructed along the western bank of the Volga. It was twelve miles long but only two and a half miles wide. Architecturally it was characterized by stone and concrete government buildings, ugly, unpainted wooden houses, and large factories. Paulus thought it was an easy target.[21] Map 15 shows the initial German dispositions and the principal features of the city.

The Siege of Stalingrad began on September 2 when the Soviet General Chuikov withdrew into the city with his 62nd Army. General Shumilov's 64th Army, which was also under Chuikov's command, withdrew to positions on his adjacent southern flank, opposing the northern wing of 4th Panzer Army. Both Soviet armies were heavily reinforced throughout the battle by the Volga Flotilla, which ferried supplies, equipment, and men across the river.[22]

Weichs felt it was essential to attack immediately, before the Soviets had time to build up their defenses, but Paulus was tied down for several days by hastily launched counterattacks from the Stalingrad Front (1st Guards, 24th and 66th armies) on his northern flank. Under such circumstances Paulus hesitated to launch an assault on the city. This hesitation cost him thousands of casualties later on, and perhaps the battle itself, for Stalin used the respite to pour thousands of reinforcements into his city. Finally, on September 7, General Walter von Seydlitz-Kurzbach assembled the two divisions of his LI Corps at Gumrak and advanced towards the 300-foot Mamayev Hill in the center of the city, the dominant topographical feature in the sector. Seydlitz-Kurzbach's advance was very methodical: his front was very narrow and he had to clear a block at a time, because the Russians fought for every building and launched numerous local counterattacks. Fifty-one Corps finally took the hill on September 13 and the next day advanced as far as Railroad Station Number 1, only one-third of a mile from the Volga. Then the street fighting began in earnest. It took 6th Army

Map 15

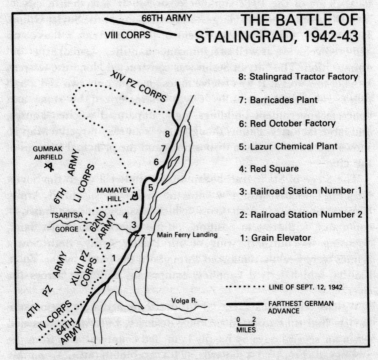

THE BATTLE OF STALINGRAD, 1942–43. General Paulus, Commander of the 6th Army, attacked the city on a broad front in September 1942 and bled his army white in bitter house-to-house fighting. Sixth Army held 90 percent of the city when it was surrounded on November 22. Paulus surrendered near Red Square on January 31, 1943, only hours after he had been promoted to field marshal. He became the first officer of that rank in German history to be captured by the enemy.

another six days to penetrate to the Volga, cutting the Soviet 62nd Army in two on September 20.[23]

Meanwhile, five miles further south, General Werner Kempf's XLVIII Panzer Corps of the 4th Panzer Army joined the battle on September 10. It advanced to the outskirts of the city along the 62nd/64th Army boundary, through scrub brush, deep ravines and steep gullies, against fanatical resistance. It was the toughest fighting the corps had yet encountered, but Kempf's men knocked out dozens of dug-in T-34 and T-60 tanks, cleverly camouflaged artillery positions, machine-gun nests, bunkers, and other positions. By September 14, however, Kempf's XLVIII had linked up with Seydlitz's LI Corps south of the Tsaritsa Gorge and severed Shumilov's forces from those of Chuikov.[24] The XLVIII Panzer was then handed over to Paulus, who used it to clear the southern half of Stalingrad – a mission for which it was totally unsuited. Paulus was wasting good mobile units on a job that foot soldiers should have handled. Casualties were very high, but the task was completed on September 26. That same day, other 6th Army detachments raised the swastika flag over the government buildings in Red Square. But the battle was far from over.

Stalingrad was a battle fought in the rubble. The Luftwaffe had pounded it with tons of bombs two months earlier (on the night of August 23/24), in a terror raid that killed tens of thousands of civilians. The craters and ruined buildings provided hundreds of positions that the Red Army units – platoons, sections, squads, fire-teams and sniper detachments – used against 6th Army. Each of these positions had to be cleared, one at a time. The battle deteriorated into a series of local actions against individual positions under the most savage conditions. Few prisoners were taken by either side. The German infantry called it *Rattenkrieg*: a War of the Rats.

Hitler staked his reputation on taking Stalingrad. "You may rest assured," he said in a broadcast to the German people, "that nobody will ever drive us out of Stalingrad."[25] From that moment on, there would be no retreating from the Volga.

With Army Group A diverted toward the Caucasus, there were not enough German forces available to cover Paulus's flanks. The 6th Army was now at the apex of a gigantic bulge, extending from the Don to the Volga. Its sides were covered by the Rumanians,

Italians and Hungarians – unreliable and ill-equipped foreigners whose ability to withstand heavy Russian attacks was questionable. General Victor von Schwelder, the commander of IV Corps, said so. He called upon Hitler to abandon Stalingrad and concentrate elsewhere. Hitler sacked him immediately. He was replaced by Lieutenant General Erwin Jaenecke.[26] General Gustav von Wietersheim, the commander of XIV Panzer Corps, also objected to the way in which the battle was being conducted. Paulus relieved him of his command on September 15 and replaced him with Hans Valentin Hube, the tough, one-armed commander of the 16th Panzer Division.[27] The battle continued.

Stalin must have been delighted that Hitler had allowed himself to be lured into a battle of attrition in a fortified urban area, where all the advantages of terrain and position accrued to the defense. The tactical skill of the Sixth Army's splendid, veteran infantry was minimized here, for there was no room for maneuver and the fighting was a house-to-house struggle with rifles, pistols, machine guns, and hand grenades. Stalin had reinforced Chuikov with nine infantry divisions, two tank brigades, and a rifle brigade by early October. When these were gone, he threw in more. Sixth Army bled its strength into the ruined streets of Stalingrad.

Paulus, unable or unwilling to see that he was stuck, threw his entire strength eastward into the cauldron in late September, handing his far-left flank over to the Rumanian 3rd Army. From September 20 to October 4 he made four separate reports on his declining infantry strength, and called upon Hitler to reinforce him still further. On October 6 he finally suspended his attack because of his low infantry strength. Since crossing the Don, he had lost 40,000 men, mostly in the infantry. The foot battalions in one division were down to an average strength of three officers, eleven NCOs and sixty-two men. Sixth Army was also low in ammunition. Since the battle began it had fired 25 million rounds of small-arms ammunition, over 500,000 anti-tank shells, and 750,000 artillery projectiles.[28]

The Battle of Stalingrad was not confined to the city limits. North of the city, on the Don-Volga land bridge, Stalin threw in about three more armies. Eight and XI corps had to be diverted against this new threat, which they halted. Stalin nevertheless continued attacking, pinning down five more divisions. Soviet losses were much heavier than those of the Germans, but Stalin could afford them; Paulus could not. Meanwhile, the Rumanian 4th Army (Rumanian VI and VII corps) under General Constantinescu took over defensive sectors in the 4th Panzer Army's zone, south of Stalingrad.[29]

BARON WOLFRAM VON Richthofen, Commander of 4th Air Fleet, was already highly critical of Paulus's handling of the Stalingrad battle. He also reported a lag in 6th Army's previously exemplary morale. He even called on General Kurt Zeitzler, the Chief of the General Staff of the Army, to replace Paulus with a more energetic leader.[30] Nothing was done, however. During the second week of October, Hitler reinforced 6th Army with five special engineer battalions[31] and a panzer division from 4th Panzer Army. Paulus also took another infantry division from his left flank and resumed the offensive on October 14, using the same tactics as before. There was no general offensive all along the line but rather a series of local attacks against specific points. The Russians, however, were at last running out of real estate, so they resisted with even greater tenacity. The next two weeks saw some of the most bitter house-to-house fighting of the war.[32]

The tractor factory in Stalingrad's northern quarter finally fell to the depleted XIV Panzer Corps on October 15, despite a massive Soviet artillery bombardment from the eastern bank of the Volga. The weather was already turning cold. The heavy rain of October 18 turned into wet snow a day later. To the west, the roads once more turned into seas of mud and 6th Army's supply convoys bogged down to their axles. Paulus continued to attack nonetheless, using up the supplies he had accumulated in the first half of October.[33] The Fuehrer had given him an order, and he was going to carry it out! The Fuehrer, after all, was always right. By October 23 the barricades plant had fallen, and half of the Red October metallurgical works was in German hands. By November 1, the Russians held only a few small bridgeheads; 90 percent of the ruined city was in Paulus's hands, but he had shot his bolt. His units were depleted and he was almost out of ammunition. Stalin threw in more troops, more replacements. Paulus regrouped and attacked again on November 10, in four separate offensives, led by four newly arrived engineer battalions. One attack broke through the northernmost Russian bridgehead and wiped out the remnants of an enemy division, but the new formations were also cut to ribbons within forty-eight hours.[34] Paulus's last offensive had failed.

THE RUSSIAN OFFENSIVE against the Rumanian 3rd Army began on November 19. The following day XLVIII Panzer Corps, now under Lieutenant General Ferdinand Heim – until recently Paulus's Chief of Staff – was routed, and the Rumanian 4th Army on Paulus's southern flank disintegrated, splitting 4th Panzer Army in two. Paulus assembled a force under XIV Panzer Corps to cover his rear and withdrew XI Corps on his left wing to better (and shorter) defensive positions, but he could do nothing to prevent the impending encirclement. The next day, November 21, the Red armies to the north pivoted 90 degrees, into the rear of 6th Army, and by noon one of its armored spearheads was within sight of Paulus's command post at Golubinsky. General Paulus and his staff hurriedly fled southward, where they set up a new CP at Gumrak Airfield. That same day Hitler sent him a fatal order: 6th Army was to stand fast, despite the danger of encirclement.[35] The Luftwaffe would resupply Stalingrad by air, he declared.

Later that day, Paulus and his Chief of Staff, Major General Arthur Schmidt, met General Martin Fiebig, Commander of VIII Air Corps, who told them frankly that the airlift was impossible. Paulus and, especially, Schmidt were unconvinced.[36] In Arthur Schmidt, Paulus had found another strong-willed man to guide him. He would be under the spell of Schmidt's dominant personality until the end of the battle.

November 22 was a fateful day in the history of Nazi Germany. The two Soviet spearheads joined hands near Kalach, surrounding 6th Army in a pocket thirty miles in length and twenty-four miles in width (i.e., north to south). To the north, massive Russian attacks had almost overwhelmed XI Corps and had forced it to retreat toward the city. At 6 P.M. that evening, Paulus and Schmidt met with Hoth and Luftwaffe Major General Wolfgang Pickert, the commanders of the 4th Panzer Army and 9th Flak Division, respectively. Paulus did not speak during the entire conference, except to agree with Schmidt. The Chief of Staff told Hoth and Pickert that 6th Army had insufficient fuel to break out of

Stalingrad and would have to be supplied by air. Pickert argued that the army should break out to the southwest immediately, because he did not believe air resupply on such a massive scale was possible during the Russian winter. "It simply has to be done!" Schmidt responded. The troops in the pocket could help, he said, by eating their horses first, to give the Luftwaffe time to organize the airlift.[37] Paulus agreed. He was deceiving himself.

As any second lieutenant knows, the best time to break any encirclement is immediately after it is completed. The enemy has not had time to consolidate his gains or shore up his weak points. The corps commanders of 6th Army knew this, of course. On November 27, at 6th Army Headquarters, they unanimously urged Paulus to order a breakout on his own initiative. General von Seydlitz-Kurzbach urged him to "take the course of the Lion," a reference to General Karl von Litzmann who, in November 1914, had made a daring breakout against orders when encircled by the Russians. General Hans Hube, the one-armed commander of XIV Panzer Corps, said: "A breakout is our only chance!" General Karl Strecker (CG, XI Corps) pleaded with Paulus. "We can't just remain here and die!" he said. General Walter Heitz (CG, VIII Corps) called for an immediate breakout, regardless of casualties. It would be better, he said, to break out, even if only five divisions made good their escape, than to die with twenty. General Jaenecke commented: "Reichenau would have brushed aside all doubts."

"I am no Reichenau," Paulus replied gravely.

The argument continued. Jaenecke, a personal friend of Paulus's, put heavy pressure on him. "We shall go through the Russians like a hot knife through butter," he predicted. Seydlitz revealed that he had already ordered his corps to destroy all surplus equipment that could not be carried on a long march. He had set the example himself by burning everything he had except the uniform he was wearing. All of the corps commanders expressed their approval and urged a breakout, in spite of Hitler's orders.

"We must obey," Schmidt said.

"I shall obey," Paulus responded.

Later, General Jaenecke, who escaped the fall of Stalingrad at the last moment, wrote: "In spite of his intelligence, Colonel General Paulus was far too pliable to cope with Hitler. I am convinced that this is the real and deeper cause of his failure."

General Seydlitz refused to accept Paulus's decision as binding. This disobedience was in keeping with his family tradition. One of his ancestors, General Friedrich Wilhelm von Seydlitz, had won the Battle of Zorndorf in the Seven Years' War by disobeying the orders of Frederick the Great. Later, Major General Florian von Seydlitz had taken part in the unauthorized negotiations with the Russians during the Napoleonic Wars. These negotiations had led to a Russo-Prussian truce and eventually resulted in the Prussian defection from Napoleon in 1813. Now, General of Artillery Walter von Seydlitz bypassed Paulus and demanded that Baron Maximilian von Weichs, the commander of Army Group B, order the breakout on his own initiative.[38] "To remain inactive," Seydlitz signaled, "is a crime from the military viewpoint, and it is a crime from the point of view of responsibility to the German people."[39]

Weichs did not respond. Sixth Army did not move.

THE STALINGRAD AIRLIFT failed, just as Richthofen and the other experts said it would. The 4th Air Fleet, without enough aircraft and hampered by bad weather and the Red Air Force, could deliver an average of only 70 tons of supplies a day as of December 11. Sixth Army demanded 750 tons a day, and needed a minimum of 300.[40] On that day Paulus and Schmidt again met with Fiebig. The troops, they said, had been on one-third rations since November 23. They would have to issue their last food reserves on December 16 and would be out of food by January 18, 1942. Almost all the horses had been eaten. The soldiers' general physical condition had deteriorated to a dangerous level. Of the 270,000 men in the pocket, the effective infantry strength was down to 40,000. Soviet troops in the siege line were walking about freely because the German soldiers would not shoot at them; they were saving what little ammunition they had left for beating off attacks. Many slept in shell holes or on the frozen ground with a single blanket because only one-third of the men had bunkers. There were tens of thousands of cases of frostbite, and thousands froze to death. Heating materials, of course, were not flown into the pocket, and available supplies were exhausted.[41] As of December 7, 6th Army was living on one loaf of stale bread for every five men. On December 26, Wilhelm Hoffmann of the 267th Infantry Regiment, 94th Infantry Division, wrote in his diary: "The horses have already been eaten. I would eat a cat; they say its meat is tasty. The soldiers look like corpses or lunatics . . . They no longer take cover from Russian shells; they haven't the strength to walk, run away and hide."[42] Even now, however, Paulus was to have one last opportunity to save at least part of his army.

HQ, ARMY GROUP Don (formerly HQ, 11th Army), was set up under Field Marshal Erich von Manstein in late November to rescue 6th Army. Despite tremendous odds, Manstein used all of his military genius and managed to push a relief column from 4th Panzer Army to within thirty miles of Stalingrad, but here he was halted. He called on Paulus to break out, and even Hitler gave conditional approval, but Paulus hesitated; he estimated that he had only enough fuel to travel eighteen miles – no more. The colonel general (he had been promoted on December 1) refused to budge.

Manstein sent Major Eismann, his Ic, to Stalingrad to reason with Paulus but found him unimpressed. "What ultimately decided the attitude of 6th Army Headquarters," Manstein wrote later, "was the opinion of the Chief of Staff . . . 'Sixth Army,' he told Eismann, 'will still be in position at Easter. All you people have to do is to supply it better.' " Manstein concluded that all of Eismann's remonstrances "were like water off a duck's back."[43]

By Christmas 1942, 28,000 men had died in Stalingrad since the encirclement was completed less than a month before. Sixth Army's strength stood at 246,000, including 13,000 Rumanians and 19,300 Russian auxiliaries. Infantry strength was very low. Supply and service troops had been converted to infantry, but they were not very combat-effective. The temperatures in Stalingrad dipped to minus 5 degrees Fahrenheit, further reducing infantry strength.[44] To make matters worse, 4th Air Fleet's Morozovskaya and Tatsinskaya airfields were overrun, making the airlift more and more difficult.

On December 27, 4th Panzer Army's relief column was forced to withdraw to prevent being encircled. Sixth Army rejected two surrender demands on January 8 and 9, 1943, and on the next day was attacked by seven Soviet armies. Two days later Pitomnik, the better of the two airstrips left to 6th Army, fell. Gaps appeared in the front, and Paulus, down to fewer than one hundred tanks and almost out of fuel and ammunition, was unable to close them.

Nevertheless he fought on, with steadily dwindling resources. Gumrak, the last airfield, fell on January 22, and the Soviets tore a three-mile gap in the southwestern sector, which Paulus could not close. The Russians broke through the western perimeter the next day and penetrated to the tractor works, cutting the pocket in two and isolating XI Corps to the north. Paulus reported more than 12,000 unattended wounded, many of whom were lying in the streets.[45] Shortly after, Paulus ordered that the wounded no longer be fed. Only those who could still fight would be given food. He signaled Hitler: "Your orders are being executed. Long live Germany!"[46]

Paulus was in despair. He complained to a Luftwaffe pilot that his men had had nothing to eat for four days. "Can you imagine soldiers falling upon the carcass of a horse, smashing its head open and eating its brains raw?"[47] But the Fuehrer had ordered him not to surrender, and the Fuehrer must be obeyed, no matter what the cost. Sixth Army fought on. By January 25 there were 20,000 unattended wounded in the streets.[48]

The southern pocket was cut in half on January 28. HQ, 6th Army was now situated in the southernmost of the three pockets, in the ruins of a large department store in Red Square, guarded by the remnants of Major General Alexander von Hartmann's 71st Infantry Division.[49] Two days later Paulus signaled Hitler from here: "On the anniversary of your assumption of power, the 6th Army sends greetings to the Fuehrer. The swastika still flutters over Stalingrad. May our struggle stand as an example to generations yet unborn never to surrender, no matter how desperate the odds. Then Germany will be victorious. Heil, Mein Fuehrer!"[50]

That same day the 76th Infantry Division was overwhelmed. Near Railroad Station Number 1, the Headquarters, XIV Panzer Corps, was surrounded and forced to surrender. General Hube had been flown out on Hitler's orders a few days before and had been replaced by Lieutenant General Hellmut Schloemer, who surrendered the corps. In the northern pocket Soviet T-34 tanks broke through to the command bunker shared by VIII and LI corps. Walter von Seydlitz, Walter Heitz, and five other generals surrendered.[51]

That night, on General Zeitler's recommendation — but not without misgivings — Hitler promoted Paulus to field marshal and sent him a message reminding him that no German field marshal had ever been captured. Hitler was clearly putting a pistol in Paulus's hands, inviting him to commit suicide.

Meanwhile, 71st Infantry Division had been overrun and General von Hartmann had been killed. He may have deliberately exposed himself to Russian fire. At 6:15 A.M. on the morning of January 31, the radio operator at 6th Army Headquarters signaled that there were Russians outside the door. The last transmission came at 7:15 A.M., announcing to OKH that they were destroying their radio equipment.[52] Shortly thereafter, Field Marshal Paulus surrendered. Hitler never forgave him for this, commenting that he had done an about-face on the threshold of history.

At 8:40 A.M. on February 2, 1943, General Karl Strecker surrendered the last pocket and the remnants of XI Corps to the Russians.[53] The Battle of Stalingrad was over. Of the 274,000 men encircled on November 22, 13,000 were Rumanians and 19,700 were Russian auxiliaries. About 25,000 German sick and wounded had been flown out and 91,000 surrendered, which meant that more than 150,000 Germans were killed or died in the siege, from a total casualty figure of just over 240,000 (excluding evacuated wounded). Both Paulus and Manstein, however, insisted that the total killed and captured did not exceed 220,000. Soviet estimates of German losses vary from 258,000 to one and a half million.[54] Two hundred and thirty thousand is the commonly accepted figure. This, of course, excludes thousands killed or captured prior to and during the encirclement. By any measure, the disaster was enormous.

The Russians never made public their own casualty figures for Stalingrad. Eight and III Cavalry corps, however, lost 36 percent and 45 percent of their troops, respectively.[55] If their casualties are in any way representative, Soviet losses were also enormous.

The survivors of 6th Army underwent a series of forced marches rivaling the Bataan Death March. Only about half of them ever reached the prisoner-of-war camps in Siberia. Only about 7,000 lived to see Germany again. Even they were not repatriated for another decade.

Sixth Army's courageous last stand did have one benefit for the Germans: it bought time for Manstein. By tying down seven Russian armies, it allowed him time to partially stabilize the southern sector of the Eastern Front, which seemed on the verge of total collapse in December 1942.

FRIEDRICH PAULUS INITIALLY refused to cooperate with his captors who wanted him to make anti-Nazi broadcasts to the German troops, but in 1944 he was persuaded. In mid-July he called on the officers of Army Group North to desert or to disobey Hitler's "murderous orders" to stand fast against the Russians.[56] He also joined the National Free Germany Committee. As a result, his entire family was arrested on Hitler's personal orders under *Sippenhaft*, the doctrine of collective family responsibility, which was used by the Nazis.[57]

Field Marshal Paulus appeared as a witness for the Russian prosecution at Nuremberg in 1946, but was not released from prison until 1953. His wife had died in Baden-Baden four years before. He settled in Dresden, East Germany, and was for a time an inspector in the People's Police. He died (apparently of cancer) in Saxony on February 1, 1957.[58]

12

Erich von Manstein

"HITLER'S RESPECT FOR Manstein bordered on fear," David Irving wrote in 1977.[1] From his point of view, Hitler had reason to fear Manstein. "The general verdict among the German generals I interrogated in 1945," B. H. Liddell Hart wrote in January 1958, "was that Field Marshal von Manstein had proved the ablest commander in their Army, and the man they had most desired to become Commander-in-Chief."[2] This was the opinion of Gerd von Rundstedt, the senior German field marshal, of Heinz Guderian, the leader of the panzer army, and many others. Even Hitler said: "Manstein is perhaps the best brain that the General Staff Corps has produced."[3] This is precisely why Hitler feared him. He was universally respected and even held somewhat in awe by the German generals – a class not exactly known for its lack of personal ego. If anyone could have led a successful military revolt, it was Manstein.

HE WAS BORN Fritz Erich von Lewinski in Berlin on November 24, 1887. His father, General of Artillery Eduard von Lewinski, later became a corps commander in the Imperial German Army. The Prussian military tradition of his family went back to the Teutonic knights. Erich, however, was Eduard's tenth child, and Frau von Lewinski's sister was childless, so Lewinski allowed her to adopt him. Erich's stepfather was Lieutenant General Manstein, a divisional commander in the Kaiser's army. Erich eventually took his name and became Fritz Erich von Lewinski gennant von Manstein – Erich von Manstein for short.[4]

Manstein was educated at Strasburg and in various cadet schools. He entered the Army as a matter of course, as an officer-cadet in the élite 3rd Prussian Foot Guards Regiment ("Dritte Garderegiment zu Fuss") in 1906, and was commissioned on July 1, 1907. Second Lieutenant Manstein attended the War Academy (1913-14), earned his General Staff credentials, and was a first lieutenant and adjutant of the 2nd Guards Reserve Regiment when World War I broke out.[5]

Young Manstein fought in Belgium, then in East Prussia and Poland (under his uncle, Field Marshal Paul von Hindenberg), and was badly wounded in November 1914. He returned to duty in May or early June 1915 and served successively as Adjutant to the Headquarters, 12th Army, and as a General Staff Officer with the 11th and 1st armies on the Eastern and Western Fronts. After fighting at Verdun, he became GSO I (Chief of Operations) of the 4th Cavalry Division in Estonia and Courland and in May 1918 was named GSO of the 213th Assault Infantry Division on the Western Front. He emerged from the war as a captain with the Iron Cross, 1st Class, and the Hohenzollern House Order.[6]

Manstein's natural brilliance and inbred military aptitude had now been supplemented with valuable operational experience. He spent the Reichswehr era in various staff appointments except for three years as an infantry company commander (1921-24) and one year in command of an infantry battalion (1931-32). He was promoted to full colonel in 1933 and was appointed Chief of Staff of Wehrkreis III in Berlin in early 1934. The following year he was named Chief of the Operations Branch of the General Staff of the Army. He was promoted to major general on October 1, 1936. General Beck appointed him Deputy Chief of the General Staff (Oberquartiermeister I) in October 1936.[7]

Manstein first ran afoul of the Nazis in early 1934, when the first racial restrictions order was issued by the Minister of War, General Blomberg. Manstein wrote a letter of protest to Reichenau, stating that it was cowardice for the Army to surrender to the Nazi Party and discriminate against its Jewish soldiers, who had demonstrated by their enlistments that they were willing to sacrifice their lives for Germany. Reichenau was furious. He showed the letter to Blomberg, whom Manstein had, in effect, called a coward. Blomberg called General Fritsch, the C-in-C of the Army, and demanded Manstein be disciplined. Fritsch, the tough Prussian infantryman, was unmoved. Perhaps he agreed with Manstein. In any event, he told Blomberg that Army disciplinary matters were none of Blomberg's business. He did nothing to Manstein.[8]

Major General Manstein was on Hitler's list of reprobates when he met with Brauchitsch in early 1938. The same day Brauchitsch replaced Fritsch, Manstein was relieved of his staff appointment. Manstein was apparently considered too brilliant to cashier altogether, however, so he was given command of the 18th Infantry Division at Leipzig; in effect, he had been sent into exile. He was nevertheless earmarked to be Chief of Staff of Leeb's 12th Army in the invasion of Czechoslovakia in September 1938 and was promoted to lieutenant general on April 1, 1939.[9]

In April 1939 Manstein was named Chief of Staff of *Arbeitsstab Rundstedt* (Working Staff Rundstedt) and, with Colonel Guenther Blumentritt, planned the invasion of southern Poland and the capture of Warsaw.[10] He retained his divisional command until August. During the invasion of Poland he was Chief of Staff, Army Group South.

As we have seen (chapter 2), Manstein originated the plan that led to the fall of France in 1940. Possibly acting out of revenge for the damage it did to his own career, von Brauchitsch "kicked him upstairs" and transferred him to the command of XXXVIII Corps, then in the process of forming in Stettin. Manstein was on leave in Leipzig, eastern Germany, when the invasion of France began. He learned over the public radio that it had started. Thirty-eight Corps was attached to Army Group A shortly thereafter, and Manstein played a minor role in the mopping-up operations after Dunkirk and spent the next eight months on occupation duty on the Channel coast.[11] He was promoted to general of infantry on June 1, 1940.[12]

AT THE END of February 1941, Manstein was named commander of LVI Panzer Corps, then being formed in Germany.[13] Initially controlling the 8th Panzer, 3rd Motorized, 3rd SS Motorized, and

290th Infantry divisions, it was part of Hoepner's 4th Panzer Group, Army Group North, during the invasion of the Soviet Union.[14] Manstein distinguished himself by penetrating more than two hundred miles into Russia and took the Dvina River bridge at Dvinsk intact on the fifth day of the campaign. His rescue of the German X Corps and the subsequent destruction of the Soviet 34th Army near Demyansk was a brilliant maneuver (see chapter 5). After that, Manstein was engaged in beating off Soviet counterattacks between Lake Ilmen and Lake Peipus.

Meanwhile, on the morning of September 12, a thousand miles to the south, Colonel General Ritter Eugen von Schobert was in a Storch reconnaissance plane, directing his 11th Army's attack on the Perekop Isthmus on the northern approach to the Crimea, when the engine failed. The pilot attempted a forced landing, but came down in a Russian minefield. Both he and the general were killed instantly.[15] The attack failed. Manstein was given command of the 11th Army that same evening.

When he took over 11th Army, it had been assigned two divergent missions: to overrun the Crimea and to take Rostov. His available forces included LIV, XLIV Mountain, and XXX Corps: six infantry and two mountain divisions, and the 1st SS Motorized Brigade "Leibstandarte Adolf Hitler," as well as the Rumanian 3rd Army (three mountain and three cavalry brigades). The 1st SS was his only mobile unit.[16] He saw at once that he did not have the strength to take both objectives, so he decided to attack the Crimea first because it represented a base from which Stalin could bomb the Rumanian oil fields and/or threaten the deep right flank of Army Group South.[17]

On September 24, 1941, Manstein attacked south into the Perekop with General Erik Hansen's LIV Corps. General Ludwig Kuebler's XLIX Mountain Corps was in reserve nearby, ready to exploit any breakthrough and drive to Sevastopol, the Red naval fortress on the southwestern tip of the peninsula. All Manstein had to defend his eastern flank was General Hans von Salmuth's XXX Corps and six unreliable Rumanian brigades.

After bitter fighting against six Soviet divisions, Hansen's LIV Corps stormed the Perekop on September 28, capturing 10,000 prisoners, 112 tanks, and 135 guns in the process. The victory could not be exploited, however, because the Russians attacked

Manstein's eastern flank with two armies on September 26. Thirty Corps held, but the Rumanians collapsed, and Manstein had to rush Kuebler's Corps to the Nogav Steppe.

By attacking in such a manner, the Russians north of the Sea of Azov saved the Crimea but at the same time exposed their own right flank to an attack by Kleist's 1st Panzer Army to the north. He and Manstein co-operated in a battle of encirclement on the Sea of Azov from October 5–10. They destroyed the Soviet 18th Army, killed its commander, routed the Soviet 9th Army, took 65,000 prisoners, and destroyed or captured 212 tanks and 672 guns.[18] The cost of this victory was high, however, for it gave the Russians three weeks to reinforce Sevastopol and the Crimea.

South of Perekop, the Soviets concentrated eight infantry and four cavalry divisions, blocking the road to Sevastopol. Army Group South had detached XLIX Mountain Corps from 11th Army, so Manstein had only six divisions left – all infantry, with little room to maneuver. The battle lasted for ten days, before the Russians retreated on October 28. Manstein pursued quickly and captured more than 100,000 prisoners, 700 guns, and 160 tanks.[19] He could not, however, take Sevastopol.

The Siege of Sevastopol lasted 247 days. Manstein launched an attack on October 30 and took the Balaklava Hills. On December 17 he launched what he hoped would be the final assault, but as the attack was entering a critical phase the Soviets staged an amphibious assault on the Kerch peninsula (on the eastern end of the Crimea), forcing him to call off the attack and divert units from Sevastopol to the Kerch. There the lines remained until the end of the Russian winter.

Manstein, a colonel general as of New Year's Day, 1942, was now operating on interior lines between Sevastopol and the Soviet bridgehead in the Kerch. In early May he suddenly shifted the bulk of his forces to the east and launched a surprise attack on the Kerch bridgehead with five infantry divisions and the 22nd Panzer Division, plus a Rumanian corps. He was also well supported by the Stuka dive-bombers of Wolfram von Richthofen's VIII Air Corps. In ten days he destroyed two Soviet armies, captured 170,000 prisoners, 1,133 guns, and 258 tanks, with a loss of only 7,500 casualties himself.[20] It was a brilliant victory. Now, with his rear secure, Manstein turned against Sevastopol one last time.

Manstein struck Sevastopol on June 3 with a massive artillery and mortar concentration: 1,300 tubes in all. Then, supported by the Stukas of VIII Air Corps, the infantry went forward against fanatical Soviet resistance. The fortress finally fell on July 3. Two more Soviet armies had been annihilated and 90,000 prisoners taken, along with 467 guns, 758 mortars, 26 tanks, 141 aircraft, and 155 anti-tank guns. Shortly after, Hitler promoted Manstein to field marshal, to rank from July 1, 1942.[21]

Instead of sending 11th Army to Army Group A or B, to lend weight to the main thrust of the 1942 summer offensive, Hitler sent it to Army Group North for an attack on Leningrad. He was confident that the city would be captured – but Manstein was less optimistic. The attack was scheduled for September 14, but the Soviets forestalled it by launching an offensive of their own, against the southern flank of Colonel General Georg Lindemann's 18th Army, on August 27. The 11th Army had to be diverted to the threatened sector. Manstein severed the Russian penetration at its base, destroying seven infantry divisions, six infantry brigades, and four armored brigades of the élite 2nd Shock Army. The Russians suffered extremely heavy losses in unsuccessful breakout attempts and most of their men were killed. Only 12,000 prisoners were taken, but more than 300 guns, 500 mortars, and 244 tanks were captured or destroyed.[22]

After the fighting ended, Manstein attended the funeral of his son, twenty-year-old Gero Erich von Manstein, a lieutenant in the 51st Panzer Grenadier Regiment, who fell victim to a Russian shell in the last days of the battle. They buried him on the shore of Lake Ilmen. Then the field marshal went on leave to Leipzig to comfort his wife. He had been back at the front only a short time when the Russians burst through the Rumanian 3rd and 4th armies and encircled the 6th Army in Stalingrad on November 22.[23] Manstein's HQ was redesignated Army Group Don and given the mission of rescuing 6th Army and restoring the southern sector of the Eastern Front. Manstein had entered the most critical and demanding phase of his military career.

EVEN BEFORE HIS headquarters was activated on November 27, Manstein was already hinting to Zeitzler and OKH that 6th Army should be allowed to break out. Hitler refused to allow it, however,

Table 5

ORDER OF BATTLE, ARMY GROUP DON, January 1, 1943

6th Army: encircled at Stalingrad
Army Detachment Hoth:
  4th Panzer Army:
    LVII Panzer Corps:
      17th Panzer Division
      23rd Panzer Division
      Parts of 16th Motorized Division
      5th SS Panzer Division*
    Reserve:
      16th Motorized Division (–)**
      15th Luftwaffe Field Division
  4th Rumanian Army:
    Remnants of six Rumanian divisions
Army Detachment Hollidt:
  Group Mieth:
    336th Infantry Division
    7th Luftwaffe Field Division
    Three miscellaneous battle groups
  XVII Corps:
    22nd Panzer Division
    294th Infantry Division
    8th Luftwaffe Field Division (–)
  XLVIII Panzer Corps:
    6th Panzer Division
    Elements, 306th Infantry Division
  XXIX Corps:
    Elements of 62nd Infantry Division
    Elements of 298th Infantry Division
    Remnants of eight Rumanian and Italian divisions
  Reserve:
    11th Panzer Division
    306th Infantry Division (–)
Rear Area Command Don: 403rd Security Division (–)
Army Group Reserve: 7th Panzer Division (en route)

SOURCE: *Kriegstagebuch des OKW*, Volume II, p. 4.

---

*En route from Army Group A.
**"(–)" means some division units detached or destroyed.

so Manstein was faced with three tasks: 1) restore the front line, which was then in remnants; 2) prevent the Russians from reaching Rostov and cutting off Army Group A in the Caucasus; and 3) relieve 6th Army. To do all of this, Manstein had only (north to south) XVII Corps on the Chir; the remnants of the Rumanian 3rd Army; the remnants of the XLVIII Panzer Corps; the weak 4th Panzer Army; and the remnants of the Rumanian 4th Army. Table 5 shows his entire order of battle as of January 1, 1943, after he had been reinforced. He was facing ten Soviet combined-arms armies, a tank army, four air armies, several independent cavalry, tank and mechanized corps, and over one hundred independent tank, artillery, anti-tank, combat engineer, and other regiments.[24]

Manstein did a masterful job. He gave ground in the Chir sector when he had to but held his front largely intact; stopped the Soviets at Rostov by committing his last reserves; and came within thirty miles of reaching Stalingrad. Paulus refused to break out and Hitler would not order him to, so 6th Army died. Manstein, however, kept his escape routes open long enough for 4th Panzer Army to withdraw. Had Hitler given Manstein the reinforcements he requested from Army Group A – and a free hand – he might well have saved a large part of 6th Army.

It would be useful if there were enough space to discuss Manstein's operations more fully, but there is not. They were characterized by genius, complexity, and almost emotionless nerve. To completely understand them, one must study individual troop movements day by day, a suitable subject for an entire book, but not an individual chapter.

Manstein's imperturbability was legendary. On January 7, 1943, for example, his orderly officer, Captain Annus, burst into his room. "Herr Feldmarschall, Soviet tanks have crossed the Don only twelve miles from here and are making straight for us. . . . Our Cossack covering parties have been overrun. We've nothing left."

"Is that so?" Manstein said calmly, and smiled. "We've got all sorts of things left, Annus. That tank repair shop next door – surely there are bound to be a few more or less operational tanks there. Collect whatever can be used and go and knock out the Soviets. Get the staff organized for defense. We're staying put. I'll leave you to cope with this little disturbance." Captain Annus did in fact halt the Russians within ten miles of GHQ.[25]

Rostov was the real key to the campaign, for Hitler had not

allowed the timely retreat of Army Group A, and Stalin burst through toward the Sea of Azov with nine armies. Had he reached the city, he would have cut off the 4th Panzer, 1st Panzer, and 17th armies, plus part of the Rumanian 4th Army – 900,000 men in all! This disaster would have exceeded that of Stalingrad for the Germans. As it happened, Manstein shifted his forces, once again committed his last reserves, and halted the Soviets within twenty miles of the city.[26]

RESISTANCE ENDED IN in Stalingrad on February 2, 1943. Manstein flew to Fuehrer Headquarters with the intention of demanding that Hitler resign as Supreme Commander. He did not make the demand, however, because of the dictator's mood and his ready acceptance that Stalingrad was his responsibility alone. After a four-hour conference, Hitler acceded to Manstein's request to abandon the eastern Donets, in order to release 4th Panzer Army for a counter-offensive.[27]

The winter battles had left Army Group Don battered but in better shape than reasonably could have been expected. Several panzer units still had enough strength to launch counterattacks. Manstein pulled all of his tank units out of the line and placed them under Hoth's 4th Panzer Army. He had correctly predicted that the headlong Soviet advance on Kharkov would leave them in a state of near supply exhaustion. Also, they would not expect such a bold offensive. Of that Manstein was sure.

Hitler was very nervous about Manstein's audacious plan. He flew to Army Group Don's Headquarters at Zaporozhye on February 16 and was at the point of watering down the attack; but then the news arrived that the Russians had broken through nearby. With enemy tanks advancing unopposed only six miles away, Hitler had to make a hasty exit, leaving a relieved Manstein free to conduct his own operations.[28]

Manstein's counteroffensive was a huge success. It ended the Soviet winter offensive, recaptured Kharkov, destroyed the Soviet 3rd Tank Army and supporting formations, and captured or destroyed 615 tanks, 354 guns, and large quantities of other equipment between the Donets and the Dnieper. On March 10 Hitler once more flew to Manstein's HQ and decorated him with the Oak Leaves to the Knight's Cross.[29]

At the end of the German offensive, a huge bulge existed in the

Kursk sector that Hitler wanted to pinch off. Manstein favored an offensive aimed at retaking the Donets, but finally agreed to the Kursk attack – but only if it could be launched in May 1943, before Stalin could adequately reinforce the bulge. Hitler, however, delayed the offensive until July. The result was the greatest tank battle in history – and a German defeat. The Soviets then broke through the southern flank of Army Group Center and headed west. It was the end of Hitler's last major offensive in the East.

From this point on, all roads led back for Manstein. On July 17 his twenty-nine infantry and thirteen panzer or panzer grenadier divisions faced 109 Soviet infantry divisions, ten tank corps, seven mechanized and seven cavalry corps, twenty independent tank brigades, and eight anti-tank brigades, plus assorted other troops. By early September, these had been reinforced by fifty-five more infantry divisions, two tank corps, and about a dozen tank brigades. Manstein was outnumbered roughly six to one by September 7. Army Group South (as Manstein's HQ had been redesignated) was opposed by twenty-one Soviet armies.[30]

Manstein fell back from the Mius to the Donets to the Dnieper. By August 24 he had only 257 panzers and 220 assault guns to hold a 1,300-mile front.[31] Hitler constantly demanded that Manstein hold every foot of territory, but he would not – could not. He did, however, relieve General Franz Werner Kempf (CG, Army Detachment Kempf, later 8th Army), following the loss of Kharkov, even though Manstein knew it could not have been held with the forces available.

If Erich von Manstein was a magnificent military commander, his character did not always match his genius. He used Kempf as a scapegoat for the loss of Kharkov in August 1943, just as he had used General Count Hans von Sponeck, commander of XLII Corps, as a scapegoat for the loss of the Kerch and the failure of the Sevastopol attack in December 1941. Manstein no doubt knew it was unreasonable to expect Sponeck to hold off two Soviet armies with a single division, but he sacked him just the same and did not object when Hitler threw him into prison as a result. Sponeck was later executed without trial after July 20, 1944.[32] Manstein's attitude toward the Jews also seemed to change in Russia, or perhaps he drew a distinction between foreign Jews and German soldiers who happened to be Jewish. It will be remembered that he ran afoul of the Nazis in early 1934 for his outspoken defense of Jewish servicemen in the German Army; yet as early as November 20, 1941, he issued an order to his divisions, stating that the German soldier in the East was "the bearer of a ruthless national ideology . . . therefore the soldier must have understanding of the necessity of a severe but just revenge on subhuman Jewry."[33] He would not, however, condone or assist the Nazis in their mass murders.[34]

Possibly Manstein's changing attitude toward the Jews represents a compromise for the sake of his own advancement. Manstein's ambition remained overwhelming, and he made no secret of the fact that he wanted to be Commander-in-Chief of the Eastern Front, and a great many generals supported him for the post. On September 3, 1943, backed by Kluge, Manstein made a series of radical proposals to Hitler. They included a unified command in the East (presumably under Manstein himself), the abolition of OKW, and the placing of all theaters of the war under the Chief of the General Staff of the Army. Hitler, of course, rejected all of the proposals.[35]

BY EARLY OCTOBER 1943, Army Group South had thirty-seven divisions, with an average strength of one thousand men each, or an average of eighty men per mile of front. Manstein was unable to hold the Dnieper line. He fell back and then suddenly launched another brilliant counterattack, smashing the Soviet 5th Guards Army at Krivoy Rog. When the remnants of the 5th Guards escaped on October 28, they left behind more than 350 tanks, 350 guns, 5,000 prisoners, and 10,000 dead. Manstein's skillful maneuvering had once again temporarily stabilized the Eastern Front.[36]

The Soviet winter offensive of 1943/44 began on December 24, and Zhitomir was lost again on December 31. On January 4, 1944, Manstein flew to Rastenburg and demanded permission to pull back his entire southern wing, but Hitler refused. Manstein asked everyone except Hitler and Zeitzler to leave the room. He then began a devastating critique of the Fuehrer's direction of the Eastern war. Hitler tried to stare him down, but Manstein continued to speak as if he were lecturing a none-too-bright second lieutenant. He concluded by once again demanding a C-in-C, East (i.e., himself). Hitler told Manstein that not even he, the Fuehrer, could get the field marshals to obey his orders. Did Manstein believe he could do better? Yes, Manstein answered – his orders were always obeyed. Hitler, taken aback, promptly brought the meeting to an end. He turned down both of Manstein's requests for a C-in-C and for permission to withdraw his left flank.[37] As a result, XLII and XI corps of 8th Army were surrounded near Cherassky. Hitler ordered General Wilhelm Stemmermann, the pocket commander, to hold at all costs, rather than stage a breakout.

On January 27, at General Schmundt's suggestion, the principal Eastern Front commanders were summoned to Posen for two days of speeches by Goebbels, Rosenberg, and others. The object was to rekindle their faith and enthusiasm for the war and for National Socialism. Then the military leaders were shipped off to Rastenburg, where Hitler himself delivered a powerful oration on the duties of officers. If, he said, he were ever abandoned as Supreme Commander, it was the duty of the entire Officer Corps to gather around him with daggers drawn, just as it was the duty of their regiments, divisions, corps, and armies to stand with them in their hours of crisis.

"And so it shall be, Mein Fuehrer!" Manstein shouted. Hitler was visibly shaken by this unprecedented interruption. It was a brilliant piece of ambiguity. Did Manstein mean it as a spontaneous expression of loyalty? Or did he mean that the events Hitler was describing were going to happen? No one knew. Hitler hoped it was the former; however, Bormann and Hitler's own adjutants later told him that the generals took it the other way.[38] General of Cavalry Count Erwin von Rothkirch und Trach, rear area commmander in White Ruthenia, described what happened next:

It was *so* awful; it was so quiet you could have heard a pin drop. And afterwards when the speech was ended, good old Keitel finished up with the usual claptrap about the Fuehrer, and we had to shout "Sieg Heil!" but that was awfully feeble. The Fuehrer had lunch with half the "Generals," and he was to have coffee with the other half – I was one of those with whom he had lunch – he didn't get round to the other half.[39]

Shortly afterward, Hitler called Manstein in and told him never to interrupt him in a speech again.

MANSTEIN, HAMPERED BY the Russian mud and fuel shortages, pushed relief columns to within five miles of the Cherassky Pocket, despite furious Russian counterattacks. Unable to go further, Stemmermann was told he would have to cover the last five miles on his own. The XI and XLII corps broke out on the night of February 16/17, losing all their tanks, artillery, and heavy equipment. The rear-guards were sacrificed. Thirty thousand of the 54,000 men in the pocket escaped, but General Stemmermann was killed and the two corps were smashed. Manstein sent all the shaken survivors back to Poland to rest and reorganise.[40]

On March 19 Manstein again went to Obersalzburg and demanded freedom of maneuver. Hitler again refused. Four days later, 1st Panzer Army (now under General Hans Hube) was surrounded on the Bug. The Fuehrer once more issued a no-retreat order, but Manstein protested vehemently. On March 25, after a heated series of telephone calls, Hitler summoned him to the Berghof, where Manstein threatened to resign. Hitler reluctantly backed down and consented to the breakout. Hube formed a floating pocket and reached the German lines on April 6, saving ten divisions.[41] When he returned, however, he found Manstein gone.

Hitler called Manstein and Kleist to Obersalzburg on March 30, 1944, presented them with the Knights' Cross with Oak Leaves and Swords – and relieved them of their commands. Manstein was replaced by Field Marshal Walter Model. A few days later, Army Group South was redesignated Army Group North Ukraine.

Manstein left without bitterness. Hitler said that if he ever launched great offensives again, he wanted Manstein to command them. As the Fuehrer extended his hand to him for the last time, Manstein told him he hoped his decision of that day turned out right for him. Hitler is said to have given the retired marshal a large estate that autumn.[42]

FIELD MARSHAL ERICH von Manstein was captured by the British at the end of the war and brought before a British military court at Hamburg in 1949, after four years in prison. He was cleared of two indictments concerning the massacre of Jews but was convicted of neglecting to protect civilian life. The trial was a very questionable affair, however. Not only did the defense have to present its case first (as was common in war crimes trials after World War II), but the prosecution was allowed to alter the charges after the defense had rested its case. B. H. Liddell Hart, an originator of the theories of armored warfare and one of the earliest consultants to the Israeli Army, was outraged and publicly denounced the trial as an example of "gross ignorance or gross hypocrisy."[43]

Manstein was convicted and sentenced to eighteen years' imprisonment on December 19, 1949. His sentence was later commuted to twelve years, and in August 1952 he went home on a medical parole. Finally released in May 1953, he worked as a military advisor for the West German Army. He also wrote his memoirs, *Verlorene Siege (Lost Victories)*, which is an excellent book, although he glosses over certain events such as the dismissal of Count von Sponeck and the Battle of Kursk. Erich von Manstein died at Irschenhausen, Bavaria, on June 12, 1973, at the age of eighty-five.[44]

13

Georg von Kuechler

BRETT-SMITH WROTE: "Of all Hitler's Field Marshals, the one who seems to us most shadowy today is Georg von Kuechler."[1] His entire World War II career, except for the campaign of 1940, was associated with the east. Despite the fact that he held army-level or higher commands from the outbreak of the war until 1944, relatively few Westerners know anything about him, and many have never even heard of him.

Georg von Kuechler was born into an old Prussian Junker family at Schloss Philippsruh on May 30, 1881. Educated in cadet schools, he entered the Imperial Army as an artillery *Fahnenjunker* in the 25th Field Artillery Regiment at Darmstadt on March 12, 1900.[2] He received his commission the following year and served in the artillery until 1907, when he was detailed to the Military Riding School at Hanover for two years. Promoted to *Oberleutnant* (first lieutenant) in 1910, he spent the next three years at the War Academy in Berlin, undergoing General Staff training. Following his graduation in 1913, he was assigned to the topographical section of the Greater General Staff in Berlin. He was promoted to captain and given command of an artillery battery when World War I broke out.[3]

Captain Kuechler fought on the Western Front in the First

World War and took part in the battles on the Somme, at Verdun, and in Champagne. He served on the General Staff of IV and VIII Corps, and in 1916 he was named First General Staff Officer (Ia) of the 206th Infantry Division. Later he served as Ia of the 8th Reserve Division in Germany and in 1918 was a General Staff Officer to General Count von der Goltz in the Baltic States. At the end of the war he remained in the Baltic region, fighting Russians and Poles as a member of the Freikorps. Joining the Reichsheer in 1919, he was initially assigned to I Corps (later Wehrkreis I) at Koenigsberg, East Prussia.[4]

Kuechler's postwar career was characterized by steady but unspectacular advancement. He served as battery commander in the 5th Artillery Regiment, and in 1924 he was named Commandant of Muenster. Later he was an inspector of schools in the Defense Ministry[5] and was on the staff of the Jueterbog Artillery School in 1930. He was promoted to major in 1924, to lieutenant colonel in 1929, and to full colonel in 1931. In 1932 he was Artillerie fuehrer I and Deputy Commander of the 1st Infantry Division in East Prussia, and on April 1, 1934, he was promoted to major general. In 1935 he was named Inspector of Army Schools and promoted to lieutenant general. Georg von Kuechler succeeded Walter von Brauchitsch as commander of Wehrkreis I in 1937, and was promoted to general of artillery effective April 1, 1937.[6]

Kuechler, isolated in East Prussia, had a very responsible command for he was surrounded on three sides by Poland. He co-ordinated with the Nazis in matters of frontier defense, expanded the military forces in his district, and supported Hitler in the Blomberg-Fritsch crisis of 1938. Accompanied by Himmler and Gauleiter Erich Koch, his forces incorporated the Lithuanian port of Memel into the Reich on March 23, 1939, in the last of Hitler's bloodless conquests.[7]

When war came in September 1939, his Wehrkreis HQ was redesignated 3rd Army, and controlled seven infantry divisions, an *ad hoc* panzer division, and four brigade-size commands. Kuechler divided his forces under three corps: Nikolaus von Falkenhorst's XXI (228th and 21st Infantry divisions), Lieutenant General Walter Petzell's I (11th and 61st Infantry divisions and Panzer Division Kempf), and Corps Wodrig (later XXVI Corps) under Lieutenant General Albert Wodrig (1st and 12th Infantry divisions).

He used Brigade Eberhard to seize Danzig, and the rest of his forces he kept in reserve or used to screen the southern and eastern Prussian frontier.[8]

Third Army's role in Poland was not defensive, nor was its primary mission to seize Danzig or to link up with the rest of Army Group North, which struck toward East Prussia on September 1. Kuechler committed only XXI Corps on his extreme right flank to a southwestern advance and struck due south with his main body (I Corps and Corps Wodrig: five infantry divisions and one panzer division) against the Polish Modlin Army in the Mlawa area, in the direction of Warsaw. By September 3, the day Army Group North and XXI Corps made contact at Graudenz (Grudziadz), Kuechler had already taken 10,000 prisoners and was forcing the Modlin Army back. Panzer Division Kempf had broken through and its spearheads were only fifty miles from Warsaw.[9] One panzer division was hardly considered sufficient to take the city, however, so 3rd Army was reinforced with Guderian's XIX and General Adolf Strauss's II Corps and was diverted to eastern Poland, to insure the main Polish armies did not withdraw to the east and form a new front. Kuechler's forces overran the Polish defenders on the Narew and Bug and linked up with the Russians, who invaded eastern Poland on September 17. Later, II Corps took Modlin (at the confluence of the Vistula and the Narew, about twenty miles northeast of Warsaw), and netted 24,000 prisoners.[10]

Kuechler remained in Poland until mid-October as Commander, Army Frontier Command North. Then he was named CG, 18th Army, and sent to Northern Germany, on the right wing of Army Group B for the Western campaign.

Kuechler's mission in May 1940 was to conquer Holland. Speed, surprise, and air superiority were the keys to this battle, as Kuechler had only five infantry divisions, a motorized division, and one weak panzer division (the 9th, equipped mainly with captured Czechoslovakian tanks). If the Dutch Army were given time to mobilize, they would be as strong as 18th Army. They were not given time, however. Spearheaded by the 9th Panzer, the SS Verfuegungs Motorized Division, and the Brandenburg Lehr Battalion, Kuechler's forces broke across the Dutch frontier at 5:30 A.M. on May 10.[11] Key towns and bridges in the Dutch rear were seized by the 7th Air and 22nd Air Landing divisions, which paved the way for the motorized advance. Dutch resistance was crumbling by May 13. The Netherlands surrendered on the evening of May 14.[12] Kuechler then turned his units south, where his forces occupied Antwerp and launched the final assault on Dunkirk,[13] capturing 40,000 French soldiers the Royal Navy had been unable to evacuate.

Georg von Kuechler's 18th Army was given a historic mission in the second phase of the French campaign, when it was assigned the task of capturing Paris. Initially in reserve with six infantry divisions, it was not committed to the battle until the French were already in full retreat. The French declared Paris an open city on June 13, and on the morning of June 14 the 218th Infantry Division took possession of it, marching down the Champs-Elysées in parade formation.[14] It was a high point in Kuechler's military career. For his services in Poland and the West, he was promoted to colonel general on July 19, 1940.

General von Kuechler had performed brilliantly in the Low Countries and France, leading his men forward from the sidecar of a motorcycle. His men loved him, according to American correspondent Louis P. Lochner, Chief of the Berlin Bureau of the Associated Press (and later editor of part of the Goebbels Diaries), who wrote of Kuechler's "fatherly care" of his soldiers. Often the general exposed himself to enemy fire in order to help rescue wounded enlisted men, a habit well calculated to inspire the admiration of his troops.[15]

After the fall of France, Kuechler was sent back to northern Poland where he guarded the Reich's eastern boundaries against possible Soviet provocations.[16] For the invasion of Russia, his 18th Army was part of Field Marshal Ritter Wilhelm von Leeb's Army Group North and consisted of eight infantry divisions under I, XXVI, and XXXVIII Corps.[17] On the far-left (northern) wing of the German armies, Kuechler conquered the old Baltic States of Lithuania, Latvia, and Estonia, destroyed the bulk of the Russian 8th Army, and drove on Leningrad but was unable to take the city (see chapter 5). On January 12, 1942, with the Soviet winter offensive in full swing, a disgusted Ritter von Leeb asked to be relieved of his command. He was replaced by Georg von Kuechler on January 17.

IN JANUARY 1942, Army Group North consisted of 18th Army (now under General Georg Lindemann) and 16th Army (Colonel General Ernst Busch). North to south, 18th Army included XXVI Corps, besieging the Soviet 8th Army at Oranienbaum; L, XXVIII, and I corps, holding the southern approaches to Leningrad; and, south of Lake Ilmen, 16th Army's XXXVIII, X, II, and XXXIX Panzer corps held a thin line from Lake Ilmen to Ostashkov. Lindemann faced the Soviet 42nd, 54th, and 55th Armies, while Busch was under

Map 16

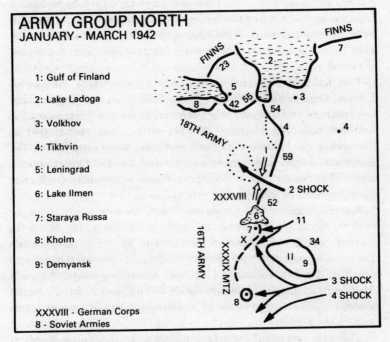

ARMY GROUP NORTH
JANUARY - MARCH 1942

1: Gulf of Finland

2: Lake Ladoga

3: Volkhov

4: Tikhvin

5: Leningrad

6: Lake Ilmen

7: Staraya Russa

8: Kholm

9: Demyansk

XXXVIII - German Corps
8 - Soviet Armies

THE BATTLES OF ARMY GROUP NORTH, JANUARY–MARCH 1942. Under heavy Russian attack during the winter of 1941/42, Army Group North held the major crossroads and maintained the Siege of Leningrad. Later, Field Marshal Georg von Kuechler managed to counterattack, rescue II Corps (encircled near Demyansk), restore his front and, destroy the Soviet 2nd Shock Army. Army Group North held roughly the same line until January 1944.

attack from the Volkhov Front (4th, 52nd, 59th, and 2nd Shock armies) and the Northwest Front (11th, 34th, 3rd Shock, and 4th Shock armies).[18]

Kuechler's situation was already desperate (see Map 16). He had virtually no reserves and was ill-equipped for a winter war. Temperatures reached −49 degrees Fahrenheit. He lost thousands of men to frostbite and many of the wounded froze to death because there were not enough blankets available to protect them from the cold.

The winter offensive in the northern sector was a battle for the crossroads. Kuechler simply did not have enough men to hold a continuous line against the heavy Russian assaults, so he tried to hold the major crossroads, reasoning that the Soviets would not be able to resupply their spearheads without them once the spring thaw set in.

The fighting centered on the road junctions of Novgorod, Kholm, Demyansk, and Starya Russa. The 281st Security Division (−) (reduced in strength) was encircled at Kholm on January 21, and the entire II Corps − 100,000 men − was surrounded at Demyansk on February 8. Both garrisons were supplied by the Luftwaffe, despite the terrible weather and Russian fighter opposition.[19] The Soviet attacks on Starya Russa were turned back after hand-to-hand fighting in the streets.

Kuechler resorted to many patchwork measures to prevent or contain breakthroughs and to hold strongpoints. He threw in recently organized battalions of Latvian SS volunteers, service troop units converted to infantry, Luftwaffe ground troops, and other *ad hoc* formations, but he held his strongpoints. By early March the crisis was generally under control, and Kuechler began a series of counterattacks aimed at destroying Russian penetrations and re-establishing his line.

The first successful counterattack came in the Volkhov sector, where two Soviet armies had penetrated fifty-five miles, even though the base of their penetration was only five miles wide. Kuechler dispatched Lieutenant General Dr. Friedrich Altrichter's 58th Infantry Division to the sector and ordered it to strike the southern base of the penetration, while the 4th SS Motorized Division "Police" attacked the northern base. The offensive began on March 15, and the two divisions linked up four days later, trapping two Soviet armies. Fighting in the Volkhov Pocket was fierce and continued until July, but seventeen Russian divisions and eight independent brigades were wiped out. Most of the Russians fought until the end; only 32,000 of them surrendered.[20]

In Kholm, Lieutenant General Theodor Scherer's 5,500-man garrison was besieged by the entire 3rd Strike Army. Two attempts to relieve it failed, but on May 5 Lieutenant General Baron Horst von Uckermann's 122nd Infantry Division reached the ruined city and rescued the survivors. Scherer had only 1,200 effectives left, and 2,200 wounded, after a siege of 103 days.[21]

Meanwhile, Kuechler also re-established contact with General Count Walter von Brockdorff-Ahlefeldt's II Corps at Demyansk. He formed a special assault force of five divisions near Starya Russa, under Lieutenant General Walter von Seydlitz-Kurzbach, and sent it forward on March 21. Progress was slow because the Russians had constructed five separate defensive lines to thwart any attempt to relieve the fortress; nevertheless, Group von Seydlitz struggled through twenty-four miles of mud to reach II Corps lines on April 20. By May 2, the German gains had been consolidated and the first land-delivered supplies reached Demyansk.[22]

For his part in halting the Russian winter offensive of 1941/42, Hitler promoted Kuechler to field marshal on June 30, 1942.[23] He now faced the problem of Leningrad.

In August 1942 Hitler moved Manstein's 11th Army from the Crimea to the northern sector, with an eye to launching another attack on Leningrad. With him (as of November 15) Manstein had four infantry, two panzer, and two Luftwaffe divisions, plus a mountain division.[24] The Russians attacked first, however, and the 11th Army was pinned down in defensive fighting. Then Stalingrad was surrounded, and Manstein and several of his divisions were transferred to the south; no major offensive against Leningrad was possible.

The Soviets attempted to break the Siege of Leningrad with massive attacks by several armies in October, but they were repulsed. The Reds immediately began building up for another offensive. They struck at Schluesselburg with twelve divisions on January 12, 1943, and one week later had established a six-mile corridor to Leningrad, linking the city to the outside world for the first time in seventeen months. The 41st and 277th Infantry divisions of Wodrig's XXVI Corps were almost completely destroyed. Russian attacks continued until early April 1943 but with little or no further gains. The entire Leningrad corridor was within range of German artillery, but Army Group North's hold on the city had been significantly weakened.[25]

Table 6

STRENGTH OF ARMY GROUP NORTH
(in divisions), January 2, 1942–October 10, 1943

Date	Inf	Pz	Mtz	Mtn	Jaeg	Lw Fld	Tng	Secu	Total
Dec. 22, 1942	33	2	3	2	3	4	1	3	51*
Jan. 1, 1943	30	0	2	1	3	4	1	3	44*
Apr. 9, 1943	31	0	2	1	3	6	1	3	47*
Jul. 7, 1943	32	0	2	1	3	6	1	3	48**
Oct. 10, 1943	30	0	1	1	3	4	1	3	43

SOURCES: *Kriegstagebuch des OKW*, Volume II, pp. 1396–97; Volume III, pp. 7, 260, 734, 1158.

Army Group North was neglected by Hitler and the High Command throughout 1943. Several of Kuechler's best divisions were diverted to the southern sector, the main crisis point of the Eastern Front. Table 6 shows his declining strength from December 22, 1942, to October 10, 1943. Note that he lost all of his panzer units and all but one of his mobile divisions. These units were largely replaced by Luftwaffe Field units, made up of excess Air Force personnel who were inadequately trained for ground fighting. By mid-July there were only forty-nine panzers in all of Army Group North, against a Soviet total of over one thousand. The Red Air Force had also established a limited air superiority over the entire zone of operations. The Soviets launched another offensive against Kuechler in July and August but had failed again by the middle of September; when it was over, however, Kuechler had only seven operational panzers left.[26]

Stalin committed another front (army group) to the northern

*Excludes 2nd SS Brigade and 17th Police Regiment
**Excludes SS Brigade "Latvia"

sector of the Eastern Front in the fall of 1943, convincing Kuechler that a major offensive was about to take place. Hitler, however, had overextended himself everywhere and was unable to send Kuechler even the six infantry divisions he requested.[27] He did, however, give Kuechler responsibility for the Nevel sector, formerly on the northern wing of Army Group Center. This move increased Army Group North's strength by three divisions but increased its frontage by forty-eight miles, making Kuechler's situation worse than it had been before.[28]

On October 6 the Soviet 3rd Shock Army struck the 2nd Luftwaffe Division on the far left flank of Army Group Center. The inexperienced division collapsed immediately. Advancing rapidly, the Soviets turned northeast and captured the critical city of Nevel on the southern flank of Army Group North early that evening. A fifteen-mile gap was created between Army Groups North and Center.

Hitler demanded to know why Nevel had fallen. Kluge explained that the 2nd Luftwaffe Field Division had panicked in its first battle and concluded that the High Command must realize that the armies in Russia were increasingly being forced to operate with troops who would not hold up against heavy attacks. Kluge requested that the 2nd Field be merged with an Army division, but Hitler disapproved on the grounds that he did not want to water down good Luftwaffe troops with bad Army troops![30] Shortly thereafter, Kluge was injured in an automobile accident. He was replaced by Field Marshal Busch.

At Hitler's insistence, Kuechler committed the equivalent of five infantry divisions to the Nevel fighting in the first half of November 1943. He protested this depletion of his reserve, for he feared an imminent Russian attack in the Leningrad sector, but was overruled by the Fuehrer. He never was able to retake Nevel and in the end set up a screen west of the city, using nineteen mixed battalions of police, security, and Latvian troops under the brutal SS Major General Erich von dem Bach-Zelewski.[31]

Hitler blamed the failure of the Nevel counterattacks on the "petty egoism" of the army group commanders, especially Kuechler. There may be some truth in his charges, for Kuechler never did work well with Busch, who had previously commanded 16th Army under Kuechler. In fact, two weeks after he assumed command of

Army Group North, Kuechler was asking permission to sack the pro-Nazi Busch, but it was not forthcoming. Their joint counter-attacks in late 1943 showed a distinct lack of co-operation and co-ordination.[32]

In late December, OKH transferred two more divisions from Army Group North to the left flank of Army Group Center. Meanwhile, Generalissimo Franco insisted that the excellent 250th (Spanish) Infantry Division be returned home, which it was. These units were replaced by non-German formations of dubious quality.[33]

Army Group North now had only forty divisions to defend more than five hundred miles of frontage. Several of these formations were non-German or Luftwaffe Field units, all of which were unreliable. The best German units were concentrated under the 16th Army in the Nevel sector, some five hundred miles from Leningrad. There was not a panzer division or brigade in the entire zone of operations.[34]

At Fuehrer Headquarters on December 30, Kuechler asked Hitler's permission to withdraw to the "Panther" position, more than one hundred miles to the west. This move would shorten his frontage to 440 miles, 120 of which were behind Lake Peipus and fifty more of which would be behind the mouth of the Narva, where it joined the Gulf of Finland. Construction of this line had been in progress since September and had made rapid headway. Kuechler felt this line could easily be held, but Hitler refused to allow a retreat because he knew that Finland and the Soviets were already carrying on peace negotiations in Stockholm, and a retreat here might well take Finland right out of the war. Meanwhile, OKH transferred the veteran East Prussian 1st Infantry Division from the 18th Army to Army Group South.[35] Kuechler also lost the experienced 96th and 254th Infantry divisions, which had first seen action in the West in 1940. All three were taken from 18th Army, then besieging Leningrad. He protested, but to no avail.[36]

Kuechler might have won his points on December 30, 1943, had he not made the mistake of taking Colonel General Georg Linde-mann with him to the conference. Lindemann was convinced that he could maintain the Siege of Leningrad in his well-prepared entrenchments, despite the loss of the three infantry divisions. On January 4, 1944, Kuechler visited Lindemann's headquarters and almost begged the 18th Army commander to reconsider his stand, but Lindemann remained optimistic.[37]

The Soviets attacked 18th Army's five Luftwaffe Field divisions and fifteen understrength Army divisions on January 14. They had a three to one superiority in infantry and artillery, and a six to one superiority in armor and aircraft. The battle seemed to be going Lindemann's way for the first three days, but then the weight of numbers began to tell. On January 17 he had to commit his entire reserve – the 61st Infantry Division – to hold together the remnants of the 10th Luftwaffe Field Division. Lindemann asked permission to retreat that morning, but Hitler would not sanction it. The following morning Lindemann reported that the battlefronts east of Oranienbaum and west of Leningrad were on the verge of collapse. Two divisions of III SS Panzer Corps between Oranienbaum and Leningrad were in danger of being annihilated.[38]

That evening, Kuechler signaled OKH that he intended to retreat that night, whether Hitler approved or not. Hitler did approve, but only after General Zeitler informed him that the retreat was already in progress. The Fuehrer would consent only to small-scale retreats, however; no general withdrawal to the "Panther" position was permitted.

The retreat order came too late for two divisions between Leningrad and Oranienbaum: they were trapped and destroyed between the Soviet 2nd Shock and 42nd armies. Meanwhile, five infantry battalions of XXXVIII Corps were surrounded at Novgorod, on the right flank of 18th Army, a defeat that unhinged Lindemann's southern flank and separated it from 16th Army. Kuechler realized that 18th Army must be allowed to retreat at least to the Luga River, or it too would face encirclement.[39]

At the front, the trench fighting resembled World War I. The Luftwaffe Field units collapsed, and the Army divisions were simply pounded to pieces by wave after wave of Soviet infantry and tanks. Some divisions lost all of their regimental commanders and were reduced to strengths of about five hundred men. Eighteenth Army was in danger of being overwhelmed.

On January 27, 1944, Kuechler attended a National Socialist Leadership Conference at Koenigsberg. In a private conference afterward, Kuechler reported to the Fuehrer that 18th Army had already suffered 40,000 casualties and was fighting with great determination everywhere, but must be allowed to retreat behind the Luga. Hitler disputed Kuechler's statements and reserved the right to order a withdrawal for himself.[40]

Kuechler's effectiveness as a commander was destroyed after the Koenigsberg conference. The next day his Chief of Staff, Lieutenant General Eberhard Kinzel, took matters into his own hands and verbally ordered 18th Army to retreat, as if the order had come from Kuechler himself. Hitler approved the order on January 30 but insisted that the Luga line be held. This would have been possible three days earlier, but was not possible now; 18th Army had been split into three pieces; its infantry strength had been reduced by casualties from 58,000 to 17,000, including 14,000 killed.[41]

Hitler made Kuechler the scapegoat for the whole disastrous affair. He summoned him to the noon situation conference at Fuehrer Headquarters on January 31 and relieved him of his command. Kuechler was temporarily replaced by Field Marshal Walter Model.[42] In March 1944 Model halted the Soviet advance on the Panther Line, just as Kuechler had planned six months before. In the meantime, two-thirds of 18th Army had been lost. Map 17 shows the ground lost by Army Group North during this period.

AFTER HIS RETIREMENT, Kuechler faded into obscurity. He was approached by Dr. Carl Goerdeler and Johannes Popitz about joining the anti-Hitler conspiracy. He expressed sympathy for their goals but refused to join them himself.[43]

THE MONOCLED KUECHLER was described as "a thoroughgoing Prussian by birth and mentality," despite "a curious un-Prussian untidiness in his personal appearance."[44] During World War II he dealt with enemy civilians in a civilized manner. He refused to co-operate with the SS murder squads in Poland and had violent arguments with Gauleiter Erich Koch over Nazi conduct in that country.[45] In Russia, in the fall of 1943, he ordered that the evacuation of civilians from eastern Estonia be halted because it was causing too much suffering among the civilian population.[46] Partisans, however, were an entirely different matter. His rear areas in Russia were thickly infested with guerrillas, and he treated them harshly, like the criminals he considered them to be. Arrested at

Map 17

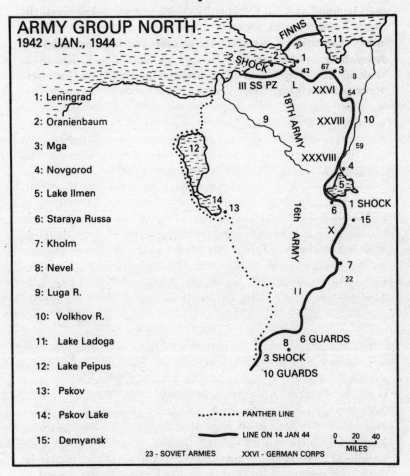

ARMY GROUP NORTH
1942 - JAN., 1944

FINNS

11

23
2 SHOCK — 2
1
42   67   3
III SS PZ   L   XXVI   54

1: Leningrad

2: Oranienbaum
9   18TH ARMY   XXVIII   10

3: Mga
59

4: Novgorod   XXXVIII   4

5: Lake Ilmen   5

6: Staraya Russa   6   1 SHOCK
16th   15

7: Kholm   ARMY   X

8: Nevel   7
22

9: Luga R.   II

10: Volkhov R.

11: Lake Ladoga   8   6 GUARDS

12: Lake Peipus   3 SHOCK

13: Pskov   10 GUARDS

14: Pskov Lake   •••••••• PANTHER LINE

15: Demyansk   ——— LINE ON 14 JAN 44   0   20   40
MILES
23 - SOVIET ARMIES   XXVI - GERMAN CORPS

12
14
13

ARMY GROUP NORTH, JANUARY–MARCH 1944. Under Field Marshal Georg von Kuechler, Army Group North besieged Leningrad for some nine hundred days. The siege was broken in January 1944, and Kuechler was retired in disgrace. He was replaced by Colonel General Model, who fell back to the Panther Line, which he reached on March 10. The Soviets were unable to penetrate this position, and their advance was temporarily halted. The 18th Army suffered especially heavy casualties during this retreat.

the end of the war, Kuechler was tried at Nuremberg as a minor war criminal and, on October 27, 1948, was sentenced to twenty years' imprisonment for his "cold-blooded and ruthless" treatment of partisans in Russia.[47] He was freed in February 1955 and faded back into obscurity.[48] In 1961 he was living in retirement with his wife at the village of Zurueckgezogenheit in the Garmisch-Partenkirchen area.[49] He died in 1969.[50]

14

Ernst Busch

STALINGRAD IS GENERALLY considered to be the greatest military disaster suffered by Hitler's armies, but it was not. Paulus lost only 230,000 men at Stalingrad; Ernst Busch lost at least 300,000 men in the Vitebsk-Minsk battles, which Paul Carell called "The Cannae of Army Group Center,"[1] Here is his story.

HE WAS BORN on July 6, 1885, at Essen-Steele, in the Ruhr industrial district of western Germany. He had the usual education for a future German officer, and in 1904 he graduated from the Gross Lichterfelde Cadet Academy and joined the Imperial Army as an officer-cadet in the Westphalian 13th Infantry Regiment at Muenster. He was commissioned second lieutenant in the 57th Infantry Regiment in 1908 and in 1913 was promoted to first lieutenant and assigned to the War Academy at Kassel for further training.[2]

Busch spent almost the entire World War I period as an infantry commander on the Western Front. He was appointed company commander upon the outbreak of hostilities and in 1915 was promoted to captain. Shortly afterward he was given command of a battalion in the 56th Infantry Regiment. Busch fought in the battles of Reims and Namur, in the Artois sector, and in Flanders, at La Bassée, Arras, and Verdun, and in the Champagne area in

1918. He was awarded the *Pour le Mérite* ("Blue Max") for his exceptional courage. Selected for retention in the 100,000-man Army, he held various staff and command assignments in the 1919–32 era. He was named Inspector of Transport Troops in the Reichswehr in 1925, and in 1930, while serving as a battalion commander in the 9th Infantry Regiment, he was promoted to lieutenant colonel. Two years later he was promoted to colonel and given command of the 9th Infantry Regiment at Potsdam.[3]

Ernst Busch was an "out-and-out" Nazi who followed Hitler with blind obedience. He was a brutal man who said that he enjoyed sitting on the People's Court tribunal,[4] a body that frequently invoked the death penalty. His career was unexceptional until Hitler assumed power in 1933, after which it was characterized by rapid promotion. He was a lieutenant colonel and number 176 on the German Army seniority list of 1932.[5] Nevertheless he was promoted to colonel soon after Hitler's rise and in 1935 was a major general, commanding the 23rd Infantry Division at Potsdam. He was promoted to lieutenant general in 1937 and was a rabid supporter of Hitler during the Blomberg-Fritsch crisis. On February 2, 1938, at the relatively early age of fifty-three, he received an accelerated promotion to general of infantry and soon after replaced Ewald von Kleist as commander of Wehrkreis VIII during the Brauchitsch purges.[6] Later that year he blindly supported Hitler's plans to invade Czechoslovakia, despite the risks involved and the objections of the more senior and experienced commanders.

In the invasion of Poland, Busch's VIII Corps (8th, 28th, and 239th Infantry divisions, 5th Panzer Division, and SS Regiment "Germania") was on the left flank of List's 14th Army, Army Group South. It took Krakow, advanced along the Vistula, and ended the campaign near Lvov.[7]

Busch replaced Georg von Kuechler as commander of the 16th (formerly 3rd) Army for the invasion of France. He did not understand tank tactics and did not believe the panzer thrust proposed by Guderian would get beyond the Meuse, much less reach the English Channel, but his most significant assignment in the campaign was to cover Guderian's left flank in the initial advance.[8] In the second (mopping-up) phase of the campaign, he directed thirteen divisions (all infantry) and followed the panzers south into the French interior.[9] After the French surrender he was promoted to colonel general on July 19, 1940.[10]

Busch's 16th Army remained in France until the spring of 1941, when it was sent to Poland. It was on the southern flank of Army Group North during the invasion of Russia. On June 27, 1941, it was controlling seven divisions – again, all infantry.[11] Later that year it received significant reinforcements. Busch's forces penetrated the Soviet frontier defenses and advanced to Staraya Russa, which the three divisions of 16th Army's X Corps took in the second week of August, after bitter street fighting. Then, in mid-August, X Corps was counterattacked by the Soviet 34th Army (eight infantry divisions, a cavalry corps, and an armored corps). Manstein's LVI Panzer Corps had to be diverted from the advance on Leningrad to clear up the situation.[12] When Manstein reported to 16th Army HQ at Dno on August 16, he described conditions there as "shitty". The brilliant Manstein nevertheless managed to reverse the situation and surround the Soviet 34th Army, which was destroyed on August 23.[13]

Busch faced the Russian winter offensive of 1941/42 with XXXVIII, XXXIX Panzer, X, and II corps: nine infantry divisions, one motorized division, and one SS motorized division on the line, with the 18th Motorized Division in reserve.[14] On January 9, in temperatures of minus 60 degrees Fahrenheit, he was struck by the 52nd, 11th, 34th, 3rd Shock, and 4th Shock armies. Busch signaled his commanders that he had no reserves; they would have to hold where they were. General Count von Brockdorff-Ahlefedt's II Corps was surrounded near Demyansk on February 8, with the 30th, 32nd, and 123rd Infantry divisions, the remnants of the 290th Infantry Division, plus SS Motorized Division "Totenkopf" and elements of the 12th Infantry Division. To the south, on January 28, Lieutenant General Scherer was encircled at Kholm with the HQ of his 281st Security Division and some 5,500 men from various units. Meanwhile, in a heroic resistance, Lieutenant General Theodor von Wrede's isolated 290th Infantry Division held up a large part of the 34th Soviet Army south of Lake Ilmen for weeks but was nearly wiped out in the process. Busch managed to save the vital city and supply base of Staraya Russa only by committing his last reserves (the 18th Motorized Division under Colonel Werner von Erdmannsdorff), and even then there was hand-to-hand fighting in the streets, right up to the doorstep of 16th Army's main supply depot. Contact with the left flank of Army Group Center was completely lost during this struggle. Kuechler, the recently appointed C-in-C of Army Group North, was so dissatisfied with Busch's leadership that he requested authorization to relieve him of his command. Permission was not forthcoming, however. Fortunately for the Germans, the main Soviet strike forces turned south, into the rear of Army Group Center, and headed for Vitebsk and Smolensk.[15] They were halted short of their objectives by General Model (see chapter 17).

As the Soviets exhausted themselves by attacking on a broad front and attempting to destroy all three German army groups, rather than contenting themselves with less ambitious objectives, Hitler and Kuechler reinforced the sagging 16th Army. That summer Busch was able to rescue Group Scherer at Kholm and re-establish ground contact with II Corps near Demyansk. Two Corps, however, did not regain its freedom of maneuver until March 1943, when the Demyansk salient was evacuated.[16]

From the spring of 1942 until 1944, the Soviet armies on the northern sector concentrated mainly against 18th Army, which was besieging Leningrad. Busch faced only secondary Soviet attacks and, except for the loss of Nevel in early October, suffered no more serious defeats. He did not score any major victories either. Nevertheless, on February 1, 1943, he was promoted to field marshal, despite his rather mediocre record.[17] He owed his advancement strictly to his pro-Nazi background and Hitler's favoritism, rather than to any distinguished performance on his part.

On October 28, 1943, Field Marshal Guenther von Kluge was seriously injured in an automobile accident. The next day Hitler named Ernst Busch to succeed him as Commander-in-Chief, Army Group Center. Busch had been promoted well beyond his capabilities. The results would be disastrous, as we shall see. Hitler valued Busch as a confirmed Nazi and as a yes-man. Busch knew he had not really proven himself, so he tended to rely on Hitler's judgment, even in tactical affairs. A Fuehrer order, to Busch, was something to be obeyed without question or thought of evasion. With this attitude, Busch was a thoroughly incompetent army group commander, a fact he would prove beyond a shadow of a doubt before 1944 was out.

FROM NORTH TO South, Army Group Center consisted of Colonel General Georg-Hans Reinhardt's 3rd Panzer Army (five infantry and four Luftwaffe Field divisions); Colonel General Gotthard Heinrici's 4th Army (eighteen infantry and four Luftwaffe Field divisions, plus the 18th Panzer and 25th Panzer Grenadier divisions); General Hans Jordan's 9th Army (fourteen infantry divisions and the battered 20th Panzer Grenadier Division) and Colonel General Walter Weiss's 2nd Army (eleven infantry and four panzer divisions, plus a security division). Busch also had six Hungarian infantry divisions, three German and one Slovak security divisions, and two field-training divisions, for an army group total of seventy-six divisions. This figure is very misleading, however. The Hungarian and Luftwaffe Field units were next to useless, and the security and training divisions were not equipped for frontline combat. Security divisions, for example, normally consisted of two security regiments, small reconnaissance, engineer and signal components, and no artillery at all. Of the remaining fifty-five divisions, none were at full strength and twenty-two were classified as in remnants or as *Kampfgruppen* – reduced to battle group strength by casualties but not without some combat value.[18] But the following summer, Busch had combined and consolidated several of these units and would have thirty-eight infantry divisions on June 15, 1944. The average infantry division would still have only two thousand men in six frontline battalions by that date.[19]

The Soviets attacked Army Group Center several times in the winter of 1943/44, and Busch actually managed to win several defensive victories. In the 4th Army's zone, the Soviets made four attempts to take Orsha (from October to the end of December 1943, but were defeated each time in heavy fighting, and the 3rd Panzer Army managed to hold Vitebsk – barely – against attacks by three Soviet armies. Busch's role in these victories was largely passive, however. When Reinhardt requested permission to withdraw his northernmost division, Busch referred the matter to Hitler, who turned it down. As a result, the division was encircled and escaped only when Reinhardt ordered it to break out against the Fuehrer's orders. It needlessly lost two thousand men and all of its artillery, heavy equipment and vehicles in the process.[20]

Hitler also ordered 2nd Army on Busch's southern flank to stand firm, despite the fact that Model's Army Group North Ukraine was retreating to the Dnieper, exposing Busch's right flank. Rather than question the Fuehrer's judgment, Busch held the line by extending his frontage and committing the bulk of his panzer divisions to the south. As a result of this "stand fast" order, a sixty-mile gap developed between 2nd Army and Model's northern flank.[21]

The fighting in the winter of 1943/44 was heavy, but Army Group Center managed to hold Vitebsk and Orsha, which guarded the fifty-mile land bridge between the Dvina and the Dnieper – the historic key to the Russian heartland. This represented a significant propaganda victory for the Germans, but elsewhere they were in serious trouble: the Siege of Leningrad was broken in mid-January; Army Group North was hurled back and lost contact with the northern wing of Army Group Center; and in the spring of 1944 the Ukraine was lost to Germany.[22] When the spring thaw brought a lull on the Eastern Front, Germany's strategic situation was at a low ebb.

In May 1944 Germany had 2,242,649 men on the Eastern Front – the lowest total since the invasion began. They were opposed by 6,077,000 Soviet troops – the highest total ever. The Third Reich had completely lost the initiative on all sectors. The Red Air Force had obtained aerial superiority, especially over Army Group Center, where 6th Air Fleet had only forty operational fighters against about three thousand Soviet aircraft. Army Group Center was in a particularly bad position. True, it was the strongest army group, with 792,196 men, as opposed to 540,965 in Army Group North, 400,542 in Army Group North Ukraine, and 508,946 in Army Group South Ukraine, but it was occupying a salient with both flanks exposed, and it barred the direct route to Berlin. At its closest point, Army Group Center was still only 290 miles from Moscow. At their closest point, the Russians were 550 miles from Berlin.[23]

In early May 1944, OKH's Eastern Intelligence Branch predicted that the Soviet summer offensive would come south of the Pripyat Marshes, through Rumania, Hungary, and Slovakia, and into the Balkans, if they could get that far. Intelligence estimates stated that the sector north of the Pripyat would remain quiet, even though Busch was concerned about signs of a troop buildup in the Kovel-Tarnopol area. Zeitzler agreed that the buildup here could not be taken lightly and proposed creating a reserve army on

Busch's right flank to deal with a possible attack. OKH began reinforcing General Friedrich Hossbach's LVI Panzer Corps (the nucleus of the reserve army) on Busch's right with tanks, artillery, and assault-gun units.[24]

On May 10, when Zeitzler suggested using the proposed reserve army for a surprise offensive, Model, the C-in-C of Army Group North Ukraine, saw an opportunity to take LVI Panzer Corps away from his less alert colleague, Busch. On May 15 he asked the Fuehrer to give him LVI Panzer so he could try "an offensive solution." This idea, of course, appealed to the offensive-minded dictator. Over the next few days Model bombarded Hitler with intelligence reports (from his own Ic) suggesting the offensive north of the Carpathians would fall on Army Group North Ukraine and miss Army Group Center altogether. Hitler was convinced, and on May 29 he transferred LVI Panzer Corps to Model. Army Group Center gave up only 6 percent of its front, but lost 15 percent of its divisions, 88 percent of its panzers, 23 percent of its assault guns, half of its tank destroyers, and 33 percent of its heavy artillery. General Weiss warned Busch that Model was trying to abscond with LVI Panzer, but Busch ignored him. He surrendered the corps without a single protest.[25]

Meanwhile, Stalin concentrated the 1st Baltic and 1st, 2nd, and 3rd Belorussian fronts opposite Army Group Center. He increased their troop strength by 60 percent, their tank and self-propelled gun strength by 300 percent, their artillery strength by 85 percent, and their already abundant air strength by 62 percent. By June 21, the 700,000 men of Army Group Center were facing 2,500,000 Russians, who were supported by 4,000 tanks, 24,400 guns and mortars, and 5,300 aircraft.[26]

Ninth Army was alarmed over the buildup, but Busch hardly reacted at all. He was more concerned about his right flank and the chances of getting LVI Panzer Corps back after Model completed his offensive. Busch turned down General Reinhardt's request to pull back his left flank in order to shorten his front and gain more divisions. Using one of Hitler's favorite arguments, he told Reinhardt that such a move would free more Russian than German troops. "Under Busch," Ziemke wrote, "Headquarters, Army Group Center had become a mindless instrument for transmitting the Fuehrer's will."[27]

In April, Hitler designated Vitebsk, Orsha, Mogilev, and Bobruisk "fortified places," to be defended to the last man. All were to have a frontline division assigned to them except Vitebsk, which was to be defended by a corps of at least three divisions. Busch again accepted the Fuehrer's order without question.[28]

Back at the front, General Hans Jordan, the acting commander of the 9th Army, appealed to Busch to question the "fortified places" concept and to retreat to the Dnieper or the Beresina, forty-five miles farther west, a move that would reduce the army group's frontage by one hundred and fifty miles.[29] Jordan's arguments must have been convincing, for on May 20 Busch visited Fuehrer Headquarters and requested permission to withdraw to the Dnieper or the Beresina, although he never questioned the "fortified places" policy. Hitler coolly rejected Busch's appeal, cynically remarking that he had not supposed Busch to be one of those generals who was always looking back over his shoulder. The remark was well calculated to influence Busch's attitude and subsequent behavior. Never again, he resolved, would he appear "disloyal": he would accept the Fuehrer's utterances without question and force his generals to do the same, even if the orders went against his own better judgment.[30]

Stalin deliberately waited until after the Allies landed in Normandy to launch his offensive. Then, on June 22, after a devastating aerial and artillery bombardment, the Soviets struck along a three-hundred-mile front. On the northern flank, X Corps of the 3rd Panzer Army was hit by twenty-nine infantry and eight tank divisions. Six Corps south of Vitebsk was attacked by eighteen infantry and nine tank divisions. Their objective was clear: they wanted to encircle General Friedrich Gollwitzer's LIII Corps at Vitebsk, which was being pinned down by the Soviet 43rd and 39th armies (Map 18). Meanwhile, in the army group's center, 4th Army was also under heavy attack. General Paul Voelckers's XXVII Corps was facing twenty-five infantry and eleven tank divisions, and XXXIX Panzer Corps met sixteen infantry and two armored divisions. The next day the offensive was extended to the zone of 9th Army, where XLI Panzer Corps was smashed by twenty-three infantry and seven tank divisions, and XXXV Corps tried to hold against twenty-seven infantry and six tank divisions.[31] By now, Stalin had committed almost two hundred divisions, with six

Map 18

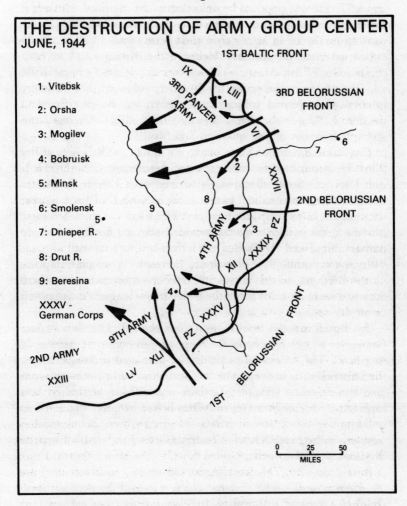

THE DESTRUCTION OF ARMY GROUP CENTER
JUNE, 1944

1ST BALTIC FRONT

1. Vitebsk

2: Orsha

3: Mogilev

4: Bobruisk

5: Minsk

6: Smolensk

7: Dnieper R.

8: Drut R.

9: Beresina

XXXV - German Corps

3RD PANZER ARMY

3RD BELORUSSIAN FRONT

2ND BELORUSSIAN FRONT

4TH ARMY

9TH ARMY

2ND ARMY

1ST BELORUSSIAN FRONT

IX   LIII   VI   XXVII   PZ   XXXIX   XII   XXXV   PZ   XLI   LV   XXIII   1ST

0   25   50
MILES

THE BATTLE OF VITEBSK-MINSK, JUNE 1944. The destruction of Army Group Center was a direct result of Field Marshal Busch's insistence that Hitler's hold-at-all-costs orders be obeyed to the letter. Fourth and 9th armies were virtually annihilated, and the 3rd Panzer Army was smashed. Busch was made the scapegoat for this defeat, and was retired in disgrace on June 28. He was replaced by Field Marshal Model.

thousand tanks and assault guns, supported by seven thousand aircraft.[32] He was opposed by only thirty-four divisions with a few depleted tank regiments and forty aircraft. Army Group Center was outnumbered in armor by a ratio of five and a half to one.[33]

Colonel General Gotthard Heinrici, the distinguished veteran commander of 4th Army, was away on sick leave. General Kurt von Tippelskirch, the acting commander, proposed that his army be allowed to retreat behind the Dnieper, but Busch refused to consider it. "Any voluntary abandonment of parts of the main line still intact is out of the question," he said.[34]

Tippelskirch had no choice but to try to halt the Russians at the front. He committed his main reserve, Lieutenant General Fried-rich-Karl von Steinkeller's newly arrived 60th Panzer Grenadier Division "Feldherrnhalle," to the sector of XXXIX Panzer Corps, with orders to stop up the hole east of Mogilev. General Robert Martinek, the panzer corps commander, who did not have a single panzer unit, asked Steinkeller just which hole he proposed to plug. "We've got nothing but holes here," he said. "Your place is back on the Beresina, so that we should have an interception line there for when we can't hold out on the Dnieper any longer. And that will be pretty soon!"

But Busch insisted that the front line be held. The 60th Panzer Grenadier was caught up in the Russian onslaught and needlessly sacrificed. Three days later Steinkeller managed to escape across the Dnieper with the remnants of his command but was captured near the Beresina. General Martinek was killed in action. He was replaced by Lieutenant General Otto Schuenemann, who tried to break out to the west, but it was too late by then. Schuenemann was also killed, and XXXIX Panzer Corps disintegrated, and its divisions ceased to exist.[35]

Busch met with Zeitzler at Army Group HQ in Minsk on June 24. Even now the field marshal did not appeal for permission to conduct a general withdrawal, but, weakening from his previous resolution, he did ask permission to abandon Vitebsk and pull 3rd Panzer Army back to the southwest. Zeitzler put this proposal to Hitler that afternoon but was turned down. All the Fuehrer would do was order the 212th Infantry and 5th Panzer divisions to Army Group Center. It would take days for them to arrive. Busch telephoned Hitler personally that evening, but the Fuehrer would not be persuaded: LIII Corps was to stay in Vitebsk, he commanded.[36]

"What can I do? What can I do?" Busch muttered to his Chief of Staff, Lieutenant General Hans Krebs. It never occurred to him to take matters into his own hands. It was probably too late now in any event; the "fortified place" was already surrounded, and the Russians were rapidly pushing the rest of 3rd Panzer Army – IX and VI corps – away from Vitebsk.[37]

That night, Hitler finally decided to allow General Gollwitzer to break out of Vitebsk with three of his four divisions, leaving only Lieutenant General Alfons Hitter's 206th Infantry Division behind. Gollwitzer cut his way out on June 25 but only got a dozen miles before being surrounded again the next day. Lieutenant Generals Pistorius and Rudolf Peschel, the commanders of the 4th and 6th Luftwaffe Field divisions, were both killed. Gollwitzer surrendered on the morning of June 27, as did Hitter. Thirty-five thousand men were lost, most of them killed during the breakout.[38]

On the southern edge of the cauldron, the 1st Belorussian Front threw its full weight into the attack on June 24. General Jordan hesitated twenty-four hours before committing his reserve, the 20th Panzer Division, to the battle. As a result the Russians broke through General Edmund Hoffmeister's XLI Panzer Corps with strong armored forces and headed for Bobruisk. Busch sacked Jordan for irresolute leadership, and replaced him with General Nikolaus von Vormann. But it was again too late: the Russians took Bobruisk on June 29 and fanned out behind 9th Army.[39] Of the 100,000 men in that command, only 30,000 escaped. Hoffmeister and Lieutenant General Baron Kurt-Jurgen von Luetzow, the commander of XXXV Corps, were captured. Lieutenant Generals Ernst Philipp and Karl Zutavern, the commanders of the 134th Infantry and the 18th Panzer Grenadier divisions, respectively, committed suicide rather than surrender to the Russians.[40]

On June 25, 4th Army faced an impossible situation. Its center (XXXIX Panzer Corps) was penetrated and overwhelmed, and the armies to its north and south – 3rd Panzer and 9th – were collapsing. General von Tippelskirch took matters into his own hands and ordered a retreat to the Dnieper on his own authority. Busch quickly countermanded the order and instructed 4th Army to retake its old front (!), but Tippelskirch ignored him and continued his retreat. Only on June 28 did Busch signal Tippelskirch to fall back behind the Beresina. He was already there by this time, but he had lost 130,000 of his 165,000 men.[41] He left behind

Voelckers's XXVII Corps and Lieutenant General Vincenz Mueller's XII Corps, trapped east of Minsk. They tried to break out, but were unsuccessful, and had to break up their commands into small groups. Almost none of these ever reached German lines. Both Voelckers and Mueller were captured.[42] Had Tippelskirch obeyed Busch, as Busch obeyed Hitler, 4th Army would have been completely wiped out. As things were, 4th and 9th armies were mere shells and 3rd Panzer Army was down to three understrength divisions with a total of only seventy guns.[43]

Hitler sacked Busch later on June 28 and replaced him with Field Marshal Model. Busch was deeply hurt by his dismissal, for he had just been obeying orders. This was true enough, but in the process he had lost 300,000 men and twenty-eight divisions,[44] as well as 215 tanks and more than 1,500 guns.[45] It was the greatest disaster Germany ever suffered on the Eastern Front. By the time Model managed to halt the Soviets, they had gained 435 miles and were on the Memel and the Vistula – on the very borders of the Reich itself.[46]

BUSCH FADED INTO obscurity after the Vitebsk-Minsk battles, and it seemed that his career was over. In July 1944 he was described as "broken and depressed."[47] On September 10, however, Reinhardt, who had succeeded Model as C-in-C of Army Group Center on August 16, wrote to Guderian. There were many rumors about Busch's fate, he informed the chief of the General Staff of the Army, including that he had committed suicide or had even defected to the Russians. He asked Guderian to persuade Hitler to give Busch some token of the Fuehrer's continued esteem. Early the next month General Rudolf Schmundt, the chief of the Army Personnel Office and Hitler's chief adjutant, died of wounds he had received in the July 20 assassination attempt. Hitler allowed Busch to give the oration at Schmundt's funeral.[48] Slowly he worked his way back into the Fuehrer's good graces and, on March 20, 1945, was named Commander-in-Chief, OB Northwest.[49]

Although his title sounded impressive, all Busch commanded was a single battle group, a few Labor Service (RAD) battalions impressed into the Army, Senior Engineer Command XV, and a few Hitler Youth, Volksturm, and miscellaneous units.[50] His area of operations included the North Sea coast, Schleswig-Holstein, and a fringe of eastern Holland still held by the Germans. The Western Front was already disintegrating. Although Busch tried to hold his sector by flying courts-martial and issuing impossible directives, there was nothing he could do. His men were thoroughly demoralized, and even the few troops and junior officers who still fought with tenacity had no respect for him and his methods. The final act of his military career was to sign the German surrender to British Field Marshal Montgomery on May 4, 1945.[51]

Taken to the United Kingdom, Busch survived his Fuehrer by only a few weeks. He died a broken man in British captivity on July 17, 1945, and was buried without ceremony on waste ground in Aldershot, under a false death certificate in an unmarked grave.[52] It was an end without honor.

15

Gerd von Rundstedt

THE SENIOR GERMAN officer in the Second World War was Karl
Rudolf Gerd von Rundstedt. He was born in Aschersleben, near
Halle, the descendant of an old Prussian Junker family from
Mecklenburg that dated back to 1109. His father was a major
general. Gerd, as he was called, entered the junior school for cadets
at Oranienstein in 1888, at age twelve.[1] He joined the Army as a
Fahnenjunker in the 83rd (2nd Upper Alsatian) Infantry Regiment at
Kassel on March 3, 1892, and was commissioned second lieutenant
the following year.[2] Erich von Manstein was six years old at the
time, Hitler was three, and Erwin Rommel was still in diapers.

Rundstedt served as battalion and regimental adjutant before
being promoted to first lieutenant and being assigned to the War
Academy in 1902, to undergo General Staff training. That same
year he married Louise von Goetz, the daughter of a retired major.
They had one son, who broke with family tradition and became a
historian. Dr. von Rundstedt, a reserve lieutenant in World War
II, later served as his father's aide from 1943 on, but this is getting
ahead of our story.[3]

After earning the red stripes of a General Staff Officer, Gerd
von Rundstedt spent three years on the Greater General Staff in
Berlin (1907–10) and two years on the General Staff of XI Corps

(1910–12), before joining the 171st Infantry Regiment as a company commander (1912–14). He spent the early months of World War I as a General Staff Officer (Ia) with the 22nd Reserve Division, and fought in the Battle of the Marne before being promoted to major at the end of November 1914.[4] He was assigned to the staff of the General Government of Antwerp in late 1914, but the following spring he was with a division on the Eastern Front, where he took part in the drive on Narev in Russia. At the end of the year he was assigned to the Polish General Government at Warsaw.[5]

Major von Rundstedt was sent to Hungary in 1916 as a corps Chief of Staff.[6] Apparently he did a brief tour of duty with the Turkish General Staff in early 1917,[7] before returning to the northern sector of the Eastern Front that fall, as Chief of Staff of LIII Corps, and fighting in the Lake Peipus battles. In 1918 he returned to France as Chief of Staff of XV Corps, a post he held at the end of the war.[8] Rundstedt emerged from the war with the Iron Cross, 1st Class, and the Hohenzollern House Order.[9] Naturally he was selected for the Reichsheer in 1920.

Rundstedt, who was considered an extremely capable General Staff officer, advanced rapidly in the Reichsheer and was given the most challenging and responsible assignments, including the task of investigating the causes for Germany's defeat. (He concluded that the economic power of Great Britain was the major reason Germany lost the war.) Rundstedt was successively named Chief of Staff of the 3rd Cavalry Division (1920–23) and Wehrkreis II on Germany's eastern border (late 1923–1925). Then he was named commander of the 18th Infantry Regiment (1925–26), with which he ruthlessly suppressed Communist and left-wing riots in Thuringia (central Germany) during the civil unrest of the mid-1920s. He then returned to Kassel as Chief of Staff of Army Group 2 (1926–28), was commander of the 2nd Cavalry Division at Breslau (1928–32), commander of Wehrkreis III (1932), and was Commander-in-Chief of Army Group 1 in Berlin when Hitler came to power in 1933. He was promoted to lieutenant colonel (1920), colonel (1923), major general (1927), lieutenant general (1929), and general of infantry (1932).[10]

Gerd von Rundstedt was an aristocrat who believed the Army should stay out of politics. He successfully blocked the promotion of the politically minded pro-Nazi General Walter von Reichenau to the post of Commander-in-Chief of the Army in 1934 and 1938. In the early years of the Nazi régime he was a major influence in the shaping and organization of the Wehrmacht, advocating military expansion, Prussian discipline, and motorized warfare. He nevertheless ran afoul of the Nazis, backing anti-Nazi Generals Fritsch and Beck, strongly protesting Fritsch's treatment in 1938, and opposing war over the Sudetenland, because he considered Germany militarily unprepared.[11] He also deeply offended Hitler by bluntly advising him to have nothing to do with that "Negroid asshole," Mussolini.[12] As a result, Rundstedt was retired in November 1938 with the rank of colonel general. For him, it was the first of four retirements.[13]

Colonel General von Rundstedt was recalled to active duty in May 1939, as Hitler's principal military adviser on the question of invading Poland. He told the Fuehrer that the Poles must be destroyed west of the Vistula and Narev rivers, by concentric attacks from Silesia and Pomerania. A surprise attack, characterized by a rapid advance, would be the best method, as it would prevent the Poles from mobilizing and retreating behind the rivers. The advance of Kuechler's 3rd Army from East Prussia against Warsaw was Hitler's own idea. Rundstedt left the detailed planning to the other members of "Working Staff Rundstedt": Lieutenant General Erich von Manstein and Colonel Guenther Blumentritt.[14] Of Rundstedt at this point, Manstein recalled:

As an exponent of grand tactics he was brilliant – a talented soldier who grasped the essentials of any problem in an instant. Indeed, he would concern himself with nothing else, being supremely indifferent to minor detail. He was a gentleman of the old school. . . . The General had a charm about him to which even Hitler succumbed. The latter seems to have taken a genuine liking to him. . . . What probably attracted Hitler was the indefinable impression the general gave of a man from a past which he did not understand and to the atmosphere of which he never had access.[15]

Like most of the German generals, Gerd von Rundstedt definitely favored the invasion of Poland. Most German officers agreed with Colonel General von Seeckt, the Commander-in-Chief of the

Reichswehr, when he said: "Poland's existence is intolerable and incompatible with Germany's essential needs: she must disappear . . . with help from ourselves."[16] Rundstedt played a key role in this disappearance, commanding almost a million men in the invasion of Poland. His Army Group South included the 8th, 10th, and 14th armies and the majority of the panzer and motorized formations, backed by most of the Luftwaffe. Most of the Polish Army was destroyed by his forces, and Colonel General Johannes Blasko- witz's 8th Army, under Rundstedt's general direction, captured Warsaw on September 28, 1939. Rundstedt was then transferred to the West, where his HQ was redesignated Army Group A and given the key role in the conquest of France.

As before, and, indeed, throughout his career as an army group commander, Gerd von Rundstedt did not concern himself with the "nuts and bolts" of the western operation, but rather left the details to his staff and subordinates. One staff officer recalled his love for cheap detective novels. He always read them with a desk drawer open, so he could quickly hide them when a visitor entered his office.[17]

He also had the curious habit of dressing in the uniform of a colonel. When he had been retired in 1938, he was given the singular honor of being named honorary colonel of the 18th Infantry Regiment, and he frequently wore this uniform, even after he had been promoted to field marshal. When someone did not recognize him and referred to or addressed him as "colonel," Rundstedt merely laughed.

He did not originate the plan that led to the conquest of France; its author was his Chief of Staff, General Erich von Manstein. Rundstedt did, however, push for its immediate adoption and eventually executed it in May 1940. The fighting of the battle he entrusted to his subordinate commanders, primarily Kleist (CG, Panzer Group Kleist), Kluge (CG, 4th Army), List (12th Army), and Busch (16th Army). Even when Guderian, the panzer spear- head commander, was relieved by Kleist, Rundstedt did not intervene personally, but sent General List to straighten out the matter – with happy results. Less happy was Rundstedt's decision to halt the panzers on the Aa Canal on May 23, to give the infantry time to close up with his armored vanguards. The army group commander was clearly nervous after the unsuccessful British counterattack at Arras on May 21, and his conservative directions gave the Allies seventy-two hours to reorganize their defenses. This delay played a major role in the subsequent escape of the British Expeditionary Force. After the war, however, Rundstedt unfairly blamed this "incredible blunder"[18] solely on the Fuehrer, who initially acted on Rundstedt's advice.[19] The plan to liquidate the pocket using just the Luftwaffe was Goering's idea alone.

After the fall of France, Rundstedt was promoted to field marshal on July 19, 1940, and was nominated to command the 6th, 9th, and 16th armies (led by von Reichenau, Strauss, and Busch, respectively) in the invasion of Britain. The Luftwaffe, however, was unable to obtain the necessary air superiority, and plans for the invasion were cancelled in October. Rundstedt served as Commander-in-Chief, West, for a time, but was sent back to the east in April 1941[20] to command Army Group South in the invasion of the Soviet Union.

Gerd von Rundstedt was against the Russian adventure from the beginning. His initial task there was the toughest of all the army group commanders, for he faced two Soviet fronts under Marshal Semen Mikhailovich Budenny. Army Group South consisted of (north to south) Kleist's 1st Panzer Group, Reichenau's 6th Army, Heinrich von Stuelpnagel's 17th Army, the Rumanian 3rd Army, Schobert's (later Manstein's) 11th Army, and the Rumanian 4th Army, a total of twenty-six infantry, five panzer, three motorized, six mountain or light, and three security divisions, plus fourteen Rumanian divisions, a grand total of forty-three German and fourteen Rumanian divisions.[21] He was opposed by fifty-one infantry, twenty-one cavalry and five armored divisions, plus fourteen mechanized or motorized brigades.[22]

Because of the strength of the Soviet opposition, and the difficult, forested terrain through which he advanced, Rundstedt did not score the tremendous successes that his neighbor, Fedor von Bock, enjoyed to the north. Rundstedt was subjected to heavier and more frequent counterattacks. Also, most of his combat units were non-motorized infantry. James Lucas wrote later: "Despite the propaganda pictures and stories which were put out regarding Germany's armed might, it cannot be accepted that its Army of World War II was a modern, that is, a motorized force, for the movement of the great mass of its units was on foot or hoof and thus the main [body] moved little faster than it had under Kaiser Wilhelm during World War I."[23]

Rundstedt did capture 150,000 men, 1,970 tanks, and 2,190 guns on the Russo-Rumanian frontier,[24] and managed to encircle and destroy most of the Soviet 6th and 12th armies and part of the 18th Army (about twenty divisions) at Uman, a battle that ended on August 8, 1941. He took 103,000 prisoners, as well as over three hundred tanks and eight hundred guns.[25] The following month his forces and the 2nd Army and 2nd Panzer Group of Army Group Center surrounded the bulk of Budenny's forces at Kiev and captured 667,000 men, 884 tanks, and 3,178 guns.[26] Then he sent Kleist south, into the rear of the Soviet concentration at Dnepropetrovsk, resulting in another battle of encirclement in the Osipenko-Mariupol sector on the Sea of Azov. The 1st Panzer Group and 11th Army took 107,000 prisoners, as well as 212 tanks and 672 guns.[27] In late October, Manstein's 11th Army took more than 100,000 prisoners on the Perekop isthmus and drove on Sevastopol, on the southern tip of the Crimean peninsula, but could not take the city.[28]

By early November 1941 Rundstedt had overrun the Ukraine, the Crimea, and the Donets industrial basin. Now he wanted to halt, before the Russian winter descended in earnest. Hitler ordered him to seize Rostov, the gateway to the Caucasus, instead. Rundstedt correctly estimated that he could take Rostov but would not have the strength to hold it. Still, he had no choice but to send Kleist's 1st Panzer Army to take the city, which he did. Then, as predicted, Kleist was brought under strong counterattack and could not hold. On November 28 Rundstedt ordered a general retreat.[29]

The withdrawal was already in progress on November 30, when Rundstedt received his first "hold at all costs" order from the Fuehrer. Despite his aristocratic manners, Rundstedt had a temper, especially when someone tried to intervene in what he considered his business. He immediately signaled back to Hitler that his order was "madness." If Hitler did not rescind the order, the message continued, he should find someone else to carry it out. That very night Rundstedt was relieved of his command.[30] Eleven days later he celebrated his sixty-sixth birthday in retirement. He was replaced by Field Marshal Walter von Reichenau.

Twenty-four hours after assuming command, Reichenau asked for and received permission to resume the retreat. In early December, Hitler visited Kleist's advanced HQ to see the situation for himself – and intent on relieving Kleist and his Chief of Staff (Major General Kurt Zeitzler) of their positions. To his great surprise, he found that Rundstedt's decision had, in fact, been the correct one; even the former chief of Hitler's bodyguard, SS General Sepp Dietrich, who had commanded the 1st SS Motorized Division at Rostov, said so. Hitler admitted to Jodl that he had been wrong. His confidence in the old Prussian field marshal was thus restored.[31]

HITLER APPOINTED GERD von Rundstedt Commander-in-Chief, West (OB West) and C-in-C, Army Group D on March 8, 1942.[32] His forces included 15th and 7th armies on the French Atlantic and Belgian coasts, and 1st Army in the interior. This appointment suited Rundstedt very well, for he liked Marshal Pétain and the French, possibly because he had Huguenot blood in his veins from his mother's side of the family.[33] However, Rundstedt did little to prepare the French coast for an Allied invasion, partially because of a lack of construction materials and labor battalions, and partially because of a lack of energy and foresight on his own part.

In France, Rundstedt adopted a very *laissez-faire* attitude. Unlike Rommel, he never believed that the British and Americans could be halted on the invasion beaches, so he was not particularly concerned about the Atlantic Wall, which he dubbed the "Propaganda Wall." He thought the decisive battle should be fought in the interior of France, out of the range of the big guns of the US and Royal navies. He was, in fact, preparing for a 1941-style battle in 1944, not realizing that the Anglo-American air forces had made the days of the great panzer victories a thing of the past. He was also disgusted by Hitler and OKW, which would not allow him to move his resources without the Fuehrer's permission. He engaged in frequent outbursts of sarcasm against the Nazis and Hitler, whom he habitually referred to as "the Bohemian corporal," but he refused to join the conspiracy against him. Indeed, he was usually paralyzed by apathy, frustration, and disgust.

Rundstedt's age was beginning to tell on him, and he knew it. By 1944 he had been in the Army fifty-two years; he was worn out physically, and his mental powers were declining, although it would be going much too far to suggest that he was growing senile. Most of the time he simply did nothing. Baron Geyr von Schweppenburg, the commander of Panzer Group West, characterized him as "incredibly idle."[34] When Erwin Rommel tried to induct him into the anti-Hitler conspiracy, he replied: "You are young. The people know you and love you. *You* do it."

At the beginning of 1944, Germany had 304 divisions in the field: 179 were in Russia, twenty-six in the Balkans, twenty-two in Italy, sixteen in Scandinavia, and eight in Finland. Rundstedt had only fifty-three.[35] By June 6, he had been reinforced to fifty-eight, many of which were second-rate, but some of which were excellent. Ten of them were panzer or motorized. Rundstedt's order of battle on D-Day is shown in Table 7.

Table 7

ORDER OF BATTLE, OB WEST, June 6, 1944

OB West: Field Marshal Gerd von Rundstedt
   Army Group B: Field Marshal Erwin Rommel
      15th Army: Col. Gen. Hans von Salmuth
      7th Army: Col. Gen. Friedrich Dollmann
   Army Group G: Col. Gen. Johannes Blaskowitz
      19th Army: Gen. Georg von Soderstern
      1st Army: Gen. Kurt von der Chevallerie
   Panzer Group West: Gen. Baron Leo Geyr von Schweppenburg
   1st Parachute Army: Luftwaffe Col. Gen. Kurt Student

Rundstedt left the details of the fighting in the Normandy campaign to his gifted subordinate, Erwin Rommel. The US Army's official history records:

> The evidence indicates that Rommel had an energy and strength of conviction that often enabled him to secure Hitler's backing, whereas Rundstedt, who was disposed whenever possible to compromise and allow arguments to go by default . . . relaxed command prerogatives that undoubtedly remained formally his. It is possible, of course, that he too came under Rommel's influence because he was content to allow Rommel to assume the main burden of responsibility. In any case the

clear fact is that after January, 1944, Rommel was the dominant personality in the west with an influence disproportionate to his formal command authority.[36]

Unlike Rundstedt, Rommel wanted to fight the decisive battle at the water's edge, correctly believing that Germany would never defeat the Western Allies if they were allowed time to consolidate their initial beachheads. Consequently, according to Rommel, everything depended on launching an armored counterattack as soon as possible. When the Allies landed on June 6, 1944, Rommel was away from his post. Rundstedt took it upon himself to order the 12th SS Panzer and Panzer Lehr divisions to rush to Normandy for the counterattack, even though this move was in conformance with Rommel's plans and not his own. Moreover, it was in violation of Rundstedt's own orders, for these units were not supposed to move without Hitler's personal approval. When OKW countermanded Rundstedt's orders later in the day, his Ia recalled that the old field marshal "was fuming with rage, red in the face, and his anger made his speech unintelligible."[37] As a result of the delays caused by the High Command and Rommel's own absence, the counterattack could not be launched until June 9, and it failed.

"I knew all along the German position in France was hopeless [after June 9]," Rundstedt said later, "and that eventually the war would be lost. But if I had been given a free hand to conduct operations, I think I could have made the Allies pay a fearful price for their victory. I had planned to fight a slow retiring action, exacting a heavy toll for each bit of ground I gave up. I had hoped this might have brought about a political decision which would have saved Germany from complete and utter defeat. But I did not have my way . . ."[38]

Rundstedt became more and more agitated over the constant interference of Hitler and his lackeys in the Normandy battle. On July 1 Rundstedt telephoned Berlin and reported to Field Marshal Keitel the failure of a local counterattack. They then began discussing the overall strategic situation, which appeared to be hopeless.

"What shall we do? What shall we do?" the Chief of OKW moaned.

"Make peace, you fools!" Rundstedt shouted. "What else can you do?" Then he hung up.[39]

The next day Colonel Heinrich Borgmann arrived at Rundstedt's

Headquarters in Paris, presented him with the Oak Leaves to his Knights' Cross, and handed him a letter relieving him of his command.[40] He was replaced by Field Marshal Guenther von Kluge.

RUNDSTEDT'S THIRD RETIREMENT lasted only two months. During that time Rommel was critically wounded, the Normandy front collapsed, Paris fell, most of France and Belgium were lost, the enemy was at the Dutch border, Kluge committed suicide, and the job of C-in-C, OB West, proved too much for his successor, Field Marshal Model, who also commanded Army Group B. On July 20, a group of Army officers, led by Colonel General Beck and Colonel Count Claus von Stauffenberg, narrowly failed to assassinate Hitler. No less than three field marshals – Witzleben, Rommel, and even Kluge – were implicated or directly involved. Now even a defeatist like Rundstedt was acceptable to the thoroughly paranoid Fuehrer, provided he was loyal. Hitler knew that Rundstedt had nothing but contempt for himself and the Nazis, but he was so nonpolitical that he would not actually do anything about it. On September 4 Rundstedt once again became Commander-in-Chief, OB West, now headquartered in Koblenz, Germany. Model stayed on in a reduced capacity, as C-in-C, Army Group B.

Almost as soon as Rundstedt assumed command, the Western Front stabilized. Eisenhower diverted most of his resources to Montgomery's 21st Army Group, leaving Bradley and Patton with insufficient supplies to continue their advance on a large scale. Then Model defeated Montgomery's ambitious ground-airborne offensive at Arnhem. Hitler, for his part, had another brainstorm: he would rebuild his decimated panzer divisions, marshal his reserves, create a new panzer army (the 6th, later 6th SS, under SS Colonel General Sepp Dietrich), and launch a major offensive through the Ardennes. His strategic objective was Antwerp. If he could capture that port, he could disrupt Allied preparations for the invasion of Germany for months. By then his "miracle weapons" would be ready, he declared, to win the war for Germany.

While Hitler built up his forces, Rundstedt used the relatively quiet period following Arnhem to build up the West Wall. His men fought a two-month battle at Aachen, which fell on October 21, gaining more time for the buildup.[41] His 15th Army (General

Gustav von Zangen) fought a delaying action in the Scheldt estuary, which Montgomery could not clear until November 8.[42] That same day, Patton began an offensive against General Hermann Balck's Army Group G. Although outnumbering the Germans three to one, he could only gain fifteen miles in eight days due to the rain, mud, minefields, fuel shortages, and Balck's mobile defenses. Patton was halted in the fortifications around Metz.[43] Eisenhower's other attacks in October and November resulted in some local successes, especially around Aachen, but Rundstedt held the West Wall basically intact, without having to use Hitler's panzer reserves. The stage was set for his most famous battle.

FIELD MARSHAL GERD von Rundstedt opposed the Ardennes offensive from the beginning. He saw at a glance that it was too ambitious for the forces involved. He thought it might be possible to pinch off the Allied salient at Aachen, which would have been a major American defeat in itself, but Hitler insisted upon driving on Antwerp. Rundstedt considered this plan "stupid" and divorced himself from it completely. Later it became a source of irritation to him when the Allies dubbed the Battle of the Bulge "Rundstedt's offensive." The old field marshal simply handed over the battle to his gifted pro-Nazi subordinate, Field Marshal Walter Model, who did not believe in it either, but commanded it with his typical determination and loyalty to the Fuehrer.

The battle began on December 16, 1944. Rundstedt was calling on Hitler to halt it on December 24, because XLVII Panzer Corps had failed to take the vital communications center of Bastogne from the encircled US 101st Airborne Division. Hitler would have none of it and threw in his last, irreplaceable reserves. The tide began to turn against the Germans on December 26. By January 9, 1945, even Hitler was ready to admit defeat and withdrew the 6th Panzer Army for employment on the Eastern Front. He had lost 103,000 men, and almost six hundred panzers and assault guns.[44] The war was lost.

The Battle of the Bulge broke German morale on the Western Front. Eisenhower began his final offensive on February 2. A week later, 25,000 men of the 19th Army were surrounded at Colmar, on the west side of the Rhine. The Allies broke through the Siegfried Line on February 20, and Rundstedt fell back behind the Rhine.

Then, on March 7, the US 9th Armored Division seized the Rhine River railroad bridge at Remagen intact. Bonn fell the next day, and Model's local reserves were unable to eliminate the American bridgehead at Remagen. The next day, March 9, Field Marshal von Rundstedt, who was as defeated as his men, was replaced by Kesselring.

GERD VON RUNDSTEDT was captured by the Americans on May 2, 1945, at the hospital at Bad Tolz, where he was undergoing treatment for arthritis.[45] He was indicted for war crimes in 1948 and scheduled to stand trial before a British military court, but he was released the following year due to ill health. He died in Hanover on February 24, 1953.[46]

HOW GOOD A military commander was Field Marshal Gerd von Rundstedt? He was undoubtedly capable but not of the first class. He almost never visited the front, rarely used the telephone, and left the day-to-day direction of operations to his staff officers and principal subordinates, concerning himself with only the most general matters. Although there is something to be said for his approach, Rundstedt probably overdid it, for he lost contact with the men at the front and did not always have a "feel" for the battle. He certainly did well until late 1941, but after that he never acted – he reacted. Sometimes he did not even do that. His period as commander of occupied France was characterized by neglect. The Atlantic coast was unprepared for the Allied invasion, and for this Rundstedt must bear full responsibility, along with Hitler. Kesselring referred to him as "the remote High Priest who was referred to only with a certain awe."[47] Colonel Seaton's verdict seems correct: "Von Rundstedt has some reputation as a strategist, but, although very able, it is doubtful whether he was a commander of the first rank or an outstandingly strong personality. He had a very impressive presence and possibly for this reason he was highly esteemed by the Fuehrer, who, in point of fact, scarcely knew him."[48]

16

Guenther von Kluge

GUENTHER HANS VON Kluge was born in Posen, Prussia, on October 30, 1882. After attending cadet schools, he joined the Imperial Army at the turn of the century and was commissioned second lieutenant in the 46th Field Artillery Regiment at Wolfenbuettel on March 22, 1901. He was a first lieutenant and battalion adjutant by the early 1910s, when he was sent to the War Academy to undergo General Staff training. In 1913 he was on the Greater General Staff in Berlin and went to war in 1914 as a captain on the staff of XXI Corps. Kluge led a battalion on the Western Front (November 1915–April 1916) before resuming his General Staff assignments with the 89th Infantry Division (1916–18) and the Alpine Corps (1918).[1] Captain Kluge fought in the battles around Artois and in Flanders. He was seriously wounded at Verdun in 1918.[2]

From his wartime service Guenther von Kluge was recognized as an excellent and energetic staff officer. He was selected for the Reichsheer and in 1921 was assigned to the staff of the 3rd Infantry Division. He served in staff positions in the Defense Ministry (1923–26), as commander of V Battalion, 3rd Artillery Regiment at Sagan (1926–28), and Chief of Staff of the 1st Cavalry Division Frankfurt-an-der-Oder (1928–30). Kluge succeeded Baron von Fritsch as commander of the 2nd Artillery Regiment in 1930 and on October 1, 1931, was named Artilleriefuehrer III and deputy commander of the 3rd Infantry Division. He was successively promoted to major (1923), lieutenant colonel (1927), and colonel (1930). In February 1933 he was promoted to major general and named Inspector of Signal Troops. The following year he was promoted to lieutenant general (on April 1, 1934), and was named commanding general of the 6th Infantry Division at Muenster in October. He continued his rapid advancement in September 1934, when he was given command of Wehrkreis VI at Muenster, controlling the 6th Infantry Division and Frontier Zone Command 9. Later the 16th and 26th Infantry divisions (at Rheine and Cologne, respectively) were created under his general direction. Guenther von Kluge was promoted to general of artillery on August 1, 1936.[3]

Kluge was a firm supporter of Werner von Fritsch, the Commander-in-Chief of the Army from 1934 to 1938. Fritsch was retired on trumped-up charges of homosexuality in February 1938, and Kluge was retired later that month in the Brauchitsch purges. With war on the horizon in October 1938, however, Hitler needed his experienced commanders, and Kluge was brought out of retirement and given command of the newly created Army Group 6, headquartered at Hanover. His north German command included Wehrkreise IX, X, and XI, with six infantry divisions.[4]

General Kluge was a traditionalist Prussian officer who showed considerable talent for his chosen profession. He was also marked, as Robert Wistrich wrote, by a "vacillating character and weak-minded opportunism."[5] His sharp mind recognized the monstrosity of the Nazi régime, but he also saw considerable personal and professional advantages in co-operating with it. Throughout World War II, Kluge realized he should join the anti-Hitler conspiracy but vacillated between duty and personal gain. He never really made a decision.

FOR THE INVASION of Poland, Brauchitsch redesignated Kluge's Army Group 6 headquarters as 4th Army. Hermann Goering hated Kluge and persuaded Hitler to veto his appointment. Hitler did so, but allowed himself to be overruled in this matter by the C-in-C of the Army. Hitler still doubted Kluge's ability, however, and the Prussian general was clearly on trial during the Polish campaign.[6]

Kluge passed the test of Poland with flying colours, cutting the Polish Corridor in three days and then driving on Warsaw from the northwest. He had convinced Hitler of his abilities, which the

Fuehrer would never question again, by the time injuries sustained in an airplane crash rendered him *hors de combat* for the rest of the campaign.[7]

Promoted to colonel general after Poland, Kluge quickly recovered his health and led 4th Army in the French campaign, although in a secondary role. He played a part in the delay at Dunkirk, advising Rundstedt to halt Kleist's armor on May 23.[8] The magnitude of this mistake was not apparent until later, however, and did not affect Kluge's advancement. After the French campaign he was promoted to field marshal on July 19, 1940. He was fifty-seven years old.

Guenther von Kluge was one of the few German generals who favored the invasion of the Soviet Union, which began on June 22, 1941. His 4th Army was initially the largest one, containing twenty-one infantry and two security divisions. On June 26, however, Hitler ordered Kluge to take direct control of both the 2nd and 3rd Panzer groups and hand his infantry over to HQ, 2nd Army, against the express wishes of Field Marshal Fedor von Bock, the army group commander. Kluge directed five panzer corps in the drive on Smolensk and has been severely criticized by Guderian for his handling of tank units. Guderian's remarks must be taken with a grain of salt, for he was hypercritical of people he did not like, and he did not get along with Kluge at all. (The two were even considering fighting a duel at one point, before cooler heads intervened.) However, the more objective General Hoth, the commander of the 3rd Panzer Group, is another matter; he, too, was highly critical of Kluge, who advanced on too broad a front and did not seal the Smolensk Pocket quickly enough, allowing a number of Soviet formations to escape.[9] By early August, Kluge was commanding infantry corps again.

In September, Kluge objected to the final drive on Moscow, saying it was too close to winter to try it. Bock ordered the advance anyway. Kluge directed the main infantry assault, but in such a slow and half-hearted manner that he came under criticism, particularly from Colonel General Erich Hoepner, whose 4th Panzer Army bore the brunt of the fighting while Kluge remained pretty well inactive.[10] The Russians counterattacked on December 6, and on December 18 Field Marshal Bock was relieved of the command of Army Group Center. He was replaced by Guenther von Kluge.

During the retreat from Moscow, Kluge got his revenge on the generals with whom he had clashed. Within a week he signaled Fuehrer Headquarters that either he or Guderian must be relieved of his command. Since Kluge was trying to hold every foot of ground, in accordance with Hitler's dictates, and Guderian did not hesitate to abandon hopeless positions whether higher head-quarters ratified his decisions or not, Hitler decided Guderian must go. He was relieved of his command on December 25,[11] and Germany lost one of its best tank commanders.

Kluge obeyed Hitler's orders blindly. "If scapegoats were needed," Colonel Albert Seaton wrote later, "von Kluge could find them; if heads must fall, von Kluge took good care to see that his would not be among them."[12] Among those replaced were General Ludwig Kuebler, the commander of 4th Army, Hoepner, and Colonel General Adolf Strauss, the commander of 9th Army. "Kluge had in fact replaced von Brauchitsch as the Fuehrer's postman," Seaton recorded.[13] In justice to Kluge, however, it must be noted that he was usually able to get approval for the necessary withdrawals, in 1941 at least, even if the Fuehrer gave permission only with the greatest reluctance.

Most of the battered Army Group Center escaped destruction in front of Moscow, despite Hitler and temperatures of below minus 25 degrees Fahrenheit, largely because Stalin also ignored his generals and attacked everywhere, instead of concentrating against the weakened Army Group Center. The cost was tremendous in any case. The Wehrmacht lost 981,895 men killed, wounded, or captured during the winter offensive: 30.68 percent of the total 3,200,000 men on the Eastern Front.[14]

Because of his heavy casualties, Hitler could launch an offensive on only one sector in the summer of 1942. He chose the southern sector. Kluge nevertheless played a significant role in the offensive by feinting. He successfully deceived Stalin into believing that the major German thrust would come against Moscow, not against Stalingrad and the Caucasus. The Russians concentrated against Kluge. When the German attack came, Stalin's huge reserves were in the wrong place.

Army Group Center faced several minor offensives in 1942 and defeated them all. Most notably, Kluge destroyed the Soviet Cavalry Corps Belov (20,000 men) at Kirov after it had broken through, and the Soviet 39th Army and XI Cavalry Corps (40,000 men) at Bely, also after they had broken through the front. Ninth Army and 2nd Panzer Army also faced major attacks at Rzhev and Belev, respectively, and defeated them. Second Panzer (now under Colonel General Rudolf Schmidt) destroyed 289 Soviet tanks in six days.[15]

Kluge also launched a minor offensive himself – and against his own wishes. In early August Hitler ordered him to pinch off the Russian salient at Sukhinichi with the 9th and 11th Panzer divisions, which Hitler had just sent him from Army Group B. Kluge said the offensive would fail because the attacking forces were too weak. Hitler overrode Kluge's objections, whereupon the field marshal told him that the responsibility for the failure would lie solely with the Fuehrer. The attack did fail, in mid-August. Hitler nonetheless reprimanded Kluge for the setback.[16] He could not have been too upset with Kluge, however, because on October 30 he gave the marshal a check for 250,000 Reichsmarks, as a sort of bonus and birthday present. Half of the money was to be used in improving Kluge's estate.[17]

During the winter of 1942/43, Army Group Center fought several severe defensive battles, especially on the left wing, in the zones of the 3rd Panzer and 9th armies. They lost Velikiye-Luki with its 7,000-man garrison, but in large part managed to hold their lines.

Kluge liked to play both sides of any issue, which is why he obtained the nickname "Der kluge Hans" – Clever Hans, a play on words with his name. No better example of this character trait can be seen than in his attitude toward Operation Citadelle, the Kursk offensive of 1943. In early May, he arrived at Fuehrer HQ in favor of delaying the start of the offensive. Then he was informed that Hitler had already decided upon a postponement. When he saw Hitler, Kluge spoke out strongly *against* the delay, to avoid future blame if the offensive failed.[18]

Field Marshal Kluge also played up to both sides in the anti-Hitler conspiracy, to which he gave noncommittal encouragement. His chief of operations, the exceptionally capable Major General Henning von Treschow, was a leader in the movement, and Kluge indicated his sympathy for it, but never committed himself 100 percent. This was typical of the man. Treschow killed himself on July 21, 1944, the day after the plot miscarried.

Meanwhile, Operation Citadelle failed. Kluge had never been an enthusiastic supporter of it, so he left command of the northern pincers to Colonel General Model. Manstein's Army Group South was responsible for the other pincer, so Kluge escaped blame when the operation misfired in early July 1943. Kluge was the first to call for a suspension of the attacks.[19]

After Kursk, Germany completely forfeited the initiative on the Eastern Front. On July 15, strong Soviet forces broke through Army Group Center's lines at Orel. Kluge slowed, but could not halt, the Soviet advance by sending in most of the depleted panzer units Model had hurled into the Battle of Kursk. Despite heavy odds, Kluge retreated gradually to the Hagen Line, along the Dnieper, which he reached on August 17. Three days later, OKH took five divisions from 9th Army and sent them to Army Group South. Kluge informed them that he could not guarantee to hold his positions without them, but Manstein's situation was even more desperate. The Russians did, in fact, break the Hagen Line on August 29. As of September 7, Kluge had only 108 tanks and 191 assault guns left. Bryansk fell on September 17, and Smolensk and Roslavl were lost on September 24. Kluge then retreated to the Panther Line in Belorussia.[20]

The Soviets renewed their offensive against Army Group Center on October 6. Although they still outnumbered Kluge, most of their strength was committed to the south, against Manstein, while Kluge still had the strongest German army group (forty-two infantry and eight panzer or panzer grenadier divisions, of which twelve infantry and four panzer divisions were at battle group strength).[21] Kluge lost Gomel and Nevel but managed to repulse the Russians elsewhere.

On October 28, 1943, Kluge's car hit a patch of ice and ran off the road. Kluge was severely injured and had to be sent home. It took him quite some time to recover, and he did not return to duty for eight months.

KLUGE WAS SUMMONED to Berchtesgarden in late June 1944, and on July 2 was appointed C-in-C, OB West. This force included Army Group B under Field Marshal Rommel, then fighting desperately in Normandy. Hitler and his cronies convinced Kluge that the German failures on the Western Front since D-Day were due to poor or irresolute leadership. Kluge headed for Paris on July 4, confident that he could restore the situation by putting backbone into his subordinates by the force of his own dynamic personality. He was full of baloney.

Guenther von Kluge had no idea of what he was in for as Commander-in-Chief of the Western Front. Influenced by the Fuehrer, Kluge believed that much of the problem lay with Erwin Rommel. The two clashed immediately. On July 5, Kluge greeted Rommel with the words: "Now you, too, will have to get accustomed to obeying orders!" Rommel did not take this insult lying down, and a terrible verbal row ensued. Kluge criticized Rommel for being too pessimistic and failing to follow Hitler's orders as wholeheartedly as he should. Rommel suggested (loudly) that Kluge visit the front before he drew any conclusions. The marshals' argument became so personal and insulting that Kluge ordered everyone else to leave the room.[22]

Kluge did visit the front shortly thereafter. "Field Marshal von Kluge was a robust, aggressive type soldier," Lieutenant General Guenther Blumentritt, the Chief of Staff of OB West, recalled later.

Table 8

ORDER OF BATTLE, OB WEST, July 1944

OB West: Field Marshal Guenther von Kluge
    Army Group B: Field Marshal Erwin Rommel*
        15th Army: Col. Gen. Hans von Salmuth
        7th Army: SS Col. Gen. Paul Hausser**
        Panzer Group West: Gen. Leo Geyr von
            Schweppenburg***
    Army Group G: Col. Gen. Johannes Blaskowitz
        19th Army: Gen. Friedrich Wiese
        1st Army: Gen. Kurt von der Chevallerie
    1st Parachute Army: Luftwaffe Col. Gen. Kurt Student

---

*Wounded July 17; replaced by Kluge.
**Col. Gen. Dollmann died of a heart attack on June 29.
***Replaced by Gen. Heinrich Eberbach, July 2. Panzer Group West redesignated 5th Panzer Army on August 6.

"At the start he was very cheerful and confident – like all newly appointed commanders . . . [he] clearly thought at first that the dangers of the situation had been exaggerated, [but] his view soon changed. . . . Within a few days he became very sober and quiet. Hitler did not like the changing tone of his reports."[23]

Kluge did not interfere a great deal with Rommel's conduct of operations from early July until the Desert Fox was critically wounded on July 17. Then Kluge assumed command of Army Group B, in addition to OB West. His last battle can properly be said to have begun on this date. His Order of Battle for July 1944 is shown in Table 8. Map 19 shows the battle lines on July 24, as well as the ground lost since the first of the month, when Kluge assumed command of OB West.

On July 20, 1944, Kluge drove to Panzer Group West's HQ at Mittois (thirteen miles northeast of Falaise), to confer with General Heinrich Eberbach and SS Colonel General Hausser, the commander of 7th Army. He did not return to Army Group B Headquarters at La Roche Guyon until 6:15 P.M., where he found two messages. One from Witzleben, dated 5 P.M., said Hitler was dead; the second (later) message was a broadcast that claimed that the Fuehrer was alive and would speak to the nation that evening.[24] Clearly the long-awaited coup was underway, but the outcome was in doubt. Kluge sat firmly on the fence, waiting to see who would win before he committed himself. Later that evening he telephoned Keitel, who assured him that the Fuehrer was in perfect health. A few minutes later General Karl Heinrich von Stuelpnagel, the Military Governor of France, appeared, along with his Chief of Staff, Luftwaffe Lieutenant Colonel Caesar von Hofacker. They tried to induce Kluge to act, but the field marshal denied all knowledge of the conspiracy and told them it had failed: Hitler was alive. He then calmly invited them to dinner. During the meal, only Kluge spoke.[25] "They ate in silence by candlelight, as if they sat in a house just visited by death," Lieutenant General Hans Speidel, the Chief of Staff of Army Group B and a member of the conspiracy, later recalled. "Those who survived never forgot the ghostly atmosphere."[26]

Kluge was completely composed until after the meal, when Stuelpnagel informed him that he had already ordered all SS and Gestapo men in Paris arrested. Kluge was shocked – how was he

Map 19

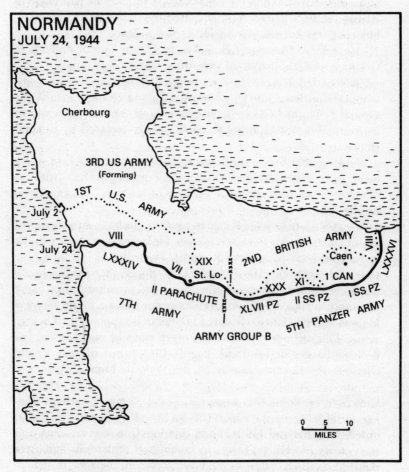

THE NORMANDY FRONT, JULY 1944. Following the successful Allied landings on D-Day, June 6, Army Group B had contained their bridgehead in Normandy for more than six weeks. The opposing dispositions are shown as of July 24. The next day the Allies attacked the Panzer Lehr Division on the right flank of LXXXIV Corps (just west of St. Lô) with some three thousand aircraft, including hundreds of heavy bombers. Field Marshal Kluge reacted slowly and allowed the Americans to exploit their breakthrough and end the stalemate in Normandy. Paris fell a month later.

going to cover *this* up? Hofacker then interrupted to remind Kluge of his agreement to join the conspiracy, a promise he had made in Russia the year before. Yes, admitted the flabbergasted marshal, but that was conditional on Hitler being dead.

"Herr Field Marshal," Hofacker said, "the fate of millions of Germans and the honor of the Army lies in your hands!"

"No!" cried Kluge. He then relieved Stuelpnagel of his command and ordered him to release the SS and Gestapo men in his custody.[27] Privately Kluge advised the former military governor to go into hiding. Stuelpnagel was temporarily replaced by General Blumentritt.

Not long after Stuelpnagel and Hofacker departed, Kluge sent a message to Hitler, calling the conspirators of July 20 "ruthless murderers" and assuring the Fuehrer of his own "unchangeable loyalty."[28]

It was too late now for Kluge to cover up his halfhearted support of the conspiracy, however. When Hofacker was arrested, he implicated both Kluge and Rommel. From that point on, Kluge walked a tightrope. He did not fail to notice that the Fuehrer's dispatches to him were becoming more and more insulting. There was more at stake now than just winning or losing a battle: his very life was in the balance. He dared not fail or disappoint the Fuehrer again! This attitude characterized every move he made during the decisive battles of July and August 1944, when disaster finally overtook the German armies on the Western Front.

SHORTLY BEFORE HE was wounded, Erwin Rommel, perhaps fearing an offensive by the Americans on his left (western) flank, had ordered the 2nd and 116th Panzer divisions into reserve, south and west of St. Lô. Kluge, however, committed these units against a British-Canadian attack in the Caen sector, in the zone of Panzer Group West. Little did he dream that this was not the main offensive; it was to come west of St. Lô, in the 7th Army's sector.

On July 24, there were seven panzer divisions and four heavy tank battalions facing the British 2nd Army in the Caen area, but only two depleted panzer divisions in the St. Lô area, facing General Omar Bradley's US 1st Army. Seventh Army had twenty-three infantry battalions in seven divisions on line, but only three in reserve (under HQ, 275th Infantry Division). In the past twelve days, 7th Army had inflicted ten thousand casualties on the

Americans in what General Dietrich von Choltitz, the commander of LXXXIV Corps, called a "tremendous bloodbath." Seventh Army's losses were also high, and its men were nearing exhaustion. The panzer divisions of 7th Army – 2nd SS and Panzer Lehr – had only 109 tanks remaining, and the infantry divisions were all at battle group strength. They were facing fifteen American divisions, with four divisions of General George S. Patton's newly activated 3rd US Army in reserve.[29]

The weather was so poor on July 24 that some Allied heavy bombers actually dropped their loads on their own side of the line. General Hausser was convinced that something was afoot and wanted to withdraw, but Kluge did not dare ask Hitler's permission for such a move. Besides, he was still convinced that the next major attack would come in the Caen sector – so much so that he committed 2nd Panzer Division to this sector the same day.[30] Hausser would have to fend for himself.

The next day, July 25, beginning at 9:40 A.M., Lieutenant General Fritz Bayerlein's Panzer Lehr Division west of St. Lô was attacked by wave after wave of bombers. Almost three thousand aircraft, virtually the entire US 8th and 9th Air Forces, pounded the division into near oblivion in repeated relays of carpet bombing. In all, more than 3,300 tons of bombs were dropped on a single German division.[31] The command post of the 902nd Panzer Grenadier Regiment took a direct hit, and everyone in it was killed. Tanks were hurled through the air like toys; every panzer in the division's forward area was destroyed. Over 70 percent of the élite Panzer Lehr Division were casualties. The landscape resembled the face of the moon. When the US VII Corps began its advance later that day, many of its units were delayed longer by the hundreds of bomb craters than by the few survivors who still put up sporadic resistance.

Kluge was slow to react. He promised to send Bayerlein an SS panzer battalion of sixty tanks, but when it arrived that night it had only five. Bayerlein had managed to scrape together fourteen more. The next day, July 26, the Americans committed their armor. Nineteen worn panzers and a few hundred dazed grenadiers faced five American divisions, two of which were armored. The Americans gained only three miles that day, but Panzer Lehr was virtually wiped out.

All Kluge sent Bayerlein on July 26 was a message ordering him to hold his positions. Bayerlein, the former Chief of Staff of the Afrika Korps, looked at Kluge's messenger and replied bitterly: "Out in the front every one is holding out, Herr Oberstleutnant. Every one. My grenadiers and my engineers and my tank crews – they're all holding their ground. Not a single man is leaving his post. Not one! They're lying in their foxholes mute and silent, for they are dead. Dead! Do you understand? You may report to the Field Marshal that the Panzer Lehr Division is annihilated."[32]

Hausser, who realized the danger, threw in his last reserves: Battle Group Heinz, which included the three remaining battalions of the 275th Infantry. By nightfall it, too, was wiped out.[33]

The following day, July 27, the US VII Corps (1st, 4th, and 30th Infantry and 2nd and 3rd Armored divisions) began to gain ground rapidly. Kluge finally ordered the 2nd and 116th Panzer divisions to march quickly toward the threatened sector and counterattack, but before they could arrive LXXXIV Corps had been overrun.[34] The front had burst.

General Patton's US 3rd Army took charge of the pursuit the next day. He ordered VII Corps to expand the gap in the German line and sent VIII Corps straight through it, for the coast. Its spearhead, the US 4th Armored Division, advanced twenty-five miles in thirty-six hours and seized Avranches on the coast on the evening of July 30. By the following day it was fanning out into the deep rear of 7th Army. Some units even crossed into Brittany, which had been almost stripped of defenders during the Normandy fighting. The 2nd and 116th Panzers struck the US VII Corps and prevented it from advancing further east (thus saving the right wing of 7th Army), but could not prevent the disaster on the left. General Patton, interpreting his orders rather liberally, pushed seven divisions down a single road in a seventy-two-hour period. They headed north into Brittany, south into the interior of France, and east – into the rear of Army Group B. An envelopment was taking shape.[35]

Meanwhile, Field Marshal Kluge behaved characteristically: he found a scapegoat. General Dietrich von Choltitz, whose LXXXIV Corps had been cut off by the rapid American advance, broke out with some of his troops – elements of the 2nd SS Panzer and 17th SS Panzer Grenadier divisions and the 6th Parachute Regiment. A few others managed to trickle out, in small groups or even individually, but the bulk of the 243rd and 353rd Infantry and 91st

Air Landing divisions were destroyed. Kluge quite unjustly blamed Choltitz for the disaster and relieved him of his command. He was replaced by Lieutenant General Otto Elfeldt.[36]

While Patton overran Brittany, Bradley took Mortain and established a firm blocking position. Bradley had by now taken command of the US 12th Army Group and handed 1st Army over to Lieutenant General Courtney Hodges. He ordered Patton to attack eastward with his main strength, into the deep rear of Army Group B.

Hitler thought he saw an opportunity in all of this. All Kluge had to do was smash the US 1st Army at Mortain and seize Avranches. Then Patton would be cut off and the front restored. Blissfully ignoring Patton's drive to the east and Montgomery's heavy attacks from the north, as well as the overwhelming Allied air supremacy, on August 4 he instructed Kluge to launch the attack with eight panzer divisions.[37]

Kluge recognized this order for the terrible piece of folly that it was, but he dared not protest. Five of the panzer divisions he had been ordered to assemble were already decisively engaged to the north, against Montgomery's 21st Army Group (2nd British and 1st Canadian armies). Only one, the 1st SS Panzer, could be disengaged. Since he dared not wait, with the encirclement already taking shape, he asked for and received permission to attack on the night of August 6/7.[38] Significantly, Hitler had already sent Jodl's deputy, General Walter Warlimont, to "sit in" at Kluge's HQ, and General Walter Buhle, a man Hitler trusted, was en route to "observe" the attack.[39] Map 20 shows Kluge's situation on August 6, 1944.

Kluge was "almost in despair" that night,[40] when General Baron Hans von Funck (CG, XLVII Panzer Corps) attacked with the 116th Panzer, 2nd Panzer, 2nd SS Panzer, and 1st SS Panzer divisions. Funck's order of battle sounds impressive, but these units had been in constant combat for weeks. In addition, the 84th Infantry Division did not arrive in time to relieve the 116th Panzer at the front as planned, so the latter unit hardly moved at all. According to Colonel von Kluge, the marshal's son and an observer of the attack, Funck moved out with only eighty tanks. He was fortunate enough to hit a weak spot in the American line and actually retook Mortain, but was then plastered by US fighter bombers. By 1 P.M. on August 7, Funck had lost fifty tanks and was being counterattacked

Map 20

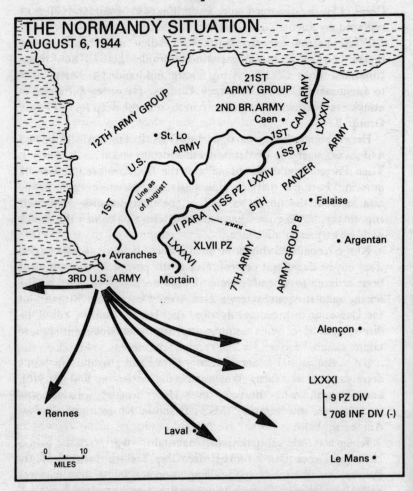

THE NORMANDY SITUATION
AUGUST 6, 1944

21ST
ARMY GROUP

2ND BR. ARMY
Caen •

12TH ARMY GROUP

CAN ARMY

1ST

• St. Lo
U.S.
ARMY

LXXXIV ARMY

I SS PZ

Line as
of August 1

II SS PZ LXXIV

PANZER

1ST

II PARA

5TH

• Falaise

xxxx

XLVII PZ

• Argentan

LXXXVI

ARMY GROUP B

• Avranches

3RD U.S. ARMY   Mortain

7TH ARMY

Alençon •

LXXXI

• Rennes

9 PZ DIV

708 INF DIV (-)

Laval •

0   10
MILES

Le Mans •

THE NORMANDY SITUATION, AUGUST 6, 1944. With the
US 3rd Army under General Patton driving into the interior of
France and the rear of Army Group B, Hitler ordered Field Marshal
Guenther von Kluge to restore the situation by counterattacking
and retaking Avranches, thus cutting off the American break-
through forces. The counterattack of XLVII Panzer Corps retook
Mortain but was halted soon after. Hitler blamed Kluge for this
failure and relieved him of command eleven days later.

by four infantry divisions and an armored division of the US VII Corps.[41] He was stopped cold. Hitler's verdict was summed up in one acid comment: "The attack failed because Kluge *wanted* it to fail."[42] He ordered a second attack for August 11 or 12. It was to be launched by Eberbach under a temporary HQ (Panzer Group Eberbach, formerly HQ, XLVII Panzer Corps). Sepp Dietrich was to temporarily take charge of 5th Panzer Army. This time all the units were to assemble, the Fuehrer decreed, and launch a deliberate attack. They were not to charge until they were ready.

Events rapidly overtook both the Fuehrer's strategy and Kluge. The US XV Corps of Patton's army drove seventy-five miles in three days and seized Le Mans on August 6. It was being delayed only by Major General Erwin Jolasse's 9th Panzer Division, which had been en route from the south of France to join Army Group B but, fortunately for the Germans, had been sucked into the battle on the southern flank, against four strong divisions of Patton's army. Without this piece of luck, Patton would not have been delayed at all. Jolasse could not, however, prevent the Americans from taking Alençon on August 12. They were now only twenty miles from Montgomery's spearheads. Eberbach had to commit his attack forces at Argentan, north of Alençon, to prevent a link-up. All thought of another counterattack was abandoned – except, of course, in Berlin.[43]

Fifth Panzer and 7th armies, as well as Panzer Group Eberbach, were now in imminent danger of being encircled, and the only remaining escape route was the bottleneck between Falaise and Argentan. It was high time to get out, but Kluge again did not dare ask permission to do so. He merely requested to be allowed to concentrate all of his armor near Argentan, to hold open the base of the salient, but Hitler refused even this. He still insisted on the Avranches attack. By nightfall on August 14 less than eighteen miles separated the British and American spearheads (Map 21).[44]

The next day, Kluge left his HQ to confer with Hausser and Eberbach in the Falaise Pocket – and disappeared for twelve hours. He arrived at Eberbach's headquarters that night "in a very shaken condition," saying that he had been attacked by fighter-bombers, his radio truck had been destroyed, and he had spent most of the day in a ditch. Hitler, however, strongly suspected that he had been trying to make contact with the enemy to arrange a capitulation.

Map 21

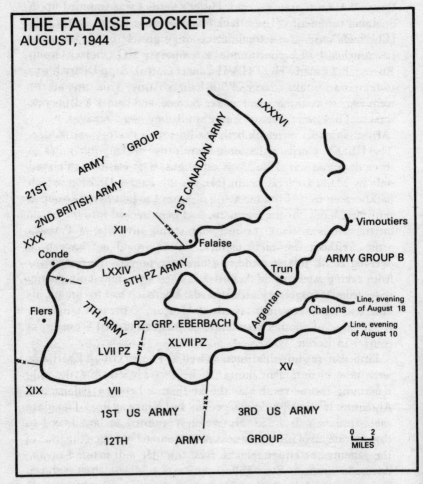

THE FALAISE POCKET
AUGUST, 1944

21ST

ARMY   GROUP

2ND BRITISH ARMY

1ST CANADIAN ARMY

LXXXVI

XXX

XII

Conde

Falaise

LXXIV

5TH PZ ARMY

Vimoutiers

ARMY GROUP B

Trun

7TH ARMY

Flers

PZ. GRP. EBERBACH

LVII PZ

XLVII PZ

Argentan

Chalons

Line, evening
of August 18

Line, evening
of August 10

XIX

VII

XV

1ST US ARMY

3RD US ARMY

12TH   ARMY   GROUP

0 2
MILES

THE BATTLE OF THE FALAISE POCKET, AUGUST 1944.
Trapped between the 21st Army Group (Montgomery) and the 12th
Army Group (Bradley), Army Group B was crushed. Field Marshal
Model assumed command of Army Group B as the battle neared its
climax and managed to get Hitler's permission to evacuate the
pocket in time to save half of the soldiers, but so much equipment
was lost that all hope of holding Paris and most of France was
abandoned.

He sent for Kesselring and Model in order to choose a permanent successor for Kluge.[45]

Ignorant of all of this, Kluge (under pressure from Hausser, Eberbach, and Dietrich) finally worked up enough nerve to ask permission to abandon the pocket before the pincers closed on his twenty-three divisions.[46] He even sent some units out of the pocket on his own initiative. OKW neither confirmed nor denied the request, but ordered Kluge out of the pocket. He was to direct the rest of the battle, they said, from the headquarters of the 5th Panzer Army, now located east of the threatened area. General Hausser took charge of all of the forces inside the pocket. Then, on the evening of August 17, Field Marshal Model appeared with a letter relieving Kluge of his command.

The rest of the Battle of the Falaise Pocket was directed by Walter Model. A confirmed Nazi whom Hitler trusted, he was hampered by none of the restrictions imposed on Kluge. Model evacuated units as rapidly as he could until the pocket was closed on August 19; then he ordered Hausser to break out immediately, with everything he could, before the encirclement could solidify. He also ordered Dietrich to attack toward Falaise with II SS Panzer Corps, to help rescue survivors.

Of the 100,000 men breaking out, about 10,000 were killed and 40,000 captured. Half of them escaped. Hausser was seriously wounded in the attempt, as was General Eugen Meindl, the tough commander of II Parachute Corps. The LXXXIV Corps was destroyed and General Elfeldt was captured. The Germans also lost 344 tanks, self-propelled guns, and armored vehicles; 2,447 motorized vehicles; 252 towed guns; and thousands of horse-drawn vehicles and horses. Approximately 50,000 veterans of the Western Front escaped to fight another day,[47] but it would not be in France – after Falaise, she was lost to the Third Reich. Guenther von Kluge knew none of this, however: he was already dead.

KLUGE BEGAN HIS journey back to Germany on August 19 under no illusions as to what his fate would be. He ordered his driver to halt at Metz, the scene of some of his World War I battles. Here he spread out a blanket and quietly took a cyanide capsule. He left behind a farewell letter. It read:

My Fuehrer:

When you receive these lines I shall be no more. . . . I do not know if Field Marshal Model, who has proved himself in all respects, will be capable of mastering the situation. I hope so with all my heart. If that is not to be the case and if the new weapons – especially air weapons, which you are so eagerly awaiting, are not to bring you success, then, my Fuehrer, make up your mind to finish the war. The German people have endured such unspeakable sufferings that the time has come to put an end to their terrors. There must be ways to arrive at this conclusion and, above all, to prevent the Reich from being condemned to the hell of Bolshevism. . . . I have always admired your greatness and your iron will to maintain yourself and National Socialism. If your destiny overcomes your will and your genius, it will be because Providence has willed it so. You have fought a good and honorable fight. History will bear witness to this. If it ever becomes necessary, show yourself great enough to put an end to a struggle which has become hopeless.

I depart from you, my Fuehrer, as one who stood nearer to you than you perhaps realized, in the consciousness that I did my duty to the utmost.

Hitler read the letter without comment. He ordered that Kluge be buried quietly, with military pallbearers but without military honors. He was officially pronounced dead of a cerebral hemorrhage.[48]

17

Walter Model

A WHOLE BOOK should be written about his campaigns. He was the most effective of the Nazi generals – the one Hitler sent to the most critical spots in his crumbling empire time and again. The other field marshals are associated with particular places: Rundstedt is associated with the Western Front, Bock with Moscow, Paulus with Stalingrad, Weichs with the Balkans, Rommel with North Africa, Manstein with southern Russia, and so on. Model is associated with the second half of the war. He received only the most dangerous assignments.

WALTER MODEL WAS born in Genthin, near Magdeburg, on January 24, 1891, the son of a music teacher. He grew up in poverty. He was a Prussian, author John Eisenhower wrote, and he certainly looked the part: tough, shorter than average but somewhat thickset, close-cropped "whitewall" haircut, and, of course, the indispensable monocle, which he wore constantly![1] To be frank, he was ugly. He joined the Imperial Army on February 27, 1909, as a *Fahnenjunker* in the 52nd Infantry Regiment, and was commissioned second lieutenant on August 22, 1910.[2] He served in the infantry on the Western Front for much of the war. Model was wounded several times and was awarded the Iron Cross, 1st Class, for bravery.[3] Late in the war he was appointed to the Greater General Staff in Berlin without having attended the War Academy – an unusual distinction. Although certainly no aristocrat, Model was chosen for the Reichsheer in 1919, and was assigned to the 2nd Infantry Regiment at Allenstein, East Prussia.[4] He first made a name for himself when, as a young officer, he wrote a book about Field Marshal August Neithardt Gneisenau (1760–1831).[5] Model was promoted slowly in the Reichsheer, attaining the rank of lieutenant colonel on November 1, 1932, only two months before Hitler came to power. He was promoted to colonel on October 1, 1934.[6]

Between the wars, Model established a reputation for himself as an expert on technical matters and visited the Soviet Union to study the technical aspects of rearmament.[7] Model served as Chief of the Training Department of the Defense Ministry before becoming Chief of the Technical Department of the Army in 1935. He was a loyal Nazi, and later a fanatical one. He met and impressed Dr. Goebbels, who introduced him to Hitler, who was also impressed. In 1938 he was promoted to major general and earmarked to be the chief of staff of an army for the invasion of Czechoslovakia, but this campaign proved unnecessary after Munich. He was Chief of Staff of General Victor von Schwelder's IV Corps in the Polish campaign and Chief of Staff of Ernst Busch's 16th Army in France in 1940. Promoted to lieutenant general in November 1940, he led the 3rd Panzer Division into Russia on June 22, 1941,[8] as part of Guderian's 2nd Panzer Group.

From the moment he assumed command, Walter Model showed great physical courage, singlemindedness of purpose, and an excellent grasp of tactical situations, but above all he was marked by incredible energy. Always at or near the front, he inspired his troops, who loved him. He led the 3rd Panzer across the Bug, then the Beresina and the Dnieper, captured Bobruysk, and took part in the battles of encirclement at Bialystok, Minsk, and Smolensk. It was Model who spearheaded Guderian's panzer group at Kiev in September 1941. When he linked up with the 9th Panzer Division of Kleist's 1st Panzer Group at Sencha on September 15, he had completed the largest encirclement of the Second World War. Obviously capable of greater things, he was given command of XLI Panzer Corps of the 3rd Panzer Group on the upper Volga in October 1941 and took part in the final drive on Moscow,[9] during which he was promoted to general of panzer troops.

On January 12, 1942, 9th Army on the northern wing of Army Group Center was threatened with encirclement. Its commander, Colonel General Adolf Strauss, was relieved of his command for reasons of health. To everyone's surprise he was replaced by Walter Model, a divisional commander only three months before, and a rather junior one at that.[10]

"It was a strange thing," Paul Carell wrote later, "but the moment Model assumed command of the Army the regiments seemed to gain strength. It was not only the crisp precision of the new C-in-C's orders – but he also turned up everywhere in person. . . . He would suddenly jump out of his command jeep outside a battalion headquarters, or appear on horseback through the deep snow in the foremost line, encouraging, commending, criticizing and occasionally even charging against the enemy penetrations at the head of a battalion, pistol in hand. The live-wire general was everywhere. And even where he was not his presence was felt."[11]

From the standpoint of morale, General Model was to the German Army what General Patton was to the American Army later on. When he took over, 9th Army seemed to be doomed to conducting a hopeless defense around Rzhev. The XXIII Corps was cut off southeast of Lake Volga, west of Rzhev. Model rescued it in a counterattack on January 22 and simultaneously cut off and then surrounded the Soviet 39th Army, which had broken through to the south. The Russians tried desperately to free the encircled force. Model's understrength and badly supplied units were under continuous attack from the 22nd, 29th, 31st, 30th armies and the 1st Strike Army. They came at him with little tactical skill, but rather in large frontal assaults, unit after unit, wave after wave – human waves – in temperatures of minus 73 Fahrenheit. Meanwhile, the 39th Army tried to break out with fanatical counterattacks.

During this battle, Model had his first run-in with Hitler – and won. On January 20, 1942, he flew to see the dictator at Fuehrer Headquarters. Model wanted a corps to be sent up immediately to support his battered army. Hitler agreed but wanted the unit sent into action in the vicinity of Gzhatsk, northeast of Vyazma. Model wanted it committed near Rzhev, nearly one hundred miles to the north. According to General Friedrich Wilhelm von Mellenthin, an "acrimonious argument" developed. Finally Model stared coldly at Hitler through his monocle and asked: "Who commands the 9th

Army, my Fuehrer – you or I?" Without waiting for an answer, Model informed the startled Hitler that he knew the situation at the front better than Hitler, who had only maps. The surprised Fuehrer let Model have his way. The Russians attacked just where Model predicted they would and were defeated.[12]

In this attack, as in so many others, the Russians attacked with great fierceness. Model met the Russians with the same fanatical determination – perhaps with even more – and with incredible energy. Two ruthless ideologies clashed in the dirty snow outside Rzhev. At the critical point Model stationed the SS Regiment "Der Fuehrer" of the 2nd SS Motorized Division "Das Reich" and ordered it to hold at all costs. It did. By the time the battle was over, only thirty-five of the fanatical SS men were left alive.

Fanatical. It is not good for an author to overuse such a word, but fanatical is the only one that can be used to describe the Battle of Rzhev, where the fate of Army Group Center was decided in the brutal winter of 1941/42. This adjective was justified over and over again as the wild-eyed SS men and the equally determined Wehrmacht troops cut down wave after wave of Soviet troops in the waist-deep snow outside Rzhev. The battle did not end until February 24, 1942. Of the 32,000 men in the Soviet 39th Army, only five thousand surrendered. The rest were killed in the desperate fighting outside Rzhev. Six Soviet divisions were wiped out, another four virtually so, and dozens more were badly shot up.[13] The Soviet effort to cut the Moscow Highway had failed. Stalin's winter offensive had met a decisive and totally unexpected defeat at Rzhev. Walter Model had saved Army Group Center – of this there was no doubt in anybody's mind. For his amazing victory, Model was promoted to colonel general, his fourth promotion in three years. Hitler personally decorated him with the Knights' Cross with Oak Leaves.[14]

Stalin was still determined to destroy 9th Army, which occupied a salient only 112 miles from Moscow. He launched offensives in March, April, and late July through mid-October 1942. Model stopped them all. After the fall of Stalingrad, however, it no longer made sense to hold Rzhev, because it was clear that it would not be used as a springboard for an offensive against Moscow. From March 1–21, 1943, in the face of ten Soviet armies, Model pulled twenty-one divisions back one hundred miles, reducing his frontage from 330 to only 125 miles, freeing an entire army for Hitler's next major operation in the East. Contrary to what the Soviet official history says, it was one of the best planned and executed retrograde operations of the war.[15] Model suffered few casualties. The Soviets could not say the same. All their efforts to overwhelm 9th Army while it was on the move met with bloody defeats.

FOLLOWING THE RZHEV withdrawal, HQ, 9th Army was transferred from the northern to the southern wing of Army Group Center and placed in charge of the northern wing of Operation Citadelle, Hitler's last major offensive in the east. Its objective was to pinch off and destroy the huge Soviet bulge at Kursk. It was originally scheduled to begin on May 3.[16]

Kursk was largely Model's battle, and he must be given the lion's share of the responsibility for losing it. He wanted to delay the start of the operation until absolutely everything was ready and the promised new-model tanks – Ferdinands – were delivered to him. He persuaded Hitler to delay the starting date until May 5, then to May 15, then to mid-June, then to July 3, and finally to July 5.[17] Manstein and Zeitzler, who favored Citadelle when the attack was scheduled for early May, wanted to forget the whole thing by then, but Hitler would not hear of that. Guderian opposed the operation from its inception, and Kluge, as usual, was on both sides.

Model did improve his tank strength considerably during this period, but any gains were more than counterbalanced by the Russian preparations. By the time Model was ready, the Soviets had constructed three main lines of defense, each two to three miles in depth. They had three full fronts (army groups) in the salient, with 11th, 4th Tank, and 3rd Guards Tank armies in reserve.[18]

Kursk was the largest tank battle in history. Model struck in a wedge formation, with five panzer divisions under XLVII Panzer Corps (led by General Erhard Raus) at the apex. In all he had eight panzer divisions with more than one hundred tanks each, plus nine infantry divisions and several independent formations. Counting assault guns, he had some three thousand armored vehicles.[19] Manstein, directing the southern flank, had about fifteen hundred more.

Model's half of the offensive started badly and then deteriorated. The Soviets were warned of zero hour by a deserter, and twenty minutes before jump-off time Model's units were hit in their assembly areas by a massive Soviet artillery bombardment. Then the Ferdinands proved to be a terrible disappointment. Not only were they mechanically unreliable, but they had no machine guns, so they could not deal with Soviet infantrymen. Raus could gain only six miles on the first day of the offensive, and his supporting corps, stalled in Soviet minefields, gained even less. By the end of the second day of the offensive, 9th Army had only gained nine to ten miles along a seven-mile front. Then on July 7, only the third day of the attack, XLVII Panzer Corps was halted at Olkhovatka, less than twelve miles from its starting line. Here the entire 9th Army was halted.[20] It had lost 20,000 men and had gained very little. By being stopped here, it also allowed the Soviets to concentrate against the southern pincer.

Model planned to resume the offensive on July 12, but Zhukov, the Soviet theater commander, preceded him by launching a massive attack against 2nd Panzer Army on Model's north the day before. His objective was clearly to surround both 2nd Panzer and 9th armies. The Soviets broke through near Orel, and Kluge hurriedly gave Model command of both armies and ordered him to halt the breakout using the mobile forces then employed in the Battle of Kursk. Citadelle was lost.

Hitler's faith in Model seemed little diminished by his failure at Kursk. The Fuehrer even allowed him to conduct an "elastic defense" in the Orel sector. Although faced by eighty-two Soviet infantry divisions, fourteen tank corps, and twelve artillery divisions, Model's superior rear-guard tactics, aided by heavy cloudbursts, enabled him to contain the Russian breakthrough. He then retreated slowly to the Hagen position, which he reached in mid-August. As he retreated, Model instituted a "scorched earth" policy. He burned Russian crops (which were ready for harvest) and herded up 250,000 civilians, with whatever they could carry, and forced them to trek westward. He also confiscated their cattle and laid waste anything he could not carry with him.[21] Model was undeniably harsh in his dealings with Russian civilians and also co-operated with the SS murder squads and with their Jewish "resettlement" programs.

Model increased his reputation as a defensive fighter in the second half of 1943. Hitler sent him on an extended leave in November, with the expectation that he would return refreshed to assume command of Army Group South, for Hitler planned to have him replace Manstein. However, Model was back with 9th Army in late November, after the Soviets forced a fifty-mile gap between 9th and 2nd armies. Model and Weiss (CG, 2nd Army) planned to close the gap via a joint counteroffensive but were unable to do so because of the speed of the Russian advance. Model directed 9th Army's retreat behind the Dnieper and successfully launched his counterattack in the December 21–26 period. The gap, which had existed for three months, was closed at year's end.[22]

HITLER WAS USING Model as a troubleshooter again on January 31, 1944, when he named him Commander-in-Chief, Army Group North, replacing Field Marshal Georg von Kuechler. As we have seen (chapter 13), Army Group North (16th and 18th armies) was badly beaten when the Russians broke the Siege of Leningrad earlier that month. Colonel General Lindemann's 18th Army was down to 17,000 infantrymen, and only its 12th Panzer and 58th Infantry divisions were intact. Model's first step was to introduce his "Schild und Schwert" (Shield and Sword) policy, which stated that retreats were tolerable, but only if they paved the way for a counterstroke later. This was a brilliant piece of psychology, because it made withdrawal palatable to Adolf Hitler. Staffs were frequently amazed by this development. Hitler would sack a commander for suggesting a retreat; then Model would appear, and the Fuehrer would approved anything he suggested. A week after the pro-Nazi Model arrived at Army Group North, the Fuehrer even went so far as to send him a communication instructing the colonel general to request permission to withdraw to the Panther Line as soon as he felt it was necessary.[23]

Model tried desperately to hold the Russians on the Luga River, east of the Panther Line. He collected stragglers and sent them back to the line, cancelled leaves, sent walking wounded to their units, and sent 5 percent of the rear-echelon troops to the front. He restored the morale of the frontline units by seeming to be everywhere at once. Without hesitation he demanded more divisions from Hitler, more experienced SS replacements from Himmler, more naval coastal batteries from Admiral Doenitz, and more Luftwaffe troops from Goering, all to deal with the partisan menace. On February 17 he began his retreat to the Panther Line, which he occupied on schedule on March 1, 1944, the same day Hitler promoted him to field marshal. The Russians, in rapid pursuit, struck the Panther Line that day with the Leningrad, Volkhov, and 2nd Baltic fronts. The battle lasted ten days before the spring thaw set in, but all of the Russian efforts were in vain.[24] Temporarily at least, Walter Model had stabilized the northern sector of the Eastern Front.

Besides being energetic, innovative, and courageous, Model tended to oversupervise and often meddled in the internal affairs of subordinate units – affairs that were really none of his business. He was friendly and popular with his enlisted men but was sometimes too harsh with his officers. He could be quite selfish and was not above pirating units from other commanders. On March 28, 1944, for example, Model had just written a situation report that stated that Army Group North might be able to spare two divisions for Army Group South, which was under heavy attack. Then General Schmundt, Chief of the Army's Personnel Office, called to tell Model that he would replace Manstein as C-in-C of Army Group South in a few days. Model quickly rewrote his estimate, saying Army Group North could give up five divisions and a corps headquarters immediately, and also the 12th Panzer Division as soon as two assault-gun brigades and a panzer battalion arrived from Germany to replace it. The next day he raised the total to six divisions and ordered Lieutenant General Eberhard Kinzel to begin the transfer immediately. Only the intervention of General Zeitzler, Chief of the Army General Staff, prevented the rape of Army Group North.[25]

MODEL WAS INSTALLED as C-in-C, Army Group South, on March 30, less than a week before it was redesignated Army Group North Ukraine. The crisis here was just about over, however, for Hube's 1st Panzer Army had just escaped a Soviet encirclement in Galicia. Model did send the 9th SS Panzer Division to rescue the four-thousand-man garrison surrounded at Tarnopol and even went so far as to take the tanks from the SS unit and place them under an Army officer when their progress did not please him. Tarnopol could not be saved, however, and only fifty-three men managed to break out on the night of April 15/16 and reach German lines.[26]

THE SOVIET SUMMER offensive struck Army Group Center on June 22. One week later, twenty-eight of its thirty-seven divisions had been destroyed or surrounded. Hitler sacked Busch that day and sent Model in to minimize the extent of the disaster. Model retained control of Army Group North Ukraine as well (under his deputy, Colonel General Josef Harpe), so he came as close as anyone ever would to realizing Manstein's dream of a Commander-in-Chief of the Eastern Front. He had forty-three divisions (five of them panzer and one panzer grenadier) in his two army groups on July 13.[27]

With Army Group Center in remnants, Model's strategy was simple: give ground rapidly and save what was left, until the Soviets outran their supply lines and he could be reinforced with divisions then forming in Germany. Pinsk fell on July 14, Lublin on July 23, Bialystok and Lvov on July 27, and Brest-Litovsk the next day. On July 31 the Russians reached Praga, across the Vistula from Warsaw. On August 1 the Soviets reached Kalvariya, only fifteen miles from the East Prussian border.

However, the Russians were now exhausted, were out of gas, and had outrun their supplies and air support. Meanwhile, Model had been reinforced with the Hermann Goering Panzer, 3rd SS Panzer, 5th SS Panzer, and Grossdeutschland Panzer divisions, as well as several infantry units. Model counterattacked, retook Praga, smashed the Soviet 2nd Tank Army, and pushed the Russians back thirty miles. With only about forty-five depleted divisions, he had halted 143 Soviet infantry divisions, twelve cavalry divisions, and more than two thousand tanks – one-third of Stalin's total strength – along a four-hundred-mile front. The situation in the East was temporarily stabilized again, but since June 22 the Soviets had gained four hundred miles and were only 350 miles from Berlin. The Germans had lost 916,860 men since June 1.[28]

After the battle, Hitler was referring to Model as "the savior of the Eastern Front."[29] Throughout the Army he was now known as "the Fuehrer's fireman." He now received his most difficult assignment: on August 16, 1944, he was named C-in-C of Army Group B and OB West. He was replaced at Army Group Center by Colonel General Reinhardt. Table 9 shows his order of battle.

Model showed up at Kluge's headquarters on August 17, relieved him of his command, and immediately ordered the evacuation

Table 9

ORDER OF BATTLE, OB WEST, mid-August 1944

OB West: Field Marshal Walter Model
   Army Group B: Model
      7th Army: Gen. Heinrich Eberbach
      5th Panzer Army: SS Col. Gen. Sepp Dietrich
      15th Army: Col. Gen. Hans von Salmuth*
   Army Group G: Col. Gen. Johannes Blaskowitz
      1st Army: Gen. Kurt von der Chevallerie
      19th Army: Gen. Friedrich Wiese
   1st Parachute Army: Luftwaffe Col. Gen. Kurt Student

---

of the Falaise Pocket, an order Kluge had been unable to get from the Fuehrer. He managed to get half of the 5th Panzer and 7th armies out of the pocket before the Allies closed it, but he immediately faced three more crises. Patton's US 3rd Army south of Paris was sweeping eastward against minimal opposition; the US 6th Army Group (Lieutenant General Jacob L. Devers) had landed on the French Mediterranean coast, was rapidly destroying Kurt von der Chevallerie's 1st Army, and was threatening to cut off Soderstern's 19th Army on the south Atlantic coast; and Model still had to get his battered forces behind the Seine, in spite of the rapid pursuit of the victorious British and Americans. The fact that Paris was in revolt did not seem to alarm Model because he knew he could not hold it anyway. When the Fuehrer ordered him to defend it, Model signaled back that the 20,000 troops he had there could not keep a lid on a city of 3,500,000.[30] Hitler then maliciously ordered the City Commandant, General Dietrich von Choltitz, to destroy the city, but he did not. It fell on August 25, 1944.

Meanwhile, Model got the remnants of Army Group B behind the Seine – barely. "From the point of view of equipment abandoned," Sepp Dietrich said later, "the Seine crossing was almost as great a disaster as the Falaise Pocket."[31] According to General Blumentritt, only 100 to 120 of the 2,300 tanks and assault guns

---

*Later Gen. Gustav von Zangen

committed to the Battle of Normandy ever made it back across the Seine. The panzer divisions' strength was now down to an average of less than ten tanks per division. The Germans had also lost at least 15,000 other vehicles in this battle.[32]

The paradox of Hitler's "strategy" in France was now abundantly clear. He had used up his panzer divisions in the hedgerows of Normandy (ideal infantry terrain), while Rommel cried for infantry. Now that the Allies were in good tank country, Model had nothing with which to stop them, except infantry, which was of marginal value here. The Ruhr was now definitely vulnerable, and if this vital industrial district fell, Germany's ability to continue the war would be questionable.

Everywhere resistance was collapsing. By August 26 the British were across the Seine in strength, while Patton crossed the Marne on August 28, the same day that Marseilles and Toulon fell in southern France. On August 30 Nice and Amiens fell, the Somme River line was breached before Model could man it, 7th Army Headquarters was overrun, and General Eberbach was captured. Nice fell on September 1, and Lyons was liberated the next day, as the Allies pushed up the Rhône River valley against weak opposition. Brussels fell on September 3, and British tank forces took the important harbor of Antwerp on September 4.[33] That same day Hitler, realizing that Model could not possibly command Army Group B and OB West effectively under such circumstances, recalled Field Marshal Rundstedt as C-in-C, West. Model retained command of Army Group B, with the duty of defending the all-important Ruhr against the Allied juggernaut. Then, as if by a miracle, the Allies stopped.

The enemy halt was no miracle: Eisenhower was simply out of gas. No one had expected the Germans to collapse as they had, so the Allies had not brought enough transport ashore from England, and the British and Americans had outrun the ability of their rear echelon to supply them. The Allied air forces' destruction of the French railroad system had turned out to be a two-edged sword. It was a major contributing factor to Rommel's defeat in Normandy in June and July, but now that the Allies had it, it was useless. Montgomery had a plan to continue the drive to the Ruhr, however: an ambitious airborne landing by the 1st Allied Airborne Army, in concert with a British land drive to secure a foothold across the Rhine at Arnhem. If successful, it might well continue the German rout.

The plan was this: the US 101st, US 82nd, and British 1st Airborne divisions would land near Eindhoven, Nijmegen, and Arnhem, respectively, while the British XXX Corps, spearheaded by the Guards Armored Division, would break through the center of the newly committed German 1st Parachute Army in the center of Model's line and advance rapidly to the north, up the single road leading to Arnhem, linking up with the paratrooper divisions in turn. The key objective was the Rhine River bridge at Arnhem. Once XXX Corps reached this point, Montgomery planned to land the British 52nd (Airportable) Infantry Division to reinforce the Arnhem bridgehead and continue the drive.[34] Much to Patton's disgust, Eisenhower approved the plan and gave Montgomery supply priority.

The ground phase of Market Garden, as this operation was named, began at 2 P.M. on September 17, with XXX Corps attacking Division Walther of Kurt Student's 1st Parachute Army. They broke through fairly quickly and headed north, where the parachute drops had begun at 1 P.M.

Although the element of surprise was definitely on his side, Montgomery's daring plan had a number of flaws in it. First, intelligence was faulty. A few low-grade battalions had been reported in the Arnhem-Nijmegen area, but they missed the entire II SS Panzer Corps (9th and 10th SS Panzer divisions), which was refitting northeast of Arnhem after being mauled at Falaise. Second, the advance focused on a single road. If it could be cut, the entire advance would stall. Third, the British 1st Airborne was dropped six to eight miles from its objective, the Arnhem bridge. Finally, the Dutch resistance had failed to report that Field Marshal Model's tactical headquarters was now at Oosterbeck, a suburb on the western edge of Arnhem, less than a mile from the easternmost drop zone.[35]

Model was eating lunch when the first wave of paratroops floated down from the sky. He hurriedly left for Arnhem to organize the local defenses and order up reinforcements. Thanks to the on-the-spot intervention of the energetic field marshal, the German reaction was much more rapid than could reasonably have been expected. The 9th SS Panzer Reconnaissance Battalion and the SS Panzer Grenadier Replacement-Training Battalion "Krafft" were already moving into blocking positions before the British moved out of their drop zones.[36]

Model entrusted the defense of the bridge to an elderly member of his operations staff, Major Ernst Schleifenbaum. The major's emergency battle group consisted of World War I veterans from twenty-eight different commands, mostly rear-area units, but they were all the troops immediately available in Arnhem. He armed them with captured rifles and twenty rounds of ammunition each. They held the city for a while, but could not prevent the British 2nd Parachute Battalion from seizing the northern end of the bridge late that afternoon. Group Schleifenbaum did, however, maintain its hold on the southern end and repulsed several British attempts to dislodge them that night.[37] By late afternoon the British drop zones were already under German mortar fire. By evening 9th SS Panzer had completely cut off the six hundred paratroopers on the bridge from the rest of the division and had a battle group in the city, where they were joined by the 10th SS Panzer Reconnaissance Battalion and a heavy mortar battalion from the 10th SS Panzer Division.[38]

The British paratroopers were tough and superbly trained but lightly equipped. Model and Student knew that II SS Panzer (under SS General Willi Bittrich) would destroy them unless XXX Corps arrived in time. To prevent the Allied rescue, they attacked the Arnhem Road with every reserve they could muster. Model also committed Division von Tettau — an *ad hoc* formation of six battalions, mostly of marginal value — to the battle on the western side of the British drop zones. Model and Student threw the 59th Infantry Division and 107th Panzer Brigade into immediate counterattacks against XXX Corps and the two US airborne divisions. Both cut the road at different points, causing more delays on September 18 and 20, and even the Luftwaffe contributed with a rare seventy-airplane raid, damaging the Eindhoven bridge and causing a great deal of traffic congestion and confusion (the British had little experience against tactical air raids). Hitler also gave Model two divisions (the 170th and 180th Reserve), and he quickly threw them into action against the Allied tank corridor. By September 20, XXX Corps had 20,000 vehicles strung out for thirty miles on a single road. Logistical problems reached nightmare proportions.[39]

The 2nd Parachute Battalion put up a truly heroic resistance, but on September 20 it ran out of anti-tank ammunition and had to surrender its wounded to the Germans, to prevent them from being burned to death in the flames that were engulfing that part of Arnhem. The 1st, 3rd, and 11th Parachute and 2nd South Stafford battalions tried to rescue them, but were slaughtered in the open terrain by the mobile SS troops. The combined strength of these four battalions was reduced to four hundred men before the survivors made their way back to the landing zones. In a similar attempt, the 10th and 156th Parachute battalions suffered even heavier losses.[40]

Shortly after daybreak on September 21, the survivors of the 2nd Parachute Battalion surrendered. Montgomery's ambitious plan had failed. The rest of the battle centered on efforts to get the remnants of the British 1st Airborne back across the river. The battle ended on the morning of September 27, when the 1st Airborne's perimeter finally collapsed. About the same time, XXX Corps at last overcame the 59th Infantry Division and reached the river.

Of the 10,000 men of the British 1st Airborne, 2,587 were successfully evacuated and 240 more (most of them hidden by the Dutch) escaped in the next few days. The rest were lost. The British 2nd Army lost 3,716 men, and the US 82nd and 101st Airborne divisions suffered 3,542 casualties. Two SS Panzer lost only 1,100 killed and 2,200 wounded in heavy fighting.[41] The losses of the other German units involved are unknown, but the 107th Panzer Brigade had to be rebuilt.

Some popular writers in recent years have played down or minimized Model's role in this victory, or ignored it altogether, presumably because Model was a Nazi sympathizer. The British official history, however, is more objective in this instance and gives Model the lion's share of the credit for the victory. Due to the speed of his reaction, it points out, only 600 of the 10,000 paratroopers dropped at Arnhem ever reached the bridge.[42] The 1st Airborne was disbanded after this battle.

As a result of the Battle of Arnhem, the last Allied chance for victory over Germany in 1944 was eliminated. Hitler would now have the time necessary to build up his forces for the Ardennes Offensive. Arnhem was also Walter Model's last major victory in the field.

MODEL OPPOSED HITLER'S plan for the Battle of the Bulge from the beginning. The field marshal wanted to use the reserve to annihilate the American salient at Aachen, but this time the Fuehrer could not be swayed. Walter Model then threw all of his considerable energies into trying to make the operation a success, like a good subordinate and faithful Nazi. He was now reportedly drinking heavily at night, but this did not stop him from getting up at 5 A.M. every day to inspect his troops. He continued to drive himself and his men unmercifully.[43]

Model attacked at 5:30 A.M. on December 16, 1944, with twenty divisions forward and five more in reserve: a total force of 300,000 men, 1,900 guns, and 970 tanks and assault guns under the 7th, 5th Panzer, and 6th Panzer armies (General Erich Brandenburger, General Hasso von Manteuffel, and SS Colonel General Sepp Dietrich, respectively). The US 106th Infantry Division was surrounded and destroyed, the US 28th Infantry and 7th Armored divisions were mauled, and the 101st Airborne Division was surrounded at Bastogne. The offensive reached its apex on December 23. Then the Americans reacted. The poor flying weather, considered essential for a German victory, lifted on December 22, and many of Model's units were smashed by fighter-bombers. Patton's 3rd Army shifted direction with incredible quickness, broke through the southern edge of the bulge, and relieved Bastogne on December 26. The fighting continued to be heavy, but by January 8, 1945, with Houffalize (the last escape route) already under American attack, Hitler authorized Model to abandon the area west of that town. Hitler's last major offensive had failed.[44]

Model had inflicted 76,000 casualties on the Americans, but had lost about 103,000 men himself, along with 600 tanks and assault guns.[45] Worse than this, the morale of his men was broken. On February 8, when the US 9th Army (Lieutenant General William H. Simpson) crossed the Roer, the resistance was so light that he suffered fewer than one hundred casualties in four divisions.[46]

It is perhaps fitting that the Fuehrer's fireman in the end fell victim to one of Hitler's "hold at all costs" decrees. He was ordered to stand fast in the Ruhr with fifteen divisions. Model still had 320,000 men (counting 100,000 flak troops), but most of these were ill-trained Hitler Youth or old men, recently inducted into the Army, who had little stomach for fighting. Model himself was seized by a strange apathy, perhaps because he realized the war was lost and he was on the Soviet war criminals' list because he had so faithfully carried out Hitler's scorched-earth policy in Russia. Possibly Model's attitude was fatalistic because he knew that he was just prolonging the agony, at the cost of thousands of lives. He had believed Hitler's stories about his "miracle weapons," but now he knew that they would not be forthcoming.

For whatever reasons, he did not conduct the Battle of the Ruhr Pocket with his customary energy or even with intelligence. For example, he located his headquarters on the extreme right wing of the battle, where he could not properly direct the left wing of his army group, where the main attack came. He turned down General von Zangen's request to reinforce Remagen before the US 9th Armored Division captured the bridge there on March 7. Model then failed to launch prompt counterattacks against the Allied bridgeheads at Remagen and Wesel, and when he did strike his attacks were not as powerful as they could have been.[47]

Army Group B, with the 5th Panzer and 15th armies, was attacked by the US 1st, 9th, and 15th armies. Model made only one attempt to get the "stand fast" order withdrawn, and that to Kesselring, the new Commander-in-Chief, OB West, not directly to Hitler. Kesselring, of course, had no authority to revoke the order, so Army Group B stood fast. Model might have used his considerable personal influence with Hitler to get the order rescinded, but he did not even try.

The Battle of the Ruhr Pocket was definitely the worst operation ever directed by Walter Model. "To this day even," Kesselring wrote later, "the operations of Army Group B remain incomprehensible to me."[48] Model counterattacked at the wrong places and at the wrong times. He had ignored Hitler's "stand fast" orders before, but he did not this time. The Ruhr Pocket was encircled at 1 P.M. on April 1. The fighting lasted three weeks, during which Model ignored Hitler's orders to destroy all of the factories in the Ruhr, but he also refused to consider American surrender proposals. Rather than that, he issued orders sending his older men and young boys home, and on April 17, with his medical supplies exhausted, he disbanded his army group.[49] He and his staff were now little more than fugitives, wandering around the ruined industrial district. "A field marshal," he said, "does not become a prisoner. Such a thing is not possible."[50]

Several times during the battle, Model went to the front lines and deliberately exposed himself to enemy fire, hoping to get himself killed in action.[51] Finally, on the morning of April 21 he told his intelligence officer: "My hour has come."[52] With the Americans only a mile or two away, the two officers walked into a woods near Duisburg, where the field marshal asked his aide to shoot him as one last service.[53] When the major refused, Model drew his pistol. "Anything is better than falling into Russian hands," he said. "You will bury me here." Walter Model then fired a single bullet into his head.[54]

He lay for years in a secret, unmarked grave near Duisberg until after the Federal Republic of Germany was created, because his staff feared that the victors would scatter his ashes to the winds, as they had done to the war criminals hanged at Nuremberg. Years later his son, Major Hansgeorg Model, had the body reinterred in a soldiers' cemetery in the Huertgen Forest, not far from the final resting place of George S. Patton. Model is now buried among the soldiers he commanded.[55]

18

Erwin von Witzleben

ERWIN JOB VON Witzleben, the scion of a very old Prussian family, was born in Breslau, Silesia (now Wroclaw, Poland), on December 4, 1881.[1] He is not noted for his victories, or even his defeats, but rather for his simple devotion to the Prussian military ideal of service for folk and country. He had moral as well as physical courage, would never compromise his lofty ideals, and was perfectly willing to take decisive action against any person or political faction that tried to subvert the Officer Corps for his or its own political objectives. Had he seen the light of day a century earlier, he would have been a worthy colleague of Gerhard Scharnhorst, August von Gneisenau, and Count Johann Yorck von Wartenburg, the officers who freed Prussia from Napoleon. Born when he was, he was born to be hanged.

AFTER BEING EDUCATED in cadet schools, Witzleben joined the Imperial Army on March 22, 1901, at the age of nineteen, as a second lieutenant in the 7th Grenadier Regiment at Leipzig, where he remained for seven years.[2] In late 1908 he was appointed Adjutant of Area Command Hirschberg and was promoted to *Oberleutnant* in 1910 – after nine years as a second lieutenant. When the war broke out he was named Adjutant of the 19th Reserve

Infantry Brigade, and was promoted to captain later that year. He spent the war on the Western Front, winning the Iron Cross, 1st Class for valor. In early 1915 he was given command of a company in the 6th Infantry Regiment, and fought in the trenches for at least a year and a half. He was appointed to the General Staff in August 1916, but his exact assignment after this is not clear; apparently he remained with the 6th Infantry. In any event, he assumed command of a battalion in that unit on April 15, 1917, and did not take up a staff appointment until August 2, 1918, when he became General Staff Officer to the 108th Infantry Division in the closing days of the war.[3]

Captain Erwin von Witzleben returned to his parent unit, the 7th Grenadier, as a company commander in early 1919 but was given a General Staff appointment two months later. He was named commander of the 8th Machine Gun Company, 8th Infantry Regiment, in January 1921.[4]

Witzleben's Reichsheer career was divided between the staff and the line. It was characterized by steady but unremarkable assignments and advancements. He was on the General Staff of Wehrkreis IV (1922–25), was with the 12th Cavalry Regiment (1925–26), on the General Staff of Infantry Command III at Berlin (1926–28), and then CO, III Battalion, 6th Infantry Regiment (1928). He was the Chief of Staff of Wehrkreis VI at Muenster (1929–31) and the commander of the 8th Infantry Regiment (1931–33) and Area Command Hanover (1933–34). He was promoted to major in 1923, lieutenant colonel in 1929, and full colonel in 1931.[5]

Erwin von Witzleben entered the stage of history on February 1, 1934, when he was promoted to major general and named Commander of Wehrkreis III, replacing General Baron Werner von Fritsch, who was named C-in-C of the Army. This critical military district was headquartered in Berlin. Prior to the Roehm purge, Witzleben – this simple but tough and experienced infantry officer – let it be known that he was perfectly willing to use his troops against the SA if Hitler did not control them. Hitler did – via the Blood Purge of June 30, 1934.[6] When he first heard that the SA leaders were being shot, Witzleben was delighted and wished aloud that he could be there to see it. Later he learned that the SS murder squads had also killed retired Generals Kurt von

Schleicher and Kurt von Bredow during the bloodbath. Witzleben demanded a military inquiry into their deaths, as did his Chief of Staff, Colonel Erich von Manstein, as well as Generals Gerd von Rundstedt and Ritter Wilhelm von Leeb. The pro-Nazi Defense Minister, General Werner von Blomberg, would not allow it, however.[7]

Witzleben was promoted to lieutenant general in late 1934 and general of infantry on October 1, 1936.[8] He continued to disapprove of the Nazis and, indeed, favored a restoration of the monarchy, but basically took no interest in politics until his friend Werner von Fritsch was dismissed as Commander-in-Chief of the Army on trumped-up charges of homosexuality in January 1938. Witzleben considered this act to be an affront to the honor of the service, something he could never forgive or forget. From that moment on, Witzleben was a dedicated anti-Nazi who advocated the overthrow of the régime by military force. He did not exclude the use of violence or assassination, if necessary.

It was fortunate for Hitler that Witzleben was on sick leave in Dresden at this time, for Colonel Paul von Hase volunteered to use his 50th Infantry Regiment to suppress the government, the SS, and the Gestapo, and Witzleben probably would have used it. As Deutsch remarked later, Witzleben and his subordinate, Colonel Count Walter von Brockdorff-Ahlefeld, were "two of the most determined men ever to function in Opposition ranks."[9] Without Witzleben, however, there was "no leadership in Berlin," as Peter Hoffmann writes.[10] Hitler was successful in removing the staunch anti-Nazi Fritsch and installing his puppet, Werner von Brauchitsch, as C-in-C of the Army.

Witzleben was one of the first to be retired in the Brauchitsch purges, robbing the anti-Hitler conspirators of the best power base they would ever have. He was recalled to active duty in August 1938, to command 1st Army on the Franco-German frontier during the Czechoslovakian crisis. Meanwhile, anti-Hitler conspirators gathered in Berlin. They included General Ludwig Beck, the Chief of the General Staff of the Army; his deputy, General Franz Halder; Admiral Wilhelm Canaris, the Chief of the *Abwehr* (the Military Intelligence Branch of the High Command of the Armed Forces), and his Chief of Staff, Colonel Hans Oster,[11] as well as Count von Brockdorff-Ahlefeld, the commander of the Potsdam garrison;

Count Helldorf, the Police President of Berlin; Colonel General Kurt von Hammerstein, the former C-in-C of the Army; and Lieutenant General Erich Hoepner, the commander of the 1st Light (later 6th Panzer) Division in Thuringia.[12]

Hans Oster traveled to Witzleben's headquarters to try to convince him to join the conspiracy. Canaris's deputy had barely begun to explain the reason for his visit (Hitler's preparations for invading Czechoslovakia) when Witzleben interrupted him and offered his unconditional support. If Halder (the unofficial head of the conspiracy) decided to act, Witzleben said, he would act with him; if not, he would act without him. In any event he was willing to take orders from General Beck.[13]

It was quickly decided that Witzleben, who could be counted upon to take decisive action, would be the military commander of the coup. The plan was this: on the signal of Halder the Potsdam garrison, supported by the Berlin Police, would seize the government quarter and arrest Hitler as soon as he issued the order to invade Czechoslovakia. Hoepner's tanks would prevent interference by the Munich SS, should they attempt to rescue Hitler. The dictator was to be put on trial before the Police Court. Meanwhile, a panel of psychiatrists was to conduct secret inquiries into Hitler's sanity. They had already obtained a copy of Hitler's previous mental history from the Pasewalk Military Hospital, and it was considered good evidence for removing Hitler from office and putting him into a lunatic asylum.[14]

A second version of this plan also existed. It called for Witzleben and certain members of his staff to go to the Reich Chancellery and demand that Hitler resign. Major Friedrich Wilhelm Heinz, the leader of Witzleben's assault squad, would provoke (or stage) an incident, during which Hitler would be assassinated, presumably by Heinz himself. Witzleben apparently approved of this version of the plan.[15]

The planned coup of 1938 was the best of all the plans the anti-Hitler conspirators came up with in the entire history of the German resistance movement. The fatal flaw lay in Hitler's own unpredictability. The man hopped around like a flea and had the instincts of a rat. Without warning he suddenly left Berlin and conducted most of his diplomatic efforts against Czechoslovakia from the Eagle's Nest in Bavaria.[16] He did not return to the capital until after the Munich Accords had been signed and Germany had acquired its territorial demands in the Sudetenland without bloodshed. Suddenly, Adolf Hitler was a genius again. The pretext for military action had been removed; the coup was defused.

After Munich, Colonel Oster still wanted to go through with it. Witzleben went to Oster's home, where the leading conspirators had assembled, and opposed any action against Hitler at this time. He said: "You see, gentlemen, for this poor, foolish nation he is again our hotly beloved Fuehrer, the unique, the Godsent, and we, we are a small group of reactionary and discontented officers and politicians, who have dared in the moment of the highest triumph of the greatest statesman of all times to throw pebbles in his path. If we do something now, then history, and not only German history, will report on us that we deserted the greatest German in the moment when he was greatest and the whole world recognized his greatness."[17]

THE OUTBREAK OF the war took Witzleben by surprise.[18] He went to Berlin shortly thereafter and tried to organize another putsch attempt, but neither Brauchitsch nor Halder were interested. Brauchitsch was especially fearful and even confided to Witzleben that he actually feared arrest by Reinhard Heydrich, the chief of the SD. Witzleben's response was typical for him. "Why don't you arrest *him*?" he asked directly. His question was followed by a painful silence.[19]

Witzleben maintained his contacts with the people who were still members of the opposition, but he gradually became disillusioned. He took little pleasure in his promotion to colonel general in November 1939. In late 1939, when his 1st Army was headquartered at Kreuznach, his health was not good (he suffered from severe haemorrhoids), and he looked tired and depressed. He had no confidence in his ability to influence either Brauchitsch or Halder into acting against Hitler and predicted that they would not act.[20] He was right.

GENERAL WITZLEBEN'S 1ST Army manned the Siegfried Line during the invasion of Poland and feinted against the Maginot Line in the first phase of the Western campaign. He participated in the mopping-up operations of June 1940 and was instrumental in surrounding the French Army Group 2 shortly before the end of hostilities. Perhaps because of his seniority he was promoted to field marshal on July 19, 1940. He was on occupation duty in France after that.

As the German armies moved east for the planned invasion of the Soviet Union, Erwin von Witzleben was named Commander-in-Chief, Army Group D (and was simultaneously Oberbefehlshaber West, or OB West) in April 1941. His forces included the much-reduced 7th and 15th armies, disposed along the Atlantic coast from Antwerp to the Spanish frontier, and the 1st Army, headquartered in Paris, occupying the interior.[21]

Witzleben took steps to secure the French coast from an Allied invasion, even though that threat seemed very remote in 1941. When he proposed that permanent coastal defenses be constructed in the West, however, OKH would not give him any construction battalions. He ordered his subordinate units to begin the project themselves, despite their limited resources for such work. Not much was accomplished, however.[22]

Field Marshal Erwin von Witzleben went on leave in March 1942 to undergo a haemorrhoid operation. Hitler used this as a pretext to retire him on March 21, 1942. He was replaced by Gerd von Rundstedt and never re-employed.

WITZLEBEN RETIRED TO the Lynar estate at Seesen, a few miles from Potsdam, where he maintained his interest in the conspiracy. He was hospitalized for a gastric ulcer in July 1943 but, despite his declining health, was on the conspirators' lists to be Commander-in-Chief of the Armed Forces in an anti-Nazi government.[23]

The coup finally began at 12:30 P.M. on July 20, 1944, when the one-armed, one-eyed Colonel Count Claus von Stauffenberg, the Chief of Staff of the Replacement Army (also called the Home Army), arrived for a Fuehrer conference in East Prussia with a bomb concealed in his briefcase. He planted it under Hitler's feet and left the room. Unfortunately, Colonel Heinz Brandt, a member of the OKH staff and a former Olympic horseman, found its position inconvenient and moved it behind a large table support, thus saving Hitler's life, but not his own. A few minutes later the bomb exploded. The table support deflected the blast away from Hitler, who was only slightly wounded.

In Berlin, General Friedrich Olbricht, the Chief of the Army Office of the Home Army, was in charge of the conspiracy. Due to a previous false start a few days before, he did not want to initiate the military takeover until he was sure Hitler was dead. The codeword for the military phase of the takeover ("Valkyrie") was not issued until shortly after 4 P.M. Three and a half critical hours had been lost.[24]

Witzleben, in full uniform and driven by Reserve Major Count Wilhelm-Friedrich zu Lynar, arrived at Bendlerstrasse, the HQ of the Replacement Army, at 4.30 P.M. Colonel General Fromm, C-in-C of the Replacement Army, refused to support the putsch and was arrested. Witzleben installed himself in Fromm's office. Now acting as C-in-C of the Armed Forces, Witzleben's first act was to appoint Colonel General Erich Hoepner Commander of the Home Army. Ten minutes later General Joachim von Kortzfleisch, the pro-Nazi commander of Wehrkreis III, arrived and demanded to see Fromm. He also was arrested. Witzleben issued an order naming Lieutenant General Baron Karl von Thuengen-Rossbach Commander of the Berlin Military District. At 5 P.M. Witzleben ordered General von Stuelpnagel, the Military Governor of France, to arrest all of the SS and SD men in Paris.[25] He also sent a telegram to Field Marshal Guenther von Kluge at OB West, saying simply: "The Fuehrer is dead. Carry out your instructions as planned." He signed it "Witzleben, Supreme Commander of the Wehrmacht."[26] Kluge was momentarily prepared to join the conspirators, but his Chief of Staff, General Blumentritt, managed to get through on the telephone to Major General Helmuth Stieff, the Chief of the Organizational Section of OKH. Although a member of the plot, Stieff told Blumentritt the simple truth: Hitler was only slightly wounded. Kluge remained "loyal" to Hitler.[27]

The late beginning robbed the conspiracy of whatever chances of success it had after Hitler escaped death. At about 10 P.M. it was clearly falling apart. "This is a fine mess!" Witzleben snapped at Stauffenberg. He then met with General Beck in Fromm's office. Stauffenberg was summoned a few minutes later and both were violently "chewed out" by Witzleben for forty-five minutes.[28] The exact nature of the conference is unknown, as all the participants would be dead within three weeks. Witzleben let it be known that he would not participate in such a badly organized affair. As soon as he had said his piece, Witzleben dissociated himself from the conspiracy altogether and returned to Seesen. He was arrested there the next day.

Beck, Olbricht, and Stauffenberg were executed by Fromm when the conspiracy collapsed at midnight on July 20. Witzleben was expelled from the Army by the Court of Honor and was brought to trial before the Peoples' Court on August 7, along with Hoepner, Stieff, General Paul von Hase (the commandant of the Berlin garrison), and four junior officers. They faced Judge Roland Freisler. Witzleben was spared nothing. The Gestapo had taken away his false teeth and belt. He was "unshaven, collarless and shabby." Witzleben seemed to have aged ten years in two weeks of Gestapo captivity, which is understandable. He stared vacantly into space.[29]

Author Robert Wistrich called Witzleben "the most broken and pathetic of the conspirators."[30] His pants were too large for him, so he had to pull them up continuously. "You dirty old man!" Judge Freisler screamed at him, "why do you keep fiddling with your trousers?" The specially selected audience of Nazis cackled with malicious delight. When he was called as the first defendant, Witzleben attempted to give the Nazi salute. The judge yelled at him again. "The Hitler salute is only given by citizens whose honor is still unimpaired."[31] His court-appointed defense attorney, Dr. Weissmann, also got into the act. He praised Hitler and Judge Freisler, screamed insults at Witzleben, and applauded the fairness of the trial.[32]

Field Marshal Witzleben freely admitted his part in the assassination attempt. He and the others were found guilty the next day and sentenced to hang that afternoon. Hitler had ordered that they be hung like cattle. "I want to see them hanging like carcasses in a slaughterhouse!"[33] he commanded. The entire event was filmed by the Reich Film Corporation. Witzleben was first. Despite his poor showing at the trial, Witzleben met his death with courage and with as much dignity as was possible under the circumstances. A thin wire noose was placed around his neck, and the other end was secured to a meat hook. The executioner and his assistant then picked up the sixty-four-year-old soldier and dropped him so that his entire weight fell on his neck. They then pulled off his trousers so that he hung naked and twisted in agony as he slowly strangled. It took him almost five minutes to die, but he never once cried out. The other seven condemned men were executed in the same manner within an hour. They were followed over the next eight months by hundreds of others.[34]

19

Ferdinand Schoerner

HE WAS THE most brutal of Hitler's field marshals, a man who, one author wrote, "shot privates and colonels with equal zeal for the smallest infractions."[1] He dealt as harshly with his own men as he did with the Russians, whom he considered subhuman.

Ferdinand Schoerner was born in Munich on June 12, 1892, into a lower-middle-class family. His father was a police officer.[2] He joined the Army as a private in the Bavarian Lifeguards Regiment in October 1911 and by 1914 had received his commission as a second lieutenant in the reserves.[3] Although intending to be a primary schoolmaster[4] (Schoerner studied at the universities of Munich, Lausanne, and Grenoble),[5] he rejoined his regiment when World War I began and was part of the German Alpine Corps for most of the war. He fought on the Italian Front in 1915 and took part in the Verdun battles of 1916. He briefly returned to Munich in 1916 but was then sent to Rumania and fought in the southern Carpathians.[6] Sent back to Italy as a mountain company commander in 1917, he distinguished himself by storming the mountain fortress of Monte Kolonrat and taking the important Hill 1114. For this action he was awarded the *Pour le Mérite*, Imperial Germany's highest decoration for courage. Second Lieutenant Schoerner was sent back to the Western Front in 1918 and fought at Verdun and Rheims, where he was badly wounded. Toward the end of the war he was promoted to *Oberleutnant* (first lieutenant) and given a staff assignment in Serbia.[7] He was there when the war ended.

In 1919, Lieutenant Schoerner joined Freikorps Epp and fought against Communist revolutionaries in the Ruhr and against the Poles in Upper Silesia. The following year he was selected for the Reichsheer and was assigned to the 19th Infantry Regiment in Munich.[8] After this he was associated with the mountain troops for much of his career. He was a south German, like Hitler, and shared his ruthlessness and prejudice. He was certainly no aristocratic snob or typical General Staff officer, characteristics which endeared him to Hitler later on. Ironically, Ferdinand Schoerner helped suppress the Beer Hall Putsch in Munich in 1923, even though he was sympathetic to the movement and belonged to several racial (anti-Semitic) organizations himself. Sometime after Hitler was released from prison in 1924, Schoerner became a supporter of the Nazi movement.[9]

Lieutenant Schoerner did attempt to become a member of the *Truppenamt* (clandestine General Staff) but failed his entrance examination. This, coupled with his lower social origins, caused him to bear a great resentment toward the aristocratic gentlemen of the General Staff, who tended to look down upon him. Hitler shared these resentments, and the two were drawn to one another.[10]

Meanwhile, Schoerner served as a company commander in the 21st Jaeger Battalion and the 19th Infantry Regiment, and he was attached to the Italian Alpine Corps in the early 1930s. He did a tour with the General Staff (1934–37), and in 1937 was named commander of the 98th Mountain Infantry Regiment (of the 1st Mountain Division) in Mittenwald. He was promoted to captain (1922), major (1934), lieutenant colonel (1937), and colonel (1939).[11]

As commander of the 98th Mountain, Schoerner distinguished himself on September 13, 1939, by capturing Hill 374 and the Zbolska Heights, commanding the fortress-city of Lvov. He held these positions throughout the night, despite desperate counter-attacks by the Polish garrison. The next day the city surrendered.[12]

Schoerner continued to lead his regiment in Belgium and France. (After the war the Belgians would attempt to get their hands on him, to try him as a war criminal, but they never succeeded – there were too many in line ahead of them.) I have been unable to find out what kind of atrocities he committed there. In any case Schoerner was named commander of the 6th Mountain Division on June 1, 1940.[13] This unit had only recently been formed and consisted primarily of Austrians. Schoerner was promoted to major general on August 1, 1940. He and his unit were sent to Poland on occupation duty in the winter of 1940/41.[14] Hurriedly sent to the Balkans for the invasion of Greece in the spring of 1941, the 6th Mountain Division played the key role in breaking the Metaxas Line by crossing a 7,000-foot snow-covered mountain range and breaking through at a point the Greeks considered inaccessible. On the evening of April 7, the second day of the invasion, it cut the railroad to Salonika, the main supply route of the Greek 2nd Army.[15]

Following the surrender of the 2nd Army on April 9, Schoerner pushed his men on to Athens, which his division and the 2nd Panzer Division captured on April 27. Later, in May, the 6th Mountain Division was lightly engaged in the last phases of the Battle of Crete.[16]

After the conquest of the Balkans, Schoerner was awarded the Knights' Cross. He remained in Greece on occupation duty until Hitler ordered his division north, to the Arctic sector of the Russian Front, on July 30. The 6th Mountain had to be transported back to Germany, then by the Baltic Sea and the Gulf of Bothnia to northern Finland. Because of the British command of the sea, it could not sail to northern Norway via the easy route, but instead had to march four hundred miles across northern Finland and Lapland, to the Murmansk sector. It did not arrive in its zone of operations until early October 1941, when it relieved the depleted 2nd and 3rd Mountain divisions. Schoerner's unit was now part of General Eduard Dietl's Mountain Corps Norway and was given the task of holding the line thirty miles from Murmansk throughout the Russian winter in a tundra wilderness.[17]

The Russian winter hit the Murmansk sector eight weeks before it arrived in Moscow. Schoerner had an extremely difficult time just keeping his men supplied. Within a few weeks 1,400 of his horses had died, as well as every one of the small Greek mules he had brought with him from the Balkans. On December 21, spearheaded by Siberian divisions, the Soviets opened their offensive in the far north. Schoerner was ready, however, and the Russians were repulsed with terrible losses in the bitter cold. They did not gain an inch of ground. After this defensive victory, he was promoted to lieutenant general on January 15, 1942, and simultaneously given command of Mountain Corps Norway, which was later redesignated XIX Mountain Corps. His predecessor, Dietl, moved up to the command of the Army of Lapland (later 20th Mountain Army) at the same time.[18]

Schoerner repulsed another major Soviet offensive in April but was unable to mount a major offensive on Murmansk due to a lack of troop strength and supplies. He did, however, manage to hold the important Pechenga Nickel Works, despite strong Russian efforts to take them. Schoerner fought these battles strictly on his own, since his nearest neighbor was XXXVI Mountain Corps, more than a hundred miles away. His left flank rested on the Arctic Ocean.[19]

Ferdinand Schoerner – a general of mountain troops since June 1, 1942 – was named commander of XL Panzer Corps on October 23, 1943, despite the fact that he had no training or experience in tank warfare, and was sent from a backwater sector to the center of action on the Eastern Front. In doing so, he came into his own. From the first his combination of Nazi fanaticism and brutality impressed Hitler, and he moved steadily up in the hierarchy of the Nazi Army.

Forty Panzer Corps was almost immediately given the temporary redesignation Group Schoerner, and was given command of XXX, XVII, and IV corps in the Nikopol bridgehead on the east bank of the Dnieper. This was a critical position, for the Soviets dared not attempt to crush the 17th Army in the Crimea with Schoerner's force intact. On the other hand, the bridgehead itself invited double envelopment.[20]

Three bridges connected Group Schoerner to the rest of the German front. When the ground froze in January 1944, the Soviets attacked in force. Schoerner's paper strength was nine infantry divisions, with the 24th Panzer Division in reserve; but all of the infantry divisions were only at regimental strength, and the 24th Panzer was down to five tanks. He was attacked by twelve infantry and two tank divisions. The battle began on January 10 and lasted six days. Schoerner, as usual, held his positions.[21]

The Soviets shifted their attacks to the north, and Schoerner's superior, 6th Army Commander Colonel General Hollidt, had to transfer the 24th Panzer Division to 8th Army, despite Schoerner's weak and exposed position. Group Schoerner was seriously weakened. On the morning of January 30, the Soviets attacked the Nikopol bridgehead with the entire 4th Ukrainian Front and drove a deep wedge in Schoerner's lines. Meanwhile, other units pushed back 6th Army. By February 2 the Russians were only five miles north of the vital railroad connecting Nikopol to the rest of the Eastern Front. It was now high time for Schoerner to get out of there.[22]

Whatever else he was, Schoerner was an excellent defensive tactician, especially when he did not have to maneuver too much. He now faced the problem of withdrawing battered units over a swollen river, under heavy enemy pressure and simultaneously evading encirclement to the rear. On February 4, 1944, the railroad was cut, and Schoerner gave the order to destroy all heavy equipment, except horse-drawn artillery, in order to get his troops out more quickly. All but surrounded, in knee-deep Ukrainian mud, he got his men out of Nikopol and simultaneously broke out through Russian lines to the west – a brilliant achievement.[23] To keep his last units from panicking as they neared the only Dnieper bridge still in German hands, Schoerner personally took charge of a light flak unit and periodically fired over the heads of his own men, clearly indicating that he would fire into their ranks if they seemed too eager to make the crossing. It was a brutal but effective maneuver. The last units escaped on the night of February 15/16. Nine divisions had been saved. "No one who fought at Nikopol will ever forget what he owes Schoerner," Major Kandutsch, the Ic of XL Panzer Corps, wrote in his diary.[24]

On February 18 Schoerner was given the only staff appointment he would hold in the Second World War. He was named Chief of the National Socialist Leadership Corps under OKW, where his job was to spread the Nazi doctrine throughout the armed forces. Here he quickly came into conflict with Martin Bormann, the Chief of the Nazi Party. Bormann wanted party men in the National Socialist Leadership Officers' slots, not soldiers who were also Nazis.[25] Unlike most others, Schoerner in general prevailed against the sinister Bormann. Schoerner held this staff post less than six weeks, however. At Himmler's recommendation, Hitler promoted him to colonel general and named him Commander-in-Chief of Army Group A, replacing the Prussian cavalryman, Ewald von Kleist, who was retired. Six days later his command was renamed Army Group South Ukraine.[26]

When Schoerner took over, Army Group South Ukraine was retreating to the west. His armies (north to south) consisted of the Rumanian 4th, the 8th, the 6th, and the Rumanian 3rd, with the 17th Army isolated on the Crimean peninsula. Schoerner faced three major tasks: 1) save his main forces in the face of the Soviet offensive; 2) keep the Rumanians in the Axis; and 3) decide what to do about the Crimea.

Schoerner handled the first problem by retreating to the Bug, then to the Dnestr, and finally to the Carpathians and the Rumanian frontier by mid-April 1944. Far from being dissatisfied with this performance, Schoerner was quite pleased to get out of the Ukraine with his German forces intact. The days of superior German mobility were long past. The Russians, equipped largely with American trucks, were now much faster. Most of Schoerner's forces were foot soldiers, and he was lucky to do as well as he did.

He was concerned that the Rumanian dictator Ion Antonescu might try to withdraw his forces from the front, so Schoerner thoroughly intermixed them with the German units and set up an elaborate chain of command that, in reality, subordinated the Rumanian 4th Army to the German 6th, and the Rumanian 3rd to the German 8th. Antonescu could not withdraw his units now, even if he wanted to.[27]

Antonescu himself was another matter. Schoerner learned that some of the leading personalities in Rumania were attempting to contact the Russians and recognized that Antonescu was losing his grip on the country. He recommended that Hitler intervene personally to shore up his position, but Hitler ignored the warning.[28]

The Crimean problem he handled with less satisfactory results. On April 7 he inspected the Crimean defenses on the Perekop Isthmus and reported that they could hold "for a long time." Ziemke called this "one of the least accurate predictions of the war."[29] The Russians attacked the next day with thirty divisions and four armored corps. Colonel General Erwin Jaenecke's 17th

Army met them with five weak German and seven demoralized Rumanian divisions. The Germans held, but the Rumanian 10th Infantry Division collapsed almost immediately. By April 10 Jaenecke was in full retreat toward Sevastopol.[30]

By April 16, 17th Army was in Sevastopol with its back to the sea. Schoerner, accompanied by Jaenecke, flew to Berchtesgaden to personally urge Hitler to order the naval evacuation of the Crimea. Hitler refused; and on April 27 he sacked Jaenecke and replaced him with General Karl Allmendinger.[31]

Seventeenth Army was now defending the twenty-five-mile Sevastopol perimeter with five divisions, all at regimental (*Kampfgruppe*) strength. Schoerner continued to urge the city's evacuation, but he also took energetic measures to defend it. Any soldier who knocked out a Russian tank, he ordered, was to get an immediate three-week leave on the mainland. Since such a leave would be tantamount to salvation, this order no doubt directly increased Soviet tank losses. On the other hand, Schoerner decreed that troops who abandoned their positions were to be shot for cowardice.[32]

Schoerner's Draconian methods had little effect on the outcome of the Battle of Sevastopol, which began on May 5. By May 8 German resistance was weakening, and even Hitler was ready to concede defeat. He ordered a naval evacuation, but as usual he had waited too long. When the fighting ended on May 13, only 26,700 of the 64,700 men trapped at Sevastopol had escaped. Almost 26,000 Rumanians were also lost. Hitler made Jaenecke and Allmendinger scapegoats for the disaster, and they were retired in disgrace, pending an investigation by a court-martial.[33] Schoerner, of course, knew where the real responsibility lay, but he did not hesitate to join the Fuehrer in blaming the catastrophe on Jaenecke, for his lack of faith.[34]

FOLLOWING THE FALL of the Crimea, a lull descended on the southern sector, interrupted only by Schoerner's "strenuous training and fitness programs."[35] In Belorussia, however, Army Group Center was crushed, and its remnants were in full retreat by early July. This disaster exposed the right flank of Army Group North; its commander, Colonel General Lindemann, also wanted to retreat. As a result, Hitler sacked Lindemann on July 2 and replaced him with General Johannes Friessner, who was soon under heavy attack himself. Estimating the odds as eight to one against him, Friessner demanded freedom of action to retreat. Hitler was furious over this request. Heinz Guderian, now Chief of the General Staff of the Army, suggested a solution: Friessner should exchange commands with Schoerner. Hitler accepted this idea, and on July 23, 1944, Schoerner was named C-in-C of Army Group North.[36]

Friessner definitely got the worst of the trade. On August 20 the Soviets attacked in overwhelming strength; three days later Antonescu was overthrown and arrested; and Rumania defected. In league with the Soviets, many of the Rumanian commanders opened their lines to the Russians. The Soviet spearheads were already miles behind German lines before the defenders knew what was going on. Some twenty divisions of 6th Army were encircled and destroyed, a loss of approximately 180,000 men. Only the mobile 13th Panzer and 10th Panzer Grenadier divisions escaped, and little remained with which to defend Hungary.[37] Such was the price Hitler paid for ignoring Schoerner's warnings about Rumania.

Meanwhile, Schoerner was having his own problems. When he took over, he had thirty divisions under (north to south) Army Detachment Narva, 18th Army, and 16th Army. A gap of more than thirty miles existed on his right flank, between 16th Army and the remnants of 3rd Panzer Army, on the northern wing of Army Group Center. The Russians were precariously close to reaching the Baltic Sea and cutting him off in Estonia and Latvia. In addition, Schoerner's divisions had been in more or less continuous action since the breaking of the Siege of Leningrad six months before. They were exhausted, depleted, and under attack by twelve Soviet Armies with more than eighty divisions.[38] By this time Schoerner had virtually no reserves left.

The Bavarian mountain general initially paid little attention to his explosed flank. His first priority was to keep his front from collapsing entirely. From his commanders he demanded "Draconian intervention" and "ruthlessness to the point of brutality." A typical order to a divisional commander (quoted by the distinguished military historian, Earl F. Ziemke) read:

Lieutenant General [Walter] Charles de Beaulieu is to be told that he is to restore his own and his division's honor by a courageous deed or I will chase him out [of the Army] in disgrace. Furthermore, he is to report by 2100 which commanders he has shot or is having shot for cowardice.[39]

By brutality and by his talent for getting the very last drop of strength from his combat divisions, Schoerner managed to keep his front from collapsing – barely. He could not, however, prevent the Soviet 1st Baltic Front from reaching the Baltic just west of Riga at the end of July. Army Group North was isolated. Schoerner wanted to evacuate Estonia, but Hitler demanded that every foot of territory be held. The Fuehrer stripped Army Group South Ukraine of its entire reserve of two panzer divisions (just three weeks before the fatal Russian offensive, described above) and sent them to Colonel General Raus's 3rd Panzer Army, which he ordered to attack and restore contact with Schoerner.[40]

Raus attacked on August 16 with surprising success. By August 20 he had covered 120 miles and established a solid link with 16th Army. By now, however, Schoerner was facing 130 Russian divisions (three full fronts) with only thirty-two divisions (one of which was panzer and two panzer grenadier) and three SS brigades. To make matters worse, Finland made peace with Moscow on August 25, freeing the Leningrad Front – and even more Russian armies.[41]

After August 20 a lull descended on the northern sector, but it was clear to everyone that it would not last long. The Soviet offensive built up slowly enough for Schoerner to follow it and determine its strength and objectives. The Russians planned to break through 18th Army with their 2nd and 3rd Baltic fronts, cutting off both it and Army Detachment Narva, while the 1st Baltic Front attacked 16th Army and reached the sea near Riga, once again isolating Army Group North. Meanwhile, the Leningrad Front would attack Army Detachment Narva and clear northern Estonia. An entire front – the 3rd Belorussian – would remain in reserve.[42] Map 22 shows Schoerner's situation on September 1 and his subsequent retreat.

Colonel General Schoerner held a strategically useless and tactically dangerous position, holding a coastal strip seventy to eighty miles wide on a front nearly five hundred miles long. Both Schoerner and Guderian tried to convince Hitler to evacuate Estonia and eastern Latvia, but Hitler rejected all their appeals.[43]

Map 22

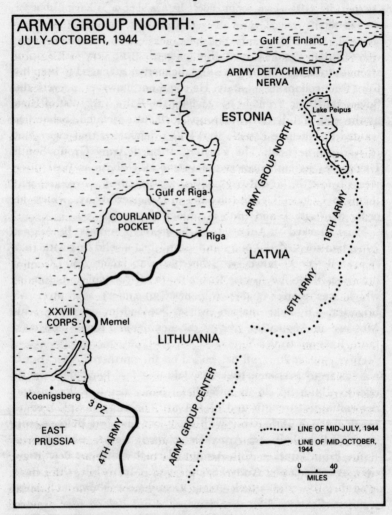

ARMY GROUP NORTH:
JULY-OCTOBER, 1944

Gulf of Finland

ARMY DETACHMENT
NERVA

ESTONIA

Lake Peipus

ARMY GROUP NORTH

18TH ARMY

Gulf of Riga

COURLAND
POCKET

• Riga

LATVIA

16TH ARMY

XXVIII
CORPS • Memel

LITHUANIA

• Koenigsberg

3 PZ

EAST
PRUSSIA

4TH ARMY

ARMY GROUP CENTER

•••••••• LINE OF MID-JULY, 1944

⸺ LINE OF MID-OCTOBER, 1944

0   40
MILES

ARMY GROUP NORTH, JULY–OCTOBER 1944. Faced with overwhelming odds, Field Marshal Ferdinand Schoerner conducted a masterful retreat, successfully abandoning Estonia, eastern Latvia, and Lithuania. Memel was not lost until January 1945. The 16th and 18th armies remained isolated in Courland until the end of the war.

Accordingly, Schoerner made secret retrograde plans without Hitler's knowledge.

The Soviets attacked on all sectors on September 14, 1944. They were checked at all points, but the attacks continued. The next day the Russians penetrated to within twenty-five miles of Riga, and Schoerner called for the evacuation of Estonia, stating that this was the last possible moment to escape. On September 16 he personally flew to Fuehrer Headquarters and finally obtained permission to retreat – if Schoerner would wait two days and he could still cancel the order in the meantime. Schoerner agreed to these conditions.[44]

The evacuation began on September 18 and was a masterpiece. It was over by September 27. Schoerner succeeded in extracting all of his German units, and 100,000 Estonians as well. Meanwhile, on the other flank, 16th Army halted the Russians only ten miles south of Riga on September 19. The Soviets called up their reserves and tried to break through to the sea on September 22. By now, however, the forces withdrawing from Estonia were becoming available to Schoerner at Riga. The 11th SS Panzer Grenadier Division "Nordland" force-marched 250 miles in four days and arrived just in time to check the Soviet breakthrough and prevent disaster. By September 27 Army Group North's frontage had been reduced from more than four hundred miles to approximately seventy miles.[45]

Until this point, Schoerner's handling of the defense of the northern sector had been flawless. Now, however, he made a serious mistake. Hitler transferred 3rd Panzer Army to Schoerner, and Guderian sent him a directive, allowing him to concentrate the 3rd Panzer to the south, against an attack on Memel. Schoerner refused to do this because he did not believe Memel was in any danger. He ignored Guderian's pleas to properly cover this flank. On October 5 the Soviets struck at the exact point Guderian predicted they would, with fourteen divisions and four armored corps (more than five hundred tanks). The German sector here was defended by the understrength 551st Volksgrenadier Division, which was defending twenty-four miles of frontage, which meant it could only cover strongpoints. The 551st was overwhelmed and the front broke. The command post of the 3rd Panzer Army was overrun and the staff had to fight its way into Memel, where

XXVIII Corps maintained a small bridgehead. The 3rd Panzer was split into three parts: one corps held at Memel, one corps escaped north into the pocket now formed by Army Group North, and the third escaped south, to join Army Group Center in East Prussia. The Soviets reached the sea north and south of Memel, isolating Army Group North in the Courland Pocket.[46]

Schoerner tried to re-establish contact with XXVIII Corps and East Prussia by organizing a counterattack. To obtain the necessary divisions, he shortened his line by evacuating Riga on October 11. Before he could strike, however, the Soviets launched another offensive against East Prussia, and Hitler cancelled the plan. The Fuehrer began to withdraw divisions from Army Group North by sea at the end of October although he would not consent to evacuate the entire army group. It would remain isolated in the Courland Pocket for the rest of the war.

Six battles of the Courland Pocket followed, in which the Soviets tried to crush Army Group North (later Courland). The first began on October 27. By the eleventh day of the battle, Schoerner's troops had knocked out 522 Russian tanks against a loss of only twenty field pieces and anti-tank guns.[47] Schoerner fought the second and third battles with similar results.

ON JANUARY 17, 1945, Hitler appointed Colonel General Schoerner to the command of Army Group A (formerly North Ukraine), replacing Colonel General Josef Harpe, who took over the 5th Panzer Army in the West. Colonel General Heinrich von Vietinghoff replaced Schoerner in Courland and was eventually succeeded by Colonel General Dr. Lothar Rendulic and then Karl Hilpert, who surrendered its 200,000 survivors to the Russians at the end of the war.[48]

Schoerner's last command consisted of the 9th, 4th Panzer, 17th, and 1st Panzer armies (north to south), holding a three-hundred-mile line from north of Warsaw to the Carpathians in Czechoslovakia, with only eighteen weak infantry divisions and elements of six panzer and panzer grenadier divisions. On January 26 Hitler changed the name of Army Group A to Army Group Center.[49] Schoerner had 400,000 men, 1,150 tanks, and 4,100 guns, with which to oppose 2,200,000 Russians with 6,400 tanks and 46,000 guns. He was outnumbered approximately six to one in men, six to one in armor, and more than eleven to one in guns.[50]

When Schoerner took over, a major Soviet offensive was already underway. Schoerner met it with typical ruthlessness. When Warsaw fell on January 18, he sacked General Baron Smilo von Luettwitz as Commander of the 9th Army and replaced him with General Theodor Busse.[51] Drumhead courts-martial and summary executions were the order of the day. Dozens of men were hung from light poles with a placard, "Coward" or "Deserter," around their necks. These actions had little effect on the outcome of the Third Reich's last battle, however.

Ninth Army was soon transferred to Army Group Vistula for the defense of Berlin. This group originally was commanded by Himmler, who was replaced on March 20 by Colonel General Gotthard Heinrici.[52] Schoerner's primary mission was to hold the Silesian industrial area, which had replaced the bombed-out Ruhr as Germany's main armaments-producing region. Schoener fought with the utmost energy but could not stem the tide. Breslau, the heart of Silesia, was surrounded on February 16.[53] Schoerner made Lieutenant General Hermann Niehoff commander of the besieged city, because he knew Niehoff had five children who could be executed under the principle of collective family responsibility if the general failed to obey his orders. "Failure in Breslau means your head," Schoerner told Niehoff as he departed for the city, where 250,000 civilians and about 35,000 soldiers were trapped. Led by Niehoff and the ruthless Nazi Gauleiter, Karl Hanke, the fortress of Breslau would not surrender until May 7 – long after Berlin fell – despite the fact that the Russians bombed and shelled it day and night. The suffering and death totals among the civilian population were incredible, as it was throughout Silesia, which was raped and plundered with terrible brutality.[54] The Russians did this deliberately, in order to induce a mass exodus of the population from what would become the Soviet satellite of Poland. Of the 4,700,000 civilians living in Silesia in early 1944, only 620,000 remained in mid-April 1946.[55]

Schoerner lost the Battle of Silesia and retreated into Saxony and Czechoslovakia. In late March Schoerner parroted Hitler, who proclaimed the target of the next Soviet offensive would be Prague, not Berlin. Hitler reinforced Schoerner to a strength of about 600,000 men, making his the strongest army group on the Eastern Front. On April 5, 1945, the Fuehrer promoted Schoerner to field marshal, the last Army officer to attain this rank. Hitler personally gave him his baton on April 10.[56]

The final Soviet offensive began on April 16, against Army Group Vistula and Berlin. Schoerner launched several relief attacks from April 19–27 and made some local progress, but could not save the Fuehrer, now surrounded in the ruins of the capital.[57]

On April 27 Hitler called Schoerner "the only man to shine as a real warlord on the entire Eastern Front." The next day he signed an order appointing Schoerner Commander-in-Chief of the Army upon his death.[58] At 3:30 P.M. on April 30, with the Russians less than a mile from his bunker, Adolf Hitler shot himself.

Schoerner never exercised the power bestowed on him by Hitler, and his last days in command come under a cloud of controversy. There are two versions of his actions during the final, chaotic days of the Third Reich: one version is based on the testimony of Lieutenant General Oldwig von Natzmer, the Chief of Staff of Army Group Center. The other version – quite a different story – was presented by Lieutenant Helmut Dirning, a collateral cousin of the field marshal and his aide-de-camp from March 17, 1945, until the end of the war. Both will be presented here.

In late April or early May, Army Group Center came under heavy attack and was virtually encircled east of Prague. With his Fuehrer dead and his cause lost, Schoerner's courage left him, according to General von Natzmer. On May 7, with the cease-fire ending the war scheduled to take effect at 9 A.M. on May 9, Schoerner ordered his men to flee to the west, packed his briefcase with money, and flew off for the Bavarian Alps. He had a cabin there, he told General Natzmer, that no one knew about. Here he would go into hiding.

Natzmer appealed to him not to flee. The army group would be marching for its life the next day, he said, to escape Russian captivity, and needed centralized control now more than ever. But Schoerner was thinking only of himself. He deserted his command and, clad in a traditional Bavarian costume, flew off to the south-west.[59] Most of Army Group Center fell into Soviet hands; a great many men were subsequently massacred by Czech partisans.

Lieutenant Dirning told my friend Friedrich von Stauffenberg quite a different story in 1946, when they were both employed in Argentina. Although Dirning agreed that Schoerner was bad-tempered and sacked commanders without proper justification, he insisted that Schoerner left Czechoslovakia in early May 1945 on the direct orders of the Fuehrer. Hitler had chosen the "Central Redoubt" (also called the "National Redoubt") in the Bavarian Alps as the site of the last stand of the Nazi armed forces. Just before he committed suicide, Hitler dictated that Schoerner, as Supreme Commander of the Wehrmacht, would immediately fly out of his army group command post and take over the "army" supposedly gathering in the "Alpine Fortress." This is exactly what Schoerner attempted to do, according to Dirning.[60]

Lieutenant Dirning, incidentally, did not accompany Field Marshal Schoerner on his flight but, in the company of a few other officers, managed to elude the Russians and escape to western Austria, where his party surrendered to the Americans.

Stauffenberg concludes: "The conduct described by Dirning certainly is in accord with what else we know of the Marshal. Surely no General who could engage in hand-to-hand fighting in Finland, and mastermind the defense and successful evacuation of the Nikopol Pocket would show himself a coward in 1945; von Natzmer's criticism does not ring true – at least about [Schoerner's] departure from his headquarters."[61]

Was Schoerner attempting to join his new command in Bavaria, or was he attempting to desert and reach a secret hideout in the same general area? This author tends to agree with Dirning and von Stauffenberg, although we will probably never know for sure, because Schoerner never reached his destination. His small airplane crash-landed in eastern Austria, where the field marshal wandered for several days, trying to avoid capture. Then, on May 18, he was recognized by some civilians who reported him. He was arrested by troops of the 1st Panzer Army. They turned him over to the Americans, who transferred him to the Russians, who had been looking for him.[62]

The Russians sentenced Schoerner to twenty-five years' imprisonment as a war criminal. On January 25, 1955, after serving only nine years of his sentence, Schoerner was released and returned to Munich. Here he found that General von Natzmer had denounced him and that he was widely abhorred as a commander who had deserted his men in their hour of need in order to save his own neck. The Association of Returned Prisoners of War was also after him. They charged him with the murder of thousands of German soldiers during the drumhead courts-martial in the last years of the war. In 1957 he was found guilty of manslaughter and sentenced to four and a half years in prison by a Munich court for executing a soldier without trial – the man had been found drunk at the wheel of an Army truck. After his release he lived another decade, dying in Munich on July 6, 1973, at the age of eighty-one.[63]

FERDINAND SCHOERNER WAS a capable defensive commander, but he did less well in the attack against a determined enemy. He could hardly be classified as a military genius. Certainly his record does not compare with that of Manstein, Guderian, or Rommel, or even of Kleist or Model. His reputation will be forever tarnished by his brutality and by his alleged desertion of Army Group Center in May 1945 – especially since he executed so many for doing exactly what he is accused of having done himself. If his action in early May was in fact desertion, then it must be further noted that the common soldiers who he had killed as deserters did not by their actions leave hundreds of thousands of their comrades to the mercy of the Russians.

Schoerner's methods were unquestionably vicious. It must be conceded that they achieved results, but it must also be pointed out that other commanders (notably Manstein, Heinrici, and Kleist) achieved equal or superior results under similar circumstances without resorting to barbarism. Schoerner will probably go down in history as a good defensive commander and a thoroughly despicable human being.

20

The Luftwaffe Marshals

THE STORY OF the Luftwaffe field marshals involves an entirely different sphere than that of the Army: air rather than ground operations. In addition, Luftwaffe operations were generally more technologically oriented than those of the Army. The battles of the Luftwaffe marshals will be the subject of another book; however, they were German field marshals, so at least a thumbnail description of their careers is in order.

THERE WERE SIX Luftwaffe field marshals. In order of seniority, they were Hermann Goering, Erhard Milch, Albert Kesselring, Hugo Sperrle, Baron Wolfram von Richthofen, and Ritter Robert von Greim. All served in World War I, where Goering, Richthofen, and Greim became fighter aces. Greim scored twenty-eight aerial victories and was given a knighthood. Goering shot down twenty-two enemy aircraft and ended the war as commander of the Richthofen Fighter Wing (*Geschwader*). Wolfram von Richthofen, the nephew of Manfred von Richthofen, the famous "Red Baron," served in the cavalry on the Eastern Front and did not transfer to the Flying Corps until late 1917. He "received his wings" in the spring of 1918, joined his uncle's famous group, and scored eight victories before the armistice. Hugo Sperrle led aerial reconnaissance units on the Western Front and was in charge of all flying units under 7th Army on the Western Front at the end of the war. Erhard Milch was an aerial observer and, at the end, was in command of a fighter squadron, although he did not yet know how to fly himself. Albert Kesselring's entire service was on the ground in artillery units or as a General Staff officer, although he had previous aerial experience as a balloon observer in the artillery.

Hermann Goering was a stunt pilot and a charter pilot in Sweden after the war. In the early 1920s he returned to Germany and joined the Nazi Party. He became Adolf Hitler's second-in-command and President of the Reichstag. When the Nazis came to power he was the unofficial Minister of Aviation and became Commander-in-Chief of the Luftwaffe in 1935, when Hitler renounced the Treaty of Versailles, which had forbidden Germany to have an air force. He became a field marshal in 1938 and in 1940 was named Reichsmarschall, the highest rank in the German military, which he alone held.

The ambitious and ruthless Erhard Milch joined the Freikorps after the war and then went into the business world, where he became head of Lufthansa, the German state airline. He began paying bribes to Goering, then a member of the Reichstag, in 1930 or 1931. Goering recognized his talent and brought him into the government as State Secretary for Aviation and number-two man in the Ministry and the Luftwaffe until 1936, when Goering learned that Milch was planning to eventually replace him as Minister of Aviation. By now Milch was too close to Hitler to be summarily dismissed, so in early 1937 Goering began to reduce Milch's power; he set up a complicated command structure, aimed at securing his own position. This organizational structure led to constant friction between Milch and the various chiefs of the General Staff of the Luftwaffe, of which there were seven between 1935 and 1945. This arrangement did irreparable damage to the Luftwaffe, for Goering grew extremely lazy and the Air Force was left without centralized guidance for most of its existence.

Spain was the turning point in the development of the Luftwaffe. Here the German Condor Legion, commanded by Hugo Sperrle and Wolfram von Richthofen, played an important role in the victory of Fascist leader Generalissimo Francisco Franco over the Republicans and their Communist supporters in the Spanish Civil

War (1936–39).[1] During this period the Luftwaffe neglected its strategic development and emphasized its role as a tactical ground support force, a mistake from which it never fully recovered. The development of the four-engine bomber was cancelled during this period, to cite but one example. With this bomber the Germans might have won the Battle of Britain, and it was precisely this sort of weapon that reduced Germany's cities to rubble in 1943–45. Several long-range fighter prototypes were also scrapped, and the full-scale development of the first jets was relatively neglected.

The Luftwaffe, functioning as a tactical ground support arm, played a major role in the German victories in Poland, France, the Balkans, and Russia (1939–41), but was defeated over the skies of Britain in 1940. It began its relative decline in late 1941, when the dreaded two-front war became a reality. The Allied strategic bomber offensive against the Third Reich began in 1943. The Luftwaffe, designed to fight short campaigns in support of ground forces, was scattered from the Arctic Ocean to North Africa, and from Russia to the Atlantic Wall in France. It was gradually crushed, and the enemy obtained almost complete aerial supremacy on all fronts.

THE AMBITIOUS MILCH thought he saw an opportunity to replace Goering in early 1943, after the Stalingrad débâcle, in which Goering promised to resupply 6th Army by air but was totally unable to do so. He went so far as to suggest to Hitler that the Reichsmarschall be removed. The effort failed, and Goering began to systematically undermine Milch's position. In June 1944, after Milch failed to develop a useable jet fighter-bomber, Goering secured his dismissal as State Secretary of Aviation and Director of the Office of Air Armament. Milch retained the post of Inspector General of the Luftwaffe (with no real power) until January 1945, when he was stripped of this post as well. He was captured by the British in May 1945 and later sentenced to fifteen years' imprisonment as a war criminal. Released in 1955, he lived in Duesseldorf, where he was employed as an aviation consultant by Fiat and by Thyssen Steel. He died at Wuppertal-Barmen on January 25, 1972.[2]

HUGO SPERRLE COMMANDED Luftwaffe Group 3 (redesignated 3rd Air Fleet in 1939) from 1938 to 1944. He did well in the Western campaign of 1940, and later that year he proposed a strategy that might have defeated the Royal Air Force in the Battle of Britain, had it been adopted. After the other major air units were transferred east in the spring of 1941, Sperrle assumed control of all aerial operations in the United Kingdom, with increasingly diminishing success. He lived like a sultan in Paris and became lazy and indolent. In August 1944 he was sacked because of his fleet's totally ineffective performance during the Battle of Normandy. Embittered by his experiences, Sperrle was never subsequently re-employed. Captured by the British on May 1, 1945, he was acquitted of war crimes at Nuremberg in 1948 and was officially declared denazified in 1949. He died in Munich on April 2, 1953.[3] Huge, thick-joweled and bearlike in appearance, he was one of Hitler's most brutal-looking generals.

WOLFRAM VON RICHTHOFEN distinguished himself as a close air support commander. As the commander of VIII Air Corps, he helped pave the way for the German victories in Poland and France, but his Stuka dive-bombers were helpless against the modern RAF fighters in the Battle of Britain, and his unit had to be withdrawn from the battle soon after the campaign began. Richthofen again distinguished himself in the conquest of Yugoslavia and Crete, where he severely hurt the Royal Navy's Mediterranean Fleet. In Russia (1941–42) he was extremely successful on all three sectors and was named Commander-in-Chief of the 4th Air Fleet in 1942. He advised against the Stalingrad airlift and bears no responsibility for its failure. Manstein had nothing but praise for him. Promoted to field marshal in early 1943, Baron von Richthofen was sent to Italy to command the 2nd Air Fleet against the British and Americans. Here he was decisively defeated. Suffering from an inoperable brain tumor, he transferred to the Fuehrer Reserve in November 1944 and died in Austria on July 12, 1945.[4]

ALBERT KESSELRING IS perhaps the best-known Air Force field marshal after Goering himself. He was Chief of the General Staff of the Luftwaffe (1936–37) but could not work with Milch, so he applied for retirement. Instead, Goering gave him command of Luftkreis III (III Air District). Later he commanded Air Force Group 1, a command that was upgraded to 1st Air Fleet in 1939. After supporting Bock's Army Group North in Poland, he was given command of 2nd Air Fleet, which he led with considerable success in the Low Countries and France (1940), Russia (1941), and the Mediterranean and North Africa (1942–43). In the Battle of Britain he was less successful.

A field marshal since 1940, Kesselring was named C-in-C, Army Group C and OB South in 1943, and directed ground operations in Sicily and Italy from July 1943 to October 1944. His retreats in Sicily and Italy and his conduct of the battles of Salerno and Cassino bear the stamp of genius, but he was also lucky. He narrowly failed to annihilate the Allied bridgehead at Anzio in February 1944. Finally outwitted by British .Field Marshal Sir Harold Alexander in the 4th Battle of Cassino, he lost Rome on June 4 to US General Mark Clark's 5th Army but managed to escape with all his forces – a major feat in itself. He retreated slowly to the Genghis Khan Line (between Rome and Florence) in October 1944. He was planning a withdrawal behind the Po River when he was critically injured in an automobile accident on October 23.[5]

After successful brain surgery, Kesselring took up his OB South command again on January 15, 1945, but on March 8 was named Commander-in-Chief, OB West, replacing Rundstedt. He was unable to salvage that hopeless situation and surrendered to the Americans at the Berchtesgadener Hotel on May 15.[6] He was tried in Italy as a war criminal for shooting 335 Italian civilians in the Ardentine catacombs on March 24, 1944.[7] Convicted by a British Military Court, he was sentenced to death, a sentence that was commuted to life imprisonment in 1947. After he developed throat cancer in 1952 he was released from prison as an act of clemency.[8]

In his last years, Kesselring wrote his memoirs, *A Soldier's Record (Soldat bis zum letzten Tag)*, and became head of the Stahlhelm, a right-wing nationalist veterans' organization that many considered to be neo-Nazi. Like all the Luftwaffe field marshals, Kesselring was a Nazi sympathizer, although he never formally joined the Party. His memoirs are not at all critical of Hitler.

Plagued by ill health for years, Kesselring died of heart failure at Bad Nauheim on July 20, 1960, at the age of seventy-four.[9] He is buried in a small cemetery at Bad Wiessee, near Munich. All that appears on his tombstone is his name and rank.[10]

RITTER ROBERT VON Greim was the last man Hitler promoted to field marshal. An artillery officer in the Imperial Army, he was a battery commander and forward observer on the Western Front in World War I, before transferring to the Flying Corps in 1916.[11] He returned to the Army in 1919 but resigned in 1920 and became a stunt pilot. Later he showed up in Canton, China, where he helped organize military aviation for Chiang Kai-shek's Nationalist Air Force. An enthusiastic Nazi who worshipped Hitler, he rejoined the service in 1934 and was commander of the Luftwaffe's first fighter wing.[12] Later he was named Inspector of Fighters and Dive Bombers.[13]

Greim served as Chief of the Personnel Branch of the Luftwaffe (1938–39) and Commander of the 5th Air Division (1939). This headquarters was progressively upgraded to V Air Corps (1940), Special Staff Crimea (early 1942), Luftwaffe Command East (1942), and 6th Air Fleet (1943). Greim did well in the west but did not come into his own until the invasion of Russia in 1941. Ritter von Greim spent four years on the Eastern Front (1941–45), broken only by one brief spell of temporary duty in Belgium. He was commanding the German air units in eastern Germany, Poland, Slovakia, Bohemia, Moravia, and Croatia when he was summoned to Fuehrer Headquarters on April 24, 1945.[14]

Berlin was already surrounded on April 25, when Greim's old training plane landed in the city. Greim himself was hit by Russian anti-aircraft shell fragments and his co-pilot, Hanna Reitsch, a fanatical Nazi stunt pilot and one of the few women to hold the Iron Cross, landed the damaged aircraft on a shell-pitted street near the Chancellery: a neat piece of flying indeed![15]

Carried into the Chancellery in great pain, Greim was astonished to learn from Hitler's own lips that Goering had sent him a message that Hitler (influenced by Martin Bormann) had decided was treasonable. Goering was sacked as C-in-C of the Luftwaffe and stripped of all his posts. He, Ritter Robert von Greim, was then appointed Commander-in-Chief of the Air Force and promoted to the rank of field marshal!

Herman Goering was arrested by the Gestapo but managed to surrender to the Americans in Austria on May 8. Convicted as a major war criminal, he committed suicide by taking cyanide in his cell at Nuremberg at 10:40 P.M. on October 15, 1946, two hours before he would have been hanged.

For Greim the end came quicker. On Hitler's orders he flew out of Berlin on April 29 to join Grand Admiral Karl Doenitz, whom

Hitler had named his successor. Doenitz was attempting to set up a Nazi government at Ploen at the time.[16] The next day, Hitler committed suicide in his bunker in Berlin. The Russians were only a few hundred yards away.

After Hitler's death, Greim no longer wished to go on living.[17] He made his way back to southern Germany, where fighting against the Russians continued until May 9. After directing these final, futile operations, despite the terrible pain caused by his wound, Greim was taken prisoner by the Americans and sent to a hospital in Salzburg. Here, true to his word, Field Marshal Ritter Robert von Greim committed suicide on May 24, probably using the cyanide capsule Hitler had given him in the Fuehrer Bunker the month before. He had commanded the Luftwaffe for less than two weeks.

Appendix I

TABLES OF EQUIVALENT RANKS

US ARMY	GERMAN ARMY
General of the Army	Field Marshal (Generalfeldmarschall)
General	Colonel General (Generaloberst)
Lieutenant General	General (General)
Major General	Lieutenant General (Generalleutnant)
Brigadier General	Major General (Generalmajor)
Colonel	Colonel (Oberst)
Lieutenant Colonel	Lieutenant Colonel (Oberstleutnant)
Major	Major (Major)
Captain	Captain (Hauptmann)
First Lieutenant	First Lieutenant (Oberleutnant)
Second Lieutenant	Second Lieutenant (Leutnant)

SS RANK	GERMAN ARMY EQUIVALENT
Reichsfuehrer SS	Commander-in-Chief of the Army
(none)	Field Marshal
Oberstgruppenfuehrer	Colonel General
Obergruppenfuehrer	General
Gruppenfuehrer	Lieutenant General
Brigadefuehrer	Major General
Oberfuehrer	(none)
Standartenfuehrer	Colonel
Obersturmbannfuehrer	Lieutenant Colonel
Sturmbannfuehrer	Major
Hauptsturmfuehrer	Captain
Obersturmfuehrer	First Lieutenant
Untersturmfuehrer	Second Lieutenant

Appendix II

GERMAN UNITS, RANKS, AND STRENGTHS

Units	Rank of Commander*	Strength**
Army Group	Field Marshal	2 or more armies
Army	Colonel General	2 or more corps
Corps	General	2 or more divisions
Division	Lieutenant General/ Major General	10,000–18,000 men 200–350 tanks (if panzer)
Brigade	Major General/Colonel	2 or more regiments
Regiment	Colonel	2 to 7 battalions
Battalion	Lieutenant Colonel/ Major/Captain	Approx. 500 men per infantry battalion; usually 50–80 tanks per panzer battalion
Company***	Captain/Lieutenant	3 to 5 platoons
Platoon	Lieutenant/Sergeant Major/Sergeant	Infantry: 20–40 men
Section	Warrant Officer/ Sergeant Major	2 squads (more or less)
Squad	Sergeant	Infantry: 7 to 10 men Armor: 1 tank

*Frequently units were commanded by lower-ranking men as the war went on.

**As the war progressed, the number of men and tanks in most units declined accordingly. SS units usually had more men and tanks than Army units.

***Called batteries in the artillery (4 or 5 guns per battery).

Appendix III

CHARACTERISTICS OF SELECTED OPPOSING TANKS

Model	Weight (tons)	Speed (mph)	Range (miles)	Armament	Crew
BRITISH					
Mark IV "Churchill"	43.1	15	120	1 6-pounder	5
Mark VI "Crusader"	22.1	27	200	1 2-pounder	5
Mark VIII "Cromwell"	30.8	38	174	1 75mm	5
AMERICAN					
M3A1 "Stuart"	14.3	36	60	1 37mm	4
M4A3 "Sherman"	37.1	30	120	1 76mm	5
				3 MGs	
GERMAN					
PzKw II	9.3	25	118	1 20mm	3
				1 MG	
PzKw III	24.5	25	160	1 50mm	5
				2 MGs	
PzKw IV	19.7	26	125	1 75mm	5
				2 MGs	
PzKw V "Panther"	49.3	25	125	1 75mm	5
				2 MGs	
PzKw VI "Tiger"	62.0	23	73	1 88mm	5
				2 MGs	
SOVIET					
T-34/85	34.4	32	250	1 85mm	4
				2 MGs	
JS II "Stalin"	45.3	23	150	1 122mm	4
				4 MGs	
ITALIAN					
L 3	3.4	26	75	2 MGs	2
L 11	10.8	21	124	1 37mm	2
				2 MGs	

Appendix IV

GERMAN STAFF ABBREVIATIONS

Ia—Staff Officer, Operations
Ib—Chief Supply Officer
Ic—Staff Officer, Intelligence (subordinate to Ia)
IIa—Chief Personnel Officer (Adjutant)
IIb—Second Personnel Officer (subordinate to IIa)
III—Chief Judge Advocate (subordinate to IIa)
IVa—Chief Administrative Officer (subordinate to Ib)
IVb—Chief Medical Officer (subordinate to Ib)
IVc—Chief Veterinary Officer (subordinate to Ib)
IVd—Chaplain (subordinate to IIa)
V—Motor Transport Officer (subordinate to Ib)
National Socialist Guidance Officer (added in 1944)
Special Staff Officers (Chief of Artillery; Chief of Projector [Rocket-Launcher] Units; Senior Military Police Officer, Gas Protection Officer, etc.)

Notes

1: Werner von Blomberg

1. Robert Payne, *The Life and Death of Adolf Hitler* (New York: Praeger Publishers, 1973, reprint ed., New York: Popular Library, 1973), p. 242; William L. Shirer, *The Rise and Fall of the Third Reich* (New York: Simon and Schuster, 1960), pp. 172–77 (hereafter cited as "Shirer").

2. Shirer, pp. 182–83.

3. Harold C. Deutsch, *Hitler and His Generals: The Hidden Crisis, January–June 1938* (Minneapolis: University of Minnesota Press, 1974), p. 8 (hereafter cited as "Deutsch 1974").

4. Robert J. O'Neill, *The German Army and the Nazi Party, 1933–1939* (New York: James H. Heinemann, 1966), p. 10 (hereafter cited as "O'Neill"); Shirer, p. 183.

5. Shirer, pp. 183, 207.

6. Norbert A. Huebsch, "Field Marshal Werner von Blomberg and the Politicization of the Wehrmacht," (Ph.D. Dissertation, Cincinnati, Ohio: University of Cincinatti, 1981), pp. 16–17 (hereafter cited as "Huebsch").

7. O'Neill, pp. 186–87.

8. Huebsch, pp. 25–31. Blomberg was very happy at Metz and was disappointed when he was transferred to the 19th Reserve Division at Hanover, even though this transfer represented a promotion.

9. Matthew Cooper, *The German Army, 1933–45* (Briarcliff Manor, New York: Stein and Day, 1978), p. 21 (hereafter cited as "Cooper"); O'Neill, pp. 186–87.

10. Huebsch, p. 44.

11. O'Neill, pp. 186–87.

12. Telford Taylor, *Sword and Swastika: Generals and Nazis in the Third Reich* (New York: Simon and Schuster, 1952, reprint ed., Chicago: Quadrangle Paperback, 1969), p. 61 (hereafter cited as "Taylor"); O'Neill, pp. 186–87; Huebsch, p. 58.

13. Richard Brett-Smith, *Hitler's Generals* (San Rafael, California: Presidio Press, 1977), p. 183 (hereafter cited as "Brett-Smith"); Taylor, p. 61.

14. John W. Wheeler-Bennett, *The Nemesis of Power: The German Army in Politics, 1918–1945* (London: Macmillan, 1964), p. 296 (hereafter cited as "Wheeler-Bennett"); Louis L. Snyder, *Encyclopedia of the Third Reich* (New York: McGraw-Hill, 1976), pp. 29–30 (hereafter cited as "Snyder").

15. O'Neill, pp. 186–87.

16. Taylor, pp. 61–62; O'Neill, p. 190; Shirer, p. 151.

17. Shirer, p. 151; O'Neill, p. 190; Taylor, pp. 61–62.

18. David Irving, *The War Path: Hitler's Germany, 1933–39* (New York: Viking Press, 1978), p. 28 (hereafter cited as "Irving 1978"). In fact, when war finally did break out, SA units fought against the Poles as part of the 3rd Army (formerly HQ, Wehrkreis I).

19. Taylor, p. 77.

20. Len Deighton, *Blitzkrieg: From the Rise of Hitler to the Fall of Dunkirk* (New York: Alfred A. Knopf, 1979), p. 28 (hereafter cited as "Deighton"); Wheeler-Bennett, p. 297.

21. Taylor, p. 76. Oskar Hindenburg was a lieutenant general and in charge of prisoner-of-war camps in Wehrkreis I in late 1944.

22. O'Neill, pp. 6–7; Wheeler-Bennett, pp. 298–300.

23. Shirer, pp. 207–08; Irving 1978, p. 28; O'Neill, p. 34.

24. Bella Fromm, *Blood and Banquets* (New York: Harper and Row, 1942), p. 140.

25. O'Neill, p. 33.

26. Ibid, pp. 32–34.

27. Cooper, p. 28; O'Neill, pp. 34–35.

28. Cooper, p. 28.

29. O'Neill, p. 36; Cooper, pp. 28, 34.

30. Cooper, p. 34.

31. Ibid., pp. 33–48.

32. O'Neill, p. 17.

33. Wheeler-Bennett, pp. 301–12; O'Neill, p. 35.

34. Shirer, pp. 214–15; Wheeler-Bennett, pp. 313–14.

35. Snyder, p. 32; Shirer, p. 223.

36. Wheeler-Bennett, p. 326.

37. Robert M. Kennedy, *The German Campaign in Poland (1939)*, United States Department of the Army *Pamphlet 20–255* (Washington, D.C.: Department of the Army, 1956), p. 11 (hereafter cited as "Kennedy").

38. Taylor, pp. 107–08. Other Wehrkreise commanders included Generals Blaskowitz (II), Geyer (V), Dollmann (IX), Knochenhauser (X), Ulex (XI), and Kress von Kressenstein (XII).

39. Kennedy, p. 20; Wheeler-Bennett, p. 340.

40. Taylor, p. 35.

41. David Irving, *The Rise and Fall of the Luftwaffe: The Life of Field Marshal Erhard Milch* (Boston: Little, Brown, 1973), p. 31 (hereafter cited as "Irving 1973").

42. Richard Suchenwirth, "Command and Leadership in the German Air Force," United States Air Force Historical Studies Number 174 (Maxwell Air Force Base, Alabama: United States Air Force Historical Division, Air University, 1969) (hereafter cited as "Suchenwirth MS").

43. Heinz Guderian, *Panzer Leader* (New York: E. P. Dutton, 1957; reprint ed., New York: Ballantine Books, 1967), p. 25 (hereafter cited as "Guderian"). Fessmann retired as an honorary (*charakterisierte*) General of Panzer Troops on September 30, 1937. Recalled to active duty in 1939, he commanded the 267th Infantry Division, a reservist unit, until June 1941. After a period of staff duty at Frankfurt-an-der-Oder, he retired again in 1942. See Wolf Keilig, *Die Generale des Heeres* (Friedberg: Podzum Pallas Verlag, 1983), p. 89 (hereafter cited as "Keilig").

44. Taylor, p. 94.

45. Shirer, pp. 285–93; Irving 1978, pp. 48–49; Cooper, p. 54.

46. Cooper, p. 54.

47. Shirer, p. 293.

48. Taylor, pp. 109–10. The organization of the original light divisions varied considerably, but they were more or less a cross between panzer and motorized divisions. Considered hard to maneuver in Poland, they were converted into panzer divisions in the winter of 1939/40. Later light divisions were basically pursuit units, with only two infantry regiments, except for those in North Africa, which had three. See Kennedy, pp. 28–30, and Samuel W. Mitcham, Jr., *Hitler's Legions: The German Army Order of Battle, World War II* (Briarcliff Manor, NY: Stein and Day, 1985), pp. 319–31 (hereafter cited as "Mitcham 1985").

49. Irving 1978, p. 63; Wheeler-Bennett, pp. 359–62; Shirer, pp. 303–08.

50. Cooper, p. 64; Wheeler-Bennett, pp. 363–64.
51. Irving 1978, p. 64.
52. Taylor, p. 147.
53. Irving 1978, p. 48.
54. Cooper, p. 59.
55. Irving 1978, pp. 3–6.
56. Deutsch 1974, p. 96.
57. Wilhelm Keitel, *In the Service of the Reich*, Walter Goerlitz, ed. (Briarcliff Manor, NY: Stein and Day, 1966), p. 43 (hereafter cited as "Keitel"); Deutsch 1974, p. 96.
58. Shirer, pp. 312–13; Deutsch 1974, p. 96; Irving (1978, p. 6) states that there is no record of her being a prostitute. It seems fairly certain that she briefly engaged in that profession, however.
59. Irving 1978, p. 5; Wheeler-Bennett, pp. 365–66.
60. See Keitel, p. 44.
61. Cooper, p. 60.
62. Shirer, p. 366; Cooper, p. 59.
63. Shirer, p. 314.
64. Harold C. Deutsch, *The Conspiracy Against Hitler in the Twilight War* (Minneapolis: University of Minnesota Press, 1978), pp. 123–24 (hereafter cited as "Deutsch 1978").
65. Ibid.
66. Ibid, p. 96.
67. Huebsch, p. 2.
68. Deutsch 1978, pp. 120–21.
69. Ibid, p. 126.
70. Ibid, p. 127.
71. Taylor, p. 151.
72. David Irving, *Hitler's War* (New York: Viking Press, 1977), p. 118 (hereafter cited as "Irving 1977").
73. Huebsch, pp. 3–4; 314–15.
74. Brett-Smith, p. 185.
75. Deutsch 1978, p. 127.
76. Robert Wistrich, *Who's Who in Nazi Germany* (New York: Harper and Row, 1965), p. 20 (hereafter cited as "Wistrich").
77. Irving 1973, p. 302. Later his remains were cremated and he was buried near his home at Bad Wiessee (Huebsch, pp. 315–16).

2: Walter von Brauchitsch

1. Brett-Smith, p. 41; Deutsch 1974, pp. 220–21.
2. O'Neill, p. 187.

3. Ibid.
4. Ibid.
5. Irving 1978, p. 79.
6. Deutsch 1974, p. 121.
7. Ibid, p. 221.
8. Ibid, p. 222.
9. Ibid, pp. 221–22.
10. Shirer, pp. 314–16.
11. Taylor, p. 167; Deutsch 1974, pp. 218–19.
12. Deutsch 1974, p. 168.
13. Ibid., pp. 219–20.
14. Taylor, p. 169.
15. Deutsch 1974, p. 261. Hans Behlendorff was named Commander of Artillery Command 31 (Arko 31) after leaving the Personnel Office. He later commanded the 34th Infantry Division and LXXXIV Corps prior to his retirement in April 1943 as a General of Artillery. Kuntzen led the 3rd Light (later 8th Panzer) Division, LVII Panzer Corps, and LXXXI Corps before his retirement as a General of Panzer Troops in mid-1944. Both survived the war (Keilig, pp. 26, 193).
16. Taylor, pp. 170–71, 238; Wheeler-Bennett, p. 373; Irving 1978, p. 161. Most of the forced retirees were recalled to active duty when the war broke out. Oswald Lutz held a minor staff appointment in 1941 but was retired again in 1942. He died in Munich in 1944. Guenther von Pogrell held a number of territorial commands before directing Corps Command XXXII in the invasion of Denmark. He remained there until his second retirement in 1942. He also died in 1944. Guenther von Niebelschuetz was in charge of the rear area command on the 3rd Army in East Prussia during the Polish campaign. He died in Russian captivity in 1949. Hermann Geyer later led IX Corps in Poland, France, and Russia. He retired again in 1942 and committed suicide in 1946. Wilhelm Ulex later commanded X Corps and Wehrkreis I before retiring again in 1941. He survived the war. Hossbach was transferred to the command of the 82nd Infantry Regiment. During the war he was Chief of Staff of XXX Corps (1939), commanded the 82nd Infantry Regiment again (1939–January 1942), was acting commander of the 31st Infantry Division (1942), and was commander of the 82nd Infantry Division (1942–43). Later he was deputy commander of LVI Panzer Corps (1943), commander of LVI (1943–44), and was named commander of the 4th Army on July 19, 1944. He was relieved of his command for direct disobedience of a Fuehrer order on January 28, 1945. He was living in

372 *Notes*

Goettingen in 1958. Wilhelm Knochenhauer was never re-employed. He died in Hamburg on June 28, 1939. See Keilig, pp. 106, 151, 175, 213, 242, 260, and 351.

17. Taylor, p. 173.
18. Deutsch 1974, p. 229.
19. Irving 1978, p. 79.
20. Taylor, p. 175.
21. Peter Hoffmann, *The History of the German Resistance* (Cambridge, Mass.: MIT Press, 1977), p. 50 (hereafter cited as "Hoffmann"); Irving 1978, p. 94.
22. Wheeler-Bennett, p. 398; Irving 1978, p. 100.
23. Taylor, p. 192.
24. Wheeler-Bennett, p. 399.
25. Cooper, p. 97; Wheeler-Bennett, p. 400.
26. Taylor, pp. 401–02.
27. Taylor, p. 242; Cooper, p. 97.
28. Cooper, p. 97; Taylor, pp. 199–201.
29. Taylor, pp. 200–01.
30. Wheeler-Bennett, pp. 402–04; Taylor, pp. 200–01.
31. Taylor, pp. 208–12.
32. Wheeler-Bennett, pp. 402–04.
33. Taylor, pp. 210–12.
34. Irving 1978, p. 134.
35. Cooper, p. 102; Hoffmann, pp. 101–03; Wheeler-Bennett, p. 421.
36. Ulrich von Hassell, *The von Hassell Diaries* (New York: Doubleday, 1947), p. 80 (hereafter cited as "Hassell").
37. Deutsch 1974, p. 229.
38. Wheeler-Bennett, p. 449.
39. Kennedy, pp. 51–54.
40. Taylor, p. 319.
41. Kennedy, p. 113; Taylor, p. 324.
42. Kennedy, p. 120.
43. Irving 1977, p. 26.
44. Ibid, p. 30.
45. Ibid, pp. 47–48.
46. Ibid.
47. Erich von Manstein, *Lost Victories* (Novato, California: Presidio Press, 1982), p. 87 (hereafter cited as "Manstein"); Guderian, p. 66.
48. Brett-Smith, p. 46.
49. United States Department of the Army, "The German Campaign in Russia—Planning and Operations (1940–1942)," US Department of

the Army *Pamphlet 20–261a* (Washington, DC: Department of the Army, 1955), pp. 3–4 (hereafter cited as "DA Pam 20–261a"). Marcks commanded the 101st Jaeger Division in Russia in 1941 and lost a leg. Later he commanded the 337th Infantry Division in Russia (1942) and LXVI and LXXXVII corps. As commander of LXXXIV Corps, he was killed near St. Lô in Normandy in June 1944.

50. Ibid, pp. 10–12.
51. Albert Seaton, *The Russo-German War, 1941–1945* (New York: Praeger, 1970), p. 54 (hereafter cited as "Seaton").
52. Manstein, p. 76.
53. Irving 1977, p. 521.
54. Ibid, p. 288.
55. Wheeler-Bennett, p. 524, citing Halder *Diary*, November 10, 1941.
56. Irving 1977, p. 351.
57. Ibid, p. 360.
58. Wheeler-Bennett, p. 525.
59. Joseph Goebbels, *The Goebbels Diaries*, Louis P. Lochner, ed. (Garden City, New York: Doubleday, 1948; reprint ed., New York: Universal-Award House, 1971), p. 157 (hereafter cited as "Goebbels").
60. Irving 1977, p. 729; Wheeler-Bennett, p. 696.

3. Ewald von Kleist

1. See David G. Chandler, *Dictionary of the Napoleonic Wars* (New York: Macmillan, 1979), pp. 226, 236–37.
2. Hermann Plocher, "The German Air Force Versus Russia, 1943," United States Air Force Historical Studies Number 155 (Maxwell Air Force Base, Alabama: United States Air Force Historical Division, Air University, 1965) (hereafter cited as "Plocher MS 1943").
3. C. R. Davis, *Von Kleist: From Hussar to Panzer Marshal* (Houston, Texas: Lancer Militaria, 1979), p. 9 (hereafter cited as "Davis").
4. Ewald von Kleist Personnel Record, Air University Archives, Maxwell Air Force Base, Alabama (hereafter cited as "Kleist Personnel Record").
5. Davis, p. 9.
6. Kleist Personnel Record.
7. Ibid.
8. Taylor, p. 379.
9. Davis, pp. 10 and 106.
10. Snyder, p. 196.
11. O'Neill, p. 206.

12. Davis, p. 10.
13. Ibid.
14. Kennedy, p. 108.
15. Jacques Benoist-Mechin, *Sixty Days that Shook the West: The Fall of France* (New York: G. P. Putnam's Sons, 1963), pp. 69–70 (hereafter cited as "Benoist-Mechin").
16. Ibid, p. 65.
17. Guderian, pp. 75–77.
18. Benoist-Mechin, p. 75.
19. Guderian, p. 77; Cooper, p. 220.
20. A. Goutard, *The Battle of France, 1940* (New York: Ives Washburn, 1959), p. 120.
21. Deighton, p. 208.
22. Goutard, pp. 120–21.
23. Guderian, p. 78; Goutard, p. 122.
24. Goutard, p. 122.
25. Ibid, p. 127, citing Grandsard, *Le 10er Corps d'Armée dans la Bataille*.
26. Deighton, pp. 218–19.
27. Goutard, p. 134; Deighton, pp. 221–24.
28. Deighton, pp. 226–27.
29. Goutard, p. 136.
30. Deighton, p. 228.
31. Goutard, pp. 156–57; Deighton, pp. 228–29.
32. Goutard, pp. 148–49.
33. Deighton, pp. 228–29; Goutard, pp. 138–39.
34. Deighton, pp. 230–31.
35. Guderian, p. 82.
36. Benoist-Mechin, p. 92.
37. Deighton, pp. 231–32.
38. Ibid, pp. 234–35.
39. Guderian, p. 85.
40. Ibid, pp. 86–87.
41. Deighton, pp. 235–36.
42. Cooper, pp. 222–23; Guderian, p. 87.
43. Guderian, p. 87.
44. Ibid, pp. 87–88.
45. Benoist-Mechin, p. 110.
46. L. E. Ellis, *The War in France and Flanders* (London, Her Majesty's Stationery Office, 1953), pp. 76–78 (hereafter cited as "Ellis 1940").
47. Goutard, pp. 193–94.
48. Irving 1977, p. 117; Goutard, pp. 201–03.
49. Benoist-Mechin, pp. 116–17.

50. Ellis 1940, p. 79; Goutard, pp. 197–98.

51. Cooper, p. 227.

52. Robert Goralski, *World War II Almanac, 1931–1945* (New York: G. P. Putnam's Sons, 1981), p. 116 (hereafter cited as "Goralski").

53. Armored losses in XLI Motorized Corps were reported as 30 percent (Cooper, pp. 230–31).

54. Brett-Smith, p. 165.

55. *Kriegstagebuch des Oberkommando des Wehrmacht (Wehrmachtfuehrungsstab)* (Frankfurt-am-Main: Bernard und Graefe Verlag fuer Wehrwesen, 1961), Volume I, p. 1122 (hereafter cited as *"Kriegstagebuch des OKW"*).

56. Ellis 1940, p. 274; Benoist-Mechin, p. 241.

57. United States Military Intelligence Service, "Order of Battle of the German Army" (Washington, DC: United States War Department General Staff, October, 1942), p. 160 (hereafter cited as "OB 1942"). Reference to other US General Staff order-of-battle data are cited by appropriate year.

58. United States Department of the Army, "The German Campaigns in the Balkans (Spring, 1941)", Department of the Army *Pamphlet 20–260* (Washington, DC: United States Army Military History Division, 1953), p. 21 (hereafter cited as "DA *Pam 20–260*").

59. Ibid, p. 32.

60. Ibid, p. 41.

61. Ibid, pp. 50–52.

62. Snyder, p. 196.

63. DA *Pam 20–260*, pp. 50–52.

64. *Kriegstagebuch des OKW*, Volume I, p. 1135.

65. Hermann Plocher, "The German Air Force Versus Russia, 1941," United States Air Force Historical Studies Number 153 (Maxwell Air Force Base, Alabama: United States Historical Division, Air University, 1965) (hereafter cited as "Plocher MS 1941").

66. B. H. Liddell Hart, *The German Generals Talk* (New York: Quill, 1979), p. 175.

67. Seaton, pp. 134–37.

68. Cooper, pp. 307–08.

69. Plocher MS 1941; Seaton, pp. 139–40; also see James Lucas, *Alpine Elite: German Mountain Troops of World War II* (London: Jane's, 1980), pp. 86–126, for a detailed description of the Battle of Uman (hereafter cited as "Lucas 1980").

70. Alan Clark, *Barbarossa: The Russian–German Conflict, 1941–45* (New York: William Morrow, 1965), p. 135 (hereafter cited as "Clark"); Plocher MS 1941.

71. Paul Carell, *Hitler Moves East, 1941–1943* (Boston: Little, Brown, 1965; reprint ed., New York: Bantam Books, 1966), pp. 123–29 (hereafter cited as "Carell").

72. Carell, pp. 303, 322–23; Plocher MS 1941.

73. Plocher MS 1941.

74. Carell, pp. 300, 324–27; Plocher MS 1941; Irving 1977, p. 342.

75. Carell, pp. 487–98.

76. Brett-Smith, p. 167.

77. Carell, pp. 134–56.

78. Paul Carell, *Scorched Earth: The Russian–German War, 1943–1944* (Boston: Little, Brown, 1966; reprint ed., New York: Ballantine Books, 1971), p. 168 (hereafter cited as "Carell 1971").

79. Davis, p. 16, citing Juergen Thorwald, *The Illusion* (New York: Harcourt Brace Jovanovich, 1975), p. 65.

80. Wheeler-Bennett, pp. 612–13.

81. Clark, pp. 318–19.

82. Davis, p. 16.

83. Goebbels, pp. 389, 532.

84. Carell 1971, pp. 154–65.

85. Earl F. Ziemke, *Stalingrad to Berlin: The German Defeat in the East*, United States Department of the Army, Office of the Chief of Military History (Washington, DC: United States Government Printing Office, 1966), p. 285 (hereafter cited as "Ziemke"); Brett-Smith, p. 168.

86. Ibid, pp. 285–89.

87. Manstein, pp. 545–46; Ziemke, p. 286.

88. Irving 1977, p. 618.

89. Davis, p. 17.

90. Plocher MS 1943; Snyder, p. 196.

91. Davis, p. 17.

92. Ibid.

93. Ibid, p. 18.

4: Walter von Reichenau

1. Brett-Smith, p. 185.

2. Brett-Smith, p. 186.

3. Plocher MS 1941.

4. Walter Goerlitz, *Paulus and Stalingrad* (Westport, Connecticut: Greenwood Press, 1974), pp. 21–22 (hereafter cited as "Goerlitz 1974"); O'Neill, p. 194; Brett-Smith, p. 185; Otto E. Moll, *Die deutschen Generalfeldmarschaelle, 1939–1945* (Rastatt/Baden: Erich Pabel Verlag, 1961), pp. 169–70 (hereafter cited as "Moll").

5. O'Neill, p. 195.
6. Brett-Smith, p. 185; O'Neill, pp. 18, 194–95.
7. Goerlitz 1974, p. 21.
8. Wistrich, p. 241.
9. Walter Goerlitz, *The German General Staff* (New York: Frederick A. Praeger, 1953: reprint ed., Westport, Connecticut: Greenwood Press, 1957) (hereafter cited as "Goerlitz 1953").
10. Cooper, p. 17.
11. O'Neill, pp. 32–34.
12. Ibid, pp. 35–36.
13. Ibid, p. 37.
14. Ibid.
15. Ibid, p. 38.
16. See Shirer, pp. 213–16, for the details of the June 30 executions.
17. Cooper, p. 48; Shirer, p. 222.
18. O'Neill, p. 194.
19. Taylor, p. 104.
20. Ibid.
21. O'Neill, p. 194; Taylor, p. 149.
22. Keitel, pp. 48, 65; Taylor, p. 169.
23. Cooper, p. 22.
24. Goerlitz 1953.
25. Kennedy, ff. 74.
26. Kennedy, pp. 78–86.
27. Ibid, pp. 86–87.
28. Ibid, pp. 103–04.
29. Kennedy, p. 104; William L. Shirer, *Berlin Diary* (New York: Alfred A. Knopf, 1941), pp. 371–73 (hereafter cited as "Shirer *Diary*").
30. Kennedy, pp. 104–06 and Map 10.
31. Ibid, pp. 111–12, 118.
32. O'Neill, p. 195.
33. Ellis 1940, p. 345; Brett-Smith, p. 187.
34. Hoffmann, p. 133; Irving 1977, pp. 37, 43–44.
35. Goutard, pp. 108–09; Deighton, p. 200; Benoist-Mechin, p. 75.
36. Benoist-Mechin, p. 94.
37. Goutard, pp. 111–13.
38. Benoist-Mechin, p. 94.
39. Goutard, p. 114; Benoist-Mechin, pp. 103, 110.
40. Shirer *Diary*, p. 372.
41. Ellis 1940, situation map dated 27 May 1940; Benoist-Mechin, pp. 142–43.
42. Ellis 1940, pp. 146–50; Goutard, p. 222.

43. Ellis 1940, pp. 175–77, 182.
44. Goutard, pp. 235–37; Benoist-Mechin, p. 170; Goerlitz 1953, p. 24.
45. *Kriegstagebuch des OKW*, Volume I, p. 1122.
46. Brett-Smith, p. 187.
47. *Kriegstagebuch des OKW*, Volume I, p. 1140.
48. O'Neill, p. 18.
49. Irving 1977, p. 327.
50. Wistrich, pp. 241–42.
51. O'Neill, p. 18.
52. Albert Kesselring, *Kesselring: A Soldier's Record* (Westport, Connecticut: Greenwood Press, 1970), p. 11 (hereafter cited as "Kesselring").
53. Irving 1977, p. 385.
54. Seaton, p. 197.
55. Goerlitz 1974, p. 44.
56. *Kriegstagebuch des OKW*, Volume I, p. 1138; Seaton, p. 192.
57. Carell, pp. 314–21.
58. Mitcham 1985, pp. 74–75.
59. Goerlitz 1974, pp. 46–47.
60. Cooper, p. 23.

5: Wilhelm von Leeb

1. Wilhelm von Leeb, *Defense* (Harrisonburg, PA: Military Service Publishing Company, 1943), p. ix (this version translated from the German by Dr. Stefan T. Possony and Daniel Vilfroy) (hereafter cited as "Leeb").
2. Snyder, p. 207; Wistrich, p. 186.
3. Leeb, p. x.
4. OB 1943, p. 299; OB 1942, p. 153.
5. Christopher Chant, Richard Humble, William Fowler, and Jenny Shaw, *Hitler's Generals and Their Battles* (New York: Chartwell Books, 1976), p. 98 (hereafter cited as "Chant et al.").
6. Leeb, p. x; Moll, pp. 103–04.
7. Leeb, p. x; OB 1942, p. 153; Snyder, p. 207; Wistrich, p. 186.
8. Leeb, p. x; Moll, p. 104.
9. Chant et al., p. 98.
10. Leeb, p. x; Taylor, pp. 377–78; Moll, pp. 104–05.
11. Deutsch 1978, pp. 209–10.
12. Leeb, p. vii.
13. Ibid, p. 2.
14. Ibid.
15. Ibid, pp. ix, 139–51.

16. Ibid, p. ix.

17. Deutsch 1978, pp. 209–10.

18. John Toland, *Adolf Hitler* (New York: Random House, 1976, reprint ed., New York: Ballantine Books, 1977), p. 403 (hereafter cited as "Toland").

19. Brett-Smith, p. 53.

20. Deutsch 1978, p. 255.

21. O'Neill, p. 211. Most of the frontier commands were reorganized as infantry divisions between 1939–43.

22. Taylor, pp. 170–71, 238.

23. Ibid, pp. 200–27. HQ, 12th Army was initially designated "Special Staff Leeb."

24. Ibid, pp. 274–76. Friedrich Dollmann commanded 7th Army in occupied France from 1940 to June 29, 1944, when he died of a heart attack during the Battle of Normandy. Curt Liebmann, who came out of retirement to command 5th Army, was retired again on October 30, 1939, and was not subsequently re-employed. He was still alive in 1958. Witzleben and Sperrle later became field marshals (see chapters 18 and 20). After being sacked by Goering in January 1940, Hellmuth Felmy commanded an army corps in the Balkans. Georg Sodenstern was promoted to lieutenant general in February 1940 and to general of infantry six months later. He was Chief of Staff of Army Group South in Russia (1941–43) and to the commanding general of the 19th Army in southern France (1944). Relieved of command in June, he was never re-employed. Sodenstern died in Frankfurt-am-Main in 1955 (Keilig, pp. 204, 326).

25. Taylor, pp. 274–75, 296; Goutard, pp. 61–62.

26. Goutard, p. 68; Taylor, p. 334.

27. Taylor, p. 334.

28. Goutard, pp. 70–71.

29. Telford Taylor, *The March of Conquest* (New York: Simon and Schuster, 1958), p. 51 (hereafter cited as "Taylor 1958").

30. Brett-Smith, p. 54; Deutsch, p. 81.

31. Taylor 1958, p. 49.

32. Deutsch 1978, pp. 211, 254–55.

33. Irving 1977, p. 116; Ellis 1940, p. 45.

34. Benoist-Mechin, p. 414.

35. Brett-Smith, p. 54.

36. T. N. Dupuy and Paul Martell, *Great Battles on the Eastern Front* (Indianapolis/New York: Bobbs-Merrill, 1982), p. 9 (hereafter cited as "Dupuy").

37. Carell, p. 6; Seaton, p. 101; Dupuy, p. 21.

38. Carell, pp. 21–22; Seaton, pp. 101–03.
39. Seaton, pp. 102–04; Carell, pp. 22–24.
40. Carell, pp. 26–29.
41. Seaton, pp. 106–07.
42. Carell, pp. 234–36; Seaton, pp. 106–07.
43. Seaton, p. 107; Carell, p. 237.
44. Carell, pp. 238–41; Seaton, pp. 108–12.
45. Seaton, pp. 108–09, 114.
46. Friedrich von Stauffenberg, "Erich Brandenberger," unpublished manuscript loaned to the author, 1985. Brandenberger was commander of the 8th Panzer Division in 1941.
47. Carell, pp. 248–49.
48. Ibid.
49. Brett-Smith, p. 57; Seaton, p. 150.
50. Carell, p. 263; also see W. de Beaulieu, *Der Vorstoss der Panzer Gruppe 4 auf Leningrad* (Neckargemuend: Kurt Vominckel, 1961).
51. Seaton, p. 100; Brett-Smith, p. 57.
52. Carell, pp. 264–65.
53. Irving 1977, p. 313.
54. Carell, p. 233.
55. Seaton, p. 151.
56. Carell, pp. 266–76; Irving 1977, p. 312.
57. Seaton, p. 151; Carell, p. 278.
58. Brett-Smith, p. 55.
59. Carell, p. 284.
60. *Kriegstagebuch des OKW*, Volume III, p. 7.
61. Carell, p. 273.
62. Carell, pp. 284–85; Seaton, p. 198.
63. Seaton, pp. 199, 285.
64. Carell, pp. 284–86; Seaton, p. 242.
65. Brett-Smith, p. 55.
66. Irving 1977, p. 290.
67. Irving, p. 357.
68. Hermann Plocher, "The German Air Force Versus Russia, 1942," United States Air Force Historical Studies Number 154 (Maxwell Air Force Base, Alabama: United States Air Force Historical Division, Air University, 1965) (hereafter cited as "Plocher MS 1942").
69. Plocher MS 1942; Seaton, pp. 242–45; also see Carell and Charles W. Sydnor, *Soldiers of Destruction: The SS Death's Head Division, 1933–45* (Princeton, NJ: Princeton University Press, 1977), for the details of the Battle of Demyansk.

49. Ibid.
50. Seaton, pp. 274–76; Brett-Smith, p. 82.
51. Irving 1977, p. 401.
52. Snyder, p. 34.
53. Brett-Smith, p. 82.
54. Irving 1977, pp. 576–77.
55. Fabian von Schlabrendorff, *Revolt Against Hitler*, Gero v. S. Gaevernitz, ed. (London: Eyre and Spottiswoode, 1948; reprint ed., New York: AMS Press, 1948), p. 58.
56. Brett-Smith (pp. 84–85) dates Bock's death as May 2. Lieutenant General Plocher (1942) states that he was killed on May 5, along with his family. The exact date probably is not known with certainty, but most sources state that it occurred on May 4.
57. Moll, p. 57.

7: Wilhelm Keitel

1. Eugene Davidson, *The Trial of the Germans* (New York: Macmillan, 1966), pp. 329–30 (hereafter cited as "Davidson").
2. Keitel, pp. 12–13.
3. O'Neill, p. 192; Keitel, p. 13.
4. Davidson, p. 331; Keitel, p. 14; O'Neill, p. 193.
5. O'Neill, pp. 192–93.
6. Wistrich, p. 168; Keltel, p. 16.
7. O'Neill, pp. 192–93; Keitel, p. 14.
8. Keitel, pp. 16–17; Davidson, pp. 330–31.
9. Keitel, pp. 17–18.
10. Ibid, p. 19.
11. O'Neill, pp. 192–93.
12. Keitel, p. 23.
13. Ibid.
14. O'Neill, p. 193.
15. Davidson, p. 331; also see Keitel, pp. 24–26.
16. Taylor, p. 149.
17. O'Neill, p. 142.
18. Keitel, p. 48.
19. O'Neill, p. 193. Bodewin Keitel was promoted to major general on March 1, 1938. He was advanced to lieutenant general on March 1, 1941, and to general of infantry on October 1, 1941.
20. Suchenwirth MS.
21. Keitel, p. 29.
22. Davidson, p. 334; Wheeler-Bennett, p. 462.

23. Wistrich, p. 169
24. Irving 1977, pp. 43–44; Keitel, pp. 100–01.
25. Keitel, p. 119.
26. Irving 1977, p. 155.
27. Davidson, p. 335.
28. Wistrich, p. 169.
29. Ibid.
30. Keitel, pp. 180–81; Irving 1977, pp. 423–24; Shirer, p. 918.
31. General Bodewin Keitel was named Commander of Wehrkreis XX (formerly part of western Poland) on March 1, 1943, and held this position until the district was overrun by the Russians at the end of 1944. He was given a minor staff post after that. He died in 1952 (Keilig, p. 166).
32. Irving 1977, p. 432.
33. Irving 1977, p. 524, citing Hassell *Diaries*.
34. Davidson, p. 338.
35. Ibid, pp. 338–39.
36. Ibid, p. 338.
37. Ibid, p. 334.
38. Roger Manvill and Heinrich Fraenkel, *The Men Who Tried to Kill Hitler* (New York: Coward-McCann, 1964; reprint ed., New York: Pocket Books, Inc., 1966), pp. 83–86.
39. Irving 1977, p. 666.
40. Davidson, p. 333.
41. Ziemke, pp. 485–86.
42. Snyder, pp. 192–93.
43. G. M. Gilbert, *Nuremberg Diary* (New York: Farrar, Straus and Cudahy, 1947; reprint ed., New York: Signet Books, 1961), p. 401.
44. Keitel, pp. 52–53.
45. Wheeler-Bennett, pp. 429–30.

8: Erwin Rommel

1. Desmond Young, *Rommel: The Desert Fox* (New York: Harper and Row, 1965), pp. 28–30 (hereafter cited as "Young"); Charles Douglas-Home, *Rommel* (New York: Saturday Review Press, 1973; reprint ed., London: Excalibur, n.d.), p. 20.
2. Young, p. 32.
3. Ibid, p. 41.
4. David Irving, *The Trail of the Fox* (New York: Thomas Congdon Books, E. P. Dutton, 1977), pp. 14–15 (hereafter cited as "Irving 1977a").

5. Young, p. 37.

6. Ibid, p. 50.

7. Ibid, pp. 56–57.

8. See Erwin Rommel, *Attacks* (Vienna, Virginia: Athena Press, 1979) for the most recent edition of this book.

9. Young, p. 61.

10. Heinz Werner Schmidt, *With Rommel in the Desert* (London: G. Harrap, 1951, reprint ed., New York: Ballantine Books, 1968), p. 89.

11. Irving 1977a, p. 41.

12. Erwin Rommel, *The Rommel Papers*, B. H. Liddell Hart, ed. (New York: Harcourt, Brace, 1953), pp. 82–84 (hereafter cited as "Rommel"); Young, pp. 76–77.

13. Rommel, pp. 94–95.

14. See Samuel W. Mitcham, Jr., *Triumphant Fox: Erwin Rommel and the Rise of the Afrika Korps* (Briarcliff Manor, NY: Stein and Day, 1983), pp. 95–114 for the details of this battle.

15. Paul Carell, *The Foxes of the Desert* (New York: E. P. Dutton, 1960); reprint ed., New York: Bantam Books, 1972), p. 114 (hereafter cited as "Carell 1972"); John Strawson, *The Battle for North Africa* (New York: Bonanza Books, 1969), p. 72; Rommel, p. 155; and Walter Warlimont, "The Decision in the Mediterranean 1942," in H. A. Jacobsen and J. Rowder, eds., *Decisive Battles of World War II: The German View* (New York: G. P. Putnam's Sons, 1965), p. 186 (hereafter cited as "Warlimont 1965").

16. Frederich Wilhelm von Mellenthin, *Panzer Battles* (Norman, Oklahoma: University of Oklahoma Press, 1956; reprint ed., New York: Ballantine Books, 1976), p. 63 (hereafter cited as "Mellenthin"); Rommel, p. 158; I. S. O. Playfair, *The Mediterranean and the Middle East*, Volume III, *British Fortunes Reach Their Lowest Ebb* (London: Her Majesty's Stationery Office, 1960), pp. 27–31.

17. Young, p. 90.

18. Rommel, p. 180.

19. Samuel W. Mitcham, Jr., *Rommel's Desert War* (Briarcliff Manor, NY: Stein and Day, 1982), pp. 22–31 (hereafter cited as "Mitcham 1982").

20. Mellenthin, p. 93.

21. Rommel, p. 197; Mellenthin, p. 190; Warlimont 1965, p. 190.

22. Mitcham 1982, pp. 37–64.

23. Young, p. 100.

24. Michael Carver, *El Alamein* (New York: Macmillan, 1962), p. 25 (hereafter cited as "Carver"); Rommel, p. 236.

25. Carell 1972, p. 249.

26. W. G. F. Jackson, *The Battle for North Africa* (New York: Mason/ Charter, 1975), p. 274; Rommel, p. 283.
27. Rommel, pp. 271, 296.
28. Andrew Kershaw and Ian Close, eds., *The Desert War* (New York: Marshall Cavendish Promotions, 1975), p. 42; I. S. O. Playfair and C. J. C. Molony, *The Mediterranean and the Middle East*, Volume IV, *The Destruction of the Axis in Africa* (London: Her Majesty's Stationery Office, 1966), pp. 2–30 (hereafter cited as "Playfair and Molony").
29. Carver, p. 177; Playfair and Molony, pp. 475–76.
30. Goralski, p. 260.
31. Brett-Smith, p. 267.
32. Rommel, pp. 446–47.
33. Gordon A. Harrison, *Cross-Channel Attack*, Office of the Chief of Military History, US Army in World War II, European Theater of Operations (Washington, DC: United States Government Printing Office, 1951), p. 138.
34. Friedrich Ruge, "The Invasion of Normandy," in H. A. Jacobsen and J. Rohwer, eds., *The Decisive Battles of World War II: The German View* (New York: G. P. Putnam's Sons, 1965), p. 330.
35. Rommel, pp. 458–59; Irving 1977a, p. 323.
36. Cornelius Ryan, *The Longest Day* (New York: Simon and Schuster, 1959, reprint ed., New York: Popular Library), p. 29.
37. Ibid, p. 279.
38. Hans Speidel, *Invasion: 1944* (New York: Henry Regnery, 1950; reprint ed., New York: Paperback Library, 1968), pp. 85–86 (hereafter cited as "Speidel"); Irving 1977a, p. 381. Dawans had previously served as Chief of Staff of XIII Corps, III Panzer Corps, and 4th Army in Russia (1941–43).
39. Martin Blumenson, *Breakout and Pursuit*, Office of the Chief of Military History, US Army in World War II, The European Theater of Operations (Washington, DC, United States Government Printing Office, 1961), p. 133 (hereafter cited as "Blumenson").
40. Speidel, p. 111. For the text of the ultimatum, see Samuel W. Mitcham, Jr., *Rommel's Last Battle: The Desert Fox and the Normandy Campaign* (Briarcliff Manor, NY: Stein and Day, 1984), pp. 163–64.

9: Siegmund Wilhelm List

1. Wistrich, p. 195; Moll, p. 114; Keilig, p. 207.
2. Moll, p. 114.
3. Taylor, pp. 377–78; Wistrich, p. 195.

4. Davidson, p. 343.

5. Carell, p. 544.

6. Guderian, p. 101.

7. O'Neill, p. 216; Taylor, p. 380.

8. Snyder, p. 212; Taylor, p. 171.

9. O'Neill, p. 216.

10. Taylor, pp. 226–27, 239–41.

11. Kennedy, ff. 74, pp. 127–28.

12. Ellis 1940, p. 345.

13. Brett-Smith, p. 59.

14. Guderian, pp. 86–88.

15. *Kriegstagebuch des OKW*, Volume I, p. 1122.

16. Guderian, p. 100.

17. DA *Pam 20–260*, pp. 70–80.

18. Ibid, pp. 81–82.

19. Ibid, pp. 86–89.

20. Ibid, pp. 91–94.

21. Ibid, pp. 94–96.

22. Irving 1977, pp. 226–27.

23. Ibid, p. 227.

24. Goralski, pp. 155–56; DA *Pam 20–260*, pp. 102–12.

25. B. H. Liddell Hart, *History of the Second World War* (New York: G. P. Putnam's Sons, 1972), Volume I, p. 137 (hereafter cited as "Hart 1972").

26. DA *Pam 20–260*, p. 112.

27. Brett-Smith, p. 61. Walter Kuntze, former commander of the 6th Infantry Division (1935–38) and XXIV Corps (1939–41), was commander of the 12th Army and OB Southeast from October 29, 1941, to August 8, 1942. Later he held a staff post in Berlin (1942–45). He was living in Detmold in 1958 (Keilig, p. 193).

28. Earl F. Ziemke, "The German Northern Theater of Operations, 1940–1945," United States Department of the Army *Pamphlet 20–271*, Office of the Chief of Military History (Washington, DC: United States Department of the Army, 1959), pp. 215–16 (hereafter cited as "Ziemke 1959").

29. DA *Pam 20–261a*, p. 180; Seaton, p. 275.

30. Goralski, p. 226.

31. Brett-Smith, p. 63.

32. Seaton, pp. 280–82.

33. Plocher MS 1942; Seaton, p. 282.

34. Plocher MS 1942, quoting Kurt von Tippelskirch, *Geschichte des Zweiten Weltkriegs*, p. 285.

35. Walter Warlimont, *Inside Hitler's Headquarters* (New York: Frederick A. Praeger, 1964), pp. 256–57; Seaton, pp. 265–86; *Kriegstagebuch des OKW*, Volume II, pp. 662–83; Davidson, pp. 342–43; DA *Pam 20–261a*, pp. 164–65.
36. Keitel, pp. 181–82; Davidson, pp. 343–44; DA *Pam 20–261a*, p 180; Plocher MS 1942. Hans von Greiffenberg was List's Chief of Staff at 12th Army from January 1, 1941, to May 1941. On October 10, 1943, he was named Military Attaché to Budapest. He was promoted to general of infantry on April 1, 1944, and was commander of German forces in Hungary from April 1944 until the end of the war. He died at Koenigstein in 1951 (Keilig, p. 114).
37. Brett-Smith, p. 65; Snyder, p. 212; Wistrich, p. 195.

10: Baron Maximilian von Weichs

1. O'Neill, pp. 196–97; Brett-Smith, p. 170.
2. O'Neill, p. 197.
3. Ibid.
4. Guderian, p. 25; O'Neill, p. 197; Brett-Smith, p. 170.
5. Kennedy, ff. 74, pp. 100–03, 112.
6. Taylor, p. 324.
7. Plocher MS 1942; Taylor 1958, p. 156.
8. Ellis 1940, p. 345.
9. *Kreigstagebuch des OKW*, Volume I, p. 1122.
10. O'Neill, p. 47.
11. DA *Pam 20–260*, pp. 39–41.
12. Ibid, pp. 37–39, 41. Second Army's training mission was taken over by 11th Army.
13. Ibid, pp. 54–60.
14. Ibid, pp. 63–64.
15. *Kriegstagebuch des OKW*, Volume I, pp. 1135–36.
16. As of June 27, 1941, these included XII, XLIII, IX, VII, XIII, and LIII corps (seventeen infantry divisions and one security division) with three infantry divisions and one security division in Army reserve (ibid).
17. Seaton, p. 125.
18. Lucas 1979, p. 176; Seaton, p. 130.
19. *Kriegstagebuch des OKW*, Volume I, p. 1140.
20. Carell, pp. 140–41.
21. Brett-Smith, p. 171.
22. Irving 1977, p. 401.
23. Walter Goerlitz, "The Battle of Stalingrad 1942–43," in H. A.

Jacobsen and J. Rohwer, eds., *Decisive Battles of World War II: The German View* (New York: G. P. Putnam's Sons, 1965), pp. 222–23 (hereafter cited as "Goerlitz 1965").

24. Ziemke, pp. 38–39.
25. Goerlitz 1965, pp. 228–29.
26. Ziemke, pp. 34–35.
27. Clark, p. 241.
28. Ziemke, pp. 48–49.
29. Ibid, p. 49.
30. Ibid, p. 50.
31. Clark, p. 242.
32. Ziemke, p. 60.
33. Ibid.
34. Clark, p. 247.
35. Ziemke, pp. 52–53.
36. Ibid, p. 53.
37. Ibid, pp. 53–54.
38. Ibid, pp. 54–55.
39. Ibid, p. 68.
40. Irving 1977, p. 476; Ziemke, p. 81.
41. Ziemke, pp. 68–85.
42. Seaton, p. 344.
43. Ziemke, p. 86.
44. O'Neill, p. 197; Seaton, p. 347; Ziemke, p. 90.
45. United States Department of the Army *Pamphlet 20–243*, "German Antiguerrilla Operations in the Balkans (1941–44)," Office of the Chief of Military History (Washington, DC: United States Department of the Army, 1954), p. 42 (hereafter cited as "DA *Pam 20–243*").
46. Ibid, p. 51. Strength figures are as of December 26, 1943.
47. Ibid, p. 46.
48. Christopher Chant, ed., *The Marshall Cavendish Illustrated Encyclopedia of World War II* (New York: Marshall Cavendish, 1972), Volume 5, p. 1170 (hereafter cited as "Chant"); DA *Pam 20–243*, pp. 44–47.
49. DA *Pam 20–243*, pp. 47–49.
50. Ibid, pp. 50–59, 65–66.
51. Chant, Volume 7, pp. 1891–92.
52. DA *Pam 20–243*, p. 68; Chant, Volume 7, p. 1893.
53. Chant, Volume 7, p. 1893.
54. Seaton, p. 497.
55. Guderian, pp. 331–32.
56. Snyder, p. 376; Moll, p. 252.
57. Guderian, p. 331.

11: Friedrich Paulus

1. Friedrich Paulus Personnel Record, Air University Archives, Maxwell Air Force Base, Alabama (hereafter cited as "Paulus Personnel Record").
2. Goerlitz 1974, p. 8.
3. Paulus Personnel Record.
4. Wistrich, p. 232; Goerlitz 1974, pp. 8–10.
5. Goerlitz 1974, pp. 10–12.
6. Ibid, pp. 14–17.
7. Goerlitz 1974, pp. 14–21; Kennedy, pp. 29–30. Erich Hoepner was the commander of XVI Motorized Corps in 1939.
8. Ibid, pp. 21–25.
9. DA *Pam 20–261a*, p. 182; Goerlitz 1974, p. 29; also see Mitcham 1982.
10. DA *Pam 20–261a*, pp. 14–19.
11. Shaw *et al.*, p. 136.
12. DA *Pam 20–261a*, p. 182; Goerlitz 1974, p. 29.
13. Shaw *et al.*, p. 136.
14. Plocher MS 1942; *Kriegstagebuch des OKW*, Volume II, p. 1367.
15. Plocher MS 1942.
16. Vasili I. Chuikov, *The Battle for Stalingrad* (New York: Holt, Rinehart and Winston, 1964), pp. 261–63 (hereafter cited as "Chuikov").
17. Shaw *et al.*, p. 124.
18. Ziemke, pp. 39–40; Shaw *et al.*, p. 121; Seaton, p. 291.
19. Ziemke, pp. 40–41.
20. Seaton, pp. 293–94; Ziemke, p. 41.
21. Ziemke, p. 41; Shaw *et al.*, p. 137.
22. Seaton, pp. 295–96.
23. Ziemke, pp. 41–43; Seaton, p. 296.
24. Seaton, p. 296.
25. Shaw *et al.*, p. 138.
26. Goerlitz 1974, p. 65.
27. F. W. von Mellenthin, *German Generals of World War II* (Norman, Oklahoma, University of Oklahoma Press, 1977), p. 112 (hereafter cited as "Mellenthin 1977"); Keilig, p. 370. Wietersheim, who had commanded XIV Corps since 1938, ended the war as a private in the Volksturm.
28. Ziemke, pp. 43–46.
29. Seaton, p. 297. As of November 15, 1942, VIII Corps consisted of the 113th and 76th Infantry divisions; XI Corps controlled the 384th, 44th, and 376th Infantry divisions. Sixth Army had no divisions in reserve (*Kriegstagebuch des OKW*, Volume II, p. 1386).

30. Irving 1977, pp. 436–37.
31. These were the 50th, 162nd, 294th, 366th, and 672nd Engineer battalions (Chuikov, p. 246).
32. Ziemke, p. 46.
33. Ibid.
34. Shaw *et al.*, pp. 153–55; Ziemke, p. 46; Plocher MS 1942.
35. Ziemke, pp. 54–57; Plocher MS 1942; Seaton, p. 318.
36. Plocher MS 1942.
37. Ibid.
38. James D. Carnes, "A Study in Courage: General Walther von Seydlitz' Opposition to Hitler," (Ph.D. Dissertation, Tallahassee, Florida: Florida State University, 1976), pp. 2–3 (hereafter cited as "Carnes").
39. Plocher MS 1942, citing Schroeter, *Stalingrad*, pp. 92–94.
40. Ziemke, p. 62.
41. Plocher MS 1942.
42. Chuikov, p. 254.
43. Manstein, pp. 332–34.
44. Ziemke, pp. 69–72.
45. Plocher MS 1942; Irving 1977, p. 477.
46. Irving 1973, p. 191.
47. Irving 1977, p. 478.
48. Plocher MS 1942.
49. Ibid.
50. Irving 1973, p. 195; Irving 1977, p. 478.
51. Ziemke, pp. 78–79; Plocher MS 1942. Schloemer had formerly commanded the 3rd Motorized Infantry Division, which was also destroyed at Stalingrad (Keilig, p. 302).
52. Ziemke, p. 79.
53. Seaton, p. 337; Ziemke, p. 79.
54. Chuikov, the commander of the 62nd Army at Stalingrad, wrote that the battle cost the German High Command 1,500,000 casualties by a "conservative estimate" (Chuikov, p. 263). For more realistic figures, see Seaton, pp. 334–36; Ziemke, p. 69; Dupuy, p. 69; Irving 1977, p. 477; and Fritz Morzik, "German Air Force Airlift Operations," United States Air Force Historical Studies *Number 167* (Maxwell Air Force Base, Alabama: Air University, 1961), p. 193.
55. Ziemke, p. 79.
56. Irving 1977, p. 654.
57. CSDIC (UK) GG Report, interrogation of Lieutenant General Heinrich Kircheim, 2 May 45. On file at the Air University Archives, Maxwell Air Force Base, Alabama.

58. Wistrich, p. 233; Plocher MS 1942; Goerlitz 1974, p. xii.

12: Erich von Manstein

1. Irving 1977, p. 81.
2. B. H. Liddell Hart in "Foreword," Manstein, p. 13.
3. Guderian, p. 241.
4. David Downing, *The Devil's Virtuosos* (New York: St. Martin's Press, 1977; reprinted ed., New York: Playboy Press Paperbacks, 1977), p. 15 (hereafter cited as "Downing").
5. O'Neill, p. 193; Downing, pp. 15–16.
6. Manstein, p. 564; O'Neill, pp. 193–94.
7. O'Neill, pp. 193–94; Manstein, p. 564.
8. Cooper, p. 29; O'Neill, p. 39.
9. Manstein, pp. 564–65; O'Neill, pp. 193–94; Taylor, p. 210.
10. Kennedy, pp. 58–59.
11. Manstein, pp. 127–47, 175.
12. O'Neill, pp. 193–94.
13. Manstein, p. 175.
14. *Kriegstagebuch des OKW*, Volume I, p. 1137.
15. Carell, p. 288.
16. *Kriegstagebuch des OKW*, Volume I, p. 1139. Figures are from Gen St H Op Abt III, Pruef-Nr. 16–284, dated 3 Sep 41.
17. Carell, p. 297.
18. Manstein, pp. 212–16; Seaton, pp. 297–302.
19. Manstein, pp. 216–21.
20. Brett-Smith, p. 224.
21. Manstein, p. 259; Carell, p. 504–11; Plocher MS 1943; O'Neill, p. 194; Shaw *et al.*, pp. 36–39.
22. Manstein, pp. 268–69; Irving 1977, p. 418.
23. Manstein, pp. 270–72.
24. Dupuy, p. 69.
25. Carell 1971, p. 131.
26. Ziemke, pp. 74–75; Carell 1971, pp. 124–34.
27. Irving 1977, p. 483.
28. Carell 1971, pp. 204–05.
29. Irving 1977, p. 497.
30. Chant, Volume 5, p. 1187.
31. Ibid, pp. 1200–01.
32. Carell 1971, pp. 320–21.
33. Wistrich, pp. 204–05.
34. Brett-Smith, p. 235.

35. Ziemke, pp. 162–63; Chant, Volume 5, pp. 1325–27.

36. Chant, Volume 5, pp. 1205–08; Ziemke, pp. 184–89.

37. Irving 1977, p. 595; Chant, Volume 5, pp. 1328–30; also see Manstein, pp. 504–05, for an interesting description of Hitler's eyes.

38. Irving 1977, pp. 597–98.

39. CSDIC (UK) SRGG 1135(C), interrogation report dated March 9, 1945. Later commander of LIII Corps on the Western Front, General von Rothkirch und Trach was captured at Bitburg on March 6, 1945.

40. Ziemke, pp. 231–38; Chant, Volume 5, p. 1335.

41. Chant, Volume 5, pp. 1342–44; Ziemke, pp. 279–82.

42. Irving 1977, p. 616.

43. Brett-Smith, pp. 234–35; Hart 1972, Volume I, p. vi.

44. Wistrich, pp. 204–05.

13: Georg von Kuechler

1. Brett-Smith, p. 94.

2. Keilig, p. 191.

3. "Georg von Kuechler," *Current Biography, 1943* (New York: H. W. Wilson Company, 1944), pp. 412–13 (hereafter cited as "Kuechler"); Brett-Smith, pp. 94–95; Taylor, p. 382; Moll, pp. 96–97.

4. Moll, pp. 96–97.

5. Kuechler, p. 413.

6. Keilig, p. 191; Brett-Smith, p. 94; Kuechler, pp. 412–13.

7. Kuechler, pp. 412–13.

8. Kennedy, ff. 74, Map 7.

9. Ibid, pp. 82–83; Map 8.

10. Ibid, pp. 93–100, 113; Map 10.

11. Winston S. Churchill, *The Second World War*, Volume 2, *Their Finest Hour* (Boston: Houghton Mifflin, 1949), p. 39; Deighton, pp. 191–92. Ellis (1940, p. 345) credits 18th Army with having the 227th, 207th, 254th, and 256th Infantry divisions, with the 208th Infantry Division in reserve.

12. Ellis 1940, p. 40.

13. Kuechler, pp. 413–44.

14. Benoist-Mechin, p. 329; *Kreigstagebuch des OKW*, Volume I, p. 1122.

15. Brett-Smith, pp. 94–95.

16. *Kriegstagebuch des OKW*, Volume I, p. 1129.

17. Ibid, p. 1137.

18. *Kriegstagebuch des OKW*, Volume II, p. 1356; Seaton, pp. 242–43.

19. Plocher MS 1942.

20. Carell, pp. 431–41; Seaton, p. 246.

21. Plocher MS 1942; Carell, pp. 435–37.
22. Carell, pp. 431–44; Plocher MS 1942.
23. OB 1943, p. 294.
24. *Kriegstagebuch des OKW*, Volume II, p. 1388.
25. Ziemke, pp. 111–12; Chant, Volume 5, pp. 1181–82.
26. Ziemke, pp. 157, 197.
27. Seaton, pp. 390–91; *Kriegstagebuch des OKW*, Volume III, p. 1243.
28. Ziemke, pp. 197–98.
29. Ibid, p. 199.
30. Ibid, p. 200.
31. Ibid, pp. 202–05.
32. Seaton, p. 246; Ziemke, p. 207.
33. Ziemke, p. 207.
34. Chant, Volume 5, p. 1356; Ziemke, p. 248.
35. Ziemke, pp. 249–50; Chant, Volume 5, pp. 1356–58.
36. *Kriegstagebuch des OKW*, Volume III, p. 1159; Seaton, p. 409.
37. Ziemke, pp. 250–51.
38. Ibid, pp. 251–53.
39. Ibid, pp. 253–54.
40. Seaton, p. 411; Ziemke, pp. 256–57.
41. Ziemke, pp. 257–58.
42. Ibid.
43. Brett-Smith, p. 98.
44. Kuechler, p. 414.
45. Goerlitz 1953, p. 359.
46. Ziemke, p. 249.
47. Brett-Smith, p. 98.
48. Plocher MS 1942.
49. Moll, p. 99.
50. Bertrum Delli, ed., *Biography Index* (September, 1976–August, 1979) (New York: H. W. Wilson Company, 1980), p. 444.

14: Ernst Busch

1. Carell 1971, p. 596.
2. Snyder, p. 47; Wistrich, p. 35; Moll, pp. 34–35.
3. Wistrich, p. 35; Moll, pp. 34–35; Snyder, p. 47.
4. Wistrich, p. 35.
5. Taylor, pp. 386–87.
6. Brett-Smith, p. 196; Taylor, pp. 386–87; Snyder, p. 47.
7. Kennedy, ff. 74, Maps 7, 9 and 10.
8. Guderian, p. 71.

9. *Kriegstagebuch des OKW*, Volume I, p. 1123.
10. OB 1942, p. 159.
11. *Kriegstagebuch des OKW*, Volume I, p. 1123.
12. Manstein, p. 248.
13. Carell, pp. 249–51.
14. As of January 2, 1942 (see *Kriegstagebuch des OKW*, Volume II, p. 1356).
15. Seaton, pp. 244–45; Carell, pp. 371–418.
16. Ziemke, p. 113.
17. OB 1943, p. 294.
18. *Kriegstagebuch des OKW*, Volume III, p. 1157, report dated 4 Oct 1943.
19. Seaton, p. 432.
20. Ziemke, p. 206.
21. Ibid, p. 193.
22. Seaton, p. 432.
23. Irving 1977, p. 647; Ziemke, pp. 311–12.
24. Ziemke, p. 313.
25. Hermann Gackenholz, "The Collapse of Army Group Center," in H. A. Jacobsen and J. Rohwer, eds., *Decisive Battles of World War II: The German View* (New York: G. P. Putnam's Sons, 1965), p. 360 (hereafter cited as "Gackenholz"); Ziemke, pp. 313–14.
26. Ziemke, pp. 314–15.
27. Ibid, pp. 205, 315–16.
28. Gackenholz, p. 360.
29. Chant, Volume 6, p. 1640.
30. Gackenholz, p. 361.
31. Ibid, p. 365.
32. Chant, Volume 6, p. 1639.
33. Brett-Smith, pp. 196–97.
34. Gackenholz, p. 369.
35. Carell 1971, pp. 575–77, 596–97.
36. Gackenholz, pp. 368–69.
37. Carell 1971, p. 581.
38. Seaton, p. 436; Carell 1971, pp. 583–86, 596.
39. Gackenholz, pp. 370–71.
40. Carell 1971, pp. 580, 597.
41. Brett-Smith, p. 197.
42. Carell 1971, pp. 595–97.
43. Chant, Volume 6, p. 1646.
44. Seaton, p. 442.
45. Chant, Volume 6, p. 1653.
46. Carell 1971, p. 596.

47. Snyder, p. 47.
48. Ziemke, p. 345.
49. Snyder, p. 47.
50. *Kriegstagebuch des OKW*, Volume I, p. 1147, report dated 30 April 1945.
51. Brett-Smith, p. 197; Wistrich, p. 35; Goralski, p. 403.
52. Irving 1973, p. 302; Brett-Smith, p. 197.

15: Gerd von Rundstedt

 1. Guenther Blumentritt, *Von Rundstedt: The Soldier and the Man* (London: Odhams Press), pp. 14–16 (hereafter cited as "Blumentritt"). Blumentritt was Rundstedt's Chief of Staff from 1942 until July 1944. Later he was commander of LXXXVI Corps (October 1944), XII SS Corps (October 1944–January 1945), and acting commander, 25th Army (January–March 1945). He was commander of the 1st Parachute Army at the end of the war (Keilig, p. 38).
 2. Wistrich, p. 261; Brett-Smith, p. 15; O'Neill, pp. 195–96. Rundstedt was promoted to captain in 1909.
 3. Blumentritt, p. 19. Dr. von Rundstedt died in 1948 or 1949. His father, who was under indictment as a minor war criminal in 1948, was released from custody long enough to visit his dying son.
 4. Wistrich, p. 261; Brett-Smith, p. 15; O'Neill, pp. 195–96.
 5. Blumentritt, p. 21.
 6. Ibid, pp. 21–22.
 7. Wistrich, p. 261; Brett-Smith, p. 15; O'Neill, pp. 195–96.
 8. Blumentritt, p. 22.
 9. O'Neill, pp. 195–96.
10. Brett-Smith, p. 16; O'Neill, p. 195.
11. Brett-Smith, p. 17.
12. Irving 1978, p. 99.
13. Brett-Smith, p. 17.
14. Manstein, pp. 22–23; Kennedy, pp. 60–62; Irving 1978, p. 210.
15. Manstein, p. 23.
16. Ibid, p. 25, citing *Seeckt, Aus Meinem Leben*, by General von Rabenau.
17. Manstein, pp. 69–70.
18. Milton Shulman, *Defeat in the West* (London: Martin Secker and Warburg, 1947; reprint ed., New York: Ballantine Books, 1968), p. 72.
19. Brett-Smith, p. 18.
20. Harrison, p. 130.
21. DA *Pam 20–261a*, pp. 38–39; Carell, p. 8.

22. Plocher MS 1941.
23. Lucas 1980, p. 86.
24. Lucas 1979, p. 176.
25. Seaton, p. 140.
26. Lucas 1980, p. 176.
27. Ibid.
28. Seaton, p. 149.
29. Seaton 1980, p. 31.
30. Brett-Smith, p. 31; Seaton 1980, p. 172.
31. Irving 1977, p. 349.
32. Harrison, pp. 131–32.
33. Brett-Smith, p. 32.
34. Ibid, p. 40.
35. L. E. Ellis, *Victory in the West*, Volume I, *The Battle of Normandy* (London: Her Majesty's Stationery Office, 1962), p. 59 (hereafter cited as "Ellis I").
36. Harrison, p. 141.
37. Irving 1977a, p. 29.
38. Cooper, p. 504.
39. Chester Wilmot, *The Struggle for Europe* (New York: Harper and Row, 1952), p. 347 (hereafter cited as "Wilmot").
40. Ellis I, pp. 321–22; Irving 1977, pp. 650–51.
41. Charles Whiting, *Bloody Aachen* (Briarcliff Manor, NY: Stein and Day, 1976; reprint ed., New York: Playboy Press Paperbacks, 1980), p. 180.
42. L. E. Ellis, *Victory in the West*, Volume II, *The Defeat of Germany* (London: Her Majesty's Stationery Office, 1968), p. 123 (hereafter cited as "Ellis II").
43. See Anthony Kemp, *The Unknown Battle: Metz, 1944* (Briarcliff Manor, NY: Stein and Day, 1981).
44. John S. D. Eisenhower, *The Bitter Woods* (New York: G. P. Putnam's Sons, 1969), pp. 179, 350 (hereafter cited as "Eisenhower").
45. Mitcham 1984, ff. 74.
46. Snyder, p. 303; Wistrich, p. 262.
47. Kesselring, pp. 305–06.
48. Seaton 1980, p. 172.

16: Guenther von Kluge

1. Guenther von Kluge Personnel Record, Air University Archives, Maxwell Air Force Base, Alabama (hereafter cited as "Kluge Personnel Record"); Keilig, p. 174.

2. Chant *et al.*, p. 86; Wistrich, p. 173; Snyder, p. 197; O'Neill, pp. 203, 211; Taylor, p. 382.
3. Taylor, p. 228; O'Neill, p. 217; Kluge Personnel Record.
4. Taylor, p. 228; Kluge Personnel Record.
5. Wistrich, p. 173.
6. Irving 1977, p. 5.
7. Kennedy, pp. 82–83; Irving 1977, p. 5.
8. Irving 1977, p. 121.
9. *Kriegstagebuch des OKW*, Volume I, p. 1136; Irving 1977, p. 305; Seaton 1980, pp. 43–45.
10. Seaton 1980, pp. 169–70.
11. Irving 1977, pp. 360–61.
12. Seaton 1980, p. 211.
13. Ibid, p. 245.
14. Plocher MS 1942.
15. Ibid.
16. Plocher MS 1942; Irving 1977, pp. 415–16.
17. Wistrich, p. 173.
18. Irving 1977, p. 538; Ziemke, p. 129.
19. Brett-Smith, p. 89; Irving 1977, p. 538.
20. Chant, Volume 5, pp. 1202–03; Ziemke, pp. 139–44, 158–63.
21. Ziemke, p. 191.
22. Rommel, p. 481; Irving 1977a, p. 403.
23. B. H. Liddell Hart, *The German Generals Talk* (New York: Quill, 1979), pp. 246–48 (hereafter cited as "Hart 1979").
24. Ellis I, p. 361.
25. Herbert M. Mason, Jr., *To Kill the Devil* (New York: Pinnacle Books, 1974), pp. 170–71 (hereafter cited as "Mason").
26. Speidel, p. 116.
27. Mason, p. 171.
28. Ellis I, p. 372.
29. Wilmot, p. 389; Ellis I, p. 384.
30. Wilmot, p. 390.
31. Blumenson, p. 234.
32. Paul Carell, *Invasion: They're Coming!* (New York: E. P. Dutton, 1963; reprint ed., New York: Bantam Books, 1964), p. 235 (hereafter cited as "Carell 1964").
33. Blumenson, p. 240.
34. Wilmot, pp. 393–94.
35. Ibid, pp. 398–99.
36. Blumenson, p. 281; Chant, Volume 7, p. 1685.
37. Wilmot, p. 401.

38. Ellis I, pp. 412–13.
39. Irving 1977, p. 684.
40. Ellis I, p. 413.
41. Ellis I, pp. 413–15; Chant, Volume 7, pp. 1691–93.
42. Irving 1977, p. 685.
43. Wilmot, pp. 417–18; Irving 1977, pp. 686–87.
44. Ellis I, p. 428.
45. Wilmot, p. 421; Ellis I, p. 432; Irving 1977, pp. 687–88.
46. Chant, Volume 7, p. 1700.
47. Alexander McKee, *Last Round Against Rommel* (New York: Signet Books, 1966), p. 328; Ellis I, pp. 447–48.
48. Irving 1977, p. 696.

17: Walter Model

1. Eisenhower, ff. 16.
2. Keilig, p. 228.
3. Mellenthin 1977, p. 147.
4. Eisenhower, ff. 16; Wistrich, p. 210; Moll, p. 137.
5. Wistrich, p. 210; Keilig, p. 174.
6. Keilig, p. 228.
7. Mellenthin 1977, p. 148.
8. Brett-Smith, p. 198; Wistrich, p. 210; Taylor, pp. 199–200; Carell, p. 17; Moll, p. 138.
9. Carell, p. 393.
10. Ibid.
11. Ibid, p. 398.
12. Mellenthin 1977, pp. 149–51.
13. Ibid, pp. 393–406.
14. Wistrich, p. 210; OB 1943, p. 210; Carell, p. 406.
15. Carell 1971, pp. 304–15; Plocher MS 1942 and 1943.
16. Ziemke, p. 128.
17. Irving 1977, pp. 513, 527; Ziemke, pp. 128–32; also see Martin Caidin, *The Tigers are Burning* (New York: Hawthorn Books, 1974; reprint ed., New York: Pinnacle Books, 1975).
18. Ziemke, p. 135.
19. Carell 1971, pp. 6–28.
20. Chant, Volume 5, pp. 1192–94; Plocher MS 1943.
21. Ziemke, pp. 139–41; Plocher MS 1943.
22. Ziemke, pp. 196, 212.
23. Ibid, pp. 257–61.
24. Ibid, pp. 257–65.

25. Ibid, pp. 265–66.
26. Ibid, pp. 288–89.
27. Chant, Volume 6, p. 1659.
28. Irving 1977, p. 679; Chant, Volume 6, pp. 1661–66.
29. Wilmot, p. 435.
30. Ellis I, pp. 451–52.
31. Wilmot, p. 434.
32. Ibid, pp. 434, 460.
33. Goralski, pp. 340–42.
34. Ellis II, pp. 29–30.
35. Wilmot, pp. 501–03; Ellis II, p. 45.
36. Ellis II, pp. 46–47.
37. Irving 1977, p. 707.
38. Ellis II, pp. 34–35.
39. Ibid, pp. 31–50.
40. Ibid, pp. 48–50.
41. Ibid, p. 56.
42. Ibid, pp. 51–52.
43. Eisenhower, ff. 16.
44. Goralski, pp. 366–71; Wilmot, p. 608. Also see John Toland, *Battle: The Story of the Bulge* (New York: Random House, 1959; reprint ed., New York: Signet, 1959) and Robert E. Merriam, *The Battle of the Bulge* (New York: Ballantine Books, 1957).
45. Brett-Smith, p. 200; Eisenhower, p. 18.
46. Wilmot, p. 673.
47. Charles Whiting, *Battle of the Ruhr Pocket* (New York: Ballantine Books, 1970), pp. 10–11, 40–44 (hereafter cited as "Whiting 1970").
48. Ibid, p. 40.
49. Charles B. MacDonald, *The Last Offensive*, US Army in World War II, European Theater of Operations. Office of the Chief of Military History (Washington, DC: United States Government Printing Office, 1973), p. 369 (hereafter cited as "MacDonald 1973").
50. Ibid, p. 372.
51. Mellenthin 1977, p. 157.
52. Whiting 1970, pp. 145–46.
53. Goerlitz 1953, p. 494.
54. Whiting 1970, pp. 145–46.
55. MacDonald 1973, p. 372.

18: Erwin von Witzleben

1. Brett-Smith, p. 208; Snyder, p. 382.

2. Keilig, p. 374.
3. O'Neill, pp. 197–98.
4. Ibid, p. 198.
5. Ibid, pp. 197–98.
6. Ibid.
7. Goerlitz 1953, p. 288; Hoffmann, pp. 25–27.
8. O'Neill, pp. 197–98.
9. Deutsch 1974, p. 36. Hase commanded the 46th Infantry Division in Poland and France and briefly directed the 56th Infantry Division (September–November 1940). He was Commandant of Berlin from November 1940 to July 20, 1944. He was hanged in August 1944 for his part in the anti-Hitler conspiracy. Brockdorff-Ahlefeldt led the 23rd Infantry Division (March 1938–June 1, 1940) and was acting commander of XXVIII Corps in June 1940. He assumed command of II Corps on June 21, 1940, and led it until early 1943. His most famous battle was the Demyansk Pocket. Relieved of command for reasons of health, Count von Brockdorff-Ahlefeldt died in Berlin in 1943 (Keilig, pp. 52 and 128).
10. Hoffmann, pp. 43–44.
11. See Heinz Hoehne, *Canaris* (Garden City, NY: Doubleday, 1979) for the story of Admiral Canaris and the German resistance.
12. Wheeler-Bennett, p. 407.
13. Pierce Galante, *Operation Valkyrie: The German Generals; Plot Against Hitler* (New York: Harper and Row, 1981), p. 66 (hereafter cited as "Galante").
14. Wheeler-Bennett, pp. 407–09, 420.
15. Hoffmann, p. 255.
16. Wheeler-Bennett, pp. 420–21.
17. Deutsch 1978, p. 41.
18. Goerlitz 1953, p. 391.
19. Deutsch 1978, p. 44.
20. Wheeler-Bennett, p. 485; Deutsch 1978, pp. 239–40.
21. Harrison, p. 130.
22. Ibid, p. 131.
23. Hoffmann, p. 627.
24. Ibid, p. 479.
25. Ibid, pp. 651–62, 666.
26. Galante, p. 24.
27. Ibid.
28. Hoffmann, pp. 497–98.
29. Wheeler-Bennett, p. 681.
30. Wistrich, p. 343.

31. Hoffmann, p. 682.
32. Ibid, p. 683.
33. Galante, p. 233.
34. Hoffmann, p. 684.

19: Ferdinand Schoerner

1. Wistrich, p. 277.
2. Mellenthin 1977, p. 175.
3. Lucas 1980, p. 247.
4. Goerlitz 1953, p. 443.
5. Mellenthin 1977, p. 173.
6. Ibid.
7. Brett-Smith, pp. 201–02; Mellenthin 1977, p. 175; Moll, p. 170.
8. Mellenthin 1977, pp. 175–76.
9. Snyder, p. 313.
10. Goerlitz 1953, p. 443; Moll, p. 170.
11. Moll, p. 170; Lucas 1980, p. 247.
12. Kennedy, pp. 106–07.
13. Ziemke 1959, p. 329.
14. Mitcham 1985, p. 339.
15. DA *Pam 20–260*, pp. 88–89.
16. Mitcham 1985, p. 339.
17. Ziemke 1959, p. 147; Carell, pp. 459–62.
18. Carell, pp. 463–66; Ziemke 1959, pp. 326 and 329. Dietl, a Bavarian, was promoted to colonel general on June 1, 1942, and commanded the 20th Mountain Army until he was killed in an air crash on June 23, 1944 (Keilig, p. 70).
19. Ziemke 1959, pp. 245–46.
20. Ziemke, p. 240.
21. Chant, Volume 5, p. 1338; Ziemke, pp. 240–41.
22. Carell 1971, pp. 448–49; Ziemke, p. 242.
23. Ziemke, pp. 242–43.
24. Carell 1971, pp. 448–49; Ziemke, p. 242.
25. Mellenthin 1977, p. 180.
26. Brett-Smith, p. 203; Irving 1977, p. 616.
27. Irving 1977, p. 612.
28. Ziemke, p. 348.
29. Ibid, p. 291.
30. Chant, Volume 5, pp. 1354–55; Ziemke, pp. 291–92.
31. Chant, Volume 5, p. 1355.

32. Irving 1977, pp. 626–27; Ziemke, p. 293.

33. Ziemke, p. 295; Chant, Volume 5, p. 1356.

34. Plocher MS 1943.

35. Ziemke, p. 346.

36. Ziemke, p. 335; Chant, Volume 6, pp. 1656–57.

37. Seaton, pp. 477–83.

38. Chant, Volume 6, p. 1656.

39. Ziemke, p. 342.

40. Seaton, p. 457.

41. Ibid, p. 523.

42. Seaton, p. 523.

43. Irving 1977, p. 706.

44. Ziemke, pp. 404–05.

45. Ibid, pp. 405–06.

46. Chant, Volume 7, pp. 1850–53; Ziemke, pp. 407–09; Seaton, pp. 525–26.

47. Irving 1977, pp. 730–31.

48. At the end of the war, Vietinghoff was commanding Army Group C in Italy, and Rendulic was leading Army Group Ostmark (formerly South) in Austria. Hilpert died in a Russian prison camp in 1946 (Keilig, p. 142).

49. Brett-Smith, pp. 203–04; Seaton, p. 539; Ziemke, p. 415.

50. Ziemke, p. 417.

51. Ibid, p. 423. Smilo von Luettwitz commanded LXXXV Corps on the southern sector of the Western Front in the last weeks of the war (Keilig, p. 212).

52. Juergen Thorwald, *Defeat in the East* (New York: Pantheon Books, 1951; reprint ed., New York: Bantam Books, 1980), p. 177 (hereafter cited as "Thorwald").

53. Ibid, p. 50.

54. Ziemke, p. 442; Thorwald, pp. 52–60.

55. Seaton, p. 560.

56. Ziemke, p. 473.

57. Irving 1977, pp. 719, 819; Ziemke, pp. 474–86.

58. Irving 1977, p. 819.

59. Thorwald, pp. 276–80; Ziemke, p. 498.

60. Friedrich von Stauffenberg to author, personal communication, August 5, 1985.

61. Ibid.

62. Thorwald, pp. 276–80; Ziemke, p. 498.

63. Clark, p. 477; Wistrich, p. 278; Snyder, p. 313; Brett-Smith, p. 204.

20: The Luftwaffe Marshals

1. General Helmuth von Volkmann also commanded the Condor Legion (from November 1937 to November 1938). He retired from the Luftwaffe soon after but rejoined the service in 1939 as a general of infantry in the Army. He was killed in an auto accident in 1940.

2. Irving 1973, p. 334.

3. "General Officers of the German Air Force," Maxwell Air Force Base, Air University Archives, declassified document dated 22 Sept 1972 (hereafter cited as "GAF Gen. Officers"); Moll, p. 245.

4. Ibid.

5. Kesselring, p. 265; for excellent accounts of the Italian campaign, see W. G. F. Jackson, *The Battle of Italy* (London: B. T. Batsford, 1967); Brian Harpur, *The Impossible Victory: A Personal Account of the Battle of the Po River* (New York: Hippocrene Books, 1981); and Fred Majdalany, *The Battle of Cassino* (Boston: Houghton Mifflin, 1957). The US and British Official Histories, by Blumenson, Fisher, Garland and Smith, and Linklater, are also good, and are listed in the bibliography.

6. Kenneth Macksey, *Kesselring: The Making of the Luftwaffe* (New York: David McKay, 1978), p. 231 (hereafter cited as "Macksey").

7. For the details of this atrocity (or reprisal), see Robert Katz, *Death in Rome* (New York: Macmillan, 1967) (hereafter cited as "Katz").

8. Macksey, p. 243; Kesselring, pp. 365, 374.

9. Brett-Smith, p. 243: Kesselring, pp. 365, 374.

10. Katz, p. 199.

11. GAF Gen. Officers.

12. Brett-Smith, p. 132; Wistrich, p. 105; GAF Gen. Officers.

13. Matthew Cooper, *The German Air Force: 1933–1945* (London: Jane's, 1981), p. 4.

14. Adolf Galland, K. Ries and R. Ahnert, *The Luftwaffe at War, 1939–1945*, David Monday, ed. (Chicago: Henry Regency, 1972), p. 243.

15. Snyder, p. 127.

16. Karl Doenitz, *Memoirs: Ten Years and Twenty Days* (Cleveland and New York: World Publishing, 1959), pp. 430–74.

17. Ibid, p. 454.

Bibliography

Anders, Wladyslaw, *Hitler's Defeat in Russia*. Chicago: Henry Regnery, 1953.

Beaulieu, W. de. *Der Vorstoss der Panzer Gruppe 4 auf Leningrad*. Neckargemuend: Kurt Vowinckel, 1961.

————. *The Tigers Are Burning*. New York: Hawthorn Books, 1974. Reprint ed., New York: Pinnacle Books, 1975.

Benoist-Mechin, Jacques. *Sixty Days That Shook the West: The Fall of France*. New York: G. P. Putnam's, 1963.

Bethell, Nicholas, and the Editors of Time-Life Books. *Russia Besieged*. Volume 6, World War II, Time-Life Books. Alexandria, Virginia: Time-Life Books, 1980.

Blumenson, Martin. *Breakout and Pursuit*. United States Army in World War II, The European Theater of Operations. Office of the Chief of Military History, United States Department of the Army. Washington, DC: United States Government Printing Office, 1961.

————. *Salerno to Cassino*. United States Army in World War II, Mediterranean Theater of Operations. Office of the Chief of Military History, Department of the Army. Washington, DC: United States Government Printing Office, 1969.

Blumentritt, Gunther. *Von Rundstedt: The Soldier and the Man*. London: Odham's Press, 1952.

Brett-Smith, Richard. *Hitler's Generals*. San Rafael, California: Presidio Press, 1977.

Carell, Paul. *The Foxes of the Desert*. New York: Bantam Books, 1972 (originally published by E. P. Dutton, New York, 1960).

————. *Hitler Moves East, 1941–1943*. New York: Bantam Books, 1966 (originally published by Little, Brown, Boston, 1965).

————. *Invasion: They're Coming!* New York: Bantam Books, 1964 (originally published by E. P. Dutton, New York, 1963).

————. *Scorched Earth: The Russian-German War, 1943–1944*. New York: Ballantine Books, 1971 (originally published by Little, Brown, Boston, 1966).

Carnes, James D. "A Study in Courage: General Walther von Seydlitz' Opposition to Hitler." Tallahassee, Florida: Ph.D. Dissertation, Florida State University, 1976.

Carver, Michael. *El Alamein*. New York: Macmillan, 1962.

Chandler, David G. *Dictionary of the Napoleonic Wars*. New York: Macmillan, 1979.

Chant, Christopher, Richard Humble, William Fowler, and Jenny Shaw. *Hitler's Generals and Their Battles*. New York: Chartwell Books, 1976.

Chant, Christopher, ed. *The Marshall Cavendish Illustrated Encyclopedia of World War II*. New York: Marshall Cavendish Corporation, 1972.

Chapman, Guy. *Why France Fell: The Defeat of the French Army in 1940*. New York: Rinehart and Winston, 1968.

Churchill Winston S. *The Second World War*. Volume 2: *Their Finest Hour*. Boston: Houghton Mifflin, 1949.

Clark, Alan. *Barbarossa: The Russian-German Conflict, 1941–45*. New York: William Morrow, 1965.

Cole, Hugh M. *The Ardennes: Battle of the Bulge*. United States Army in World War II, The European Theater of Operations. Office of the Chief of Military History, Department of the Army. Washington DC: United States Government Printing Office, 1965.

————. *The Lorraine Campaign*. United States Army in World War II, The European Theater of Operations. Office of the Chief of Military History, Department of the Army. Washington DC: United States Government Printing Office, 1950.

Cooper, Matthew. *The German Air Force, 1933–1945*. London: Jane's, 1981.

————. *The German Army, 1933–1945*. Briarcliff Manor, New York: Stein and Day, 1978.

Davidson, Eugene. *The Trial of the Germans*. New York: Macmillan, 1966.

Davis, C. R. *Von Kleist: From Hussar to Panzer Marshal*. Houston, Texas: Lancer Militaria, 1979.

Deighton, Len. *Blitzkrieg: From the Rise of Hitler to the Fall of Dunkirk*. New York: Alfred A. Knopf, 1979.

————. *Fighter*. New York: Ballantine Books, 1979 (originally published by Alfred A. Knopf, New York, 1977).

Delli, Bertrum, ed. *Biographical Index*. Volume 11 (September, 1976–August 1979). New York: H. W. Wilson Company, 1980.

Deutsch, Harold C. *The Conspiracy Against Hitler in the Twilight War*. Minneapolis: University of Minnesota Press, 1978.

————. *Hitler and His Generals: The Hidden Crisis, January–June 1938*. Minneapolis: University of Minnesota Press, 1974.

Doenitz, Karl. *Memoirs: Ten Years and Twenty Days*. Cleveland and New York: World Publishing Company, 1959.

Douglas-Home, Charles. *Rommel*. London: Excalibur (originally published by Saturday Review Press, New York, 1973).

Downing, David. *The Devil's Virtuosos*. New York: Playboy Press Paperbacks, 1980 (originally published by St. Martin's Press, New York, 1977).

Drum, Karl. "The German Air Force in the Spanish Civil War." United States Air Force Historical Studies. Maxwell Air Force Base, Montgomery, Alabama: United States Air Force Historical Division, Aerospace Studies Institute, Air University, 1965.

Dupuy, T. N. and Paul Martell. *Great Battles on the Eastern Front*. Indianapolis/New York: Bobbs-Merrill, 1982.

Eisenhower, John S. D. *The Bitter Woods*. New York: G. P. Putnam's Sons, 1969.

Ellis, L. E. *Victory in the West,* Volume I: *The Battle of Normandy*. London: Her Majesty's Stationery Office, 1962.

————. *Victory in the West,* Volume II: *The Defeat of Germany*. London: Her Majesty's Stationery Office, 1968.

————. *The War in France and Flanders, 1939–40*. London: Her Majesty's Stationery Office, 1953.

Esposito, Vincent J., ed. *A Concise History of World War II*. New York: Frederick A. Praeger, 1964.

Fisher, Ernest F., Jr. *Cassino to the Alps*. United States Army in World War II, Mediterranean Theater of Operations. Office of the Chief of Military History, Department of the Army. Washington, DC: United States Government Printing Office, 1977.

Fromm, Bella. *Blood and Banquets*. New York: Harper and Row, 1942.

Gackenholz, Hermann. "The Collapse of Army Group Center in 1944." *Decisive Battles of World War II: The German View*. H. A. Jacobsen and J. Rowher, eds. New York: G. P. Putnam's Sons, 1965: pp. 355–83.

Galante, Pierre. *Operation Valkyrie: The German Generals' Plot Against Hitler*. New York: Harper and Row, 1981.

Galland, Adolf, K. Ries, and R. Ahnert. *The Luftwaffe at War, 1939–1945*. David Monday, ed. Chicago: Henry Regnery, 1972.

Garland, Albert N. and Howard McG. Smyth. *Sicily and the Surrender of Italy*. United States Army in World War II, Mediterranean Theater of Operations. Office of the Chief of Military History. Department of the Army. Washington, DC: United States Government Printing Office, 1965.

"General Officers of the German Air Forces." Maxwell Air Force Base, Montgomery, Alabama: Air University Archives. Declassified document dated 22 Sept 1972.

"General Ritter von Greim." Maxwell Air Force Base, Montgomery, Alabama: Air University Archives. Declassified Document EO 11652.

Gilbert, G. M. *Nuremberg Diary*. New York: Signet Books, 1961 (originally published by Farrar, Straus and Cudahy, New York, 1947).

Goebbels, Joseph. *The Goebbels Diaries*. Louis P. Lochner, ed. New York: Universal-Award House, 1971 (originally published by Doubleday and Company, Garden City, NY, 1948).

Goerlitz, Walter. "The Battle of Stalingrad." Hans-Adolf and J. Rohwer, eds. *Decisive Battles of World War II: The German View*. New York: G. P. Putnam's Sons, 1965: pp. 355–83.

————. *History of the German General Staff, 1657–1945*. Westport, Connecticut: Greenwood Press, 1975 (originally published by Praeger Publishers, New York: 1953).

————. *Paulus and Stalingrad*. Westport, Connecticut: Greenwood Press, 1974.

Goralski, Robert. *World War II Almanac, 1931–1945*. New York: G. P. Putnam's Sons, 1981.

Goutard, A. *The Battle of France, 1940*. New York: Ives Washburn, 1959.

Guderian, Heinz. *Panzer Leader*. New York: Ballantine Books, 1967 (originally published by E. P. Dutton, New York, 1957).

Gundelack, Karl. "The Battle for Crete 1941." *Decisive Battles of World War II: The German View*. H. A. Jacobsen and J. Rowher, eds. New York: G. P. Putnam's Sons, 1965: pp. 99–133.

Harpur, Brian. *The Impossible Victory: A Personal Account of the Battle of the Po River*. New York: Hippocrene Books, 1981.

Harrison, Gordon A. *Cross-Channel Attack*. United States Army in World War II, The European Theater of Operations. Office of the Chief of Military History, Department of the Army. Washington, DC: United States Government Printing Office, 1951.

Hart, B. H. Liddell. *The German Generals Talk*. New York: Quill, 1979.

————. *History of the Second World War*. New York: G. P. Putnam's Sons, 1972.

Hassell, Ulrich von. *The Von Hassell Diaries, 1938–1944.* Westport, Connecticut: Greenwood Press, 1979.

Hoehne, Heinz. *Canaris.* Garden City, New York: Doubleday, 1979.

Hoffmann, Peter. *The History of the German Resistance, 1933–1945.* Cambridge, Mass.: MIT Press, 1977.

Huebsch, Norbert A., Jr. "Field Marshal Werner von Blomberg and the Politicization of the Wehrmacht." Cincinnati, Ohio: Ph.D. Dissertation, University of Cincinnati, 1981.

Irving, David. *Hitler's War.* New York: Viking Press, 1977.

————. *The Rise and Fall of the Luftwaffe: The Life of Field Marshal Erhard Milch.* Boston: Little, Brown, 1973.

————. *The Trail of the Fox.* New York: Thomas Congdon Books, E. P. Dutton, 1977.

————. *The War Path: Hitler's Germany, 1933–1939.* New York: Viking Press, 1979.

Jackson, W. G. F. *The Battle for North Africa.* New York: Mason/Charter, 1975.

————. *The Battle for Rome.* New York: Charter, 1969.

Jacobsen, Hans-Adolf and J. Rohwer, eds. *Decisive Battles of World War II: The German View.* New York: G. P. Putnam's Sons, 1965.

Jacobsen, Hans-Adolf, ed. *July 20, 1944.* Bonn: Federal German Government Press and Information Office, 1969.

Katz, Robert. *Death in Rome.* New York: Pyramid Books, 1968 (originally published by Macmillan, New York, 1967).

Keegan, John. *Waffen SS: The Asphalt Soldiers.* New York: Ballantine Books, 1970.

Keilig, Wolf. *Die Generale des Heeres.* Friedberg: Podzum-Pallas Verlag, 1983.

Keitel, Wilhelm. *In the Service of the Reich.* Walter Goerlitz, ed. Briarcliff Manor, New York: Stein and Day, 1966.

Kemp, Anthony. *The Unknown Battle: Metz, 1944.* Briarcliff Manor, New York: Stein and Day, 1981.

Kennedy, Robert M. *The German Campaign in Poland (1939).* United States Department of the Army *Pamphlet 20–255.* Washington, DC: Department of the Army, 1956.

Kershaw, Andrew, and Ian Close, eds. *The Desert War.* New York: Marshall Cavendish, 1975.

Kesselring, Albert. *Kesselring: A Soldier's Record.* Westport, Connecticut: Greenwood Press, 1970.

Kriegstagebuch des Oberkommando des Wehrmacht (Fuehrungsstab). Frankfurt-am-Main: Bernard und Graefe Verlag fuer Wehrwesen, 1961.

"Georg von Kuechler." *Current Biography.* New York: H. W. Wilson, 1980.

Leeb, Ritter Wilhelm von. *Defense.* Dr. Stefan T. Possony and Daniel Vilfroy, trans. Harrisonburg, PA: Military Service Publishing Company, 1943.

Linklater, Eric. *The Campaign in Italy.* London: His Majesty's Stationery Office, 1951.

Lucas, James. *Alpine Elite: German Mountain Troops of World War II.* London: Jane's, 1980.

————. *War on the Eastern Front.* New York: Bonanza Books (originally published by Stein and Day, Briarcliff Manor, NY, 1979).

MacDonald, Charles B. *The Last Offensive.* United States Army in World War II, European Theater of Operations. Office of the Chief of Military History, United States Department of the Army. Washington, DC: United States Government Printing Office, 1973.

————. *The Siegfried Line Campaign.* United States Army in World War II, European Theater of Operations. Office of the Chief of Military History, United States Department of the Army. Washington, DC: United States Government Printing Office, 1963.

McKee, Alexander. *Last Round Against Rommel.* New York: Signet Books, 1966.

Macksey, Kenneth. *Kesselring: The Making of the Luftwaffe.* New York: David McKay Company, 1978.

Majdalany, Fred. *The Battle of Cassino.* New York: Ballantine Books, 1958 (originally published by Houghton Mifflin, Boston, 1957).

Manstein, Erich von. *Lost Victories.* Novato, California: Presidio Press, 1982 (originally published as *Verlorene Siege*, Athenaeum-Verlag, Bonn, 1955).

Manvell, Robert, and Heinrich Fraenkel. *The Men Who Tried to Kill Hitler.* New York: Coward-McCann, 1964. Reprint ed., New York: Pocket Books, 1966.

Mason, Herbert M., Jr. *To Kill the Devil.* New York: W. W. Norton, 1978.

Mellenthin, Frederich Wilhelm von. *German Generals of World War Two.* Norman, Oklahoma: University of Oklahoma Press, 1977.

————. *Panzer Battles.* New York: Ballantine Books, 1976 (originally published by the University of Oklahoma Press, 1956).

Merriam, Robert E. *The Battle of the Bulge.* New York: Ballantine Books, 1957 (originally published as *Dark December* by Ziff-Davis, 1947).

Mitcham, Samuel W., Jr. *Hitler's Legions: The German Army Order of Battle, World War II.* Briarcliff Manor, New York: Stein and Day, 1985.

————. *Rommel's Desert War.* Briarcliff Manor, New York: Stein and Day, 1982.

————. *Rommel's Last Battle.* Briarcliff Manor, New York: Stein and Day, 1983.

—————. *Triumphant Fox: Erwin Rommel and the Rise of the Afrika Korps.* Briarcliff Manor, New York: Stein and Day, 1984.

Moll, Otto E. *Die deutschen Generalfeldmarshaelle, 1939–1945.* Rastatt/Baden: Erich Pabel Verlag, 1961.

Molony, C. J. C. *History of the Second World War.* Volume V: *The Mediterranean and Middle East.* London: Her Majesty's Stationery Office, 1966.

Morzik, Fritz. "German Air Force Airlift Operations." United States Air Force Historical Studies *Number 167.* Maxwell Air Force Base, Alabama: Air University, 1961.

Mosley, Leonard, *The Reich Marshal: A Biography of Hermann Goering.* New York: Doubleday, 1974.

O'Neill, Robert J. *The German Army and the Nazi Party, 1933–1939.* New York: James H. Heineman, 1966.

Personnel Records of Ewald von Kleist, Ritter Wilhelm von Leeb, and Friedrich Paulus. Maxwell Air Force Base: Air University Archives, n.d.

Playfair, I. S. O. *The Mediterranean and Middle East.* Volume III: *British Fortunes Reach Their Lowest Ebb.* London: Her Majesty's Stationery Office, 1960.

Playfair, I. S. O., and C. J. C. Molony. *The Mediterranean and Middle East.* Volume IV: *The Destruction of the Axis in Africa.* London: Her Majesty's Stationery Office, 1966.

Plocher, Hermann. "The German Air Force Versus Russia, 1941." United States Air Force Historical Studies Number 153. United States Air Force Historical Division, Aerospace Studies Institute. Maxwell Air Force Base, Montgomery, Alabama: Air University, 1965.

—————. "The German Air Force Versus Russia, 1942." United States Air Force Historical Studies Number 154. United States Air Force Historical Division, Aerospace Studies Institute. Maxwell Air Force Base, Montgomery, Alabama: Air University, 1965.

—————. "The German Air Force Versus Russia, 1943." United States Air Force Historical Studies Number 155. United States Air Force Historical Division, Aerospace Studies Institute. Maxwell Air Force Base, Montgomery, Alabama: Air University, 1965

Rommel, Erwin. *Attacks.* Vienna, Virginia: Athena Press, 1979 (originally published in Germany as *Infantry in the Attack*, 1936).

—————. *The Rommel Papers.* B. H. Liddell Hart, ed. New York: Harcourt, Brace, 1953.

Ruge, Friedrich. "The Invasion of Normandy," in H. A. Jacobsen and J. Rohwer, *Decisive Battles of World War II: The German View.* New York: G. P. Putnam's Sons, 1965: pp. 317–349.

Ryan, Cornelius. *The Last Battle*. New York: Popular Library, 1966 (originally published by Simon and Schuster, New York, 1966).

—. *The Longest Day*. New York: Popular Library, 1959 (originally published by Simon and Schuster, New York, 1959).

Salisbury, Harrison E. *The 900 Days: The Siege of Leningrad*. New York: Harper and Row, 1969.

Schlabrendorff, Fabian von. *Revolt Against Hitler*. Gero V. S. Gaevernitz, ed. London: Eyre and Spottiswoode, 1948. Reprint ed., New York: AMS Press, 1948.

Schmidt, Heinz W. *With Rommel in the Desert*. New York: Ballantine Books, 1968 (originally published by George G. Harrap, New York, 1951).

Schneider, Franz, and Charles Gullans. *Last Letters From Stalingrad*. New York: New American Library, 1961.

Seaton, Albert. *The Battle for Moscow*. New York: Playboy Press Paperbacks, 1981 (originally published by Stein and Day, Briarcliff Manor, New York, 1980).

—. *The Russo-German War, 1941*. New York: Praeger, 1970.

—. *The German Army, 1933–45*. New York: St Martin's Press, 1982. Reprint ed., New York: New American Library, 1985.

Shaw, John, and the Editors of Time-Life Books. *Red Army Resurgent*. Volume 20, World War II, Time-Life Books. Alexandria, Virginia: Time-Life Books, 1979.

Shirer, William L. *Berlin Diary*. New York: Alfred A. Knopf, 1941.

—. *The Rise and Fall of the Third Reich*. New York: Simon and Schuster, 1960.

Shulman, Milton. *Defeat in the West*. London: Martin Secker and Warburg, 1947; reprint ed., New York: Ballantine Books, 1963.

Snyder, Louis L. *Encyclopedia of the Third Reich*. New York: McGraw-Hill Book Company, 1976.

Spiedel, Hans. *Invasion: 1944*. New York: Paperback Library, 1968 (originally published in the United States by Henry Regnery, New York, 1950).

Stauffenberg, Friedrich von. "Panzer Commanders of the Western Front." Unpublished manuscript, n.d.

—. Personal communication, 1985.

Strawson, John. *The Battle for North Africa*. New York: Bonanza Books, 1969.

Suchenwirth, Richard. "Command and Leadership in the German Air Force." United States Air Force Historical Studies Number 174. United States Air Force Historical Division, Aerospace Studies Institute. Maxwell Air Force Base, Montgomery, Alabama: Air University, 1969.

Sydnor, Charles W., Jr. *Soldiers of Destruction: The SS Death's Head Division, 1933–45*. Princeton, New Jersey: Princeton University Press, 1977.

Taylor, Telford. *Sword and Swastika: Generals and Nazis in the Third Reich*. Chicago: Quadrangle Paperbacks, 1969 (originally published by Simon and Schuster, New York, 1952).

————. *The March of Conquest*. New York: Simon and Schuster, 1958.

Thorwald, Juergen. *Defeat in the East*. New York: Bantam Books, 1980 (originally published in English by Pantheon Books, 1951).

Toland, John. *Adolf Hitler*. New York: Ballantine Books, 1977 (originally published by Random House, New York, 1976).

————. *Battle: The Story of the Bulge*. New York: Signet, 1959 (originally published by Random House, New York, 1959).

United Kingdom CSDIC GG (Interrogation) Reports. On file at the Historical Research Center, Air University Archives, Maxwell Air Force Base, Montgomery, Alabama.

United States Department of the Army *Pamphlet 20–243*. "German Antiguerrilla Operations in the Balkans (1941–1944)." Office of the Chief of Military History. Washington, DC: United States Department of the Army, 1954.

United States Department of the Army *Pamphlet 20–260*. 'The German Campaigns in the Balkans (Spring, 1941)." United States Army Military History Division. Washington, DC: United States Department of the Army, 1953.

United States Department of the Army *Pamphlet 20–261a*. "The German Campaign in Russia—Planning and Operations." United States Army Military History Division. Washington, DC: United States Department of the Army, 1955.

United States Military Intelligence Service. "Order of Battle of the German Army." Washington, DC: United States War Department General Staff, October 1942.

————. "Order of Battle of the German Army." Washington, DC: United States War Department General Staff, April 1943.

————. "Order of Battle of the German Army." Washington, DC: United States War Department General Staff, February 1944.

————. "Order of Battle of the German Army." Washington, DC: United States War Department General Staff, February 1945.

Warlimont, Walter. "The Decision in the Mediterranean 1942." *Decisive Battles of World War II: The German View*. H. A. Jacobsen and J. Rowder, eds. New York: G. J. Putnam's Sons, 1965, pp. 185–215.

————. *Inside Hitler's Headquarters*. New York: Frederick A. Praeger, 1964.

Wheeler-Bennett, John W. *The Nemesis of Power: The German Army in Politics, 1918–1945*. London: Macmillan, 1964.

Whiting, Charles. *Battle of the Ruhr Pocket*. New York: Ballantine Books, 1970.

——. *Bloody Aachen*. Briarcliff Manor, New York: Stein and Day, 1976.

Wilmot, Chester. *The Struggle for Europe*. New York: Harper and Row, 1981.

Wistrich, Robert. *Who's Who in Nazi Germany*. New York: Macmillan, 1982.

Young, Desmond. *Rommel: The Desert Fox*. New York: Harper and Row, 1965.

Ziemke, Earl F. *Battle for Berlin*. New York: Ballantine Books, 1968.

——. "The German Northern Theater of Operations, 1940–1945." United States Department of the Army *Pamphlet 20–271*. Office of the Chief of Military History. Washington, DC: United States Department of the Army, 1959.

——. *Stalingrad to Berlin: The German Defeat in the East*. United States Department of the Army, Office of the Chief of Military History. Washington, DC: United States Government Printing Office, 1966.

Index

415

Index of Military Units

423